Letters from Prison
Part One

Angelo - nephew of Angela

Rebecca - Boss' new job

Jo - job for Brander

Jacqualene - Mom of sister's loss of grandmother

Lynne - Mother-in law - new home
Butch's stress

Julie - David & Allison divorce (to 5 kids)
f.i.o.

Michele - Sister Denise - Lost her Job
& her & mom & is Diabetic

Letters from Prison
Part One

Philippians and Philemon

Vincent M. Smiles, Philippians
Terence J. Keegan, Philemon
with Little Rock Scripture Study staff

Little Rock
Scripture Study

LITURGICAL PRESS
Collegeville, Minnesota

www.littlerockscripture.org

Nihil obstat for the commentary text by Vincent M. Smiles (Philippians): Robert C. Harren, *Censor deputatus.* *Imprimatur* for the commentary text by Vincent M. Smiles (Philippians): ✛ John F. Kinney, Bishop of St. Cloud, Minnesota, August 30, 2005.

Nihil obstat for the commentary text by Terence J. Keegan, O.P. (Philemon): Robert C. Harren, *Censor deputatus.* *Imprimatur* for the commentary text by Terence J. Keegan, O.P. (Philemon): ✛ John F. Kinney, Bishop of St. Cloud, Minnesota, December 29, 2005.

Cover design by John Vineyard. Interior art by Ned Bustard.

 This symbol indicates material that was created by Little Rock Scripture Study to supplement the biblical text and commentary. Some of these inserts first appeared in the *Little Rock Catholic Study Bible*; others were created specifically for this book by Amy Ekeh.

1   2   3   4   5   6   7   8   9

Library of Congress Cataloging-in-Publication Data

Names: Smiles, Vincent M., 1949– author. | Keegan, Terence J., author.
Title: Letters from prison : Philippians and Philemon / Vincent M. Smiles, Philippians ; Terence J. Keegan, O.P., Philemon with Little Rock Scripture Study staff.
Description: Collegeville : Liturgical Press, [2019] | Contents: Lesson one (introduction and Philippians 1:1-26) — Lesson two (Philippians 1:27–3:1) — Lesson three (Philippians 3:2–4:23) — Lesson four (introduction and Philemon) — Praying with your group — Reflecting on scripture. | Summary: "Scripture study focusing on the letters Paul wrote to the Philippians and Philemon while in prison"— Provided by publisher.
Identifiers: LCCN 2019017262 (print) | LCCN 2019980433 (ebook) | ISBN 780814664551 (pbk.) | ISBN 9780814664544 (pbk.)
Subjects: LCSH: Bible. Philippians—Criticism, interpretation, etc. | Bible. Philemon—Criticism, interpretation, etc.
Classification: LCC BS2705.52 .S65 2019 (print) | LCC BS2705.52 (ebook) | DDC 227/.607—dc23
LC record available at https://lccn.loc.gov/2019017262
LC ebook record available at https://lccn.loc.gov/2019980433

TABLE OF CONTENTS

Wrap-Up Lectures and Discussion Tips for Facilitators are available for each lesson at no charge. Find them online at LittleRockScripture.org/Lectures/LettersPartOne.

Welcome

The Bible is at the heart of what it means to be a Christian. It is the Spirit-inspired word of God for us. It reveals to us the God who created, redeemed, and guides us still. It speaks to us personally and as a church. It forms the basis of our public liturgical life and our private prayer lives. It urges us to live worthily and justly, to love tenderly and wholeheartedly, and to be a part of building God's kingdom here on earth.

Though it was written a long time ago, in the context of a very different culture, the Bible is no relic of the past. Catholic biblical scholarship is among the best in the world, and in our time and place, we have unprecedented access to it. By making use of solid scholarship, we can discover much about the ancient culture and religious practices that shaped those who wrote the various books of the Bible. With these insights, and by praying with the words of Scripture, we allow the words and images to shape us as disciples. By sharing our journey of faithful listening to God's word with others, we have the opportunity to be stretched in our understanding and to form communities of love and learning. Ultimately, studying and praying with God's word deepens our relationship with Christ.

Letters from Prison, Part One
Philippians and Philemon

The resource you hold in your hands is divided into four lessons. Each lesson involves personal prayer and study using this book *and* the experience of group prayer, discussion, and wrap-up lecture.

If you are using this resource in the context of a small group, we suggest that you meet four times, discussing one lesson per meeting. Allow about 90 minutes for the small group gathering. Small groups function best with eight to twelve people to ensure good group dynamics and to allow all to participate as they wish.

Some groups choose to have an initial gathering before their regular sessions begin. This allows an opportunity to meet one another, pass out books, and, if desired, view the optional intro lecture for this study available on the "Resources" page of the Little Rock Scripture Study website (www.littlerockscripture.org). Please note that there is only one intro lecture for two-part studies.

WHAT MATERIALS WILL YOU USE?

The materials in this book include:

- The text of Philippians and Philemon, using the New American Bible, Revised Edition as the translation.

- Commentaries by Vincent M. Smiles (Philippians) and Terence J. Keegan (Philemon), which have also been published separately as part of the New Collegeville Bible Commentary series.

- Occasional inserts ● highlighting elements of Philippians and Philemon. Some of these appear also in the *Little Rock Catholic Study Bible* while others are supplied by staff writers.

- Questions for study, reflection, and discussion at the end of each lesson.

- Opening and closing prayers for each lesson, as well as other prayer forms available in the closing pages of the book.

In addition, there are wrap-up lectures available for each lesson. Your group may choose to purchase a DVD containing these lectures or make use of the audio or video lectures online at no charge. The link to these free lectures is: LittleRockScripture.org/Lectures/LettersPartOne. Of course, if your group has access to qualified speakers, you may choose to have live presentations.

Each person will need a current translation of the Bible. We recommend the *Little Rock Catholic Study Bible*, which makes use of the New American Bible, Revised Edition. Other translations, such as the New Jerusalem Bible or the New Revised Standard Version: Catholic Edition, would also work well.

HOW WILL YOU USE THESE MATERIALS?

Prepare in advance

Using Lesson One as an example:

- Begin with a simple prayer like the one found on page 13.

- Read the assigned material in the printed book for Lesson One (pages 14–18) so that you are prepared for the weekly small group session. You may do this assignment by reading a portion over a period of several days (effective and manageable) or by preparing all at once (more challenging).

- Answer the questions, Exploring Lesson One, found at the end of the assigned reading, pages 19–21.

- Use the Closing Prayer on page 21 when you complete your study. This prayer may be used again when you meet with the group.

Meet with your small group

- After introductions and greetings, allow time for prayer (about 5 minutes) as you begin the group session. You may use the prayer found on page 13 (also used by individuals in their preparation) or use a prayer of your choosing.

- Spend about 45–50 minutes discussing the responses to the questions that were prepared in advance. You may also develop your discussion further by responding to questions and interests that arise during the discussion and faith-sharing itself.

- Close the discussion and faith-sharing with prayer, about 5–10 minutes. You may use the Closing Prayer at the end of each lesson or one of your choosing at the end of the book. It is important to allow people to pray for personal and community needs and to give thanks for how God is moving in your lives.

- Listen to or view the wrap-up lecture associated with each lesson (15–20 minutes). You may watch the lecture online, use a DVD, or provide a live lecture by a qualified local speaker. This lecture provides a common focus for the group and reinforces insights from each lesson. You may view the lecture together at the end of the session or, if your group runs out of time, you may invite group members to watch the lecture on their own time after the discussion.

Above all, be aware that the Holy Spirit is moving within and among you.

PREFACE

Welcome to Little Rock Scripture Study's *Letters from Prison, Part One*. Before we begin our study, it may be helpful to understand why some of Paul's letters are classified as "Letters from Prison" (or "Captivity Epistles," as they have also been called).

Both the Acts of the Apostles and Paul's own letters attest to multiple imprisonments endured by Paul "for the defense of the gospel" (Phil 1:16). A determined and unflagging missionary, Paul was not shy about describing the danger and discomforts of his apostleship: "with far greater labors, far more imprisonments, far worse beatings, and numerous brushes with death" (2 Cor 11:23). It seems that Paul's message about a crucified Messiah won over some but angered others, Jews and Gentiles alike, to the point of physical attacks and incarceration (e.g., Acts 14:19; 16:22-24; 28:16; 2 Cor 11:24-26).

In five of the thirteen letters attributed to Paul, the apostle remarks within the letter that he is imprisoned at the time of its composition: Ephesians (3:1, 4:1), Philippians (1:7, 13-14, 16-17), Colossians (4:3, 10, 18), 2 Timothy (1:8, 16; 2:9), and Philemon (1, 9-10, 13). For example, in Philemon, Paul refers to himself as "a prisoner for Christ Jesus" (v. 1, 9), and in Colossians, he writes, "Remember my chains" (4:18).

Of these letters, 2 Timothy is typically classified with the Pastoral Letters (1 and 2 Timothy, Titus), leaving four remaining letters classified as Prison Letters: Ephesians, Philippians, Colossians, and Philemon. The authorship of Philippians and Philemon is undisputed (Paul himself is most certainly the author), so they are treated together in Part One of our study. Because the authorship of both Colossians and Ephesians is uncertain, and because the two books share many themes and ideas, they are treated together in *Letters from Prison, Part Two*.

As you read the commentary on the letter to the Philippians (Lessons 1–3), you may notice that the author will sometimes quote the text of Philippians with a slightly different wording than you find in the outside columns of your book. In these cases, Vincent M. Smiles is providing his own translation based on the Greek text rather than quoting the New American Bible, Revised Edition. These complementary translations can work together to enhance your study and understanding of this letter.

Enjoy your study!

Letters from Prison

Part One

LESSON ONE

Introduction and Philippians 1:1-26

Begin your personal study and group discussion with a simple and sincere prayer such as:

Prayer

Lord Jesus, your servant Paul willingly endured and even rejoiced in imprisonment for the sake of the gospel. May we also find joy in a way of life that embraces your death and resurrection. As we study your word, empower us with your strength.

Read the Introduction on page 14 and the Bible text of Philippians 1:1-26 found in the outside columns of pages 15–18, highlighting what stands out to you.

Read the accompanying commentary to add to your understanding.

Respond to the questions on pages 19–21, Exploring Lesson One.

The Closing Prayer on page 21 is for your personal use and may be used at the end of group discussion.

INTRODUCTION TO PHILIPPIANS

The importance of Philippi

Philippi was located about 110 miles northeast of Thessalonica in Macedonia. It got its name in 360 B.C. from Philip II of Macedon, father of Alexander the Great. In 42 B.C. it was the scene of a great battle in the civil war that followed the assassination of Julius Caesar. One of the victorious generals—Octavian—would eventually become Caesar Augustus, the emperor at the time of Jesus' birth. In 31 B.C. he made Philippi a Roman colony, permitting army veterans to settle there. Philippi, therefore, enjoyed special status; it came under Italian law and was exempt from various taxes. Paul was aware of its prestige (see 3:20; 4:22).

According to Acts 16:9, a vision summoned Paul to preach the gospel in Macedonia. From the very beginning Paul's relations with Philippi were warm and affectionate; it was the one church that consistently supported him in his apostolic work (4:15-16, cf. 1:5). Its founding members and leaders included a number of women (4:2-3; Acts 16:13-15), but unlike other cities of Paul's mission, Philippi seems not to have included a synagogue or any large Jewish population. The issue of when and where Paul wrote his letter to the Philippians takes us into its particular difficulties.

Challenges for interpretation

Scholars are agreed that Paul wrote Philippians, but most also believe that the letter we have was originally two or three separate letters. The most obvious seam is between 3:1 and 3:2; the switch of mood is so abrupt that even those who defend the unity of the letter struggle to explain the transition. Another difficulty is the delayed thank-you (4:10-20), which interrupts what looks like a standard ending of a letter (4:8-9, 21-23).

These and other observations have given rise to numerous theories about the original *letters* to Philippi and, of course, such theories affect the question of when and where Paul wrote. A common theory of multiple letters regards 4:10-20 as *letter A*, written from prison in Ephesus, about A.D. 55. *Letter B*, from prison a few weeks later, comprises 1:1–3:1a, 4:4-7, 21-23, and *letter C* includes the polemical 3:1b–4:3, 8-9 after Paul's release and was written perhaps from another city (Corinth?). A more simple theory would be: *letter A* = 1:1–3:1; 4:1-7, 10-23 (from Ephesus, about 55), and *letter B* = 3:2-21; 4:8-9 (from Corinth, about 56). All such theories presuppose that an editor, for some reason, conflated the original two or three letters and in doing so chopped off the openings and endings of one or more letters to avoid needless repetition.

Those who reject such theories insist that, in spite of difficulties, the letter is coherent and should be read as a unity, and certainly it *can* be read as a unity. The commentary to follow will do so, without denying that the theories of division are, at least from a historical perspective, very valuable. Assuming its unity, where was Paul when he wrote Philippians? The traditional view is that he wrote from Rome in the early sixties while under house arrest (Acts 28:16-31). Philippians, however (see 1:12-20; 2:17), envisions more than house arrest, and travel between Rome and Philippi was more difficult than the ease of communication that is presumed in the letter (2:19-30). Some scholars think Ephesus was the more likely place of writing, some time in the mid-fifties. There is no explicit record of Paul being imprisoned in Ephesus, but that is not an insurmountable problem (see 2 Cor 1:8; 11:23; 1 Cor 15:32). The best guess, therefore, is that Philippians comprises one or more letters written from prison in Ephesus in the mid-fifties and perhaps also from Corinth a year or so later.

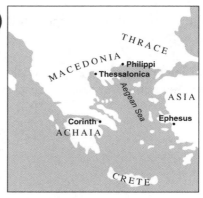

1:1-2 Greeting

The opening is brief and simple but includes interesting details. Timothy is named as co-sender, but he probably had little to do with the actual composition of the letter. From 1:3 Paul speaks in terms of his particular experience (e.g., 1:12-17); this letter, like the others that are original to Paul (Romans, 1 and 2 Corinthians, Galatians, Philippians, 1 Thessalonians, Philemon), bears the imprint of one very strong personality. It is unusual that Paul here does not claim the title "apostle." It was sometimes important for him to do so (e.g., Rom 1:1; Gal 1:1-12), but in the warm relationship he shared with Philippi, there was no such need. "Slaves" recalls Jesus' instruction about leadership (Mark 10:44).

Even more interesting, but also strange, is Paul's special mention of "the overseers and ministers." The Greek terms (*episkopos* and *diakonos*) are sometimes translated "bishop" and "deacon" (e.g., 1 Tim 3:2, 8), but in his list of primary church functions (1 Cor 12:28), these titles have no place, and in fact "overseers" are never mentioned again in the original letters. He uses "minister" (*diakonos*) to describe, among others, himself and other leading "ministers" of the gospel (1 Cor 3:5; 2 Cor 3:6), but only in the case of Phoebe (Rom 16:1) does it have an offi-

---

I: Address

CHAPTER 1

Greeting

¹Paul and Timothy, slaves of Christ Jesus, to all the holy ones in Christ Jesus who are in Philippi, with the overseers and ministers: ²grace to you and peace from God our Father and the Lord Jesus Christ.

Thanksgiving

³I give thanks to my God at every remembrance of you, ⁴praying always with joy in my every prayer for all of you, ⁵because of your partnership for the gospel from the first day until now. ⁶I am confident of this, that the one who began a good work in you will continue to complete it until the day of Christ Jesus. ⁷It is right that I should think this way about all of you, because I hold you in my heart, you who are all partners with me in grace, both in my imprisonment and in the defense and confirmation of the gospel.

continue

---

cial ring to it. These titles are so unusual that some scholars think the phrase was inserted by an editor, but this is doubtful. They must have been leaders of various house-churches—people like Euodia, Syntyche, and Clement (4:2-3).

The letter is addressed to "*all* the holy ones" (the baptized); he greets them with the standard but significant formula he employs in all his letters: "Grace to you and peace . . ." Though Paul addresses the community six times as "brothers" (e.g., 1:12), it is important to note that he is addressing women and men alike (note 4:2-3). *Adelphoi* ("brothers") in this context is best translated "believers."

1:3-11 The thanksgiving

The warmth of Paul's relationship with the Philippians is evident here: "I thank my God at *every* remembrance of you, praying *always*

> ⁸For God is my witness, how I long for all of you with the affection of Christ Jesus. ⁹And this is my prayer: that your love may increase ever more and more in knowledge and every kind of perception, ¹⁰to discern what is of value, so that you may be pure and blameless for the day of Christ, ¹¹filled with the fruit of righteousness that comes through Jesus Christ for the glory and praise of God.
>
> *continue*

with joy at my *every* prayer for *all* of you." In Greek the italicized words all begin with the letter "p," increasing the emotional and rhetorical effect. "My God" (also 4:19; Rom 1:8) denotes a personal relationship and is quite common in the psalms (e.g., Ps 22). "Joy" characterizes this letter throughout (1:18; 2:2, 17; 3:1; 4:1, 4, 10).

As a "thanksgiving," the passage is a standard feature of letter writing (cf. Rom 1:8-15; 1 Cor 1:4-9, etc.), but there is nothing standard or merely formal about Paul's "joyful" remembrance of the Philippians and of their "partnership in the gospel from the first day until now" (1:5). "Partnership" (or "participation"—see 2:1; 3:10; 4:15) refers both to their spiritual and their material sharing in the task of the gospel (see 4:15). They "defend and confirm" (1:7) the gospel by living it and by "struggling together" for its progress (1:27). They have also generously enabled Paul's missionary endeavors by their gifts to him (4:16); the phrase "until now" may refer to Paul's having just received their latest contribution.

The beginning of the "good work" that God "will continue" in them was that "first day," when Paul came to Philippi and was received, according to Acts 16:11-15, by Lydia and the other women at the "place of prayer." Lydia herself is not mentioned in Philippians, but the leadership of women seems to have remained important (4:2-3) in the intervening years. Lydia was from Thyatira (northwest Asia

Minor), says Luke (Acts 16:14), so she may no longer have been in Philippi.

The "day of Christ" is the first of several references to the expected return of Jesus (see 1:10; 2:16; 3:20-21). Some years earlier Paul had fully expected to be alive for Jesus' return (1 Thess 4:15-17), but now he realizes that he may die first (1:20-23). Nevertheless, the end will come soon, and Paul's confident prayer (1:9) is that, at the judgment, the believers of Philippi will be "pure and blameless" (1:10). In the meantime, he says, he "longs for them with the affection of Christ Jesus" (1:8); Paul's love for his churches was unmistakable (1 Thess 2:7-8; 2 Cor 11:11). His final prayer is that they "will be filled with the fruit of righteousness" (1:11). Paul will resume this theme of "righteousness through Christ" in the fiery words of 3:2-9.

Although he was in prison (1:7, 13-17), the apostle was joyful and confident. Epaphroditus, who has delivered the Philippians' gift (4:18), remains with Paul, recovering, we will discover later, from a near brush with death (2:25-30). Also with Paul is Timothy, of whom Paul will speak affectionately (2:22).

 Paul lists numerous imprisonments during his career (e.g., 2 Cor 11:23; Phil 1:7, 13-14; Phlm 1:1, 9), most of which were likely in Roman prisons. **Imprisonment in the Greco-Roman world** could occur for a variety of reasons, such as being in debt or being caught in a crime; but conditions varied somewhat, depending on the status of the person. Roman citizens might enjoy a kind of "house arrest," which allowed them to continue a modified lifestyle (e.g., Paul in Acts 28:30-31). Harsher conditions awaited hardened criminals, the poor, and runaway slaves. Prisons were generally dark, gloomy, filled with rats and other vermin, and lacking basic hygiene and ventilation. Men and women were not segregated in prison, and conditions were usually overcrowded and fostered disease. Prisoners were often kept shackled in chains, so that "chains" became synonymous with imprisonment (see Col 4:18). Some Roman officials tried to reform prison conditions because of the tendency to abuse prisoners. Early Christians were exhorted to visit the imprisoned as an act of mercy (Matt 25:36; Heb 13:3).

1:12-26 The irresistible progress of the gospel

The first paragraph here (1:12-18) is remarkable, speaking as it does of the effect of Paul's imprisonment, first among "the praetorium and all the rest" (1:13), probably denoting non-believers, and second, among believers also (1:14-18). "The praetorium" (palace guard) refers not to a place but to the soldiers and others of "Caesar's household" (4:22). Paul wants the Philippians to know that his imprisonment, although on the surface a disadvantage, "served to advance the gospel." This goes along with Paul's optimistic tone, in spite of the most difficult circumstances. Even among non-believers it has become known that Paul's imprisonment is "in Christ," meaning that they see Paul, not as a common criminal, but as a witness of Christ. And "most of the believers," far from being intimidated by his imprisonment, have gained greater confidence "to speak the word fearlessly" (1:14).

It is amazing that Paul has such equanimity in the circumstances he describes next. "Some," he says, "proclaim Christ because of envy and rivalry" (1:15), "thinking to cause me trouble in my imprisonment" (1:17). We know, then, that these opponents were Christians, but it is impossible to know much else about them or what sort of "trouble" (or "affliction") they might cause for Paul. Because he was a champion of the freedom of Gentile believers from the Jewish law, Paul ran into opposition many times, including in Antioch, Jerusalem (Gal 2:1-14; Acts 15:1-5), Galatia (Gal 1:6-9; 6:12-16), and Philippi (Phil 3:2-9; cf. Rom 3:8; 6:1-15).

II: Progress of the Gospel

[12]I want you to know, brothers, that my situation has turned out rather to advance the gospel, [13]so that my imprisonment has become well known in Christ throughout the whole praetorium and to all the rest, [14]and so that the majority of the brothers, having taken encouragement in the Lord from my imprisonment, dare more than ever to proclaim the word fearlessly.

[15]Of course, some preach Christ from envy and rivalry, others from good will. [16]The latter act out of love, aware that I am here for the defense of the gospel; [17]the former proclaim Christ out of selfish ambition, not from pure motives, thinking that they will cause me trouble in my imprisonment. [18]What difference does it make, as long as in every way, whether in pretense or in truth, Christ is being proclaimed? And in that I rejoice.

continue

The "trouble" these people sought to cause was perhaps simply distress in Paul's own mind. Their intention, however, may have been even more sinister, hoping to make his imprisonment worse and more protracted. Whatever the case, Paul refused to see it as a defeat. There was no trouble that could subdue his joy and confidence in Christ! Especially encouraging for him are those believers who preach Christ "for the sake of God's will" (1:15, not merely human "good will") and "out of love," aware that Paul was in prison "in defense of the gospel" (1:16). All that matters for Paul, whether to his advantage or not, is that "Christ is proclaimed; in that," he says, "I rejoice"!

"And I will continue to rejoice," he insists, "because I know that 'this will result in deliverance for me.'" These last words are from the book of Job (13:16). Whether or not the Philippians would recognize the reference—Philippians is almost devoid of Old Testament quotations—it seems clear that Paul sees in Job's words a reason for confidence. In the text in question, Job rebukes

Indeed I shall continue to rejoice, [19]for I know that this will result in deliverance for me through your prayers and support from the Spirit of Jesus Christ. [20]My eager expectation and hope is that I shall not be put to shame in any way, but that with all boldness, now as always, Christ will be magnified in my body, whether by life or by death. [21]For to me life is Christ, and death is gain. [22]If I go on living in the flesh, that means fruitful labor for me. And I do not know which I shall choose. [23]I am caught between the two. I long to depart this life and be with Christ, [for] that is far better. [24]Yet that I remain [in] the flesh is more necessary for your benefit. [25]And this I know with confidence, that I shall remain and continue in the service of all of you for your progress and joy in the faith, [26]so that your boasting in Christ Jesus may abound on account of me when I come to you again.

his friends because they have presumed to speak for God. Job, however, is convinced that they do not understand God's ways and that God, somehow, will vindicate him and bring him "deliverance" (or "salvation"). In applying this text to himself, Paul appears to be saying that he "knows" what will happen to him. In reality, however, he does not even know whether the outcome will be "life or death" (1:20). Either alternative will be "deliverance"!

"The prayer" of his friends in Philippi and the "support of the Spirit of Jesus Christ" (1:19) are further reasons that Paul is confident. In fact, his confidence extends to "eager expectation and hope" (1:20). "Hope" here denotes the biblical virtue that "waits with eager longing" (Rom 8:19); it is not to be understood, as so often in modern speech, as a vague and anxious desire ("I hope the weather will be nice"). Paul

fully "expects" his hope to be fulfilled. "I shall not be put to shame," he says, "in any way," meaning that there is nothing his enemies can do to defeat him. That is true for the simple reason that Paul has let go of any personal gain or advantage; all that matters is that "Christ is glorified," and whether that happens by Paul's "life or death" (1:20), it is all he desires.

Indifference to death is difficult to understand. We associate such indifference with the depths of despair and pain, but here it arises in a letter which, more than any other, exudes hope and joy. This gives a glimpse into Paul's spirit and into what motivated his long and difficult ministry. For Paul, "life" itself is nothing other than "Christ," and therefore "to die is gain" (1:21). To the Galatians he had said, "I have been crucified with Christ. I no longer live, rather, Christ lives within me" (Gal 2:19-20; cf. Rom 8:10-11). His entire life and identity are enfolded in his allegiance to Jesus. He is, therefore, content "to live in the flesh" for the sake of "fruitful labor" (1:22) for the gospel. On the other hand, he has a great desire "to depart this life and be with Christ—which is far better" (1:23). Nevertheless, he knows that it may be "more necessary for [their] benefit" to remain (1:24) and, for some reason, he seems convinced that this is the more likely outcome.

In fact, Paul is sure that he will "remain and abide with" them for their "progress and joy in the faith" (1:25), "so that" the Philippians "may boast in Christ Jesus" when Paul comes to them again. "Boasting" is closely related to the joyful hope that so fills this letter. Paradoxically, there is no such thing for Paul as "boasting" (Rom 3:27; 4:2; 1 Cor 1:29), as though humans could somehow be independent of God. On the other hand, within the relationship of faith, Paul often speaks of the joyful boast that believers can have because of what God enables within them (e.g., Rom 5:2-3; 2 Cor 1:12-14; Phil 2:16; 1 Thess 2:19).

EXPLORING LESSON ONE

1. What has motivated you to embark on a study of the letters associated with Paul's imprisonment?

_____

_____

_____

_____

_____

2. Read Acts 16:9-40. What do you learn about Paul's experience in Philippi according to Acts?

_____

_____

_____

_____

3. Why do many scholars think that Paul's letter to the Philippians as we now have it was originally two or even three letters (see Introduction)?

_____

_____

_____

_____

4. Why might Paul identify himself as a "slave" of Jesus Christ (1:1) rather than an "apostle" as he often does in letters (e.g., 2 Cor 1:1; Gal 1:1)?

_____

_____

_____

_____

5. a) Paul writes of the Philippians' "partnership for the gospel" and their partnership "with me in grace" (1:5, 7). What is the nature of the Philippians' partnership with Paul?

_____

_____

_____

_____

b) In what ways are you part of a "partnership for the gospel"?

_____

_____

_____

_____

6. How has Paul's imprisonment actually promoted the spread of the gospel (1:12-18)?

_____

_____

_____

_____

7. Have you ever shared Paul's experience of rejoicing in a difficult, uncomfortable, or painful situation (1:18-19)? If so, what was the source of your joy?

_____

_____

_____

_____

8. a) What do you think Paul means when he writes, "My eager expectation and hope is that . . . Christ will be magnified in my body" (1:20)?

_____

_____

_____

_____

b) What are some ways that Christ can be "magnified" in our bodies?

_____

_____

_____

9. a) Why is Paul content to live or die (1:21-26)?

_____

_____

_____

_____

b) Can you relate to this attitude? Why or why not?

_____

_____

_____

_____

CLOSING PRAYER

Prayer

I am confident of this, that the one who began a good work in you will continue to complete it until the day of Christ Jesus. (Phil 1:6)

Lord Jesus, guide our study and prayer as we come to know Paul through time spent with his words. Inspire in us his spirit of joy and steadfastness. Bless us with relationships as fruitful as his friendship with the Philippians. And above all, make us partners in the gospel, imitating Paul's life in Christ—a life of faith, hope, and love. We pray now for those who are part of our own communities: our families, friends, fellow parishioners, and co-workers, especially . . .

LESSON TWO

Philippians 1:27–3:1

Begin your personal study and group discussion with a simple and sincere prayer such as:

Prayer

Lord Jesus, your servant Paul willingly endured and even rejoiced in imprisonment for the sake of the gospel. May we also find joy in a way of life that embraces your death and resurrection. As we study your word, empower us with your strength.

Read the Bible text of Philippians 1:27–3:1 found in the outside columns of pages 24–29, highlighting what stands out to you.

Read the accompanying commentary to add to your understanding.

Respond to the questions on pages 30–32, Exploring Lesson Two.

The Closing Prayer on page 33 is for your personal use and may be used at the end of group discussion.

III: Instructions for the Community

Steadfastness in Faith

²⁷Only, conduct yourselves in a way worthy of the gospel of Christ, so that, whether I come and see you or am absent, I may hear news of you, that you are standing firm in one spirit, with one mind struggling together for the faith of the gospel, ²⁸not intimidated in any way by your opponents. This is proof to them of destruction, but of your salvation. And this is God's doing. ²⁹For to you has been granted, for the sake of Christ, not only to believe in him but also to suffer for him. ³⁰Yours is the same struggle as you saw in me and now hear about me.

CHAPTER 2

Plea for Unity and Humility

¹If there is any encouragement in Christ, any solace in love, any participation in the Spirit, any compassion and mercy, ²complete my joy by being of the same mind, with the same love, united in heart, thinking one thing. ³Do nothing out of selfishness or out of vainglory; rather, humbly regard others as more important than yourselves, ⁴each looking out not for his own interests, but [also] everyone for those of others.

⁵Have among yourselves the same attitude that is also yours in Christ Jesus,

continue

1:27–2:18 Encouragement and instructions

Paul now changes his tone. In a long, complex sentence (vv. 27-30), he turns emphatically to instruction: "Only [one thing]—conduct yourselves worthily . . ." "Conduct yourselves" could be translated "be citizens" (cf. 3:20) and would be relevant in Philippi, which, as a Roman colony, was proud of its full citizenship rights. Believers, however, now are citizens under "Christ's gospel," and Paul's wish is that whether he can "come and see" them or not (2:12), he should "hear about" them

that they "stand in one spirit" (1:27). "Spirit" might include reference to the Holy Spirit, but the parallel phrase "one mind" shows that Paul is primarily thinking of the spiritual unity of believers. "The faith of the gospel" (1:27) is a unique phrase; it probably means "the faith that arises from the gospel." Though the Philippians are being persecuted, they are not to "be startled in any way by the opponents" (1:28), the latter referring probably to unbelievers, the probable source of the trouble Paul himself experienced in Philippi (1 Thess 2:2).

The next part of this complex sentence gets even more difficult. "This," he says, "is proof to them of destruction, but of your salvation" (1:28). "This" must refer to the whole situation of belief opposed by unbelief. The next two phrases ("proof to them of destruction, but of your salvation") could mean (1) that unbelievers think that the outcome will be "destruction" for the church, with Paul, however, assuring believers that in reality it will be their "salvation." Alternatively, (2) Paul assures the church that the present situation shows that unbelievers are bound for destruction (cf. 1 Cor 1:18; 2 Cor 4:3), but believers for salvation (1:28; cf. Rom 8:28). "And this," he concludes, "is from God," meaning not only salvation but also the mysterious outworking of things that, on either interpretation, unbelief cannot fathom.

The next two verses (1:29-30) assert that *everything* derives from God, both the capacity "to believe"—faith is a gift (cf. Gal 3:23-25)—and "to suffer" for Christ. The Philippians share "the same struggle" which they saw in Paul when he was persecuted in Philippi (1 Thess 2:2; Acts 16:20-24) and which they now hear about as he languishes in prison. For Paul, to suffer for Christ is a privilege (Rom 5:3) and an opportunity to experience grace (2 Cor 12:8-10).

Paul's rhetoric rises to a higher pitch as he reminds the Philippians of the fundamental qualities of life "in Christ" and appeals to them to live these out in full. "If there is . . ." is purely rhetorical; there is no question of whether these qualities are present (cf. 4:8). The passage is carefully and artistically phrased, so that commentary might obscure rather than clarify. Verses 1-4 prepare for the exhortation of verse 5 and the uniquely beautiful, but also deeply theological hymn of verses 6-11. Because of its unusual wording and rhythm, some scholars believe that Paul *quotes* a hymn that he did not himself compose. In any event, he found it deeply meaningful.

⁶Who, though he was in the form of God,
did not regard equality with God something to be grasped.
⁷Rather, he emptied himself,
taking the form of a slave,
coming in human likeness;
and found human in appearance,
⁸he humbled himself,
becoming obedient to death, even death on a cross.
⁹Because of this, God greatly exalted him
and bestowed on him the name
that is above every name,
¹⁰that at the name of Jesus
every knee should bend,
of those in heaven and on earth and under the earth,
¹¹and every tongue confess that
Jesus Christ is Lord,
to the glory of God the Father.

continue

 Scholars call the famous Philippians hymn the **kenotic hymn** (from the Greek, *kenōsis*, "emptying") because it aptly describes Jesus' emptying himself to take on human flesh. The church uses this hymn regularly—in the Liturgy of the Hours (Sunday Evening Prayer) and in the solemn liturgies of Palm Sunday and Good Friday—because it expresses eloquently the theology of Christ's passion, death, and exaltation. It may subtly contrast Christ with Adam, as elsewhere in Paul (Rom 5:12-14).

Adam	Christ, the New Adam
Made in God's image	In the form of God
Grasped at equality with God	Rejected grasping for equality with God
Became filled with pride	Emptied himself
Made himself a master	Made himself a slave
Exalted himself	Humbled himself
Ultimately brought low by God	Ultimately exalted by God

Obedience and Service in the World

[12] So then, my beloved, obedient as you have always been, not only when I am present but all the more now when I am absent, work out your salvation with fear and trembling. [13] For God is the one who, for his good purpose, works in you both to desire and to work. [14] Do everything without grumbling or questioning, [15] that you may be blameless and innocent, children of God without blemish in the midst of a crooked and perverse generation, among whom you shine like lights in the world, [16] as you hold on to the word of life, so that my boast for the day of Christ may be that I did not run in vain or labor in vain. [17] But, even if I am poured out as a libation upon the sacrificial service of your faith, I rejoice and share my joy with all of you. [18] In the same way you also should rejoice and share your joy with me.

continue

The crucial phrases parallel and reinforce one another, but not merely for rhetorical effect. Paul may have in mind emerging tensions within the Philippian churches (4:2-3), which he wishes to forestall. "Encouragement in Christ" and "comfort of love" (2:1) are synonymous; "love" refers both to the love Christ has for believers and to the love he inspires in them for one another (Gal 2:20; Phil 1:9). "Participation (or 'fellowship') in the spirit" recalls Paul's blessing that has been adopted into the liturgy (2 Cor 13:13) and, more clearly than 1:27 ('in one spirit'), alludes to the Spirit of God that believers share. The words "compassion (or 'affection') and mercy" reflect Paul's insistence elsewhere on the primacy of the love-command (Rom 13:8-10; Gal 5:14).

"Complete my joy" (2:2) finishes the thought begun with all those "ifs" and recalls the great joy Paul felt with regard to the Philippians (1:4; 4:1). Being "in Christ," believers can be of "the same mind" and have "the same love," that is,

mutual love for one another. The next phrases—"united in heart (or 'mind'), thinking one thing"—repeat and reinforce the same notion. The words "Do nothing" (2:3) are actually not in the Greek text, though it is reasonable to supply them. Paul simply says, "Nothing out of selfishness nor from vainglory ('conceit'), but with humility regard others as more important . . ." "Others" here refers to believers; elsewhere Paul extends this love to outsiders (4:5; Gal 6:10; 1 Thess 3:12; 5:15). "Humility" and making others' interests more important than one's own (2:4, cf. 1 Cor 10:24, 33; 13:5) are not to be understood as groveling subservience; being humble has nothing to do with being a doormat (John 18:22-23). The humility Paul describes is self-sacrifice for others born out of unity in Christ. The basis for such humility is what Paul turns to in the Christ-hymn that follows.

A **libation** is a liquid such as wine or blood poured out upon an altar as a sacrificial offering. Old Testament texts attest to the Israelite practice of offering libations to Yнwн (Gen 35:14; Exod 29:38-41). Paul uses "libation" as a metaphor for the totally self-emptying nature of his own ministry (Phil 2:17; 2 Tim 4:6).

Paul introduces the hymn with a third use of the verb *phronein* ("think") in this immediate passage (2:1-5; see 3:15); the related noun is part of the word "humility" ("lowly thinking"—2:3). It denotes an attitude or mindset more than "thought." The New American Bible, Revised Edition translation may be correct, but more probably Paul is simply pointing to "the attitude that is also in Christ Jesus" himself (2:5), as the opening lines of the hymn suggest. Paul presents Christ's loving and humble attitude as the model for Christian morality. The hymn itself is almost impossible to interpret in a short space; we will confine ourselves to a few essentials.

Whether the hymn is poetry as such or simply rhythmic, exalted prose, it is constructed around balanced, pregnant phrases that tell and celebrate the stages of Christ's redemptive acts for the world. It can be divided into six stanzas of three lines each, dealing with: beginning—emptying—dying—being exalted—being named—being glorified. The first half comprises Christ's actions, the second half God's. The central point is the little phrase "death on a cross." The hymn evokes and may, in some respects, be modeled on the great Servant Song of the Good Friday liturgy (Isa 52:13–53:12).

The major problem of the first three lines (2:6) is whether they envisage Christ in divine preexistence ("in the form of God"), analogous to John 1:1, or as the antitype to Adam, who also was "in God's image" (Gen 1:26-27), but who, unlike Christ, "grasped at" equality with God and was disobedient (Gen 3:1-19). There are strong arguments on both sides. It is also possible—and an easy way out—that Paul might have entertained aspects of both interpretations. Other texts (notably 2 Cor 8:9; Gal 4:4; Col 1:15-17) show that the preexistence of Christ was not foreign to Paul, but Christ as the antitype of disobedient Adam is even more clearly attested (Rom 5:12-21; 1 Cor 15:22). A great deal depends on how individual phrases are translated and interpreted. "Equality with God" as "something to be *grasped at*" suggests the Adamic interpretation, but the crucial Greek word *(harpagmon)* could also be rendered "something to *be held on to*" or *"be taken advantage of."* Overall, the Adamic interpretation is more likely, but certainty is impossible.

The next stanza ("emptying") has three phrases describing Christ's entrance into the human condition (2:7). The preexistence interpretation sees here the description of the incarnation, as in John 1:14 ("the Word became flesh") and can properly say that it was precisely in being a "slave" (not in spite of it) that Jesus revealed who God is. "Emptied himself" evokes 2 Corinthians 8:9 ("though he was rich, Christ became poor for your sake"). The Adamic view focuses on the contrast between human arrogance ("You will be like gods"—Gen 3:5) and Christ's humility.

The final stanza of the hymn's first part describes Christ's self-sacrificial death (2:7-8). All can agree that Christ's "obedience to death" is, for Paul, the heart of the gospel, and, as here, he sometimes focuses on Jesus' death without explicit mention of the resurrection (e.g., 1 Cor 2:2; Gal 2:19-20). In the immediate context, Christ's self-emptying death provides the basis for the self-sacrifice that Paul wants the Philippians to practice toward one another (2:3-4). The nadir of the hymn is the little phrase "death on a cross," which many interpreters understand to be Paul's addition to the hymn he is quoting. That view may be correct; the phrase breaks the rhythm. On the other hand, standing at the center, it may be intended to stand alone as the turning point. Paul was not bound by rules as he either quoted or composed. However understood, it is a stark but powerful image: Christ crucified, the one on whom human redemption turns, seemingly abandoned (Mark 15:34; Gal 3:13).

"Because of this" (2:9) recalls the similar turning point in the hymn of the Suffering Servant (Isa 53:11-12) and does not primarily envisage reward for suffering but points to the *ways* of God, victory *through* suffering. God reveals in Jesus the *reversal* of human expectations by highly exalting the Crucified and bestowing on him "the name above every other name." This may refer to the exalting of the name "Jesus" itself (2:10), but probably it envisages God conferring on Jesus the name "Lord." Throughout the Old Testament, "Lord" *(kyrios)* is the translation for the sacred name Yʜwʜ, the sacred name for God (Exod 3:14; 20:7). The preexistence view of the hymn sees Jesus being raised again to his previous exalted status (cf. John 17:5). The Adamic view takes at face value that God "highly exalted" Jesus and "gave him a name" he did not previously have (cf. Acts 2:36; Rom 1:3-4). The latter view is not, of course, a denial of Jesus' divine nature but simply says that it was *not yet so fully* articulated. That Paul saw Jesus as "the Son of God" is quite clear (e.g., Rom 8:2, 32; Gal 4:4), but in

27

Paul's time the formulations of the Nicene Creed were far in the future.

Be that as it may, the present text provides clear precedent for later formulations. Isaiah 45:23, clearly quoted in 2:10-11 ("every knee shall bend . . . every tongue confess") applies to Jesus words that the text from Isaiah uses of God; all creation and all parts of creation will own and confess that "Jesus is Lord" (Rom 10:9; 1 Cor 12:3) and in glorifying Jesus will glorify "God the Father." So concludes this remarkable hymn. Its second half is not as relevant to Paul's point that believers are to imitate the humility of Jesus. Nevertheless, in depicting also the final stage of Christ's self-sacrifice, it enables believers to have a greater vision of the path of faith.

In the next paragraph (2:12-18) Paul uses the example of Christ to exhort the Philippians to both greater effort and a deeper vision. Of great interest is the command "Work out your own salvation." It arises from mention of Paul's "absence." When present, *he* worked for their salvation; now "all the more" he throws the responsibility on them. It is a remarkable command, however, because usually salvation, for Paul, is exclusively *God's* work (e.g., 1 Thess 5:9) and, in fact, he hastens to correct any misunderstanding by emphasizing that "*God* is the one who . . . works in you both to desire and to work" for salvation (2:13; cf. 1:29). Nevertheless, Paul also knows that humans have a part in the salvation of themselves and of those close to them (Rom 11:14; 1 Cor 7:16; 9:22); believers' conduct does matter.

The difference, therefore, between believers and the world ought to be apparent. Believers "shine like stars in the cosmos" (2:15), but not if "quarrels and disputes" (2:14) mark their behavior. The world, says Paul, is "crooked and perverse"; believers are to be "innocent." This can come across as an idyllic, unrealistic vision, but Paul presupposes a community where *every* member "works for salvation." There is here no handing over of responsibility to a class of "ministers and overseers" (1:1); all together "hold on to the word of life" and will prove the value of Paul's "labor" on "the day

of Christ" (2:16). Meanwhile, for all his apparent optimism (1:25; 2:24), Paul acknowledges that he may be "poured out as a libation," almost certainly a reference to martyrdom (2 Tim 4:6). "Sacrifice and service" is the language of temple worship and is used elsewhere both of Paul (Rom 15:16) and of believers generally (Rom 12:1; 15:27; Phil 2:30; 4:18). Paul would find death a reason for "rejoicing" (1:23; cf. 3:10), and if it happens, he asks that the Philippians "rejoice with" him (2:18)!

2:19–3:1 Travel plans

Paul often includes, usually toward the end of his letters (see Rom 15:14-32; 1 Cor 16:5-12), some indication of the travel plans for himself and others. He hopes "to send Timothy soon" (2:19) so that he will be able to bring back good news. Paul takes this occasion to speak very warmly of Timothy (1:1; Acts 16:1), who was like a devoted child to the apostle (1:22). Paul also hopes that he himself will soon be able to come to Philippi (1:24).

Timothy was a trusted co-worker, companion, and disciple of Paul. In Acts 16:1, we learn that Timothy's mother was Jewish-Christian, and his father was Greek (Gentile). Timothy is mentioned as a co-worker of Paul in the Corinthian correspondence as well as in Romans, Philippians, Colossians, 1 and 2 Thessalonians, and Philemon. According to Acts, Timothy travelled with Paul on two out of three of his major missionary journeys (16:3; 20:4) and was entrusted with various missions by Paul (17:14; 19:22; see also 1 Cor 4:17; 1 Thess 3:2). The later Pastoral Letters of 1 and 2 Timothy, though likely not written by Paul himself, are addressed to this same Timothy, who is there presented as the leader of the church in Ephesus.

He thinks it even more urgent "to send Epaphroditus," who came as "an apostle" of the

Philippians (2:25), bearing their gift (4:18). The next verses suggest regular communications between Paul in prison and the Philippians. They have heard that Epaphroditus fell seriously ill ("close to death"—2:27, 30), and word has come back of their concern, so that now Epaphroditus is concerned for *them* (2:26, 28). Though he figures nowhere else in the New Testament, he was a "co-worker" with Paul for a while (2:25). Paul regarded it as a mercy of God that Epaphroditus recovered from his illness (2:27) and is concerned that the Philippians should receive him warmly and "hold such people in high regard" (2:29; cf. 1 Thess 5:13). He "risked his life" both "for the work of Christ" and for the "service" the Philippians wished to render to Paul (2:30).

The word "finally" (3:1) can signal the near conclusion of a letter (2 Cor 13:11; cf. Eph 6:10; 2 Thess 3:1) or the conclusion of one topic and transition to another (1 Cor 7:29; 1 Thess 4:1). Here, following "travel plans," the letter should be drawing to a close, but it does not, and it is unusual that there is a second "finally" (4:8). Further, the natural sequence of "Rejoice in the Lord" (3:1) is either 4:1 or 4:4, certainly not 3:2! These observations have convinced scholars either that Philippians comprises more than one letter (the majority view) or that something has caused Paul to create a very awkward transition after 3:1. In any event, 3:1 or at least the command to "rejoice in the Lord" concludes the first (half of the) letter, recalling one of its major themes. It is "no burden" to him to repeat himself (about joy), but it is rather a "safeguard" for them (cf. Neh 8:10; Pss 81:1; 21:1).

IV: Travel Plans of Paul and His Assistants

Timothy and Paul

[19]I hope, in the Lord Jesus, to send Timothy to you soon, so that I too may be heartened by hearing news of you. [20]For I have no one comparable to him for genuine interest in whatever concerns you. [21]For they all seek their own interests, not those of Jesus Christ. [22]But you know his worth, how as a child with a father he served along with me in the cause of the gospel. [23]He it is, then, whom I hope to send as soon as I see how things go with me, [24]but I am confident in the Lord that I myself will also come soon.

Epaphroditus

[25]With regard to Epaphroditus, my brother and co-worker and fellow soldier, your messenger and minister in my need, I consider it necessary to send him to you. [26]For he has been longing for all of you and was distressed because you heard that he was ill. [27]He was indeed ill, close to death; but God had mercy on him, not just on him but also on me, so that I might not have sorrow upon sorrow. [28]I send him therefore with the greater eagerness, so that, on seeing him, you may rejoice again, and I may have less anxiety. [29]Welcome him then in the Lord with all joy and hold such people in esteem, [30]because for the sake of the work of Christ he came close to death, risking his life to make up for those services to me that you could not perform.

CHAPTER 3

Concluding Admonitions

[1]Finally, my brothers, rejoice in the Lord. Writing the same things to you is no burden for me but is a safeguard for you.

EXPLORING LESSON TWO

1. Paul encourages the Philippians to "[stand] firm in one spirit, with one mind" even in the midst of their struggles (1:27; see also 2:2). Where do you see this spirit of unity—in the church, in your parish, in your home—and what is its benefit?

_____

_____

_____

_____

_____

2. Paul speaks of faith as a gift (1:29; see also 1 Tim 1:13-14; Mark 9:24; and Luke 17:5). What do you think Paul means by this? Do you think it means that God chooses certain people to give this gift to, or do you think he is referring to faith as a mysterious grace? Reflect on this mystery, and record some of your thoughts.

_____

_____

_____

_____

_____

3. The commentary on 2:3-5 seeks to explain Paul's understanding of humility: "being humble has nothing to do with being a doormat." How would you explain Paul's understanding of Christian humility based on 2:3-5 and the hymn that follows in 2:6-11?

_____

_____

_____

_____

4. One interpretation of 2:6 (being "in the form of God") points to the preexistence of Christ. The other points to Christ as the New Adam who, "in the image of God," refuses to grasp at equality with God as Adam did. Which interpretation do you find most convincing and why? Or do you see both interpretations as possible?

_____

_____

_____

_____

5. a) The commentary on 2:7 states that "it was precisely in being a 'slave' (not in spite of it) that Jesus revealed who God is." How does Jesus reveal God's very nature by "emptying himself" and "taking the form of a slave"?

_____

_____

_____

_____

   b) What other biblical figures can you think of that exemplify this "self-emptying" attitude?

_____

_____

_____

6. What is the central phrase of the Christ-hymn (2:6-11), and why is it so significant (see also 1 Cor 1:18-25; 2:2; Gal 2:19-20)?

_____

_____

_____

_____

_____

7. How does the "journey" of Christ from incarnation and crucifixion to exaltation and glorification show believers "the path of faith"? (See Rom 6:4-5; 8:17.)

_____

_____

_____

_____

8. Why does Paul tell the Philippians to "work out [their] salvation" (2:12), and how does he clarify this statement (2:13)?

_____

_____

_____

_____

_____

9. a) What does Paul mean when he says that he may be "poured out as a libation upon the sacrificial service" of the faith of the Philippians (2:17; see also 2 Tim 4:6; Exod 25:29; 29:40-41)?

_____

_____

_____

_____

b) Have you ever known anyone who has poured out his or her own life in this way?

_____

_____

_____

_____

10. Paul speaks of his co-workers Timothy and Epaphroditus with gratitude and affection (2:19-30). What does it tell us about Paul that he has this kind of relationship with those who work alongside him? What does it tell us about the nature of ministry?

_____

_____

_____

_____

_____

CLOSING PRAYER

Prayer

Have among yourselves the same attitude that is also yours in Christ Jesus . . . (Phil 2:5)

Jesus Christ, you emptied yourself, becoming poor for our sakes, dying on a cross for our sakes, humbling yourself for our sakes. May the legacy of your incarnation and death be our own humility and service toward one another. Like you, may we lay down our lives for one another in a spirit of humility and love. Today we pray especially for those whose lives imitate yours, for those we look up to in faith . . .

LESSON THREE

Philippians 3:2–4:23

Begin your personal study and group discussion with a simple and sincere prayer such as:

Prayer

Lord Jesus, your servant Paul willingly endured and even rejoiced in imprisonment for the sake of the gospel. May we also find joy in a way of life that embraces your death and resurrection. As we study your word, empower us with your strength.

Read the Bible text of Philippians 3:2–4:23 found in the outside columns of pages 36–40, highlighting what stands out to you.

Read the accompanying commentary to add to your understanding.

Respond to the questions on pages 41–43, Exploring Lesson Three.

The Closing Prayer on page 43 is for your personal use and may be used at the end of group discussion.

V: Polemic: Righteousness and the Goal in Christ

Against Legalistic Teachers

[2]Beware of the dogs! Beware of the evil workers! Beware of the mutilation! [3]For we are the circumcision, we who worship through the Spirit of God, who boast in Christ Jesus and do not put our confidence in flesh, [4]although I myself have grounds for confidence even in the flesh.

Paul's Autobiography

If anyone else thinks he can be confident in flesh, all the more can I. [5]Circumcised on the eighth day, of the race of Israel, of the tribe of Benjamin, a Hebrew of Hebrew parentage, in observance of the law a Pharisee, [6]in zeal I persecuted the church, in righteousness based on the law I was blameless.

Righteousness from God

[7][But] whatever gains I had, these I have come to consider a loss because of Christ. [8]More than

continue

3:2-11 An urgent warning against false faith

This paragraph shows how Paul's feelings of affection can burst into anger at those who would threaten the direction of believers' faith in Christ. The threat probably comes from conservative Jewish Christians, similar to those he contended with in Galatians. In that case the opponents were already present (Gal 1:6-7; 6:12). In this case Paul seems simply to be afraid of their imminent arrival in Philippi, and he uses harsh invectives to emphasize that such persons are not to be trusted. In calling them "dogs," he turns on them a common Jewish epithet directed at Gentiles (Mark 7:27); "evildoers" may be an ironic twist on their claim to be "law-doers," and "mutilation" *(katatome)* is a sarcastic reference to their insistence on "circumcision" *(peritome*—3:2; cf. Gal 6:12). *They* are not the true "circumcision," says

Paul; *"we are,"* we "who worship through the Spirit of God" (3:3).

The opponents claim that with their adherence to the traditions and laws of Israel, *they* represent the true "Israel" ("descendants of Abraham" —Gal 3:6-9, 29). Paul insists that they are nothing of the kind and sees this as an urgent issue, because it has to do with whether believers have "confidence" in Christ—note the repetition of this word (3:3-4)—or implicitly regard Christ's death as worthless (cf. Gal 2:20-21). By his conversion Paul was convinced that the covenant, from Abraham on, was founded simply on grace and faith (Rom 4:1-5; 9:6-16); the law was secondary (Rom 4:13-17; Gal 3:15-17).

Paul's critique of these Jewish-Christian opponents must *not* be taken as a critique of Judaism, as has too often been the case. Paul's love of his heritage (e.g., Rom 9:1-5) and his confidence that God would be faithful to the covenant with them (Rom 11:1-2, 29) are well attested. The enduring value of God's covenant with the Jews was also strongly affirmed at the Second Vatican Council. This polemic has to do with particular circumstances in Philippi, not with Judaism as such.

Paul presents himself as the model to follow. If circumcision or law-obedience were crucial, Paul would have "even more" reason for "confidence" than the opponents (3:4).

There follows in verses 5-6 his recounting of the privileges he enjoyed by birth and his chosen way of life as a "Pharisee," all of which attest to his unique pedigree as a devoted member of the chosen people. His "zeal" for the law, in which he had been "blameless" (3:6), had even extended to persecution of the church (cf. 1 Cor 15:9; Gal 1:13-14; Acts 7:58–8:3; 9:1-2). But what he had once thought of as "gains," now "because of Christ" he reckons as "loss" (3:7). No human privilege or achievement "counts" for anything when compared with "the supreme good of knowing Christ Jesus my Lord" (3:8).

The key issue for Paul in all his letters is the nature of the divine-human relationship—specifically, by what is it characterized? As here, he rejects law and tradition as its foundation; elsewhere he rejects human wisdom or any kind of superior status, whether religious or social (Rom 2:17-29; 1 Cor 1:18-31). All such "gains" are simply "so much rubbish"; what matters is to "know Christ" (3:8), which means to have "faith in" him (3:9), in the sense of joyful trust. To "be found in him" looks forward to the judgment, when those who are "in Christ" will have no reason for fear (2:16).

Verses 9-11 describe the purpose of letting go of former privileges and status: it is "to know him and the power of his resurrection" (3:10). "Resurrection," however, is not merely in the future; it is a *present* experience, even in the midst of suffering (2 Cor 4:7-18; 5:17). To be "in Christ" is already to "walk in newness of life" (Rom 6:4; cf. 7:6). None of this, however, is a human accomplishment. The relationship ("righteousness") believers enjoy with God derives from a "righteousness" gained by Christ that is conferred as a gift; it is not essentially dependent on law or tradition (3:9). Even "faith" (3:9) is not the *condition* of "righteousness" but simply the *way it is lived.*

3:12-21 The ongoing journey toward Christ

Having stressed again *God's* initiative (cf. 1:29; 2:13), Paul turns emphatically to the theme of human responsibility, though even here Christ's action is prominent. He uses a

that, I even consider everything as a loss because of the supreme good of knowing Christ Jesus my Lord. For his sake I have accepted the loss of all things and I consider them so much rubbish, that I may gain Christ [9]and be found in him, not having any righteousness of my own based on the law but that which comes through faith in Christ, the righteousness from God, depending on faith [10]to know him and the power of his resurrection and [the] sharing of his sufferings by being conformed to his death, [11]if somehow I may attain the resurrection from the dead.

Forward in Christ

[12]It is not that I have already taken hold of it or have already attained perfect maturity, but I continue my pursuit in hope that I may possess it, since I have indeed been taken possession of by Christ [Jesus]. [13]Brothers, I for my part do not consider myself to have taken possession. Just one thing: forgetting what lies behind but straining forward to what lies ahead, [14]I continue my pursuit toward the goal, the prize of God's upward calling, in Christ Jesus. [15]Let us, then, who are "perfectly mature" adopt this attitude. And if you have a different attitude, this too God will reveal to you. [16]Only, with regard to what we have attained, continue on the same course.

continue

series of verbs ("received," "made perfect," "pursue") to describe the *process* of "straining forward" toward "perfection" in Christ. He is at pains to say that, to be sure, he is not totally "perfected," but that, as he wishes them to do, he makes maximum effort to "possess" that for which he is already "possessed by Christ" (3:12). Therefore, he lets go of "the past" and sets his sights only on "the prize of God's upward calling" (3:13-14). Paul may again have death in mind (cf. 1:23; 2:17), but "calling" is an important word in his letters to denote both the event of conversion and the life of faith to which it leads (e.g., Rom 4:17; 8:30; 1 Cor 1:9,

Wrong Conduct and Our Goal

[17]Join with others in being imitators of me, brothers, and observe those who thus conduct themselves according to the model you have in us. [18]For many, as I have often told you and now tell you even in tears, conduct themselves as enemies of the cross of Christ. [19]Their end is destruction. Their God is their stomach; their glory is in their "shame." Their minds are occupied with earthly things. [20]But our citizenship is in heaven, and from it we also await a savior, the Lord Jesus Christ. [21]He will change our lowly body to conform with his glorified body by the power that enables him also to bring all things into subjection to himself.

continue

26; 7:15-24). Paul considers himself and others as, in a sense, "perfect" (3:15, cf. 1 Cor 2:6; Matt 5:48), but this perfection consists in the "attitude," which he wants the Philippians to have, of *striving* for perfection! If some are inclined to disagree (cf. 1 Cor 11:16), Paul is sure that he is right and that "God will reveal this also" to them. Meanwhile they should remain constant in the progress already attained (3:16) and join together in being "imitators" of Paul and of those whose behavior is a true model.

Paul frequently asks his congregation to **"imitate" him** (1 Cor 4:16, 11:1; Phil 3:17). Paul viewed himself as a model for faith. Just as he attempted to emulate Jesus in every way, such as by embracing suffering and preaching good news, so Paul exhorted his communities to do likewise. Sometimes he commended their effectiveness in becoming models themselves (1 Thess 1:6-7).

Paul's confidence in himself, that he is a proper guide and "model" for believers, should

not be seen as arrogance. The ultimate example he has in mind is Christ in his self-emptying death (2:6-8), to which all believers are to seek to be "conformed" (3:10). Paul's self-assurance derives from long years of having lived in imitation of the self-sacrificial example of Jesus. On the other hand, "there are many" whose behavior makes them "the enemies of the cross" (3:18). Paul had "often" told the Philippians of such people; they, therefore, must have known who they were. We, however, can only plead ignorance. Perhaps they are the opponents Paul inveighs against in 3:2, but that is not clear. The criticisms of them are very vague, but they may indicate moral laxity of some kind. A warning against laxity also appears in Galatians (Gal 5:13-26) following that letter's stern teaching against being overly concerned with law. The pattern here is similar.

By contrast with such people, whose "minds are set on earthly things" (3:19), "*our* citizenship is in heaven, from where we await a *savior,* the *Lord.*" "Citizenship" (cf. 1:27) and "savior" are never found again in Paul's own letters; they are suited very specifically for this city with its "Roman" citizenry, which acknowledged the *emperor* (probably Nero) as "Lord" and "Savior." The contrasting of the emperor with Jesus is undoubtedly deliberate, though Paul is not preaching political rebellion (cf. Rom 13:1-7). His point is precisely that believers' hope is *not* in politics. Believers' hope is in Christ, who will, at his coming, "change our lowly body to conform with his glorified body" (3:21), a theme that Paul develops at length elsewhere (1 Cor 15:35-57). The *present* experience of *gradually* "being transformed" into the image of the Lord (2 Cor 3:18) anticipates that future "change" at the resurrection. Gradual transformation is what Paul has largely had in mind since 3:10.

4:1-9 Final appeals and exhortations

The opening demonstrates once again Paul's deep affection for, and joy in, the Philippians. We never hear elsewhere of Euodia and Syntyche. The appeal to them to "have the same mind" is the same plea of 2:2 (Rom 15:5). Paul asks his "true yokemate" (*Syzygos*—perhaps a proper name) to "assist them," probably meaning to act as an arbitrator. They were important leaders of the church in Philippi, having been foundational, along with Lydia (Acts 16:13-15), in establishing the church there. We cannot know what their dispute was, and in any case it was not overly serious; Paul has confidence that they will work it out. We also do not know anything more about "Syzygos." The word (name?) is masculine; this is not a reference, as is sometimes supposed, to Paul's wife.

Paul exhorts them all yet again to "rejoice." In that joy their "kindness" (or "gentleness") can and should "be known to all" (4:5). "The Lord is near" refers to the soon-expected "day of Christ" (2:16; cf. 3:20). In the meantime they must not "worry"; that would be the opposite of joy. They must simply make their prayers and requests known to God (4:6), and "the peace of God" (cf. John 14:27), which has to do with far more than the absence of conflict or suffering (1:29), "will guard their hearts and minds" (4:7). "Peace" is the gift that flows from "grace" (1:2; Rom 5:1-11). "Finally" Paul exhorts them simply to hold fast to all that is good and repeats again the theme of learning from and imitating his manner of following Christ. The "peace" blessing is also found elsewhere (Rom 15:33; 2 Cor 13:11).

 For those of us who are **anxious about many things**, Paul's words in Philippians 4:4-9 can be medicinal. If we can find something to rejoice in and be grateful for when we are anxious, our anxiety lessens. Take to heart Paul's request to focus on those things in your life that are good, beautiful, true, and right. Make your list and rejoice!

4:10-20 Thanks for the Philippians' generosity

Many commentators regard this section as "letter A," sent before the other letter(s) as a thank-you note. That could be correct, but this

VI: Instructions for the Community

CHAPTER 4

Live in Concord

[1]Therefore, my brothers, whom I love and long for, my joy and crown, in this way stand firm in the Lord, beloved.

[2]I urge Euodia and I urge Syntyche to come to a mutual understanding in the Lord. [3]Yes, and I ask you also, my true yokemate, to help them, for they have struggled at my side in promoting the gospel, along with Clement and my other co-workers, whose names are in the book of life.

Joy and Peace

[4]Rejoice in the Lord always. I shall say it again: rejoice! [5]Your kindness should be known to all. The Lord is near. [6]Have no anxiety at all, but in everything, by prayer and petition, with thanksgiving, make your requests known to God. [7]Then the peace of God that surpasses all understanding will guard your hearts and minds in Christ Jesus.

[8]Finally, brothers, whatever is true, whatever is honorable, whatever is just, whatever is pure, whatever is lovely, whatever is gracious, if there is any excellence and if there is anything worthy of praise, think about these things. [9]Keep on doing what you have learned and received and heard and seen in me. Then the God of peace will be with you.

VII: Gratitude for the Philippians' Generosity

[10]I rejoice greatly in the Lord that now at last you revived your concern for me. You were, of course, concerned about me but lacked an opportunity. [11]Not that I say this because of need, for I have learned, in whatever situation I find myself, to be self-sufficient. [12]I know indeed how to live in humble circumstances; I know also how to live with abundance. In every circumstance and in all things I have learned the secret of being well fed and of going hungry, of living in abundance and of being in need. [13]I have the strength for

continue

everything through him who empowers me. [14]Still, it was kind of you to share in my distress.

[15]You Philippians indeed know that at the beginning of the gospel, when I left Macedonia, not a single church shared with me in an account of giving and receiving, except you alone. [16]For even when I was at Thessalonica you sent me something for my needs, not only once but more than once. [17]It is not that I am eager for the gift; rather, I am eager for the profit that accrues to your account. [18]I have received full payment and I abound. I am very well supplied because of what I received from you through Epaphroditus, "a fragrant aroma," an acceptable sacrifice, pleasing to God. [19]My God will fully supply whatever you need, in accord with his glorious riches in Christ Jesus. [20]To our God and Father, glory forever and ever. Amen.

VIII: Farewell

[21]Give my greetings to every holy one in Christ Jesus. The brothers who are with me send you their greetings; [22]all the holy ones send you their greetings, especially those of Caesar's household. [23]The grace of the Lord Jesus Christ be with your spirit.

is not the first time Paul has received a gift from the Philippians (4:16; cf. 2 Cor 11:9); this is the "revival" of their generosity—not that their concern had flagged, but they "lacked the opportunity" to show it (4:10). Now, however, Epaphroditus has delivered their gift (4:18), and Paul rejoices at their concern and, as is typical, not only gives thanks for the material blessing but also reflects on the spiritual riches he has in Christ (4:13). As elsewhere, Paul can appear slightly arrogant as he assures them that he has "learned" to be "self-sufficient"

(4:11-12). He just barely says "thanks" (4:14), but his tone is not so much arrogant as embarrassed.

Elsewhere, especially in the Corinthian letters (1 Cor 9:3-18; 2 Cor 12:13-16), Paul refused to exercise his "right" to be paid for his apostolic work, "working night and day" rather than be a burden on anyone (1 Thess 2:9). For some reason, however, he had long ago entered into a financial arrangement with the Philippians (4:15) but was hesitant to accept their money. It might appear that he wanted their *possessions* rather than *themselves* (2 Cor 12:14) and be no better than other "peddlers of the word of God" (2 Cor 2:17). Further, his enemies might say that he appropriated for himself (2 Cor 8:20-21) money he had promised to collect for Jerusalem (Gal 2:10; Rom 15:25-26). So he assures the Philippians that he is "not eager for the gift" but for "the profit that accrues to *their* account" (4:17). The money is fully adequate to his needs, but, more important, it is "an acceptable sacrifice, pleasing to God" (4:18). And God will also fill their every need "according to his wealth in glory" (4:19). Paul concludes his thank-you in the manner of a prayer, giving glory to God (4:20).

4:21-23 Final greetings and blessing

The sending of greetings is common enough (see 1 Cor 16:19-20; 2 Cor 13:12), but particular here is the mention of greetings from some in "Caesar's household" (4:22), which to many suggests that Paul was in Rome. This is possible, but Caesar's officials and servants were in major cities throughout the empire, including Philippi. The mention of Caesar (only here in Paul's letters; cf. Rom 13:1-7) would be meaningful for this Roman colony. Paul ends the letter with his standard blessing (1 Cor 16:23; Gal 6:18); it echoes his opening greeting (1:2). "Grace" is the beginning and end of Christian existence.

EXPLORING LESSON THREE

1. What historical situation accounts for the change in tone and topic in 3:2-11?

_____

_____

_____

_____

2. What does Paul mean when he says that the Philippians (who are uncircumcised Gentiles) are "the circumcision"? (See Rom 2:25-29; Col 2:11.)

_____

_____

_____

_____

3. In 3:7-11, Paul talks about his righteousness being from God through Christ. But in 3:12-14, it is clear that Paul is putting forth great effort to attain "perfect maturity." How do you understand this combination of divine grace and human responsibility?

_____

_____

_____

_____

_____

4. a) Why does Paul advise the Philippians to imitate him (3:17; 4:9)? Is Paul being arrogant? (See also 1 Cor 11:1.)

_____

_____

_____

   b) Who do you imitate, and why is this person worthy of imitation?

_____

_____

_____

5. Why is Paul's language about "citizenship" and "a savior" especially meaningful in Philippi (3:20)?

_____

_____

_____

_____

6. Paul assures the Philippians that Jesus Christ "will change our lowly body to conform with his glorified body" (3:21). Read 1 Corinthians 15:35-57, a passage in which Paul writes at length about how our own bodies will share in the resurrection of Christ. What do you learn from this passage? Does this make sense to you? Why or why not?

_____

_____

_____

_____

7. a) What advice does Paul give to the Philippians about having "no anxiety" (4:4-9)?

_____

_____

_____

_____

   b) Among these verses, what do you find most helpful in dealing with stress, worry, or anxiety?

_____

_____

_____

_____

8. Joy is a major theme of the letter to the Philippians (1:4, 18, 25; 2:2, 17-18, 28-29; 3:1; 4:1, 4, 10). After reading this letter, how would you explain the source of a Christian's joy and why joy is a hallmark of Christian life?

_____

_____

_____

_____

9. What verse or passage in Philippians stands out for you as a favorite? Why?

_____

_____

_____

_____

_____

_____

CLOSING PRAYER

Prayer

Have no anxiety at all, but in everything, by prayer and petition, with thanksgiving, make your requests known to God. (Phil 4:6)

God of joy and peace, we imitate Paul by turning to you in our every need, knowing that in our struggles, we share in the cross of Jesus, and in our joys, we share in his resurrection. Fill our hearts and minds with the peace of Christ which passes all understanding. And grant peace to those who are most in need of it this day, especially . . .

LESSON FOUR

Introduction and Philemon

Begin your personal study and group discussion with a simple and sincere prayer such as:

Prayer

Lord Jesus, your servant Paul willingly endured and even rejoiced in imprisonment for the sake of the gospel. May we also find joy in a way of life that embraces your death and resurrection. As we study your word, empower us with your strength.

Read the Introduction on page 46 and the Bible text of Philemon found in the outside columns of pages 47–52, highlighting what stands out to you.

Read the accompanying commentary to add to your understanding.

Respond to the questions on pages 53–55, Exploring Lesson Four.

The Closing Prayer on page 55 is for your personal use and may be used at the end of group discussion.

INTRODUCTION TO PHILEMON

The letter to Philemon is the shortest but one of the most intriguing letters in the New Testament. Almost all scholars agree that it was written by Paul himself during one of his imprisonments. It provides one piece of an extended conversation involving Paul, Onesimus, Philemon, and others. The information the other parts of the conversation would provide remain a mystery and have been the subject of much conjecture. Fortunately most of this missing information, while interesting, is not crucial for appreciating the ongoing significance of this short and beautiful letter.

Paul is clearly in prison at the time of the letter, but the where and when of the imprisonment are not known. Discussions on these questions are usually linked to discussion about his imprisonment at the time he wrote his letter to the Philippians, and answers vary widely. Were both letters written from Rome and hence later than the letter to the Romans? Were one or both written from Ephesus or some other location? Was one written from an earlier or later imprisonment than the other? It seems most likely but hardly certain that Philemon was written during an earlier imprisonment, possibly at Ephesus, from which Paul expected to be released, and hence be able to visit Philemon and continue his ministry. Travel for both Onesimus and Paul from Ephesus to Colossae, the usually assumed location of Philemon's home, would be relatively easy, since they are only about a hundred miles apart.

Onesimus is a slave belonging to Philemon and is, at the time of the letter, with Paul. Why he has left his owner and is with Paul is also the subject of much speculation. He has done something to offend his owner, which could have been some inappropriate act while he was in his service or which may simply have been his running away. While he may have been a runaway slave, the prevailing opinion is that he was visiting Paul to appeal to him for advice and assistance in his difficulty with his owner. Some have even suggested that Philemon sent his pagan slave to minister to Paul in prison. It is also not certain what Paul expects Philemon to do. He is clearly asking him to receive Onesimus back as a brother in the Lord and to charge Paul for whatever debt Onesimus owes. Paul, however, also says that he would like Onesimus to be able to serve him and seems to be suggesting that Philemon do even more than he is explicitly asked to do, perhaps even give Onesimus to Paul as his slave.

This letter, like others in the New Testament, simply accepts slavery as an institution without discussing its morality. This letter does, however, recognize the tension that exists between the liberating message of the gospel (cf. Gal 3:26-28; 1 Cor 12:13) and the slavery that society accepted. In its treatment of Christian brotherly love, it provides a basis for later Christian understanding of the slavery issue. It calls for a reordering of relationships on a higher plane than those possible within secular society. While many questions will remain unanswered, the letter to Philemon can be read by Christians of all ages as an exposition on the new relationship that exists among people as a result of their incorporation into Christ. This relationship, which transcends all other relationships, including that of master and slave, is based on the new life that all Christians share by reason of the grace that comes from Christ. This new life involves both mutual love and partnership in promoting the gospel.

Address and Greeting

¹Paul, a prisoner for Christ Jesus, and Timothy our brother, to Philemon, our beloved and our co-worker, ²to Apphia our sister, to Archippus our fellow soldier, and to the church at your house. ³Grace to you and peace from God our Father and the Lord Jesus Christ.

continue

THE OPENING

1-2 Senders and recipients

Like all Paul's letters, the letter to Philemon opens by identifying both the senders and the recipients. The senders are Paul and Timothy. Elsewhere Paul calls himself "an apostle of Christ Jesus" (1 Cor 1:1) or "a slave of Christ Jesus" (Rom 1:1), but here he identifies himself a "a prisoner for Christ Jesus" (1). This identification refers not only to his actual status as a prisoner but even more to the reason for his being a prisoner—his preaching of the gospel of Christ—and most especially, in the context of the purpose of this letter, to Christ's total, authoritative claim on Paul and Paul's dedication to that claim. Timothy's being called a "brother" establishes his close relationship with Paul and also prepares for Paul's addressing Philemon as "brother" (7, 20) and his appealing to Philemon to accept Onesimus as a "brother" (16).

The main recipient of the letter is Philemon, but the letter is also addressed to other key individuals in his community, Appia and Archippus, and to the whole community. In the early church, communities were usually small enough to gather for worship in a private home, often that of a leading citizen like Philemon. While the immediate purpose of the letter is to persuade Philemon to do a good deed, the argument of the letter involves Philemon's understanding of his and Onesimus's relationship within the whole community. Using the terms "brother" and "sister" as well as "co-worker" sets the stage for the new relationship Paul seeks to bring about between Philemon and Onesimus. Addressing the letter to the whole community provides greater incentive for Philemon to comply with the letter's request. It also gives the letter applicability, beyond Philemon himself, to the whole community as well as to Christian communities of future generations.

3 Greeting

The formal greeting is similar to those used in Paul's other letters and has the same wording as the greeting in Paul's other letter from prison (Phil 1:2). While formal, this greeting, together with the formal blessing at the end (25), frames the body of the letter within the context of God's grace. Paul's theology of grace is nowhere developed in this letter, nor are other aspects of his theology. It is reasonable to assume, however, that Philemon and his community, having been converted by Paul, are familiar with the main aspects of Paul's teaching. God's graciousness toward Philemon and his community should inspire their graciousness toward one another.

> ### *Thanksgiving*
>
> ⁴I give thanks to my God always, remembering you in my prayers, ⁵as I hear of the love and the faith you have in the Lord Jesus and for all the holy ones, ⁶so that your partnership in the faith may become effective in recognizing every good there is in us that leads to Christ.
>
> ### *Plea for Onesimus*
>
> ⁷For I have experienced much joy and encouragement from your love, because the hearts of the holy ones have been refreshed by you, brother.
>
> *continue*

THANKSGIVING

4-5 Philemon's love and faith

The thanksgiving, which follows the opening greeting in all Paul's letters except Galatians, usually involves thanking God for some quality in the letter's recipient and serves to introduce the main themes of the letter. Here Paul thanks God for Philemon's love and faith, qualities that will be the basis of Paul's appeal in the body of the letter. Paul sees in Philemon's faith not just his assent to the gospel but the way his vital faith has been operative in his life—"faith working through love" (Gal 5:6). Philemon's love "for all the holy ones" (5) includes those in "the church at your house" (2), Paul himself (7), and will shortly be extended to include Onesimus (16).

6-7 Effects of Philemon's love and faith

In the opening of the letter, Paul referred to Philemon as "our co-worker" (1). He now strengthens that designation by referring to him as "brother" (7), associating him more closely with himself and with "Timothy our brother" (1), the co-author of the letter. Paul suggests that he and Philemon together can now do even more good for the holy ones than what Paul

has already seen Philemon doing. Thus far, Paul has drawn an extremely positive picture of Philemon. As the letter develops, Philemon will be expected to live up to this positive picture. The themes of prayer (4), love (5, 7), partnership (6), good (6), and refreshing the heart (7) will all be used as Paul develops his argument.

 In order to be as persuasive as possible, Paul uses a variety of **rhetorical (persuasive) devices** to make his case. These rhetorical devices have an effect on the minds and hearts of readers, working to convince or to create emotions that build toward accepting Paul's argument. Some examples of rhetorical devices that Paul uses in Philemon are:

- Autobiography: *"I rather urge you out of love, being as I am, Paul, an old man, and now also a prisoner for Christ Jesus" (9).*
- Wordplay: *"I urge you on behalf of my child Onesimus . . . who was once useless to you but is now useful to [both] you and me" (Onesimus means "useful") (10-11).*
- Metaphor: *"I am sending him, that is, my own heart, back to you" (12).*
- Antithesis/Paired Opposites: *"Perhaps this why he was away from you for a while, that you might have him back forever" (15).*
- Hyperbole/Exaggeration: *"[Y]ou owe me your very self" (19).*
- Flattery: *"With trust in your compliance I write to you, knowing that you will do even more than I say" (21).*

APPEAL ON BEHALF OF ONESIMUS

8-12 Paul appeals out of love

Paul claims the right to order Philemon to do the good he is about to propose, but refrains from exercising this right. This right probably derives from Paul's apostolic authority, although Paul called himself a prisoner rather than an apostle in the introduction to the letter. Because of the encouragement he has felt on the basis of the good that has come from Philemon's love, rather than order him to do what is proper, Paul urges him "out of love" (9). The love here referred to is both Philemon's love for all the holy ones (5) and Paul's and Timothy's love for Philemon (1). Paul refers to himself as an old man and as a prisoner (9) as motivation for Philemon to extend to Paul the love he has for the holy ones.

Having established the basis of his appeal as the love relationship that exists between himself and Philemon and their mutual love for the holy ones, Paul now identifies the object of his appeal. Whatever he may have been, Onesimus has become Paul's child in prison. By bringing him into Christianity, Paul has become his "father." Paul will describe him as "my own heart" (12). Onesimus has become one of the holy ones mutually loved by Paul and Philemon. Significantly, the term "child," which Paul uses to refer to Onesimus and often to Christians in general, is used in his letters for only one other individual, namely, Timothy (1 Cor 4:17; Phil 2:22), Paul's partner in spreading the gospel and a co-author of this letter.

The extensive use of family language in this letter indicates that a new model of mutual relationships has already been established within the Christian community, a model of relationships that is in tension with the master/slave relationship accepted in Roman society. Paul does not advocate the overthrow of the institution of slavery, but he does advocate overcoming the tension by fully incorporating the Christian slave into the familial relationships within the Christian community. In at least two ways Paul has described a new household in tension with the structured household of Philemon. First, in this new household Paul, not Philemon, is the head; both Philemon and Onesimus are his children. Second, Paul's father/child relationship with Onesimus has priority over Philemon's master/slave relationship with Onesimus.

> [8]Therefore, although I have the full right in Christ to order you to do what is proper, [9]I rather urge you out of love, being as I am, Paul, an old man, and now also a prisoner for Christ Jesus. [10]I urge you on behalf of my child Onesimus, whose father I have become in my imprisonment, [11]who was once useless to you but is now useful to [both] you and me. [12]I am sending him, that is, my own heart, back to you. [13]I should have liked to retain him for myself, so that he might serve me on your behalf in my imprisonment for the gospel, [14]but I did not want to do anything without your consent, so that the good you do might not be forced
>
> *continue*

The name Onesimus, a common name for slaves, means "the useful one," enabling the play on words in verse 11. Away from Philemon, Onesimus was useless to him. Now a Christian devoted to Paul, he has become useful both to Paul and to Philemon. He will become useful to Philemon when Paul sends him back, but his real usefulness to both Philemon and Paul will become clear later in the letter.

13-14 Philemon's voluntary good deed

Paul never explicitly states what it is that he expects Philemon to do. He had said that he had a right "to order you to do what is proper" (8), but here says he wants the good Philemon will do to be voluntary (14), a good deed on the part of Philemon in response to the grace of God. He says he would have liked Onesimus to remain with him, serving him in prison for the gospel, an indication that Onesimus, like many slaves at that time, was well educated and hence equipped to be of service to Paul and the gospel. However, he sends him back to Philemon and apparently expects Onesimus to be with Philemon when he is released from prison and visits Philemon (22).

but voluntary. ¹⁵Perhaps this is why he was away from you for a while, that you might have him back forever, ¹⁶no longer as a slave but more than a slave, a brother, beloved especially to me, but even more so to you, as a man and in the Lord. ¹⁷So if you regard me as a partner, welcome him as you would me. ¹⁸And if he has done you any injustice or owes you anything, charge it to me. ¹⁹I, Paul, write this in my own hand: I will pay. May I not tell you that you owe me your very self. ²⁰Yes, brother, may I profit from you in the Lord. Refresh my heart in Christ.

²¹With trust in your compliance I write to you, knowing that you will do even more than I say. ²²At the same time prepare a guest room for me, for I hope to be granted to you through your prayers.

continue

15-18 Paul's request

Paul appears to be asking Philemon to receive his slave back, charging Paul for anything that Onesimus might owe as a result of previous misdeeds or his temporary absence. Paul, however, is asking for much more. He is asking that Philemon receive Onesimus back not only as a slave but also as a brother in the Lord. He is asking that he receive Onesimus both as a man, that is, as a fellow Christian who is his slave, and in the Lord, that is, as a co-worker in the gospel. Most of all, Paul is asking that Philemon receive Onesimus back just as warmly as he would welcome Paul. Onesimus has become Paul's "own heart" (12). Just as Philemon is Paul's co-worker in the gospel (1), so too Philemon should regard Onesimus as a co-worker, like Paul, in the gospel. Verse 17 implies that Paul's primary concern was to effect a reconciliation between Philemon and Onesimus.

Modern readers are often disappointed that Paul does not ask Philemon to grant freedom to his slave. While some scholars think that there are passages (16, 21) that can be read as hinting that Paul desires Onesimus's freedom, most do not, and all agree that the letter falls far short of reconsidering the practice of slavery. In fact, recent studies in cultural anthropology have shown that Philemon's simply freeing his slave would not have fundamentally altered his relationships within the household. Paul wants to alter these relationships. The letter offers a model for transforming the way Christians view one another, now seeing other human beings with eyes reconditioned by faith in Jesus Christ. The transforming power of God's grace, personally experienced by Paul, led to his conviction about God's ability to make all things new (2 Cor 5:17). Paul was actually asking Philemon for something far more radical than freeing his slave. Paul's declaration that Onesimus is Philemon's brother both "as a man and in the Lord" (16) indicates not merely a spiritual reevaluation in the sight of the Lord but a real change in the social relationship between slave and owner.

As the father of Onesimus (10), Paul now accepts responsibility for the debts of his son. In so accepting this responsibility, however, Paul is emphasizing the intensity of his relationship with Onesimus and setting the stage for the implied request at the end of the letter. Martin Luther saw in Paul's letter to Philemon a parallel to the kenotic hymn Paul quotes in Philippians (Phil 2:6-11), his other letter from prison. Christ emptied himself of his right with the Father and instead died to bring us into favor with God. As Christ pleads our cause and takes our part, so too Paul has emptied himself of his rights and takes the place of Onesimus in order to get Philemon to waive his right to punish Onesimus and instead welcome him as a brother.

19-21 Personal appeal

Paul's letters were dictated by him and written by a scribe, but he would sometimes add a note at the end in his "own hand" (19; cf. 1 Cor 16:21; Gal 6:11). By writing in his own hand he is concluding his appeal by making his request intensely personal. He now not only restates his agreement to pay Onesimus's debt but also reminds Philemon of the debt he owes to Paul. The new life in Christ that Philemon now lives he owes to Paul, that is, he owes Paul his "very self" (19). With this comment Paul draws Philemon into the creditor-debtor relationship as a debtor as well as a creditor. The sphere of mutual relationships is expanded. Philemon, in fact, has the same relationship to Paul as does Onesimus. For both, Paul is their father in faith. For both, Paul is their partner in the gospel (1; 13).

Paul is expecting Philemon to reflect on the significance of these relationships when Paul asks to "profit from you in the Lord" (20), followed by his appeal to Philemon to "refresh my heart in Christ" (20). Paul is expecting Philemon to reflect on his love for Paul and his partnership with him in the gospel and to consider what he can do to further support him in his ministry. Near the beginning of the letter Paul thanked God for Philemon's love, faith, and partnership, noting that "the hearts of the holy ones have been refreshed by you" (7). He identified Onesimus as "my own heart" (12) and now asks Philemon to "refresh my heart" (20). Paul concludes this personal appeal by expressing his confidence that Philemon will not only do what Paul has explicitly asked, that is, receive Onesimus back as a brother in the Lord, but will do even more (21).

Paul is certainly expecting that Philemon will accept Onesimus not only as a returned slave and a brother in the Lord but also as a beloved co-worker in the gospel, a partner with Paul and Philemon. He may also be expecting that Philemon will refresh his heart by granting the wish Paul had earlier expressed: "that he might serve me on your behalf" (13). Philemon indeed may have Onesimus back forever by giving him to Paul as their mutual partner in the gospel.

This letter calls not only Philemon but all Christians to adopt new patterns of mutual respect, mutual responsibility, and mutual concern. This letter can help Christian communities today to reflect on the roles and concerns of minorities and others who might be marginalized. Accepting the transforming power of God's grace will not only alter relationships but can offer new possibilities for living out Christian faith in freedom and joy.

 Slavery in the Greco-Roman world was a universally accepted reality. In New Testament times, masters generally treated their slaves fairly well because they were considered to be valuable property. They were viewed as members of the family, and many became trusted nannies or instructors for the master's children. Slaves could eventually win freedom (*manumission*), either by saving enough money or performing heroic service. Runaway slaves, however, could be severely punished by imprisonment, flogging, mutilation by branding or cutting, being sold to a harsher master, or even sentenced to death. The New Testament nowhere condemns slavery. Indeed, slaves are instructed to be obedient to their masters (Eph 6:5-8; 1 Tim 6:1). But Paul recognizes that baptism changes even a slave's relationship to the rest of the Christian family, as they become brothers and sisters in Christ: "There is neither Jew nor Greek, there is neither slave nor free person, there is not male and female; for you are all one in Christ Jesus" (Gal 3:28; see also Phlm 16).

CONCLUSION

22 Travel plans

Travel plans are a common feature of Paul's letters, appearing just before the final greetings and blessing. Here Paul indicates his hope to be able to visit Philemon. There must have been a realistic prospect of his being released from prison, a development for which he asks the prayers of Philemon and his community. His arrival at the home of Philemon would be an appropriate occasion for Philemon to refresh his heart by granting him Onesimus. To this point in the letter, "you" has been in the singular, referring to Philemon alone. The request for prayers, however, uses "your" in the

Final Greetings

²³Epaphras, my fellow prisoner in Christ Jesus, greets you, ²⁴as well as Mark, Aristarchus, Demas, and Luke, my co-workers. ²⁵The grace of the Lord Jesus Christ be with your spirit.

23-25 Greeting and blessing

Greetings are another common feature of Paul's letters, appearing just before the final blessing. The greetings from Paul's fellow prisoner, Epaphras, and four fellow workers are addressed to "you" in the singular, that is, to Philemon alone, possibly because they were personally known by Philemon. The final blessing, however, is addressed to the entire community, using the blessing formula similar to those found in Paul's other letters and identical to that in Paul's other letter from prison, the letter to the Philippians (Phil 4:23).

plural, indicating not only that Paul is asking for the prayers of the community but also that this personal letter to Philemon is intended to be read to the entire community.

EXPLORING LESSON FOUR

1. What is the basic situation that caused Paul to write this letter to Philemon? (See Introduction.)

Onesimus, a slave who has run away from his master, Philemon, has become a Christian. Paul has convinced him to return & ask for forgiveness; (MAYBE FOR THEFT) and asks Philemon to accept him as a Brother

2. What is the double meaning behind Paul's reference to himself as a "prisoner for Christ Jesus" (v. 1)?

1- his is literally in prison for preaching Christ's good news
2- He is so committed to Christ completely - unable to leave

3. Although this letter is clearly written to Philemon, Paul adds other individuals and the entire Philippian church to his list of addressees (v. 2). Why might Paul have done this?

1- to allow other witnesses to his request of Philemon 2- Maybe to let everyone know that he sees Onesimus as a 'son' and a brother and wishes the whole community to accept him as brother

4. Why does Paul choose not to *order* Philemon to "do what is proper" (vv. 8-9, 14)?

It is much more effective to allow Philemon to make the right choice. It allows the community to respect Philemon & the relationship with Paul as brothers NOT AUTHORITY

5. a) What words does Paul use to describe Onesimus in verses 10-12? What do these words tell us about the way Paul views Onesimus and his status as a slave?

he calls Onesimus his 'child' and refers to him as " my own heart " Paul sees Onesimus as a kindred spirit.

b) How do these words imply a new vision for the traditional household of Philemon?

While Paul does not dismiss the relationship of Onesimus & Philemon as slave/master he wants Philemon to recognize them as a human and a brother worthy of the same dignity as all the community of

6. What is Paul asking of Philemon, beyond simply accepting Onesimus back without punishing him (vv. 15-18)?

to actually treat him as a brother

7. The commentary articulates a truth at the heart of Paul's letter: "seeing other human beings with eyes reconditioned by faith in Jesus Christ." What does this mean to you? In what circumstances have you been challenged to do this?

to see others as God sees us - as children as Jesus sees us - as a sibling; we are much more forgiving and loving to our family.

8. What is the effect of Paul stating that he has written the letter "in [his] own hand" (v. 19)?

these are "my words" this is important to me "I will pay"

9. Paul's letter to Philemon is packed with rhetorical (persuasive) techniques and powerful language. Do you find his letter persuasive? How do you think Philemon responded?

I think it is alway persuasive to tell someone you believe they will do the right thing; and Paul's management style seems effective to me. I would guess Philemon listened

"I urge you out of love"

10. What have you gained from studying these two letters Paul sent from prison—knowledge, a life lesson, a favorite verse, fellowship with your study group? What stands out most for you?

It makes me remember letters I have written & received and think how wonderful and special it is to read one.

CLOSING PRAYER

Prayer

I give thanks to my God always, remembering you in my prayers, as I hear of the love and the faith you have in the Lord Jesus and for all the holy ones . . . (Phlm 4-5)

Lord God, you are the Father of all. Jesus Christ, you are the brother of all. As we read Paul's letter to Philemon, may the truths it teaches take root in our hearts and in our world. May we embrace every person as our brother or our sister, judging no one based on their status or their usefulness to us. May we recognize every person as a beloved child of God. As our study comes to a close, we pray in thanksgiving for the blessings of this time together, especially . . .

Philemon effect —

How much would we Sacrifice to lead one person to Christ?

PRAYING WITH YOUR GROUP

Because we know that the Bible allows us to hear God's voice, prayer provides the context for our study and sharing. By speaking and listening to God and each other, the discussion often grows to more deeply bond us to one another and to God.

At *the beginning and end of each lesson* simple prayers are provided for individual use, and also may be used within the group setting. Most of the closing prayers provided with each lesson relate directly to a theme from that lesson and encourage you to pray together for people and events in your local community.

Of course, there are many ways to center ourselves in God's presence as we gather together in groups around the word of God. We provide some additional suggestions here knowing you and your group will make prayer a priority as part of your gathering. These are simply alternative ways to pray if your group would like to try something different from those prayers provided in the previous pages.

Conversational Prayer

This form of prayer allows for the group members to pray in their own words in a way that is not intimidating. The group leader begins with Step One, inviting all to focus on the presence of Christ among them. After a few moments of quiet, the group leader invites anyone in the group to voice a prayer or two of thanksgiving; once that is complete, then anyone who has personal intentions may pray in their own words for their needs; finally, the group prays for the needs of others.

A suggested process:
In your own words, speak simple and short prayers to allow time for others to add their voices.

Focus on one "step" at a time, not worrying about praying for everything in your mental list at once.

Step One	Visualize Christ. Welcome him.
	Imagine him present with you in your group.
	Allow time for some silence.
Step Two	Gratitude opens our hearts.
	Use simple words such as, "Thank you, Lord, for . . ."
Step Three	Pray for your own needs knowing that others will pray with you.
	Be specific and honest.
	Use "I" and "me" language.

Step Four   Pray for others by name, with love.
              You may voice your agreement ("Yes, Lord").
              End with gratitude for sharing concerns.

Praying Like Ignatius

St. Ignatius Loyola, whose life and ministry are the foundation of the Jesuit community, invites us to enter into Scripture texts in order to experience the scenes, especially scenes of the gospels or other narrative parts of Scripture. Simply put, this is a method of creatively imagining the scene, viewing it from the inside, and asking God to meet you there. Most often, this is a personal form of prayer, but in a group setting, some of its elements can be helpful if you allow time for this process.

A suggested process:

- Select a scene from the chapters in the particular lesson.

- Read that scene out loud in the group, followed by some quiet time.

- Ask group members to place themselves in the scene (as a character, or as an onlooker) so that they can imagine the emotions, responses, and thinking that may have taken place. Notice the details and the tone, and imagine the interaction with the Lord that is taking place.

- Share with the group any insights that came to you in this quiet imagining.

- Allow each person in the group to thank God for some insight and to pray about some request that may have surfaced.

Sacred Reading (or Lectio Divina)

This method of prayer invites us to "listen with the ear of the heart" as St. Benedict's rule would say. We listen to the words and the phrasing, asking God to speak to our innermost being. Again, this method of prayer is most often used in an individual setting but may also be used in an adapted way within a group.

A suggested process:

- Select a scene from the chapters in the particular lesson.

- Read the scene out loud in the group, perhaps two times.

- Ask group members to ponder a word or phrase that stands out to them.

- The group members could then simply speak the word or phrase as a kind of litany of what was meaningful for your group.

- Allow time for more silence to ponder the words that were heard, asking God to reveal to you what message you are meant to hear, how God is speaking to you.

- Follow up with spoken intentions at the close of this group time.

REFLECTING ON SCRIPTURE

Reading Scripture is an opportunity not simply to learn new information but to listen to God who loves you. Pray that the same Holy Spirit who guided the formation of Scripture will inspire you to correctly understand what you read, and empower you to make what you read a part of your life.

The inspired word of God contains layers of meaning. As you make your way through passages of Scripture, whether studying a book of the Bible or focusing on a biblical theme, you may find it helpful to ask yourself these four questions:

What does the Scripture passage say?
Read the passage slowly and reflectively. Become familiar with it. If the passage you are reading is a narrative, carefully observe the characters and the plot. Use your imagination to picture the scene or enter into it.

What does the Scripture passage mean?
Read the footnotes in your Bible and the commentary provided to help you understand what the sacred writers intended and what God wants to communicate by means of their words.

What does the Scripture passage mean to me?
Meditate on the passage. God's word is living and powerful. What is God saying to you? How does the Scripture passage apply to your life today?

What am I going to do about it?
Try to discover how God may be challenging you in this passage. An encounter with God contains a challenge to know God's will and follow it more closely in daily life. Ask the Holy Spirit to inspire not only your mind but your life with this living word.

FOREWORD AND ACKNOWLEDGEMENTS

Complete coverage of economic production is a vital aspect of the quality of the national accounts. This *exhaustiveness* is hard to achieve because of the difficulties in accounting for certain types of productive activities. Activities that are missing from the basic data used to compile the national accounts because they are underground, illegal, informal, household production for own final use, or due to deficiencies in the basic data collection system are referred to as *non-observed*. They are said to comprise the *non-observed economy* (NOE), and including them in the national accounts is referred to as *measurement of the* NOE.

Given the wide range of possible approaches to NOE measurement, there is a need to identify and promote international best practice. This is the aim of the Handbook. It presents a systematic strategy for achieving exhaustive estimates of gross domestic product that is consistent with international standards and, in particular, with the 1993 System of National Accounts.

The Handbook was put together by a team drawn from national and international statistical organisations. The principal contributors were Adriaan Bloem, Manlio Calzaroni, Jacques Charmes, Michael Colledge (editor), Ralf Hussmanns, Youri Ivanov, Brugt Kazemier, Andrei Kosarev, Ronald Luttikhuizen, Sabina Ronconi, Manik Shrestha, Seppo Varjonen, Peter van de Ven and Denis Ward. Derek Blades provided detailed comments on all chapters. Helpful advice and comments were also received from Misha Belkindas, Peter Harper, Anne Harrison, Ralf Hein, Victor Holovko, Olga Ivanova, Irina Masakova, Paul McCarthy, Brian Newson, Vitezslav Ondrus, Gerhard Reinecke, Silke Stapel, Alexander Surinov and Jiri Vopravil. Particular thanks are due to the Italian National Statistical Institute (Istat), the Russian Federation State Statistical Committee, and Statistics Netherlands for their active support of this project.

An electronic copy of the Handbook and supporting documentation are available on the Internet at *www.oecd.org*. Comments on the Handbook are welcomed and should be e-mailed to *noehandbook@oecd.org*. They will be taken into account in any future revision.

Enrico Giovannini
Chief Statistician and Director of the Statistics Directorate
Organisation for Economic Co-operation and Development

Carol S. Carson
Director
Statistics Department
International Monetary Fund

Abimbola Sylvester Young
Director
Bureau of Statistics
International Labour Organisation

Mikhail Korolev
Chairman
Interstate Statistical Committee of the Commonwealth of Independent States

TABLE OF CONTENTS

ABBREVIATIONS AND ACRONYMS

(See Annex 2 for definitions of terms)

1968 SNA	System of National Accounts 1968
1993 SNA	System of National Accounts 1993
COICOP	Classification of Individual Consumption by Purpose
CPC	Central Product Classification
CPI	Consumer Price Index
DQAF	Data Quality Assessment Framework (IMF)
ESA 1995	European System of Accounts 1995
FISIM	Financial Intermediation Services Indirectly Measured
GDP	Gross Domestic Product
GDDS	General Data Dissemination Standard (IMF)
GFCF	Gross Fixed Capital Formation
Goskomstat	State Statistical Committee (abbreviation derived from the Russian)
HES	Household Expenditure Survey
HS	Harmonised System
ICLS	International Conference of Labour Statisticians
IMF	International Monetary Fund
INSEE	Institut National de la Statistique et des Études Économiques, France
ISIC, Rev. 3	International Standard Industrial Classification, Revision 3 (United Nations)
Istat	Italian National Statistical Institute
NSO	National Statistical Office
NSS	National Statistical System
NOE	Non-observed Economy
NPISH	Non-profit Institutions Serving Households
PPI	Producer Price Index
SDDS	Special Data Dissemination Standard (IMF)
VAT	Value Added Tax

INTRODUCTION

1. INTRODUCTION

1.1.   Good quality national accounts are vital for economic policy making and research. An important aspect of their quality is the extent to which they cover all economic activities. Exhaustive coverage is difficult to achieve because of the wide range of economic activities, some of which are deliberately concealed from observation by those responsible for them.

1.2.   Lack of coverage causes problems for users both in terms of levels and trends. Levels of gross domestic product (GDP) and other data are downward biased, thus giving an inaccurate impression of the economy and impeding international comparability. This can be of great significance in situations where, for example, monetary contributions made or received by a country depend on its GDP or when poverty is measured by GDP per head or environmental standards are measured by pollutant emission per unit of GDP. Similarly, biases in trend estimates can be expected if the economic activities missing from GDP grow at different rates from those included. For example, it is often conjectured that underground and informal sector activities are expanding at precisely the time the official economy is contracting.

1.3.   For the national accountants, lack of coverage causes imbalances in the internal consistency of the accounts because parts of economic transactions may be measured whilst other parts are not. For example, household expenditures on goods and services produced underground may be measured because the purchasers have no reason to hide their purchases, whereas the corresponding production activities are not reported by the producers.

1.4.   A lot of media attention is paid to the possibility of missing economic activities, and reports often suggest that the GDP figures published by national statistical offices exclude large parts of the economy. These reports challenge the credibility of national accounts estimates and often quote assessments of the underestimation. The problem is that many media reports are based on research methodologies with one, or both, of two major weaknesses. First, these methods frequently fail to define exactly what is to be measured and thus, possibly, missed. This lack of precision regarding the measurement target is epitomised by the wide range of different terms in common use – hidden economy, shadow economy, parallel economy, subterranean economy, informal economy, cash economy, black market – to mention just a few. There is no common understanding whether they all mean the same thing, and if not, what relationships they have to one another. Capital flight, tax evasion, shuttle trade, theft and extortion are all lumped together as undesirable or illegal activities that are being grossly underestimated by the official figures.

1.5.   The second problem is the dependence of many estimation methods upon simplistic assumptions that cannot be justified. For example, the so-called "monetary models" assume that changes in the patterns of currency demand can be attributed entirely to, and reflect accurately, changes in missing economic activities. Another popular model is based on changes in consumption of electricity. Such methods make inadequate use of the wealth of pertinent economic data available and there is no obvious way in which their findings can be combined with others to provide more reliable measures.

1.6.   One of the reasons that these macro-models get so much attention is that national statistical offices do not explain their own methods sufficiently, and thus users suppose that other methods are needed and useful. This discussion also raises questions about what is meant by informal, underground, illegal, unmeasured, unrecorded, untaxed, etc., activities. How do these activities relate to one another? Are these activities part of or different from the shadow economy, the cash economy, the parallel economy, the subterranean economy, etc.? What are the best methods for estimating such activities? How reliable are the current figures? Where do capital flight, tax evasion and the shuttle trade fit in? The aim of this Handbook is to provide a common language and to put measurements of economic production on a firm footing, for the benefit of survey statisticians, national accountants, and users of macroeconomic data. The Handbook is intended to reflect a convergence of opinion amongst statisticians and national accounts experts as to what constitutes best practice.

1.2.   Scope and Objectives

1.7.   The conceptual framework for the Handbook is provided by relevant international standards, in particular the System of National Accounts 1993 (1993 SNA) produced by five international organisations (Commission of European Communities *et al.*, 1993). Thus, the scope of the Handbook is economic production as defined by the 1993 SNA. This provides a solid basis but also implies a restriction on the range of issues that are considered. In particular, as further elaborated in Chapter 2, the Handbook does not include the measurement of many services provided by household members to themselves, such as housework or preparing meals, because they are not within the 1993 SNA production boundary. These are not regarded as being missing production.

1.8.   The main focus of the Handbook (Chapters 2-7) is to provide guidance on how to produce exhaustive estimates of GDP. This means ensuring that as many productive activities as possible are *observed*, *i.e.*, directly measured in the basic data on production, incomes, and expenditures from which the national accounts are compiled. It also means ensuring that *non-observed* activities are nevertheless accounted for, *i.e.*, indirectly measured during compilation of the national accounts.

1.9.   The groups of activities most likely to be non-observed are those that are *underground, illegal, informal sector,* or *undertaken by households for their own final use*. Activities may also be missed because of *deficiencies in the basic statistical data collection programme*. These groups of activities are referred to in this Handbook as the *problem areas*. Activities not included in the basic data because they are in one or more of these problem areas are collectively said to comprise the *non-observed economy* (NOE). Thus, *measurement of the non-observed economy* involves action on two fronts:

- improvements in direct measurement by the data collection programme, resulting in fewer *non-observed* activities and hence fewer *non-measured* activities; and

- improvements in indirect measurement during compilation of the national accounts, resulting in fewer *non-measured* activities.

1.10.   Although the main goal of the Handbook is to help statisticians produce exhaustive estimates of GDP, it is recognised that there are many issues in addition to exhaustiveness closely related to the NOE. In particular, in many countries, especially developing ones, a large number of persons are involved in informal sector production, which has a very significant role in employment creation, income generation and poverty reduction. Data on the size and characteristics of the informal sector and its contribution to GDP are thus required for research and policy making. In response to this demand, the Handbook provides advice on the production of stand-alone statistics for the informal sector and of household production undertaken for own final use.

1.11.   Other issues that are sometimes considered to be related to the NOE are capital flight, shuttle trade, cross border shopping, tax evasion, and drug trafficking. Some of the concern that official statistics do not properly reflect the magnitude of such activities stems from a misunderstanding of what is included in the GDP. In particular, capital flight and tax evasion are not productive activities and thus are not measured in the GDP. Whilst it is not the aim of the Handbook to deal explicitly with these issues, it does provide some guidance. In particular, it details methods for the production of stand-alone statistics for underground production and describes its relationship to tax evasion, shuttle trade and other items commonly associated with the underground economy. It also discusses the most common types of illegal production.

1.12.   It is worth emphasising what the Handbook does *not* attempt to do. It does not lay claim to presenting new material, nor to providing the single best solution. Rather it is a compendium of existing good practices, with guidance on how they might best be used. Furthermore, it does not aim at *reduction* of underground, illegal, informal sector activities or household production for own final use. Rather it aims at ensuring that productive activities are observed to the extent possible, and that those that are non-observed are nevertheless measured in the national accounts. In doing so, the Handbook may provide some ideas regarding the causes and magnitudes of underground and illegal activities, but their reduction is a matter for government administrators, not for statisticians.

1.13.   The Handbook gives insight into tax evasion only to the extent that tax evasion is associated with activities within the 1993 SNA production boundary. However, tax evasion also occurs in connection with activities that are non-productive and which are therefore not included in the GDP. As further discussed in Chapters 4 and 9, estimates of missed tax revenues may be useful in assessing priorities for measuring the NOE and even for determining adjustments for missing production. Conversely, GDP estimates that have been adjusted to include some non-observed activities are indicative of the lower limits of the shortfall in tax receipts through tax evasion.

1.3.   Handbook Users

1.14.   The Handbook is aimed at all producers and users of macro-economic statistics. The primary audience is the staff of statistical offices involved in the collection of macroeconomic statistics and preparation of the national accounts. In addition, the Handbook may prove useful to data users who have reason to be concerned about overall levels of economic production or differences in trends between the economic activities that are directly measured and those that are indirectly estimated as part of the NOE. The Handbook may also prove useful to researchers and journalists who are confronted with a plethora of measures of the underground, hidden, shadow economy, etc., and who would like to know why they are all different and which can be regarded as the most reliable.

1.15.   Just as the 1993 SNA provides an international standard for all countries, so it is the intention of the Handbook to provide a measurement framework that is applicable in all countries, whether their statistical systems are well developed, or in development, or in transition from a planned economy.

1.4.   Concepts and Terminology

1.16.   The Handbook is anchored on the 1993 SNA and may be viewed as a supplement to it that discusses some specific measurement problems and methods. The following paragraphs introduce some of the key concepts, definitions and frequently used terms. They are further elaborated in Chapters 2, 3 and 8. A glossary of terms relevant to the Handbook is provided in Annex 2.

1.17.   The 1993 SNA defines an *enterprise* as an institutional unit, *i.e.*, corporation, government unit, non-profit institution or household, in its capacity as a producer of goods and services. This is a very broad definition. It includes, in particular, households producing goods entirely for their own final use. It goes far beyond what most economic survey statisticians would regard as an enterprise, but it is needed in order to cover all the units engaged in productive activities. It is the definition that is used in the Handbook.

1.18.   The Handbook also draws on the 1993 SNA for the definition of the terms used in the definition of the NOE, including:

- *underground production*, defined as those activities that are productive and legal but are deliberately concealed from the public authorities to avoid payment of taxes or complying with regulations;

- *illegal production*, defined as those productive activities that generate goods and services forbidden by law or that are unlawful when carried out by unauthorised producers;

- *informal sector production*, defined as those productive activities conducted by unincorporated enterprises in the household sector that are unregistered and/or are less than a specified size in terms of employment, and that have some market production;

- *production of households for own final use*, defined as those productive activities that result in goods or services consumed or capitalised by the households that produced them.

1.19.   The 1993 SNA takes its definition of *informal* directly from the International Conference of Labour Statistician (ICLS) 1993 Resolution concerning employment in the informal sector. (ICLS Resolutions are another primary source of international concepts for the Handbook.) The Resolution describes the informal sector in broad terms, and provides the framework within which each country should formulate its own specific operational definition. The Resolution uses the 1993 SNA production boundary as the starting point, defining the informal sector as a subset of the household sector and specifying the operational criteria for delineating those enterprises that belong to it.

1.20.   *National statistical system* is the term used in the Handbook to describe the ensemble of statistical organisations and units within a country that jointly collect, process and disseminate official statistics. The leading statistical agency is referred to as the *national statistical office*.

1.21.   The term *basic data collection programme* is used to describe the statistical infrastructure and survey procedures that collect and process basic economic data. Raw data obtained by survey statisticians directly from respondents by survey, or from administrative sources, are edited, imputed and aggregated to become the *basic data* that are supplied to the national accounts area, where, after appropriate transformation to national accounting concepts, they are input to the *national accounts compilation process*. Where these basic data are inadequate, the data gaps are filled and inconsistencies resolved using *indirect compilation methods* that model the missing data using other related data – *indicators* – and that enforce accounting identities.

1.5.   Measurement Strategy

1.22.   The Handbook strategy for NOE measurement draws on and combines a broad range of current ideas and practical experiences, for example as described by the Organisation for Economic co-operation and Development (1997), Goskomstat of Russia (1998), Bloem and Shrestha (2000), Calzaroni (2000), Luttikhuizen and Kazemier (2000), Masakova (2000) and Stapel (2001). It embodies the following basic principles.

1.23.   First, a national statistical system should have a NOE measurement programme with clear objectives, roles and responsibilities for the national accountants and for the survey statisticians, including those in regional offices. The major data users should also be informed and involved. Given that exhaustive coverage is an important aspect of quality, the NOE measurement programme should be blended with other quality management and improvement initiatives.

1.24.   There should be systematic analysis of NOE problems and potential solutions. This analysis should be based on a comprehensive analytical framework that helps categorise the causes of non-observed activities or the methods appropriate for their measurement. Causes may be classified, for example, as being due to non-registration, non-response or under-reporting.

1.25.   Improvement of the basic data collection programme is fundamental. The theme is upstream quality control. NOE measurement should be optimised by ensuring that the basic data include productive activities to the fullest extent possible. The national accounts compilation process should not be expected to deal indefinitely with problems in the basic data, caused, for example, by inappropriate concepts, or failure to make proper adjustments for non-response.

1.26.   Finally, full use should be made of all the basic data available rather than relying on model based assumptions. Where model based assumptions are unavoidable, they should be applied at the most detailed level available. *Macro-models* that model the entire economy in terms of variables that may relate in some way to the NOE are too crude to be accurate and the results they produce cannot be integrated with other data to provide better adjustments. They are to be avoided.

1.27.   The NOE measurement strategy recommended in this Handbook involves five lines of action.

- Identify an appropriate conceptual and analytical framework on the basis of which the NOE can be assessed.

- Assess the basic data being supplied to the national accounts and the compilation methods, identifying the extent of non-observed and non-measured activities and establishing priorities for dealing with them, both in the immediate future and the longer term.

- Identify potential improvements in the national accounts compilation process that will reduce the incidence of non-measured activities through model based adjustments and using the results of supplementary surveys. Such indirect measurement methods can be introduced relatively quickly and cheaply in comparison with changes to the basic data collection programme that may require substantial additional resources. These methods can provide short-term solutions to data problems that should ultimately be remedied by improvements in data collection. They may also be long-term solutions to chronic undercoverage and under-reporting problems that can never be solved at the data collection stage.

- Identify potential improvements in the infrastructure and content of the basic data collection programme that will reduce the incidence of non-observed activities by bringing the programme into line with international standards and best practices. This is the long-term solution to many data problems. Improvements in the basic programme are the way to deal with non-response and to reduce, if not completely eliminate undercoverage and under-reporting.

- Develop an implementation plan that includes consulting with users, prioritising the potential improvements, ensuring good communication between survey statisticians and national accountants, and dealing with revisions to national accounts estimates that may occur as a consequence of the changes.

1.6.   Roadmap to Handbook

By Chapter Content

1.28.   Chapter 2 summarises the conceptual framework provided by international standards, in particular the 1993 SNA, on which the remainder of the Handbook is based. It includes descriptions of the production boundary, transactions, units, classifications and labour related concepts.

1.29.   Chapter 3 defines the NOE problem areas, providing descriptions of underground production, illegal production, informal sector production, and household production for own final use. It introduces the notion of an analytical framework for assessing the magnitude and nature of non-observed activities, and provides some examples that have been used in practice.

1.30.   Chapter 4 outlines the procedures for assessing the basic data used in compiling the national accounts and the compilation procedures. It describes data confrontation and discrepancy analysis and techniques for estimating upper bounds for non-observed and non-measured activities. It reviews the sort of supplementary surveys that may provide additional information.

1.31.   Chapter 5 details indirect compilation methods for measuring non-observed activities (other than those associated with illegal production). It describes production approach methods that can be applied across a range of industries, of which the labour input method is a particularly important example. It also describes industry-specific methods, expenditure approach methods, and procedures based on supply and use tables.

1.32.   Chapter 6 focuses on improvements to the basic data collection programme that feeds the national accounts. It emphasises the need to evaluate the underlying statistical infrastructure – including legislation, organisational structure, business register, survey frames and survey design, use of administrative sources and metadata management. It describes a wide range of possible enhancements that may serve to reduce the incidence of non-observed activities.

1.33.   Chapter 7 provides guidance on planning and implementing measurement of the NOE. It suggests how to tailor the NOE measurement plan to particular circumstances, for example to a developing country or a country in transition. It also gives advice on revision strategies and, in particular, how to present changes in statistical estimates that result from better measurement of the NOE.

1.34.   Chapter 8 provides more details regarding the terminology and measurement of underground production, covering various activities frequently associated with the underground economy, such as shuttle trade and cross-border shopping.

1.35.   Chapter 9 is devoted to the description and treatment of illegal activities. These are not fully discussed in the context of national accounts compilation methods (Chapter 5) because it is not yet current practice to make explicit adjustments for illegal activities in the national accounts. This is due to the experimental and sensitive nature of the subject and the poor quality of the estimates.

1.36.   Chapter 10 deals with the informal sector in detail. It is in two parts. The first part explains the origins and nature of the definition of the informal sector and its policy significance. It also includes the results of recent deliberations by the *Delhi Group*, which was established by the United Nations Statistical Commission to improve measurement of the informal sector. The second part of the chapter describes how statistics for the informal sector may be obtained through use of supplementary questions added to labour force surveys and household income and expenditure surveys, or through special informal sector surveys, including mixed household-enterprise surveys.

1.37.   Chapter 11 describes the measurement of productive activities undertaken by households for their own final use, including subsistence farming, own account construction and paid domestic services.

1.38.   Chapter 12 outlines the principal macro-model methods. These include monetary methods, a model based on electricity consumption and the *latent variable method*. Estimates based on macro-model methods are often quoted in the media and attract considerable attention because they usually suggest that the GDP is much larger and is growing much faster than is shown by the official figures. The chapter describes the simplistic assumptions on which such methods are based and explains why they are usually misleading and of little practical use in compiling GDP.

1.39.   The Annexes contain a list of references, a glossary including the main terms used in the Handbook, a list of the principal national accounts aggregates and their typical data sources, and some additional material on NOE analytical frameworks and assessment tools.

By User

1.40.   Different types of users may wish to focus their attention on different chapters. Some redundancy has been introduced in the chapters to allow them to be read separately.

1.41.   Survey statisticians may find interesting material in all chapters – some chapters providing guidance on good data collection practices, others describing how the data are used to compile the national accounts.

1.42.   National accountants will certainly be familiar with the 1993 SNA material summarised in Chapter 2, so they may wish to focus on Chapters 3-5. They may also want to review Chapter 6 to the extent that they need to know what survey statisticians should be doing.

1.43.   Users of macro-economic data for policy purposes might want to focus on the NOE description and analytical framework in Chapter 3. They may also wish to skim through the remaining chapters, including discussion of issues related to the underground economy (Chapter 8) and the reasons why macro-model methods are not recommended (Chapter 12).

1.44.   Analysts and researchers interested in knowing the essence of the measurement strategy that is being presented and how it differs from the various macro-model methods should focus on Chapters 2-6 and 12.

1.45.   Journalists may find the material most pertinent to media articles in Chapters 3 and 8-12.

1.46.   Users interested in tax evasion may find some useful material in Chapters 4 and 8.

1.47.   Users with a focus on governance or dealing with capital flight, smuggling, shuttle trade, drug production or distribution may find Chapters 8 and 9 the most informative.

1.48.   Users particularly interested in the informal sector or household production for own final use should focus on Chapters 10 and 11.

Chapter 2

CONCEPTUAL FRAMEWORK

2. CONCEPTUAL FRAMEWORK

2.1. Introduction

2.1.   This chapter provides the basic knowledge to support the first line of action in the strategy for NOE measurement, namely establishing an appropriate conceptual framework. The chapter describes the concepts, definitions, classifications, and accounting rules of the 1993 SNA and other international standards that enable the NOE problem areas to be systematically defined and analysed in Chapter 3.

2.2.   In the context of the NOE, the most relevant elements of the 1993 SNA concern the measurement of GDP. Three approaches to measuring GDP can be distinguished: the production approach, the expenditure approach and the income approach. In the production approach the starting point is to measure output and intermediate consumption of goods and services, obtain value added as the difference between output and intermediate consumption, and sum the values added by different producers to obtain GDP. In the expenditure approach, GDP is measured as the sum of expenditure components (namely, final consumption expenditure, gross capital formation and net exports). The income approach directly measures the income arising from production – largely the wages paid to employees and the operating surplus/mixed income coming from productive activities. The distinction between these three approaches is somewhat artificial because they are seldom used completely independently from each other as they often share the same basic data. In practice, national accounts compilation is often a patchwork, with some elements estimated from the production approach, others from the expenditure approach, and still others from the income approach.

2.3.   Using the three approaches in conjunction also helps to alleviate their individual, inherent weaknesses. Bloem *et al.* (2001) provide details. In particular, combining data from the production side with data from the expenditure side through the commodity flow method or in a supply and use framework has proved to be a useful tool to check data and to generate estimates for missing items, including non-observed production, as further elaborated in Chapter 5.

2.4.   Because the Handbook focuses on exhaustive measurement of GDP, this chapter is concerned with those aspects of the 1993 SNA that have a direct bearing on GDP and the ways in which it can be measured. Section 2.2 describes the SNA production boundary; Section 2.3 introduces the concepts of transactions and other flows; Section 2.4 deals with the units involved in production and their classification by sector and economic activity; Section 2.5 defines the economic territory of a country; Section 2.6 discusses price and volume measures; Section 2.7 introduces labour related concepts; and Sections 2.8, 2.9, and 2.10 describe compilation of the accounts using production, expenditure and income approaches, respectively.

2.2. Production Boundaries

2.5.   One of the key concepts in the national accounts is that of production. The rules that have been developed to determine what is to be included as production and what is to be excluded – referred to as the *production boundary* – determine the scope of most current and capital transactions in the national accounts. First of all, the production boundary determines what is to be included in the accounts as output. Secondly, because the 1993 SNA recognises only uses of *produced* goods and services, the boundary also determines the scope of intermediate consumption, and thus, value added. For the same reason, the production boundary also determines what is to be included as household consumption and other final uses. Furthermore, because the 1993 SNA recognises only incomes generated through the production process, the production boundary also determines what should be included as income. Primary income is derived by the distribution of value added components (in particular, wages and salaries, and operating surplus and mixed income) on the basis of input of labour and capital. Disposable income is derived from primary incomes through the redistribution process (mainly through taxes, social contributions, and social benefits). Finally, the production boundary also determines what is saving (which is the difference between disposable income and final consumption) and net lending and borrowing (which is the final balance of the current and capital accounts).

2.6.   Because of the far-reaching importance of the production concept, the quality of national accounts is to a large extent determined by the exhaustiveness of the GDP estimates. To achieve exhaustiveness, the first step is the delineation of what should and should not be included in national accounts as production. In the first place, a boundary must be defined between those activities that are regarded as *productive* in an economic sense and those that are not. The second step is to define the boundary around the economic production that needs to be included in the national accounts. For several reasons that will be mentioned below, not all productive activities are included. With respect to productive activities, the 1993 SNA thus introduces two fundamental boundaries, namely the *general production boundary* and the SNA *production boundary*.

2.7.   The *general production boundary* draws the line between economic and non-economic production. Economic production includes all activities "carried out under the control and responsibility of an institutional unit that uses inputs of labour, capital, and goods and services to produce outputs of goods or services... of a kind that can be delivered or provided to other institutional units" (1993 SNA: 6.15 and 6.6). In short, it includes any human controlled activity resulting in outputs capable of being exchanged. For an activity to be productive in this sense, the following conditions need to be satisfied:

  * There must be a link between the activity and an institutional unit. The activity must be carried out "under the control and responsibility of an institutional unit exercising ownership rights on what is produced" (1993 SNA: 6.15). As a consequence, purely natural processes without any human involvement or direction are excluded. For example, the unmanaged growth of fish stocks is outside this general boundary, whereas fish farming is included.

  * There must be marketability (resulting in outputs capable of being exchanged). This is a weak criterion in the sense that being actually exchanged is not required as long as outputs are capable of being exchanged. Thus, production for own final use is included. Marketability also implies observance of the so-called *third-party criterion*, which states that an activity may be deemed economically productive only if it can be performed by a person other than the one benefiting from it. By this criterion, basic human activities such as eating, drinking, sleeping, taking exercise, etc. are excluded, whereas services such as washing, preparing meals, caring for children, the sick or aged fall within this general boundary because they can be exchanged between different units (1993 SNA: 6.16).

2.8.   The SNA *production boundary* is more restricted than the general boundary. It describes the range of productive economic activities that should be included in GDP estimates and is thus the boundary relevant to considerations of exhaustiveness. Activities included within the boundary are summarised as follows (1993 SNA: 6.18):

  a) the production of all individual or collective goods or services that are supplied to units other than their producers, or intended to be so supplied, including the production of goods and services used up in the process of producing such goods or services;

  b) the own-account production of all goods that are retained by their producers for their own final consumption or gross capital formation;

  c) the own-account production of housing services by owner-occupiers and of domestic and personal services produced by employing paid domestic staff.

2.9.   Regarding item (b) the 1993 SNA (Para 6.24) provides the following list of the most common types of production, that are included irrespective of whether or not they are intended for own final use:

- The production of agricultural products and their subsequent storage; the gathering of berries or other uncultivated crops; forestry; wood-cutting and the collection of firewood; hunting and fishing.
- The production of other primary products such as mining salt, peat extraction, and the supply of water.
- The processing of agricultural products; the production of grain by threshing; the production of flour by milling; the curing of skins and the production of leather; the production and preservation of meat and fish products; the preservation of fruit by drying, bottling, etc.; the production of dairy products such as butter or cheese; the production of beer, wine, or spirits; the production of baskets or mats, etc.
- Other kinds of processing such as weaving cloth; dress making and tailoring; the production of footwear, pottery, utensils or durables; making furniture or furnishings, etc.

2.10.   To decide in practice whether or not to record the production of a good within households, the 1993 SNA (Para 6.25) suggests adoption of a criterion of *significance*, meaning that if the amount produced is believed to be quantitatively important in relation to the total supply of that good in the country, then it should be estimated.

2.11.   The production of *services* for own final use by households is excluded from the accounts, with the exceptions mentioned in item *c*) of Paragraph 2.8 above. In particular, the 1993 SNA (Para 6.20) lists the domestic and personal services that are specifically excluded when produced and consumed within the same household, namely:

- the cleaning, decoration and maintenance of the dwelling occupied by the household, including small repairs of a kind usually carried out by tenants as well as owners;
- the cleaning, servicing and repair of household durables, including vehicles used for household purposes;
- the preparation and serving of meals; the care, training and instruction of children;
- the care of sick, infirm or old people;
- the transportation of members of the household or their goods.

2.12.   The 1993 SNA provides additional guidance regarding some "service like" activities. Major repairs to dwellings of the kind that a landlord would perform are included within the production boundary as gross fixed capital formation. Water carrying is regarded as part of the supply of water. The storage of crops produced by households for their own use is also included as an extension of the goods producing process. On the other hand, small-scale do-it-yourself repairs and maintenance to dwellings and consumer durables are excluded.

2.13.   The production boundary within households (1993 SNA: 6.23-6.33) was subject to considerable debate during the revision of the SNA.[1] The 1993 SNA acknowledges that certain kinds of household activities may be particularly important in some developing countries and that this issue deserves careful consideration.[2] However, as in the 1968 SNA, with the exception of housing services no values for the production of services by households for own final consumption are to be recorded in the central framework of the 1993 SNA.[3] This choice was justified on the following grounds:

- "limited repercussions on the rest of the economy;

---

1. For instance, one of the problems raised was that the SNA definition of production implies a gender bias since women typically spend more time than men in providing services to others within their immediate family and hence a smaller fraction of their contributions to society as a whole is valued within the system.
2. Expansion of the scope of the production boundary by the 1993 SNA removes some of the limitations of the 1968 version, which excluded the production of goods not made from primary products, the processing of primary products by those who do not produce them and the production of other goods by households who do not sell any part of them on the market.

- difficulty in the imputation of monetary values;
- adverse effects on the usefulness of the accounts for macroeconomic analysis and policy purposes."

2.14.   Services produced within households for own consumption were considered to have limited repercussions on the rest of the economy because of the self-contained nature of these activities. In contrast to the production of goods for own consumption – which can be sold or supplied to another unit at any point in time – the production of services for own consumption implies of necessity a simultaneous consumption of these services within the household.

2.15.   The difficulty in the imputation of monetary values arises because most household domestic and personal services are not produced for the market so that there are usually no suitable market prices available to value them. In addition to this valuation problem, it can be observed that imputed values have in any case a different economic significance from the other monetary values. The 1993 SNA (Para 6.21) notes, for instance, that "if a household member were offered the choice between producing services for own consumption and producing the same services in return for remuneration in cash, the paid employment would likely be preferred because of the greater range of consumption possibilities it affords. Thus imputing values for own account production of services ... would yield values which would not be equivalent to monetary values for analytic or policy purposes".

2.16.   As regards the usefulness of the accounts it is pertinent to note that the SNA production boundary is not only relevant for the variables explicitly recorded in the accounts, but also to related variables such as labour force and employment. The definition of the *economically active population*, as provided by the Thirteenth International Conference of Labour Statisticians (International Labour Organization, 1982), refers in fact to "all persons of either sex who furnish the supply of labour for the production of economic goods and services as defined by the United Nations System of National Accounts". This definition would become meaningless if the production boundary were to include own-account household services because this would imply most of the population was in the labour force – the distinction between employed and unemployed would be blurred, and unemployment would be virtually eliminated by definition.

2.17.   The 1993 SNA acknowledges that in most countries the own-account production of services within households undoubtedly absorbs a considerable amount of labour and their consumption contributes much to welfare. The delineation of the production boundary is explained as the result of a deliberate compromise between the desire to be as comprehensive as possible and the need not to impair the usefulness of the System for analytical and policy-making purposes in accordance with the needs of most users. Like its predecessors, however, the 1993 SNA is only a stage in the development of national accounting. Generally speaking, the debate on the scope of the production boundary is far from being over.

2.3.   Transactions and Other Flows

2.18.   Output, final uses, and incomes are all concepts known as *transactions*. As previously mentioned, what are included as transactions is largely decided by the 1993 SNA production boundary. However, there are other events that affect the economy through changes in stocks. The 1993 SNA refers to these events as *other flows*. Other flows do not constitute output or uses as such, and care must be taken to ensure that measurement of transactions properly excludes any such flows. Particular examples of other flows are *holding gains and losses*, which should be excluded from output and related transactions.

2.19.   Most transactions in the national accounts have a money value, are between different parties, and have a *quid pro quo* (something for something) character. However, the 1993 SNA also acknowledges transactions that have no money value as such, for example barter transactions, and output for own consumption. In these cases a money value is imputed, ideally, a comparable market price. In addition, the 1993 SNA recognises some transactions that are not between different parties (for example consumption of fixed capital and output for own consumption) or that do not have a *quid pro quo* (for

---

3. However, in Chapter XXI Satellite Analysis and Accounts, the 1993 SNA suggests including estimates of household production of services for own use in satellite accounts where an alternative concept of gross domestic product could be elaborated using an extended concept of the production boundary.

example taxes). However most transactions have two economic actors, whether from the same or different sectors and can thus be measured from two sides. In this sense there are two chances of measuring them, which has great significance in the compilation of the national accounts when data from many sources are brought together.

2.20.   The 1993 SNA distinguishes two main groups of transactions, namely, current transactions and accumulation transactions. Current transactions can be divided into productive transactions (transactions that concern the production process) and distributive transactions (transactions that concern the distribution, redistribution and use of income created in the production process). The distinction between productive and distributive transactions is of particular importance in defining the concept of illegal production (see Chapter 3). Accumulation transactions are relevant for the processes of capital formation and finance.

2.21.   Concerning the other flows that are not transactions and do not in any way relate to production, but, nevertheless, may have an effect on the economy, the 1993 SNA distinguishes two types:

- *other volume changes* – volume changes in stocks that are not caused by production such as new discoveries of subsoil minerals and oil deposits and destruction of stocks through catastrophic losses, *e.g.* due to floods or earthquakes;

- *changes in price* – can cause the value of stocks to increase or decrease. While this does not affect current transactions it does affect the economy through the changes in the value of the stocks.

The System does not record these other flows in the transaction accounts, but in the *other changes in assets* accounts.

2.4.   Units and Classifications of Units

2.4.1. *Institutional Units, Sectors and Subsectors*

2.22.   The concept of *institutional unit* is the starting point for consideration of the units engaged in economic activities. An institutional unit is defined as "an economic entity that is capable, in its own right, of owning assets, incurring liabilities and engaging in economic activities and in transactions with other entities" (1993 SNA: 4.2). "There are two main types of units in the real world that may qualify as institutional units, namely persons or groups of persons in the form of households, and legal or social entities whose existence is recognised by law or society independently of the persons, or other entities, that may own or control them" (1993 SNA: 4.3).

2.23.   The 1993 SNA concept of *household* is complex, not only because households can be very heterogeneous economically and socially, but also because their behaviour from an economic point of view may be more varied than that of the other institutional units. In fact, they may engage in any kind of economic activity and they may assume the role of final consumers as well as producers. Production within the household sector takes place within enterprises directly owned and controlled by members of households (individually or in partnership with others).

2.24.   In their capacities as economic production units, institutional units are referred to as *enterprises* (1993 SNA: 5.1). It should be noted that the 1993 SNA definition of enterprise is very broad. It not only includes all "businesses", as known in common parlance, but also includes government enterprises, non-profit enterprises, small market producers, and even those that do not market any of their production. These small producers can be a significant source of non-observed activities.

2.25.   A widely used definition of enterprise is contained in a European Union document – Section III of the Annex to the Council Regulation (EEC) No. 696/93 of March 1993 on the statistical units for the observation and analysis of the production system in the Community. This is directly linked to the descriptions given in the introduction to the UN International Standard Industrial Classification (ISIC, Rev.3) and the 1993 SNA: "The enterprise is the smallest combination of legal units that is an organisational unit producing goods and services, which benefits from a certain degree of autonomy in decision-making, especially for the allocation of its current resources. An enterprise carries out one or more activities at one or more locations. An enterprise may be a sole legal unit." An enterprise can be one of three types depending upon the underlying institutional unit and its activities: *corporation* (including *quasi-corporation*), *non-profit institution* or *unincorporated enterprise*.

- A *corporation* (1993 SNA: 4.23) is "a legal entity created for the purpose of producing goods or services for the market, that may be a source of profit or gain to its owner(s); it is collectively owned by the shareholders who have the authority to appoint directors responsible for its general management". "The laws governing the creation, management and operations of corporations may vary from country to country" (1993 SNA: 4.24), but the essential features of a corporation are its creation by law, its accountability for its own actions, its ownership and control by shareholders, and its purpose to produce goods and services at economically significant prices.

- A *quasi-corporation* (1993 SNA: 4.49-53) is an unincorporated enterprise that operates as if it were a corporation and, thus, must be treated as if it is one. All unincorporated enterprises owned by non-residents are defined as quasi-corporations. Quasi-corporations may also be owned by general government institutional units or by households. Since quasi-corporations owned by households may be more difficult to identify, it is worth noting that one important element of the definition is the presence of a complete set of accounts.

- *Non-profit institutions* (1993 SNA: 4.54) are "legal or social entities created for the purpose of producing goods and services whose status does not permit them to be a source of income, profit or other financial gain for the units that establish, control or finance them".

- All other enterprises are *unincorporated enterprises*. An *unincorporated enterprise* refers to an institutional unit (a household or government unit) in its role as a producer and "it covers only those activities of the unit that are directed towards the production of goods or services", whereas corporate enterprises and non-profit institutions are complete institutional units (1993 SNA: 5.1).

2.26. As noted previously, some government unincorporated enterprises are treated as quasi-corporations (1993 SNA: 4.109). However, most government unincorporated enterprises are largely or entirely non-market producers, meaning that they provide output free or at prices that are not economically significant to the general public or other government units.

2.27. The remaining unincorporated enterprises are owned and operated by households. They are referred to as "household unincorporated enterprises". The term "unincorporated" here simply emphasises the fact that the producer unit is not a separate legal entity distinct from the household itself.

2.28. Many households do not contain an unincorporated enterprise. Some households may share an unincorporated enterprise in a partnership. Household enterprises are divided into two groups: *unincorporated market enterprises* primarily producing goods or services for sale or barter; and *unincorporated non-market enterprises* producing primarily for their own final use (1993 SNA: 4.144 and 4.147).

2.29. For the purposes of data collection, the most important division of enterprises is into those that are household unincorporated enterprises and those that are not. Thus, for convenience in this Handbook, although this is not standard terminology, enterprises that are corporations, quasi-corporations, non-profit organisations, or government unincorporated enterprises may be collectively referred to as *non-household enterprises* and household unincorporated enterprises referred to simply as *household enterprises*.

2.30. Institutional units are grouped (1993 SNA: 4.6) into five mutually exclusive, exhaustive *institutional sectors*. Households constitute the *household sector*, and the other institutional units are divided into four sectors, namely: *non-financial corporations, financial corporations, general government, and non-profit institutions serving households* (NPISH).

2.31. The underlying criterion for the grouping of units to sectors is the homogeneity of the units as regards their objectives, functions and behaviour. In turn, sectors can be divided into sub-sectors depending "upon the analysis to be undertaken, the needs of policy makers, the availability of data and the economic circumstances and institutional arrangements within a country. No single method of sub-sectoring may be optimal for all purposes or all countries" (1993 SNA: 4.12). Thus, alternative methods of sub-sectoring are proposed by the 1993 SNA for certain sectors. In relation to the household sector it is noted that "it is particularly important for many developing countries to be able to distinguish between the formal and informal sectors of the economy" (1993 SNA: 4.159). This is further discussed in Section 3.2.3.

2.4.2. *Kind of Activity Units, Local Units and Establishments*

2.32.   The 1993 SNA and ISIC, Rev 3 recognise that an enterprise, particularly a large enterprise, may be engaged in a range of different activities at various different locations. In such a case, the classification of a large enterprise to a single activity, at a single location, results in a loss of detail – detail that would be useful for analytical purposes. This leads to the idea that large enterprises should be divided into smaller, more homogeneous *producing units* that can be more precisely classified and that collectively represent the enterprise as a whole.

2.33.   Partitioning an enterprise by reference to its various activities results in one or more *kind of activity units*. Partitioning an enterprise by reference to its various locations results in one or more *local units*. Using both methods of partitioning simultaneously results in one or more *establishments*. More specifically an establishment is defined (1993 SNA: 5.21-27) as an enterprise or part of an enterprise at a single location, engaged in essentially a single activity, and capable, in principle, of providing the data required for the production and generation of income accounts. The 1995 European System of Accounts (ESA 1995), produced by Eurostat (1995), defines a *local kind of activity unit* in place of an establishment, but the terms are synonymous.

2.34.   Kind-of-activity units and establishments are grouped according to their primary economic activity using an activity classification. To enable cross-country comparisons, it is essential to use an international standard. The standard specified is ISIC, Rev 3 (1993 SNA: 5.3 and 5.5). It is used to classify each enterprise, or part of the enterprise, according to its *primary activity*, defined as the activity that generates the most value added (1993 SNA: 5.7).

2.5.   Economic Territory and Residence

2.35.   Households and enterprises often engage in economic activities abroad, and foreign units often develop activities within the country. For instance, an enterprise may transport goods from the country across the border, or between two foreign countries. The 1993 SNA provides the criteria to decide which units belong to the national economy.

2.36.   The *economic territory* of a country (1993 SNA: 14.9-14.11) consists of the geographic territory administered by a government within which persons, goods and capital circulate freely. It includes islands, air space and territorial waters, also territorial enclaves in other parts of the world that the government owns or rents for diplomatic, military or scientific purposes. It excludes territorial enclaves within its geographic boundaries that are used by foreign governments or international organisations.

2.37.   The core of the residency principle is that, to belong to a national economy, an institutional unit should have a *centre of economic interest* within the economic territory (1993 SNA: 14.12). A centre of economic interest is deemed to be present when there exists a location – a place of work – within the economic territory of the country where the institutional unit engages or intends to engage in economic activities on a significant scale over an indefinite or long period of time. Long period is usually defined as the presence of the unit in the territory for at least a year (1993 SNA: 14.13).

2.38.   Output of a resident unit is included in the GDP of the country of residence no matter where that output is realised. Thus, for example, if an enterprise provides transport services between two foreign countries, this output is part of the output of the country of residence of the enterprise.

2.6.   Current Price and Volume Measures

2.39.   While the distinction between current price measures and volume measures does not affect the concepts and definitions as such, price and volume measurement pose their own problems, which should not be ignored in the context of the NOE. For many uses of the national accounts, volume measures are as least as important as current price measures. For instance, the growth rate of GDP, which is one of the main economic indicators, is usually presented in volume terms.

2.40.   In national accounts terminology, *volume measures* can be defined as current price measures from which the effects of price changes have been removed. Volume measures can have the format of constant price data (data of one year expressed in the prices of a reference year), indices (constant price data of one year divided by the constant price data of the base year), or growth rates (constant price data of one year divided by the constant price data of a previous year).

2.41.   In measuring the NOE, it is important to consider the price and volume components. It is tempting to assume that prices of transactions in the NOE behave in the same way as in the regular part of the national accounts, and thus, that the same deflators may be used. However, it is also worthwhile questioning this assumption. For instance, it is quite plausible that prices in the informal sector develop differently from those in the formal sector if the supply and demand curves are different. If this is the case, separate price indices would need to be developed to obtain accurate volume estimates or to obtain accurate current estimates if the constant price estimates have been obtained by extrapolating base year values by volume indicators.

2.7.   Labour Related Concepts

2.42.   Labour related concepts included in the 1993 SNA are population, number of jobs, total hours worked, full-time equivalent employment, and compensation of employees. The 1993 SNA refers to a Thirteenth International Conference of Labour Statisticians Resolution for definitions of the numbers of persons that are *employed, unemployed* and *not in the labour force* (International Labour Organization, 1982). Given their central role within the 1993 SNA, it is vital that labour market data are based on consistent, coherent measurements, integrated within the 1993 SNA framework. The relevant labour market concepts are summarised in Figure 2.1, which is copied from the 1993 SNA.

2.43.   The *population* of a country is the annual average number of persons (including foreigners) present in the economic territory of the country who reside or intend to remain within the economic territory for a period of time not shorter than one year. Persons who are living abroad for a period not exceeding one year are considered to be part of the population although temporarily absent.

2.44.   The total population of a country therefore includes:

- nationals present within the territory;
- nationals living abroad for a period not exceeding one year (*e.g.* seasonal workers and cross-border workers);
- foreigners (with the exception of military personnel, members of diplomatic corps and students) residing for a period exceeding one year;
- students abroad (regardless of length of stay);
- members of the Armed Forces stationed in the rest of the world;
- members of diplomatic corps stationed abroad;
- national crewmembers stationed on ships, aircraft or oilrigs located outside the economic territory.

2.45.   As previously noted, the residence of the household, as a unit, is determined according to the location of its principal centre of economic interest. This is defined as the location of one or more lodgings considered by the family as their principal residence, regardless of where the individual family members work.

2.46.   Using the concept of *labour input, i.e.*, the total amount of work performed in a productive system, analyses can be made of the performance and characteristics of the economic system and of different economic activities and/or different territorial areas.

2.47.   The population is broken down into *employed persons, unemployed persons*, and *persons not in the labour force*. The set of employed persons is then analysed according to the activities they perform, using the concept of job. A *job* is defined as an implicit or explicit contract between a person and an institutional unit. An employed person may have one or more jobs, running in parallel or at different times, within the reference period. Self-employed jobs are also included. In this case there is considered to be an

Figure 2.1. **(1993 SNA Figure 17.1) Population and labour concepts**

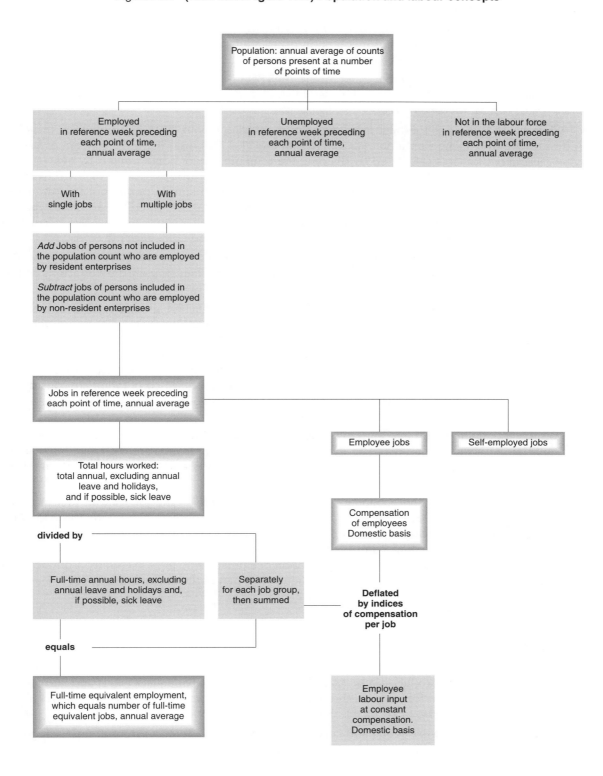

Note: Those concepts which are part of the SNA are in heavy boxes.

27

© OECD 2002

implicit contract between the self-employed persons in their capacity as owners of unincorporated enterprises and themselves as employees.

2.48.   Estimates regarding population and labour input are calculated as average values for the reference period. Persons who are not involved in production processes, even though under formal contract with the enterprise, are not counted as having jobs.

2.49.   The preferred measure of labour input for the 1993 SNA is the *total hours worked*. This excludes the time spent on annual leave, holidays, and if possible sick leave. Hours worked can be characterised as: *hours paid – hours paid but not worked + hours worked but not paid*.

2.50.   While hours worked is the best instrument for measuring labour input, there may be technical difficulties inherent in its measurement. For this reason the 1993 SNA introduces the concept of *full-time equivalent employment*, which is calculated by dividing the total number of hours worked by average full-time annual hours for each job group and summing over all job groups. The 1993 SNA gives no indication as to the exact methodology for making the estimate. It simply points out that the most appropriate procedure is to determine the average annual number of hours worked as per contract, and to use this information to convert from jobs to full-time equivalents. It also points out that this calculation should be computed separately for each branch of economic activity and/or for each job type.

2.51.   *Labour input at constant compensation* is determined by measuring employee labour input on the basis of job compensation for the base period. This is useful for focusing on the variations in the different job categories and the different branches of economic activity.

2.52.   The concepts defined thus far form the necessary and sufficient groundwork for measuring labour input. However, for a more finely tuned description, the 1993 SNA makes a distinction between employee jobs and self-employment jobs. *Employee jobs* include individuals working under an employment contract for resident institutional units and receiving compensation in return. *Self-employment jobs* refer to single proprietors or co-proprietors of unincorporated enterprises as well as contributing family workers. All persons working for a corporation or a quasi-corporation are considered employees. This means that the owner of an incorporated enterprise or quasi-corporation is counted as an employee when he or she works for that enterprise.

2.53.   Population, jobs (divided into employee jobs and self-employment jobs), total number of hours worked, full-time equivalent employment, and compensation of employees are the concepts that are an integral part of the 1993 SNA. Number of employed persons and labour input at constant compensation are viewed as auxiliary variables.

2.54.   The labour input within an economic territory is determined by the jobs within that territory, which are in turn determined by the residence of the employing or self-employed institutional unit. Consequently this does not include labour input associated with jobs belonging to non-resident units, for example workers who live in one country but work in another. Thus full-time equivalent employment cannot be compared with population. The compensation of a person who lives in country A but works in country B is part of the value added of country B although it is part of the national income of country A.

2.8.   The Production Approach

2.8.1. Introduction

2.55.   In the production approach, GDP is measured as the sum of value added by industries, augmented with *net taxes and subsidies* on products. *Value added* is the difference between *total output* and *intermediate consumption* (the goods and services used in the production process), and can be measured *gross* (before deducting consumption of fixed capital), or *net* (after deducting consumption of fixed capital).

2.56.   It is not self-evident what goods and services should be considered as output, nor what goods and services can be considered intermediate consumption. As noted earlier, it has been argued that many household activities (such as cooking and cleaning) and do-it-yourself activities (such as car maintenance) are productive, and should be included in output as measured in the national accounts. Likewise, it has been argued that the use of the environment should be recorded as intermediate consumption. As explained above, the 1993 SNA contains a very important concept, namely, the production boundary in order to decide on these issues for the purpose of GDP measurement. Although the production boundary provides a general rule, quite a few issues remain that do not immediately follow from this rule. Subsection 2.8.2 discusses the most relevant aspects from the 1993 SNA in this respect. Besides deciding what should be included in the accounts as output and intermediate consumption, it has also to be decided how these should be recorded: at what value and at what time. As well, it has to be decided how the national accounts of any particular country can be delineated *vis-à-vis* the rest of the world. The 1993 SNA rules in these respects are discussed in subsequent subsections.

2.8.2. *Output*

2.57.   Concerning output, specific issues that need to be highlighted concern the distinction between market and non-market output and the measurement of these types of output. Market output is output sold at an agreed price that, in principle, covers costs and a margin for operating surplus/mixed income. Such output can be paid for in whatever currency units partners to the sale/purchase agree upon, or be exchanged for other goods and services, which is dubbed barter trade.

2.58.   A specific case of barter is when a producing unit provides part of its output to its employees as wages in kind. Common examples of such output include free meals in restaurants, free health care services produced by the employer (or an establishment in the same enterprise), and use of holiday facilities operated by the employer (the latter two examples are particularly relevant in formerly centrally planned economies). Such output should be included in the output of the units themselves, or of specific establishments, depending on the arrangements that are in place.

2.59.   Another special case of output concerns banking services. These services are usually only partly paid for through fees, although in some countries these may be quite substantial. In any case, the 1993 SNA requires full inclusion of banking services in output, including the part that is not paid for directly. This output is dubbed *financial intermediation services indirectly measured* (FISIM) and is defined as the difference between the interest received by banks and the interest paid by them.

2.60.   Non-market output concerns output that is intended for own final use by the producer, or to be provided to users at *economically non-significant prices*, defined as prices that do not significantly affect supply and demand. Output intended for own use can be production of goods for household consumption, for fixed capital formation and work-in-progress. An important example of own account production of goods for households is agricultural production of foodstuffs to be consumed within the producing households. Another important example concerns production of owner-occupied housing services. Where households own the dwelling they live in, the System treats this as a production of housing services consumed within the same household.

2.61.   Important examples of own account fixed capital formation are computer software developed within an enterprise, and construction of dwellings for own occupation and sheds for agricultural purposes. In particular, in developing countries farmers often construct sheds near distant plots for shelter and for storage. Other examples of fixed capital formation on own account include raising cattle for reproductive purposes, and growing fruit trees.

2.62.   Work-in-progress can be seen as output for own use in the sense that it is intended for further processing before a finished product can be marketed. One can argue about the "own use" character of such output (see Bloem *et al.*, 2001), but the main issue is that, for production processes that take longer than a single accounting period, output should be recorded in the period in which it takes place rather than at the time a finished product is realised. Examples of activities in which work-in-progress is relevant are construction, production of machinery, agriculture (*e.g.* crops in the field, sheep for wool), producing movies and organising major events.

2.63.   Non-market output is mostly generated by government and NPISH. Non-market services can be for individual consumption or for consumption by society at large. It should be noted that, in cases where a government or an NPISH buys products from other producers to provide free to other units, this

29

does not affect the output of government or the NPISH themselves (except for the activities involved in distributing such products).

2.64. The gross output of enterprises/establishments is usually not the same as the value of sales. For goods-producing enterprises some of the goods sold are taken from inventories produced or purchased for resale in earlier periods. Similarly, some of the goods produced or purchased in the current period will enter inventories for sale in later periods. Inventories include work-in-progress. Goods produced or purchased may also be used for own consumption by the enterprise owner's household, or given to employees as wages in kind, rather than being sold. In developing countries such uses of goods tend to be more important than changes in inventories in generating a difference between gross output and value of sales.

2.8.3. Intermediate Consumption

2.65. In concept, intermediate consumption is a measure of the goods and services used up in a period in the production process. In practice, businesses do not directly measure their intermediate usage of goods and services; rather they record their purchases and the changes in inventories of fuels and materials. Therefore, it is necessary to estimate intermediate consumption as:

- expenditure on purchases of materials and supplies, and services used as inputs;
- less changes in inventories of materials and supplies (inventories include work-in-progress).

2.66. Specific issues to be considered in regard to intermediate consumption concern the borderline between intermediate consumption and compensation of employees, and the borderline between intermediate consumption and fixed capital formation. As with output, intermediate consumption can involve barter trade, and deliveries between establishments of the same enterprise.

2.67. Concerning the borderline between intermediate consumption and compensation of employees the main issue is whether the goods and services provided to employees are for their own use, or for use in the production process. An example of a borderline case is clothing provided to employees with a use that is not limited to the production environment but have possible off duty use (military uniforms are an example).

2.68. Regarding the borderline between intermediate consumption and fixed capital formation, the main issue is whether a product is entirely used up in a single accounting period or whether it can be used for a number of periods. As a practical convention, the 1993 SNA has adopted the rule that a product that is used for more than one year is to be considered as fixed capital, and if it is used for less than one year as intermediate consumption. If such a product is considered intermediate consumption, its whole value is to be deducted from output to derive gross value added. If a product is considered fixed capital, its use will not affect gross value added but net value added will be lower by the amount of consumption of fixed capital during the period of its use.

2.8.4. Valuation and Time of Recording

2.69. Both concerning valuation and time of recording, perspectives often differ between participants in a sale/purchase agreement, and the 1993 SNA has to offer solutions that allow consistency. In the 1993 SNA, valuation of output and intermediate consumption is basically at market prices, that is, at prices upon which willing buyers and sellers agree. Often, such prices are not available for all output (*e.g.* work-in-progress) and in such cases the 1993 SNA offers as alternatives to use prices from comparable products, or cost plus mark up.

2.70. As a general rule, non-market output of government and NPISH is valued at cost. These costs include wages and salaries, intermediate consumption and consumption of fixed capital. Government's intermediate consumption includes weapons, tanks, warships, missiles, etc. purchased by the armed forces, but excludes items such as transport vehicles, hospital equipment, computers, etc., which are treated as capital formation. Government's intermediate consumption does not include goods and services purchased in order to be provided free to other units. This is also the case for NPISH. As a general rule, according to the 1993 SNA, no taxes on products are recorded for government units and NPISH. However, such units *can* pay taxes on production (such as real estate taxes) and these should be included in output.

2.71.   Market prices differ between producers and users. For producers the most relevant price is the basic price, that is the price they receive before net taxes and subsidies on products and trade and transport margins have been included. This is also the preferred valuation for output in the 1993 SNA. Because it is sometimes difficult to measure output in basic prices, the 1993 SNA also allows the use of producer prices, which are basic prices plus net taxes and subsidies on products (exclusive of deductible value added taxes). For users the most relevant price is the purchasers price, which includes all taxes less subsidies on production and trade and transport margins. This is also the recommended valuation in the 1993 SNA for intermediate consumption.

2.72.   Total GDP also includes net taxes and subsidies on production and imports. For the production approach this means that if output has been valued at basic prices, total value added of industries has to be augmented with net taxes and subsidies on products to arrive at a GDP estimate.

2.73.   Concerning time of recording, the 1993 SNA considers two basic options namely *cash basis* and *accrual basis*. In general terms, *cash basis* is when the actual payment is made and *accrual basis* is when change of ownership takes place. The 1993 SNA requires recording on an accrual basis.

2.9.   The Expenditure Approach

2.9.1. *Introduction*

2.74.   In the expenditure approach, GDP is estimated by adding up all final uses of resident units. The 1993 SNA distinguishes seven types of final uses:

- household final consumption;
- government final consumption;
- final consumption by NPISH;
- gross fixed capital formation;
- changes in inventories;
- acquisition less disposal of valuables;
- net exports of goods and services, *i.e.*, exports less imports.

2.75.   What is included in these types of final uses is explained in subsequent subsections. Some important preliminary remarks concern the types of final expenditure in which the various institutional sectors engage, the different ways to look at consumption, and the time of recording and valuation.

2.76.   As regards final consumption it should be noted that not all institutional units engage in all types of final uses. In fact the only type of final use that all resident sectors engage in is acquisition less disposal of valuables. Evidently, households are the only units that engage in household final consumption and, because they also may have productive activities, they may also have fixed capital formation and changes in inventories. By convention government is deemed to consume its own output (to the extent that it is not sold), which is called government consumption. Furthermore, besides acquisition less disposal of valuables, government has fixed capital formation and changes in inventories. NPISH engage in the same type of expenditures, except that they are deemed to consume output of NPISH. The corporate sectors have, besides acquisition less disposal of valuables, fixed capital formation and changes in inventories as final expenditures. For the rest of the world sector only imports by resident units and exports from resident units are recorded.

2.77.   In the context of national accounts, consumption can be viewed from two perspectives, namely, the *expenditure* perspective and the actual *consumption* perspective. The expenditure perspective is at the core of the 1993 SNA. What is relevant from this perspective is who actually paid for the consumption, either by making an actual monetary payment, by barter, by incurring a liability, or by producing the product on own account. As well, some specific transfers in kind are deemed by the System to be transfers in cash so that the recipient is deemed to have paid for the products involved. For example, this is the case with international relief goods and current transfers in kind that are not from government or NPISH.

2.78. The 1993 SNA also includes the concept of *actual consumption*, which – for households – includes not only expenditures, but also social transfers in kind. Social transfers in kind are individual goods and services produced or purchased by government and NPISH that are provided free to households. In the same vein, actual consumption for government and NPISH excludes these goods and services. Examples of individual consumption goods and services are health care, education, and cultural services and, by convention, all services provided by NPISHs.

2.79. As mentioned in relation to the production approach, expenditures are to be recorded on an accrual basis and to be valued at purchasers prices.

2.9.2. *Household Final Consumption Expenditure*

2.80. Household final consumption expenditure consists of expenditure incurred by households on goods and services. Most of these are goods bought in shops and markets and services like dry cleaning, shoe repairs, hairdressing, restaurant meals, etc. Also included are:

- goods produced by households for own consumption;
- purchases or barter from other households;
- expenditures on financial intermediation services indirectly measured (FISIM);
- services of insurance companies and pension funds;
- compensation of employees paid as income in kind;
- imputed rent of owner-occupied dwellings.

2.81. Because households include households with unincorporated enterprises, care should be taken not to include expenditure for intermediate consumption and fixed capital formation of such enterprises in household consumption.

2.82. Licenses and fees have to be included in household consumption expenditures if a good or service is provided in return. Examples are tuition fees and fees for medical care. An important criterion is whether the payment is commensurate with the return. For instance, if the fee for a passport is commensurate with the costs of producing it, the payment for it can be classified as household consumption expenditure. If the fee is much higher, it is classified as a current tax.

2.83. The residency principle is also applicable to household consumption expenditures. In this case, this principle means that the expenditures of resident households made abroad should be included, but that expenditures by residents of other countries should be excluded.

2.9.3. *Government Final Consumption Expenditure*

2.84. Government final consumption expenditure comprises all non-market gross output (excluding capital goods) of government units and non-profit institutions financed by government, minus sales of goods and services to other units. Goods and services purchased by government to pass on free to the population should also be included. As mentioned in Section 2.8.2, government non-market output and non-market output of NPISH are estimated as the sum of costs, and intermediate consumption of government includes weapons and similar equipment for the armed forces.

2.9.4. *Final Consumption Expenditure of NPISHs*

2.85. Except for the issue of military goods the description of government final consumption expenditure in Subsection 2.9.3 also applies to final consumption expenditure of NPISHs.

2.9.5. *Gross Fixed Capital Formation*

2.86. Gross fixed capital formation (GFCF) consists of goods that are used in a production process for more than one year. GFCF is measured by the value of expenditure on tangible and intangible fixed assets to be used in production. The assets concerned can be purchased or produced on own account. Gross fixed capital formation is equivalent to the acquisition, less disposals, of new and existing fixed assets (tangible or intangible) plus the improvement and cost of ownership transfer associated with fixed assets and with all non-produced assets such as land and sub-soil assets.

2.87.   Tangible fixed assets include:

* dwellings and other structures such as factories;
* civil engineering works;
* machinery and vehicles;
* expenditure on fruit-bearing trees, shrubs and vines, that are producing for a number of years;
* major improvements to tangible non-produced assets (*e.g.* land);
* expenditure on, and production of, breeding and dairy livestock that continue to be used in production year after year.

2.88.   Intangible fixed assets include:

* computer software and databases;
* expenditures on mineral exploration;
* artistic products used in production (*e.g.* movies, literary or artistic originals).

2.89.   GFCF is to be valued at market prices, or, if these are not available, either at costs plus mark up, or as the present (*i.e.*, discounted) value of future earnings. GFCF should be recorded when change of ownership takes place or, in the case of own account fixed capital formation, at the time of initiation of use (before initiation of use own account output of a fixed capital asset is regarded as work-in-progress and recorded as changes in inventories). GFCF covers both newly produced assets and existing assets.

2.90.   GFCF includes expenditure made on own-account construction of dwellings and major repairs by households. GFCF excludes the acquisition of military hardware that is included in the intermediate consumption of general government.

2.9.6. *Changes in Inventories*

2.91.   Changes in inventories include:

* raw materials and other materials;
* work-in-progress;
* goods for resale;
* finished goods (that is, finished goods held by the original producer).

2.92.   A major concern in the valuation of changes in inventories is to avoid including holding gains and losses. For that purpose additions to inventories have to be recorded at the prices prevailing at the time of their entry, and withdrawals from inventories at the prices prevailing at the time of withdrawal. These valuation principles apply both to products purchased from others and products produced within the unit. The prices to be used should, ideally, be market prices, or, if these are not available, prices of comparable products or costs plus mark-up. If prices are based on costs plus mark-up, care should be taken that these also need to be corrected for price changes.

2.9.7. *Acquisition and Disposal of Valuables*

2.93.   Valuables are described in the 1993 SNA as assets that are acquired as stores of wealth, that are not used up in production, that do not deteriorate over time, and that are expected to at least retain their value. Examples are jewellery, works of art, antiques, and precious stones and metals. In some countries commercial banks acquire gold and other precious metals as financial assets. These are also included as valuables.

2.9.8. *Exports and Imports*

2.94.   Exports are goods and services provided by residents to non-residents, and imports consist of goods and services provided by non-residents to residents. Imports and exports include:

- shuttle trade;
- parcel post;
- gifts to and from individuals abroad except by parcel post;
- consumption expenditures abroad;
- construction and installation of equipment abroad;
- exports and imports of military equipment;
- foreign aid;
- supply of fuel, food, water and other products to national ships and aircraft abroad, and to foreign vessels in the country;
- value of fishery products sold by resident units operating in international waters to non-residents;
- direct purchases of goods by embassies and international organisations;
- non-monetary gold, *i.e.*, gold purchases for industrial purposes or held as "valuables" by commercial banks;
- cross-border barter goods;
- exports/imports of oil and natural gas by pipeline;
- very large items such as ships and aircraft;
- very small but high value items such as gems.

2.10.   The Income Approach

2.95.   GDP can also be estimated as the total of incomes, *i.e.*, operating surplus, mixed income, compensation of employees and rents. The *income approach* is sometimes presented as a third method of obtaining GDP, the other two being the production approach and the expenditure approach. The income approach is independent of the other two methods in the sense that the estimates of the various kinds of income may come from sources that are different from those used for the other methods. As a consequence, GDP estimates from the income approach can be used as a check on estimates from the production and expenditure sides. Conceptually, however, the income approach is the same as the production approach. Recall that for the production approach, value added is obtained as the difference between output and intermediate consumption. But this value added is nothing other than an estimate of the incomes – compensation of employees, operating surplus, mixed income and rents – that are being generated in the various kinds of productive activities.

2.96.   The production approach normally uses information from enterprise surveys on gross output and intermediate consumption. The income approach usually makes use of administrative sources for employee compensation and of company accounts and tax records for operating surplus and mixed income. In both the income and the production approaches, operating surplus and mixed income are derived in the same way as residuals by deducting intermediate consumption and employee compensation from gross output.

Chapter 3

NOTIONS OF THE NON-OBSERVED ECONOMY

3. NOTIONS OF THE NON-OBSERVED ECONOMY

3.1. Definition of Non-Observed Economy

3.1. This chapter supports the first line of action in the NOE measurement strategy. It deals with the definition of the NOE and the development of a framework for its analysis. As discussed in the previous chapter, the 1993 SNA offers a coherent, internationally accepted conceptual framework for economic statistics, which is the starting point for identifying and analysing the NOE problem areas. In aiming for exhaustive measurement of activities within the 1993 SNA production boundary, the goal of the national statistical system is to reduce as far as possible the incidence of non-observed activities and to ensure that those remaining are appropriately measured and included in the GDP estimates.

3.2. As noted in Chapter 1, the groups of activities most likely to be non-observed are those that are *underground, illegal, informal sector,* or *undertaken by households for their own final use.* Activities may also be missed because of *deficiencies in the basic data collection programme.* These five groups of activities are referred to as the NOE *problem areas,* and activities not included in the basic data because they are in one or more of these problem areas are collectively said to comprise the *non-observed economy* (NOE).

3.3. The term is used by the European Union in connection with its programme to guarantee the exhaustiveness of the GDP. A European Commission (1994) Decision notes that "within the production boundary, national accounts provide an exhaustive measure of production when they cover production, primary income and expenditure that are directly and *not* directly *observed* in statistical or administrative files".

3.4. The order in which the problem areas are listed is not intended as an indication of their relative importance. In fact their sizes and impacts vary from country to country. For example, non-observed activities in the informal sector may be relatively unimportant in developed countries and of great significance in developing countries. Neither should it be assumed that the problem areas are mutually exclusive. In particular, informal sector units may conduct activities that are underground or are non-observed because of deficiencies in the data collection programme.

3.5. Section 3.2 describes each of the NOE problem areas, drawing on the conceptual framework presented in Chapter 2. Section 3.3 discusses the characteristics of non-observed activities and the formulation of an analytical framework as the basis for NOE assessment and measurement as described in subsequent chapters.

3.2. NOE Problem Areas

3.2.1. *Underground Production*

3.6. The 1993 SNA (Para 6.34) states that "Certain activities may be both productive in an economic sense and also quite legal (provided certain standards or regulations are complied with) but deliberately concealed from public authorities for the following kinds of reasons:

  a) to avoid the payment of income, value added or other taxes;

  b) to avoid the payment of social security contributions;

    c) to avoid having to meet certain legal standards such as minimum wages, maximum hours, safety or health standards, etc.;

    d) to avoid complying with certain administrative procedures, such as completing statistical questionnaires or other administrative forms."

It also states that "Producers engaged in this type of production may be described as belonging to the 'underground economy'".

3.7.   Examples of activities belonging to the underground economy are where enterprises choose not to declare part or all of their income in order to avoid direct or indirect taxation; or choose not to respect employment regulations or immigration laws by hiring labour "off the books", or decide to operate unofficially in order to avoid long and costly bureaucratic procedures, or where self-employed workers declare fraudulently that they are unemployed in order to draw unemployment benefits.

3.8.   As noted in the 1993 SNA (Para 6.35) the borderline between underground and illegal production is not entirely clear. "For example production that does not comply with certain safety, health or other standards could be described as illegal. Similarly, the evasion of taxes is itself usually a criminal offence." Two observations help to clarify the boundary. First, the lack of administrative authorisation alone is not sufficient to define an activity as illegal. Second, a distinction can be made between the various kinds of activities that break the law. On the one hand, *illegality in a strict sense* refers to acts violating the penal code. This kind of illegality is typical of illegal activities defined by the 1993 SNA. On the other hand, *illegality in a broad sense* refers to all other activities that break the law, in particular violation of rules and standards concerning taxes, social security/pension contributions, minimum wages, maximum hours, safety or health standards, etc. So the rule of thumb is that underground activities according to the 1993 SNA are those not complying with administrative rules, whereas illegal activities are associated with criminal behaviour. Also, as further noted in the 1993 SNA (Para 6.35) "it is not necessary for the purposes of the System to try and fix the precise borderline between underground and illegal production as both are included within the production boundary".

3.2.2. *Illegal Production*

3.9.   The 1993 SNA states explicitly that illegal activities should be included in the system of national accounts, noting that "despite the obvious practical difficulties in obtaining data on illegal production, it is included within the production boundary of the System" (1993 SNA: 6.30), and that: "All illegal actions that fit the characteristics of transactions – notably the characteristic that there is mutual agreement between the parties – are treated the same way as legal actions" (1993 SNA: 3.54). Illegal activities are activities forbidden by law, for example production and distribution of illegal drugs, or activities that are illegal when they are carried out by unauthorised actors, for example unlicensed practice of medicine. Illegal production is thus classified by the 1993 SNA in two categories:

- the production of goods and services whose production, sale or mere possession is forbidden by law;

- production activities which are usually legal but which become illegal when carried out by unauthorised producers.

Both kinds of production are included within the production boundary, provided that they are genuine processes whose outputs consist of goods and services for which there is an effective market demand.

3.10.   When recommending the inclusion of illegal activities within the production boundary, the 1993 SNA makes a clear distinction between transactions mutually agreed upon by the purchaser and the seller (for example, sale of drugs, trafficking stolen goods, or prostitution), which are included within the production boundary, and other activities where such mutual agreement is missing (for example, extortion or theft), which are excluded. The 1993 SNA suggests that illegal actions for which there is no mutual agreement can be construed as an extreme form of *externality* for which, in general, no values are imputed in the national accounts. So it is *absence of consent* rather than illegality that is actually the criterion for exclusion from the production boundary. *Theft* is mentioned explicitly (1993 SNA: 3.55 and 6.33) as an example of an illegal activity that has no effect on output and value added.

3.11.   Illegal activities can be either *productive* or *distributive*. As mentioned in Chapter 2, the former have a direct impact on the level of GDP estimates whereas the latter involve redistribution among the various institutional sectors. However, for consistency between transactions, other flows and the balance sheets, illegal activities that are distributive in nature also need to be taken into account if they involve redistribution between different institutional sectors.

3.12.   A particular activity cannot always be characterised as exclusively productive or distributive. Productive activities may also have consequences for the distribution of incomes – in particular they are a source of additional income. Distributive activities may also have consequences for the level of GDP if the new distribution of goods and services and of incomes turns out to be more or less efficient than the previous one. Thus, the designation of a particular activity as productive or distributive must be based on the dominant features of that activity.

3.13.   Variations in the definition of illegal production occur across countries. What is illegal in one country may be legal in others. From the perspective of exhaustive estimates of GDP, in principle the boundary between underground and illegal activities does not need to be precise, given that both should be included within GDP estimates. However, differences in the boundary between countries, or changes in the boundary within a country over time, can cause inconsistencies in practice because GDP is often compiled without explicitly including illegal activities. Thus a difference in what is defined as illegal, or change from illegal to legal, or *vice versa* , affects the estimates. For example, prostitution and the production of alcoholic beverages are illegal in some countries and legal in others. The case of abortion in Italy is an example of a change over time. Before 1978, abortion in Italy was illegal and activities related to it were not recorded in the national accounts. Its legalisation in 1978 led to inclusion in the national accounts of outputs and household expenditures for legal abortions. As a result there was a sudden (small) increase in the size of the health sector on both the output and expenditure sides. Thus, it is important to describe what is defined as illegal production in a country in order to be aware of any limitations in the comparison of GDP estimates with other countries and over time. This is further discussed in Chapter 9.

3.2.3. *Informal Sector Production*

3.14.   The informal sector represents an important part of the economy and the labour market in many countries, especially developing countries. Thus, measurements of the informal sector are important in their own right as well as contributing towards exhaustive estimates of GDP. This section summarises the international definition of the informal sector that was adopted in 1993 by the Fifteenth International Conference of Labour Statisticians (15th ICLS) Resolution *concerning statistics of employment in the informal sector* (International Labour Organization, 1993), and that was included in the 1993 SNA (Para. 4.159). The summary is in sufficient detail for discussion of the NOE. The definition and the thinking behind it are further elaborated in Chapter 10.

3.15.   Paragraph 5(1) of the 15th ICLS Resolution describes the underlying concept. "The informal sector may be broadly characterised as consisting of units engaged in the production of goods or services with the primary objective of generating employment and incomes to the persons concerned. These units typically operate at a low level of organisation, with little or no division between labour and capital as factors of production and on a small scale. Labour relations – where they exist – are based mostly on casual employment, kinship or personal and social relations rather than contractual arrangements with formal guarantees."

3.16.   Most informal sector activities provide goods and services whose production and distribution are perfectly legal. This is the characteristic that distinguishes them from illegal production. There is also a distinction between informal sector and underground activities, although it may be more blurred. Informal sector activities are not necessarily performed with the deliberate intention of evading the payment of taxes or social security contributions, or infringing labour legislation or other regulations. However, there can be some overlap, as some informal sector enterprises may prefer to remain unregistered or unlicensed in order to avoid compliance with regulations and thereby reduce production costs.

3.17. The characteristic features of household unincorporated enterprises as described in the 1993 SNA correspond well to the concept of the informal sector. In particular, the fixed and other capital used does not belong to the production units as such but to their owners; the enterprises as such cannot engage in transactions or enter into contracts with other units, nor incur liabilities on their own behalf; the owners have to raise the necessary finance at their own risk and are personally liable, without limit, for any debts or obligations incurred in the production process; expenditure for production is often indistinguishable from household expenditure; and capital equipment such as buildings or vehicles may be used indistinguishably for business and household purposes. Accordingly, the 15th ICLS defined the informal sector in operational terms as a subset of household unincorporated enterprises.

3.18. In addition, the 15th ICLS aimed to ensure that the activities included in the informal sector were as homogeneous as possible both regarding their economic behaviour and the data required to analyse them, and also that these data could be collected in practice. Thus, it introduced further criteria for inclusion. First, an enterprise must have at least some market output. Second, an enterprise that is an employer must satisfy one or more of the following three criteria:

- The enterprise is less than a specified size in terms of persons engaged, employees or employees employed on a continuous basis.

- Non-registration of the enterprise under specific forms of national legislation, such as factories' or commercial acts, tax or social security laws, professional groups' regulatory acts, or similar acts, laws or regulations established by national legislative bodies.

- Non-registration of the employees of the enterprise in terms of the absence of employment or apprenticeship contracts which commit the employer to pay relevant taxes and social security contributions on behalf of the employees or which make the employment relationships subject to standard labour legislation.[1]

For enterprises that are not employers only the second of these criteria is relevant.

3.19. In addition, for practical reasons the 15th ICLS introduced the optional exclusion from the informal sector of household unincorporated enterprises that are classified to agriculture.

3.20. These criteria provide the framework within which the actual definition of informal sector should be constructed in any given country. Evidently, they may not necessarily result in exactly the same definition of the informal sector across countries. The criteria can be applied in different combinations, the national legislations may differ, the employment size limits and how they are measured may vary, etc. The *Delhi Group* has been trying to narrow down the options as further discussed in Chapter 10.

3.21. The 15th ICLS definition is not designed to lead to a segmentation of the economy according to a formal/informal sector dichotomy. In fact it does not explicitly define a formal sector. It recognised that certain activities excluded from the scope of the informal sector were not formal and recommended that such activities should be identified as a separate category outside a formal/informal sector distinction. Also, the 1993 SNA (Annex I, B: 2.31) notes that "depending on national circumstances, certain production units of the household sector may fall outside the distinction between formal and informal sectors (*i.e.*, units exclusively engaged in agricultural activities, the production of goods for own final use, or the production of services for own final consumption by employing paid domestic workers)". This implies a trichotomy – an enterprise is formal, informal or neither. However, the 15th ICLS Resolution was not completely reproduced in the Annex to Chapter IV of the 1993 SNA. Furthermore, the 1993 SNA contains several references to formal/informal sectors, which may be taken to imply that there are only two sectors, namely formal and informal, and that, if an enterprise does not belong to one, it must belong to the other. Thus, this alternative option for sub-sectoring the household sector can be regarded as available for national accounting purposes.

---

1. Registration of the employees is a useful criterion only in countries where it implies that the enterprise itself is also registered.

3.2.4. Household Production for Own Final Use

3.22.   Production undertaken by household unincorporated enterprises exclusively for own final use by the owners' households is not part of the informal sector according to the 15th ICLS Resolution, and is thus regarded as a separate NOE problem area in this Handbook. It includes production of crops and livestock, production of other goods for their own final use, construction of own houses and other own-account fixed capital formation, imputed rents of owners-occupiers, and services of paid domestic servants.

3.23.   Evidently, some household production activities are on a very small scale. Thus, the 1993 SNA: Paragraph 6.25 suggests a criterion of *significance* for deciding whether or not to record the production of a particular good. Only if the amount produced is believed to be quantitatively important in relation to the total supply of that good in the country should it be estimated. The 1993 SNA (Para 6.24) lists some of the most common types of production for which estimates should be made. (See Section 2.2.)

3.24.   For complete consistency this problem area should be defined as *production performed by enterprises that are not classified as formal or informal*, thereby including any other enterprise that falls outside the formal/informal distinction in addition to those producing for their own final use.

3.2.5. Production Missed Due to Deficiencies in Data Collection Programme

3.25.   This problem area is an inseparable aspect of exhaustiveness. It comprises all the productive activities that should be accounted for by the basic data collection programme but are missed due to statistical deficiencies. It is sometimes referred to as the *statistical underground* – in contrast to the *economic underground*, which comprises activities that have been concealed by the producing units for economic reasons.

3.26.   Viewed from the production approach to GDP compilation, the reasons why activities may escape direct measurement by the basic data collection system can be grouped into three main categories, as follows.

- *Undercoverage of enterprises.* Enterprises, or parts of them, are excluded from the data collection programme though in principle they should have been included. This may occur, for example, because an enterprise is new and has not yet been included in the survey frames, or it falls below the size cut-off for surveys, or it has been incorrectly classified by kind of activity or by region and thus improperly excluded from the survey frame.

- *Non-response by enterprises.* Enterprises are included in the sample but no data are collected from them (for example, because the survey questionnaire was wrongly addressed or the enterprise, or part of it, did not return the questionnaire) and no imputation is made for the missing observations.

- *Underreporting by enterprises.* Data are obtained from enterprises, but are misreported by the respondent in such a way as to underreport value added, or correct data are received but are inappropriately edited or weighted.

3.3.   Analytical Framework for the NOE

3.3.1. Introduction

3.27.   Insight into the nature of the NOE and ways to measure non-observed activities requires the use of an analytical framework. The essence of such a framework is the division of non-observed activities into groups that help their identification and proper measurement. Ideally, the groups should be mutually exclusive and exhaustive so that non-observed production can be summed across them. As previously noted, the NOE problem areas are not mutually exclusive, although mutually exclusive groups can readily be derived by selecting one of the problem areas as the first group and defining subsequent groups to exclude any activities already included in a previous group. An example of an analytical framework based on this approach would be:

- underground production;
- illegal production (which, by definition, is not underground);
- informal sector production that is not underground or illegal;
- household production for own final use that is not underground or illegal (and by definition is not informal sector);
- other missed productive activities.

3.28.   However, such a classification is too broad to provide much insight into the NOE. An analytical framework needs to provide a finer breakdown, incorporating additional characteristics of non-observed activities. The characteristics by which non-observed activities may be subdivided into mutually exclusive groups include the following.

Characteristics of enterprise carrying out the activity

- institutional sector: financial corporation/non financial corporation/government/NPISH/household;
- economic activity classification;
- size of enterprise, in terms of employment, turnover or value of assets;
- type: formal/informal/other;

Characteristics of activity

- legal and not underground/underground/illegal;

Characteristics of observation method

- compilation approach for which data are being collected: production/income/expenditure;
- GDP component for which data are being collected;
- source of data: survey/administrative source;

Cause of measurement deficiency:

- enterprise not registered/non-response/data under-reported.

3.29.   There may be other characteristics that are useful. They may be used in any combination to model NOE activities. Use of too many dimensions may obscure the main issues. Use of too few dimensions may not give enough insight. Whatever criteria are used to classify non-observed activities into groups, they must be explicitly described. The essence of an analytical framework is that it should be useful in understanding the NOE causes, or in reflecting the various measurement options, or both. There is no perfect model. As the statistician George Box once said, "All models are wrong, some are useful".

3.30.   Four examples of a NOE analytical framework are described in the following paragraphs. Two of these – the Istat and the Eurostat frameworks – have been well tried and tested. The others are presented to illustrate the range of options available.

3.3.2. Istat Analytical Framework

3.31.   From the statistical point of view, measuring the NOE is difficult because of the elusive nature of what is being measured and the approximations that have to be made in the measurement process. The Istat Analytical Framework relates the NOE to the statistical problems to be addressed by national accountants so as to identify the origins of the lack of exhaustiveness and their impact on the statistical system. The issues in constructing the framework are briefly described in the following paragraphs, which also highlight the statistical aspects of measuring the five individual NOE problem areas. More details are provided by Calzaroni (2000). In this context it should be noted that deficiencies inherent in

Figure 3.1. **Istat analytical framework**

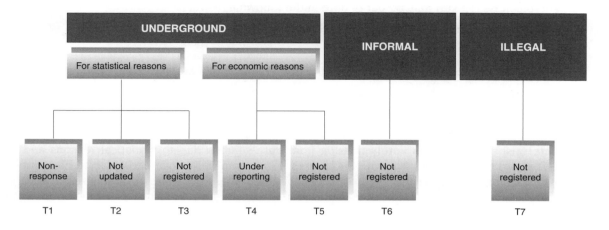

the statistical system are linked to the *underground for statistical reasons*, and the informal sector is assumed to include household production for own final use.

3.32.   The framework views the NOE problem areas in terms of three types of statistical problem.

-   *Non-registration and lack of updated information*. Non-registered production units and the inappropriate presence or absence, or misclassification, of registered units occur due to missing or incorrect updating information from statistical and administrative sources. The most important consequence is the failure to maintain a reliable, comprehensive business register. The situation may arise for a variety of reasons: high turnover rate of enterprises; lack of adequate laws and rules about statistics; inefficiency of the statistical system; deliberate failure to register totally or in part by some enterprises; or absence of an obligation to register. For example, enterprises engaged in illegal activities or small scale informal sector enterprises may not register.

-   *Non-response*. Non-response is one of the main problems affecting the quality of data. Enterprises and households may fail to respond because they do not want to waste their time in completing a questionnaire or are afraid the information they provide will be used for administrative purposes, or because the questionnaire is badly designed or unduly burdensome.

-   *Underreporting*. Even if all units are included in the survey frame and the questionnaires have been completed there may still be a problem of misreporting. Often it is because the respondent is understating income for tax purposes, either by overstating costs or understating revenues and decides to make the same false declarations to the statistical office. When misreporting is due to genuine mistakes by the respondent, the errors may go in either direction. When the misreporting is deliberate, the usual effect is to understate incomes and value added.

3.33.   Figure 3.1 shows the relationship between the NOE problem areas and the statistical measurement problems. It groups non-observed activities into seven types, which are described in the following paragraphs.

Statistical underground: non-response (NOE *type* 1)

3.34.   The main impact of non-response is the bias that is introduced into the statistical output if all non-respondents are assumed to have zero output. There is a vast literature outlining methods for encouraging response and dealing with non-response in the basic data collection programme. These are discussed in Chapter 6.

Statistical underground: units not updated (NOE Type 2)

3.35.   The business register may be out of date in the following respects:

- enterprises that no longer exist (so called *dead units*) are included;
- new enterprises are excluded;
- wrong information about enterprises, due to mergers, splits, etc.;
- incorrect details about economic activity, size of enterprise, or address.

Statistical underground: units not registered (NOE Type 3)

3.36.   Enterprises may be completely missing from data sources due to statistical reasons and not because they are trying to hide from the authorities. For example, this can occur due to high rates of enterprise turnover, which is a common problem in countries where the share of small-sized production units is particularly high or due to absence of adequate statistical laws and rules, or inefficiencies in the statistical system.

Economic underground: underreporting (NOE Type 4)

3.37.   As previously noted, value added may be understated in order to avoid taxes, social charges, etc.

Economic underground: units not registered (NOE Type 5)

3.38.   Some enterprises may be missing because the owners have deliberately avoided the obligations to register in order to avoid additional costs of various kinds such as value added taxes, social security contributions, costs related to the compliance with health and safety standards, etc. Non-registration may involve the whole enterprise being completely missing, or the enterprises being registered but one or more local units not being registered.

Informal sector: units not registered (NOE Type 6)

3.39.   As previously noted, non-registration can be a criterion for defining the informal sector and enterprises may be missing simply because they are not required to register by any kind of legislation.

Illegal production: units not registered (NOE Type 7)

3.40.   In most cases illegal production units are not registered. In a few cases they may be registered but under incorrect activity descriptions. For example, illegal brothels may be described as health-care clubs or massage shops, illegal gambling operations may be described as nightclubs, etc.

3.41.   In summary, the Istat analytical framework is built by matching the NOE problem areas with the statistical measurement problems that a statistical office must address in aiming for exhaustive measurement of GDP. Given that the NOE types are defined to be mutually exclusive, they may be grouped in various ways in order to give insight into different aspects of the NOE. For example, coverage problems are the sum of types T2, T3, T5, T6, and T7, underreporting problems are represented by T4, and non-response problems are represented by T1.

Units, Activities and Causes Variant of Istat Framework

3.42.   A variant of the Istat Analytical Framework is shown in Table 3.1. The NOE types are essentially the same as described in the Istat model but in defining them an explicit distinction is made between the type of activity and the type of unit engaged in the activity. This sharpens the conceptual boundary between the NOE types, giving a clearer separation. For a finer breakdown of non-observed activities, the types could be further subdivided according to rows and columns. The framework has not yet been tested through practical application.

Table 3.1. **Unit by activity by cause classification of non-observed activities**

Type of activity	Type of cause	Type of unit		
		Formal	Informal	Household production for own use
Illegal underground	Not registered Not registered Underreporting		NOE Type 7 NOE Type 5 NOE Type 4	
Legal and not underground	Not registered Not updated Non-response	NOE Type 3	NOE Type 6 NOE Type 2 NOE Type 1	

3.3.3. *Eurostat Tabular Framework*

3.43.   The Eurostat tabular framework was developed in the course of technical assistance to the European Union Candidate Countries in order to gauge the comparability and exhaustiveness of their GDP estimates. It is described in detail by Hein (1998) and Stapel (2001), from where the following summary is drawn.

3.44.   The framework is very similar to the Istat framework from which it was originally derived. The main difference is the introduction of an additional type (T8) of non-observed activity. T8 includes a series of reasons for the lack of exhaustiveness that are very significant in transition countries, the main ones being production for own final use, tips, wages and salaries in kind.

3.45.   An extremely useful, integral part of this framework is the accompanying documentation template comprising three tables that summarise non-observed activities by type, and the adjustments (if any) made for each of them in the national accounts aggregates. Completion of these tables encourages a systematic analysis of non-observed activities, the methods adopted to deal with them and the adjustments and estimates obtained in the national accounts.

3.46.   The first table comprises a listing of the types of NOE that affect the main components of the national accounts, together with cross-references to the adjustments that are made for each in compiling the accounts. The listing has three parts, one for the production components, one for the expenditure components and one for the income components. The production components are divided by institutional sector, and by industry group and size within sector. There is also an entry for taxes and subsidies on products. The income components have a similar structure. The expenditure components are divided as usual. There are also entries for a specified set of illegal production activities. Thus, completion of the first table involves consideration of the possible effects of, and adjustments for, each NOE type on each major component of GDP.

3.47.   The second table is also in three parts, one for each compilation approach. Each part comprises a list of the NOE adjustments by type of adjustment, GDP component, data source, size of adjustment and relative size of adjustment, also by industry group, size group or COICOP code as appropriate. The third table summarises the adjustments by NOE type for the production and expenditure components.

3.48.   A full description of the NOE types and examples of the tables, which can be adapted on a case by case basis to any specific country, are appended in Annex 4.

3.3.4. *Unit and Labour Input Framework*

3.49.   Whereas the Istat and Eurostat analytical frameworks arise from consideration of the NOE problem areas and statistical measurement problems, the *unit and labour input framework* starts from the data collection programme and the main reasons for non-observed activities. It follows a production approach perspective. It assumes the existence of a business register, data from enterprise and labour force surveys and supply and use tables. The basic idea is that for each entry (or combination of entries) in the supply and use tables, a table can be created in which the data from all sources can be confronted. The classifications on the axes of the table are chosen so as to highlight the most plausible reasons for errors and wrong observations, and hence the actions to be taken. The most practical and illustrative confrontation table for analysing the NOE is presented in Table 3.2.

3.50.   The horizontal axis (columns) provides a breakdown of the observation of activities, *i.e.*, data collection from the production side, which is mainly by means of enterprise surveys. Such surveys require a solid frame covering as many production units as possible. Nevertheless, there are units that are not in the survey frame and this is the reason for making the distinction between registered and unregistered units.

3.51.   From the perspective of data collection, the most relevant breakdown is into own account enterprises (self-employed workers), enterprises engaged in production for own use, and other enterprises. In most countries, the legal status and legal obligations for own account enterprises differ significantly from those for other enterprises. For example, the book keeping requirements are less strict and business and private book keeping is frequently combined. The data available from own account enterprises are less detailed than from other enterprises. Enterprises engaged in production for own use are not required to keep books.

3.52.   The vertical axis (rows) looks at the production process from the input side. With the exception of dwelling services provided by owner-occupiers, all production requires input of labour. Labour can be observed by various means, but the most common way to obtain an independent estimate of the volume of labour input is by labour force survey. In general, it is not very difficult to survey labour as most people will report that they are working. Moreover, their involvement in the labour market can often be checked in administrative files, for example in enterprise payrolls. However, there are situations in which people prefer to hide their income from work and special observation methods are needed. The distinction between registered and unregistered labour leads to the two rows in the table.

3.53.   Of the eight possible cells in Table 3.2, only six can be filled. The two cells at the top right are expected to be empty as registration of labour does not make sense for them. The contents of the cells are described in Annex 4.2 and further details are available in Luttikhuizen and Kazemier (2000).

Table 3.2.   **Classification of NOE by registration of units and labour input**

Labour	Production units			
	Enterprises registered in business register	Enterprises not registered in business register		
		Other	Own account	Production for own use
Registered	C1	C3		
Not registered	C2	C4	C5	C6

3.3.5. *Production Income Framework*

3.54.   A rather different analytical framework such as that shown in Figure 3.2 might be used if the focal point of the analysis were unreported income from production.

Figure 3.2. **Production income framework**

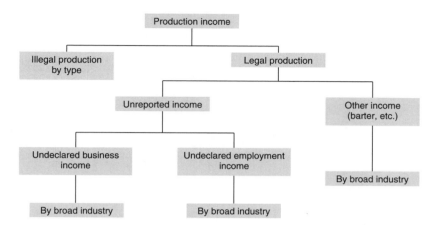

3.3.6. *Concluding Remarks*

3.55.   Each of these frameworks has limitations in the sense that some of the borderlines between the various types of NOE activities are not distinct conceptually or cannot be easily determined in practice. Furthermore, most of them are geared to a view of the NOE from the production approach and need to be supplemented by analysis from the expenditure side.

3.56.   In summary, a national statistical system should choose or develop an analytical framework that best suits its circumstances, depending upon the nature and extent of underground, illegal, informal sector and household production for own use and the coverage and quality of the basic data collection programme.

Chapter 4

ASSESSMENT OF NATIONAL ACCOUNTS

4. ASSESSMENT OF NATIONAL ACCOUNTS

4.1. Introduction

4.1.   This chapter describes methods appropriate for the second line of action in the NOE measurement strategy, namely the assessment of the national accounts from the perspective of non-observed activities. The ultimate goal of the assessment is to have a systematic and comprehensive list of all non-observed activities, broken down by type according to an appropriate analytical framework, and to have recorded their likely magnitudes and the ways in which they are currently being included (if at all) in the GDP estimates. Achievement of this objective would be exemplified by completion of all the tables in the Eurostat Tabular Framework.

4.2.   Section 4.2 deals with analysis of the incoming basic data by comparison with data from other sources, through data confrontation and discrepancy analysis. Section 4.3 outlines the approaches that can be used to estimate upper bounds to the extents of non-observed and non-measured activities. Section 4.4 describes the use of supplementary and special surveys for assessment. The last two sections present more general national accounts assessment tools, namely the Data Quality Assessment Framework and the National Accounts Process Table, being developed by the IMF and Eurostat, respectively. In each case exhaustiveness is seen as just one of several quality aspects that collectively define the overall quality of the national accounts.

4.3.   As exemplified in the following sections, many of these assessment methods can also be used to provide adjustments for the NOE using indirect compilation methods as described in Chapter 5. Equally, the adjustment procedures can be used as a basis for assessment. Thus Chapter 5 is an additional rich source of assessment methods.

4.2. Data Confrontation and Discrepancy Analysis

4.4.   Confrontation of data from different sources is an integral part of the national accounts compilation. It can also be used to identify the remaining errors and gaps in and between these data. Ideally, data confrontation should take place prior to national accounts compilation, with the aim of checking the statistics and increasing their quality. Examples of possible data confrontation are:

- Enterprise survey data *versus* taxation data; wages paid *versus* taxes raised; sales of goods and services due to VAT *versus* VAT raised; and production *versus* production related taxes.

- Enterprise survey data about the production of commodities *versus* enterprise survey data about purchases of commodities; supply of goods and services *versus* the use of them.

- Expenditure survey data *versus* retail trade survey data; household expenditures *versus* retail trade.

- Expenditure survey data *versus* income or taxation data; household expenditures *versus* available income.

- Enterprise survey data *versus* labour force survey data; use of labour *versus* supply of labour; turnover, value added, intermediate consumption, etc. *versus* the use of labour.

The following paragraphs illustrate the general approach through some specific examples.

Actual value added tax **versus** *theoretical value added tax*

4.5.   This analysis is useful if a significant amount of value added tax (VAT) is collected. The actual amount of VAT collected by the government is compared with the theoretical amount of VAT that should have been raised, calculated from the supply and use tables. In principle, the latter equals the VAT revenues that a government should raise if no VAT was evaded. In practice, there are some statistical and legal reasons for differences, such as bankruptcies, discharges and individual arrangements. Therefore, the theoretical VAT should always exceed the actual VAT by perhaps as much as 5%, depending on the particular situation in the country. If the difference is less, or even worse, if the theoretical VAT is less than the actual VAT, it may safely be assumed that there are NOE activities not included in the national accounts.

Actual tax returns **versus** *theoretical income tax*

4.6.   The income available to households computed from income tax returns is compared with that calculated from the national accounts. Apart from some differences for statistical and legal causes such as bankruptcies, discharges and individual arrangements the differences between the figures can be assumed to be a consequence of tax evasion on the one hand and NOE on the other. Such an analysis is especially useful if the national accounts do not use the income tax statistics as a data source, as in the Netherlands, for example. Van de Laan and De Waard (1985) describe how Statistics Netherlands used this type of analysis to arrive at an estimate of tax fraud. They calculated that about three quarters of the difference between the two income estimates was due to the differences in their definitions. The remaining difference averaged around 6% over the period 1977 to 1985, as summarised in Table 4.1.

Table 4.1.   **Primary income of households according to the national accounts and income tax statistics for the Netherlands 1977-1985**

(in 1 000 million guilders)

	1977	1979	1981	1983	1985
a) Income tax statistics	192.2	223.9	246.0	264.6	283.8
b) National accounts	203.0	235.3	258.2	282.9	301.6
Difference *b*) − *a*) as % of *b*)	+5.3	+4.8	+4.7	+6.5	+5.9

Source: Van de Laan and De Waard, 1985.

4.7.   In principle, the difference between the national accounts and the income tax statistics should be an indication of the size of economic activity that is concealed for income tax reasons and that has been included in the national accounts. However, at a more detailed level in this analysis, some of the differences proved to be negative, *i.e.*, had the wrong sign for such a conclusion. This shows that a detailed analysis is preferable to an aggregate one, as aggregation may hide significant details and lead to the wrong conclusions.

4.8.   A few years later, the research was repeated. The legal situation had changed. From 1987, interest payments made by financial institutions had to be reported to the tax authorities. As a consequence, the size of the interest income concealed by households from the tax records decreased dramatically from almost 30% of the total in the period 1983-1987 to about 15% in 1988-1990. This indicates the importance of checking and updating the assumptions built into adjustment models.

Income based **versus** *expenditure based estimates of national income*

4.9.   In many countries, the national accounts lend themselves very well to discrepancy analysis as they provide both income based and expenditure based estimates of national income (MacAfee, 1980; O'Higgins, 1989). The first estimate does not include income that has been concealed for tax reasons, whereas the second estimate does. Thus, the difference between both estimates can be partly attributable to tax evasion. Other causes for discrepancy are errors in timing and statistical errors. However, according to MacAfee (1980), the long run average of these latter causes is zero. Of course, there are likely to be omissions from the expenditure based estimates, for example expenditure on narcotics, gambling and alcohol.

Use of labour versus supply of labour

4.10. Wages and employment measured from the use (employer) side and from the supply (employee) side can be compared. With appropriate allowances for conceptual differences, the measures should be the same. Examination of the discrepancies can provide an indication of the size and distribution of activities that are missing from the enterprise data. In fact this approach is so effective that analysis of labour inputs is one of the mechanisms specified by the European Commission (1994) for assessing the exhaustiveness of GDP estimates. European Union Member States are required to make a systematic comparison of the estimates of employment which underlie their estimates of GDP with the alternative estimates of employment obtained from household based sources, as described by Hayes and Lozano (1998). The elements of the method are as follows.

- *Estimate the labour input underlying GDP estimates*. This means deriving the labour input that is present (explicitly or implicitly) in the data sources used to derive GDP estimates. If the data are derived from enterprise surveys, then the labour input to the production covered by these surveys must be estimated.

- *Estimate the labour input based on household survey data*. Typically these data are obtained from a labour force survey, supplemented by census data if available.

- *Standardise the labour input estimates*. Convert the enterprise based (use) and household based (supply) estimates of labour input to the same units of labour input, such as hours worked or full-time equivalent employment units, so that they can be meaningfully compared.

- *Compare the two sets of estimates*. Analyse any discrepancies taking into account the reliability of the different sources. A surplus of labour input derived from the household source over that from the enterprise source is an indication of non-observed production. It provides a lower bound as some labour input could be missing from both sources. No difference or a surplus of the enterprise-based labour input over the household-based input suggests that the household data are not providing extra coverage.

4.11. The final step in the EU exhaustiveness procedure is to compute a multiplication factor by which to adjust the output and value added estimates to account for non-observed production. This is further elaborated in Sections 5.2 and 5.4, which provide, respectively, a more comprehensive description of the labour input method as a compilation and adjustment tool, and an example of its application by Istat.

Micro discrepancy analysis

4.12. Discrepancy analysis can be carried out at micro as well as macro level. For example, data for individual persons or enterprises, retrieved from tax files or from other administrations, can be compared with data from surveys.

4.13. An example of micro discrepancy analysis is described by the US Internal Revenue Service (1979) and Parker (1984). A sample of 50 000 income tax returns was very closely examined and compared with data from *information returns*. Information returns are reports that must be completed by payers of certain types of income, for example wages and salaries paid by employers and interest paid by banks. It was found that approximately 25% of the incomes that were covered by the information returns were not reported on the tax returns.

4.14. A similar research was conducted in the Netherlands, in 1985 in a research study on concealed interest income on giro, bank and savings accounts (Kazemier, 1991). The Dutch Central Bank collected the 1981 data on interest received by 1 369 households as far as it could be traced in the accounts of the giro and the banks. The Department of Finance collected the data on interest as reported in the tax returns by the same households. Both data files were put in the same order, made anonymous and sent to Statistics Netherlands for further analysis. The results of this research were almost similar to those of the macro-discrepancy analysis between the national accounts and the income tax statistics, described above.

4.15. Another example of a micro discrepancy analysis, from the United Kingdom, was reported by Dilnot and Morris (1981). Of a sample of households, they compared the expenditures and income. The expenditures were measured in the 1977 Family Expenditure Survey. The income data were retrieved from tax forms. If expenditures inexplicably exceeded income, it was assumed that the difference between both figures equalled concealed income.

Partial integration

4.16. The extension of simple confrontation of two data sources to produce new data on a particular topic in more detail than is normal during compilation of the national accounts is commonly termed *partial integration*. For example, information on construction and the production of construction materials may be integrated, as these are two closely linked branches of industry.

4.17. Another example of partial integration is the preparation of labour accounts in which labour data from the supply and demand sides are integrated. Leunis and Verhagen (1999) provide an example. Other examples are energy accounts, which combine the results of surveys on the production, transformation and use of energy, data on the imports and exports of energy and fuels et cetera, resulting in energy balances per branch of industry and per type of fuel. More information on energy accounts can be found in Eurostat (2000).

4.3. Upper Bound Estimation

4.3.1. Introduction

4.18. The aim of upper bound estimation (sometimes termed "sensitivity analysis") is to derive an upper limit to the extent of NOE activities. The essence of the procedure is to consider systematically for each component of GDP the maximum possible amount of NOE activities and to total the results to obtain an upper bound. The procedure can be applied to GDP compiled by any or all of the expenditure, income and production approaches. It can be applied for all NOE problem areas, or just for specific types, for example, underground production or the informal sector. Analyses of this sort have been conducted in many countries. The following sections illustrate upper bound estimation for underground production using the expenditure and the production approaches, respectively, by examples from Canada and the Netherlands. Willard (1989) describes other applications in France and Italy.

4.3.2. Upper Bound – Expenditure Approach

4.19. In Statistics Canada (1994) Gervais describes the procedures used by Statistics Canada in estimating an upper bound for the underground economy in Canada in 1992. In the second part of the paper, Gervais works systematically through all the components of GDP compiled by the expenditure approach. For each component in turn an upper bound on underground (legal) production is computed and compared with the allowance for such production (if any) already made in compiling the official estimates. The differences are summed to provide an upper bound on the extent to which the published estimates underestimate the GDP due to underground production.

4.20. The following paragraphs give a flavour of the sort of reasoning that is used in this analysis. Whilst the particular reasons for underground activity and sources of data are likely to be different in other countries, the same general approach and type of reasoning will still be applicable.

4.21. Viewing GDP through the expenditure approach, Gervais argues that the main areas for underground activities are residential construction and final consumption expenditure of households. The effects of underground activities on imports and exports are small and on the other expenditure components of GDP are negligible. The reasoning goes as follows, starting with the least significant components.

Government current expenditure on goods and services and government investment

4.22. The upper bound is zero as there is no scope for underground activities.

Business investment in inventories

4.23. The upper bound is zero. Businesses may have a tax incentive to exaggerate holding losses and to understate holding gains. However, holding gains or losses are removed in the calculation of inventory changes, as they do not relate to current production. Thus if businesses exaggerate their holding losses or understate holding gains this should not affect the national accounts measure of inventory changes.

Business fixed capital investment

4.24. The upper bound is zero. Capital investment is measured on the demand side. Businesses have no incentive to hide expenditures.

Imports

4.25. In Canada the only legal goods smuggled into the country in sufficient volume to be worth considering are tobacco, alcoholic beverages and precious jewellery. Commodity related data sources provide estimates for the quantities. For example, estimates of the quantities of smuggled alcohol are obtained using data from the Liquor Board of Ontario. The black-market price in Canada is assumed to be 60% of the regular price and the import price is assumed to be between 40-60% of the black-market price.

Exports

4.26. In Canada, businesses have little or no incentive to hide exported goods. There are no export duties. Ninety per cent of Canadian exports involve vehicles and parts, crude petroleum, natural gas, lumber, pulp and paper, ores, metals and alloys. None of these are likely to be exported "under the table".

Residential construction

4.27. The ratio of domestic sales of lumber and building materials to reported value of residential construction put in place provides, over time, a broad indication of the growth of unrecorded residential construction. However, increases in this ratio may also be due to reduced profit margins and/or reduced wages, as well as to increase in underground transactions. An upper bound on underground activities is determined in terms of three components:

- New construction. Estimates for new construction are based on housing starts, average value of building permits and work put in place. It is more or less impossible to construct a house without a permit. Builders have a vested interest in understating the values, but local authorities base tax liabilities on values and will thus not issue a permit if they believe the value is too low. Hence, under-estimation is probably not more than 15% on average, plus another 5-10% for additional work done after the permit has been issued. To get upper bounds for seasonal dwellings (*i.e.*, those used only during the summer months) the number of permits issued is multiplied by five and 25% is added to stated permit values. The number of permits issued for conversion from seasonal to all-season dwelling is multiplied by two. The larger conversions have to be reported, as it is difficult to avoid detection.

- Alterations and improvements. The data source for alterations and improvements is the (Canadian) *homeowner repair and renovation survey*. Homeowners have no particular incentive to hide repairs and renovations, as they are not responsible for payment of taxes on the income earned. Thus, a maximum of 20% is assumed in the under-reporting of the total payments for materials and labour. This upper bound can be checked for plausibility by first estimating the total amount of home improvements put in place. These estimates are based on householders' purchases of materials (assuming all purchases are made legally) and the estimated ratios of material content to the total value of work. Next the estimated value of the homeowners' own work (based on time use survey data) is deducted to arrive at an estimate of the value of underground contract work.

- Transfer costs. Real estate commissions are computed by applying average commission rates to reported sales. Average commission rates are obtained from the Canadian Real Estate Association. The value of sales is not thought to be underestimated, as real estate agents prefer to advertise rather than hide their success in making sales.

Household expenditure on goods and services

4.28.   There are three aspects to underground activities in this area:

- *under the table* purchases, known by other authors as *cash settlements*;
- *skimming*, whereby businesses fail to declare part of their legitimate business income to the tax authorities and (presumably) to the statistical agency as well; and
- *tips.*

4.29.   Expenditures are divided into 140 different categories, which are grouped according to type of goods and services and the opportunities for underground transactions. For some groups of goods and services, underground transactions are virtually impossible. An important example is purchases of new motor vehicles. The expenditure groups that are singled out for special treatment are tobacco, alcoholic beverages, rent, room and board, professional services, food, childcare, and domestic and household services. Within each of these groups the maximum conceivable values of under the table purchases, skimming and tips are considered and compared with the figures already included in the official GDP estimates.

4.30.   Understatement of business receipts (skimming) does not necessarily translate into underestimation of GDP. In the case of businesses selling to other businesses, the businesses doing the purchasing will find a way of passing purchase costs onto their customers whether or not the purchases have been under the table. Thus the market prices of good and services sold to final consumers automatically embody any skimming that may have gone on at an intermediate level. This reasoning suggests that only skimming by businesses selling to households needs to be considered.

4.31.   Self-employed individuals and small businesses have more opportunity to engage in skimming than large businesses. It is very unlikely that large retail organisations with hundreds or thousands of employees indulge in skimming at all as the risk of damage to their reputation (should the skimming be discovered) would far outweigh the benefits of it. Large businesses are thus likely to focus on tax avoidance rather than tax evasion and it can be assumed that skimming is restricted to small businesses.

4.32.   Input-output tables provide a general picture because the effects of skimming can show up in balancing the tables as implausibly low values of retailers' profit.

4.33.   Skimming levels are estimated by category: 25% of gross receipts for services; 15% for taxicabs and most retail trade; 25% for vending machine operators, direct sellers, and repair shops.

4.34.   On top of skimming there are direct sales of goods and services by individuals that are not registered as businesses. These are also considered on a category-by-category basis. In the case of food, for example, direct sales by farmers reported by the provincial departments of agriculture are inflated by 20%.

4.35.   Tables 4.2 and 4.3, respectively, indicate the upper limits thus obtained of personal expenditures missing from the published estimates and of underground transactions missed from expenditure based GDP.

Table 4.2. **Upper limit of underground transactions missing from personal expenditure**

Canada 1992

	Underground $ million	Published estimates $ million	Proportion %
Skimming by businesses	10 836		
Contraband tobacco	1 057		
Contraband spirits	768		
Illegally manufactured wine	515		
Mark-ups on illegal alcohol	565		
Rent, room and board	269		
Tips	312		
Professional services	208		
Food	50		
Domestic and household services	250		
Subtotal	14 830	393 053	3.8
Goods and services tax and provincial sales tax	0	26 483	
Total	14 830	419 536	3.5

Source: (Gervais) Statistics Canada (1994).

Table 4.3. **Upper limit of underground transactions missing from expenditure based GDP**

Canada 1992

	Underground $ million	Published $ million	Proportion %
Personal expenditure on goods and services	14 830	419 536	3.5
Government current expenditure on g&s	0	148 377	
Government investment	0	16 508	
Business investment in fixed capital	3 578	113 440	3.2
Residential construction	3 578	43 992	8.1
New residential construction	1.883	20 934	9.0
Alterations and improvements	1 695	12 153	13.9
Transfer costs	0	10 905	
Non-residential construction	0	30 189	
Machinery and equipment	0	39 259	
Business investment in inventories	−15	−2 258	−0.6
Exports	1 100	181 948	0.6
Merchandise	800	156 567	0.5
Non-merchandise	300	25 381	1.2
Less Imports	1 003	185 751	0.5
Merchandise	1 003	147 588	0.7
Non-merchandise	0	38 163	0
GDP at market prices	**18 408**	**688 541**	**2.7**

Source: (Gervais) Statistics Canada (1994).

4.3.3. *Upper Bound – Production Approach*

4.36.   Broesterhuizen (1985) describes upper bound estimation (referred to in the paper as "sensitivity analysis") for underground production in the Netherlands using the production approach. The following paragraphs outline the procedure used.

4.37.   GDP is broken down into six categories, according to the estimation method and/or the sector of origin. The categories differ in the extent to which they are susceptible to underground production.

Category 1: industries where estimation is by indirect methods

4.38.   Usually a significant part of GDP is measured indirectly, *i.e.*, not based on reports from producers. In the Dutch case this applies to agriculture, crude petroleum and natural gas production and exploration, the petroleum refining and the operation of real estate.

- The production of agriculture is calculated by multiplying production volumes (measured by independent observers) by known market prices.
- The gross value added of the petroleum industry in the Netherlands is almost completely dependent on imports and exports of crude petroleum and coal products. Data on these imports and exports are retrieved from the customs declaration forms. (The case described is the situation as of 1979. Since then, things have slightly changed because intra-EC trade customs forms are no longer available.)
- The domestic crude petroleum and natural gas production and exploration are so strictly controlled by the government that concealed activities are not very likely.
- The value added of real estate is almost entirely measured by indirect methods.

The researchers concluded that whatever size underground activities in these sectors might be they had no significant effect on GDP.

Category 2: estimates for government and government controlled units

4.39.   Category 2 consists of the gross value added of all sectors that are subject to strict government supervision. These include general government, public utilities, railways, tramway and regular bus services, subsidised motor coach services, banking and insurance, hospitals, mental homes and nursing houses, subsidised welfare services, social and cultural institutions, co-operative business organisations, and communications. Underground activities are assumed to be zero. (Note that, since this study, the railways, many tramways and bus services have been privatised and government control over the communications industry has become less strict, so these services should now be analysed within the following categories, 3-5.)

Categories 3, 4 and 5: estimates for large, small and very small enterprises

4.40.   Categories 3 to 5 refer to large, small and very small businesses respectively. Estimates of the proportions of underground activities are made separately within each category. These categories contain the gross value added of enterprises that are not included in categories 1 and 2 and for which the estimates of gross value added are not based on fiscal data. Typically the data are obtained by annual surveys. The sampling frame for these surveys is a business register based on the administrative register maintained by the Chambers of Commerce. Each enterprise has to register in order to obtain licences and a value added tax-number.

4.41.   For some industries there is a cut off in the sample frame and only enterprises with over 10 employees receive a questionnaire. Other industries are fully included. For large (category 3) enterprises, *i.e.*, those with over 100 employees, the sampling rate is 100%. For the smaller (category 4) enterprises, *i.e.*, the remainder of those included within the sampling frame, the sampling rates are lower. In general, the questionnaires used in this category are shorter and ask for less detail than the questionnaires sent to the larger enterprises. More detailed information than is provided in the questionnaires is borrowed from the category 3 enterprises in the form of ratios and percentage shares. The estimates for the very small enterprises (category 5) are all obtained as extrapolations of the category 4 estimates.

Category 6: estimates based on fiscal data

4.42.   For some own account workers, the national account estimates are based on information derived from tax files. This includes, for example, the value added of own account workers in hotels, restaurants and cafés, repair of consumer goods, business services, renting of machinery and other movables, health and veterinary services, social-cultural institutions and private households with domestic servants. (Since the study, other data sources have been introduced in place of tax estimates for several of these activities.)

Summary of results

4.43.   In arriving at estimates of undercoverage of underground activities in GDP, several alternative sets of assumptions were made. The scheme giving the largest values is presented in Table 4.4 and indicates that the highest possible (but very unlikely) estimate of GDP understatement in 1979 is 5.7%.

Table 4.4.   **NOE upper bound for the Netherlands, 1979**

		Categories						
		1	2	3	4	5	6	Total
GDP	1 000 million guilder	65.2	104.6	61.1	54.0	11.3	19.7	315.9
Share in GDP	%	20.6	33.1	19.3	17.1	3.6	6.2	100.0
NOE	% of GDP	0	0	2.0	10.0	30.0	40.0	5.7
NOE	1 000 million guilder	0	0	1.2	4.4	3.4	7.9	19.9

Source: Broesterhuizen (1985).

4.44.   This analysis also shows that, although category 6 estimates are quite small as a proportion of GDP, this category contributes the largest part of the upper bound estimate. This suggests that category 6 might be the place to invest more effort in improving estimates, thus illustrating how such analyses can help in setting priorities.

4.4.   Analytical Material from Supplementary, Special Purpose Surveys

4.45.   Supplementary, special purpose surveys are another tool for assessing the exhaustiveness of the national accounts. These are surveys that are not part of the basic data collection programme. They can take a variety of forms, being special surveys of expenditure, income, labour, time use, and opinion surveys. They can be designed to target any or all of the NOE problem areas – underground, illegal, informal sector and household production for own use. They can be conducted by the national statistical office or by other agencies including, for example, sample audits by the tax authorities. However, the results must be interpreted very carefully, especially for those surveys focussed on sensitive subjects. For example, in surveys relating to tax evasion, it is very likely that the non-response is selective because people who are involved in tax evasion are more likely to refuse to co-operate than people who are not. Such non-response is difficult to reduce or to adjust for.

4.46.   Supplementary surveys in the context of assessment of GDP estimates are summarised in this section. They are further elaborated in later chapters in association with the other purposes for which they are used. In particular, they are described in considerably more detail in Chapters 8-11 in the context of standalone measurements of the individual NOE problem areas. Also, in so far as the results of such surveys provide parameters or adjustment factors for compilation of the national accounts, they are further described in Chapter 5. To the extent that they eventually become integrated within the basic statistical data collection programme, they are further discussed in Chapter 6. For example a survey of retail sales in city markets may begin as an *ad hoc* survey intended to check on the relative size of such sales. From this survey, adjustment factors may subsequently be derived for use in the national accounts expenditure estimates, and finally the survey may become a regular part of the basic programme of retail trade statistics.

Surveys of expenditure on goods and services from underground production

4.47.   Expenditure on underground production is a less sensitive topic than underground income. In the latter case the respondent is being asked to report on fraud whereas expenditure on underground production is usually not forbidden nor prosecutable. Indeed, the purchaser may well not know whether a seller is operating underground or not. For example, if one orders a beer in a café, one does not know whether the owner of the café pays all value added tax or not.

4.48.   Kazemier and Van Eck (1992) provide an example of a survey on expenditure on underground production. The survey was on the subject of home maintenance and home repair and included questions on both underground labour and underground expenditure, *i.e.*, expenditure on building materials without paying value added tax.

Surveys of labour input to underground production

4.49.   In surveying the input of labour to underground production, there are two alternative approaches, namely surveying the *demand* and surveying the *supply*. Questions on demand are less sensitive than those on supply and can thus be expected to yield larger numbers. Zienkowski (1996) provides an example.

4.50.   Experiences suggest that, in an anonymous interview, many people are willing to admit part or all of their underground (but not illegal) production activities. However, surveying supply is prone to item non-response and incorrect response and so needs careful design. Kazemier and Van Eck (1992) show how a sequence of questions, that gradually lead to the key questions on underground activities, gives the best results. The methods they describe are further elaborated in Chapter 8 on underground production.

Surveys of time use

4.51.   Time use surveys are generally used to measure the time spent on activities like household work, do-it-yourself, neighbour help and voluntary work. For examples, see Goldschmidt-Clermont (1987), Goldschmidt-Clermont and Pagnossin-Aligisakis (1995) and Organisation for Economic co-operation and Development (Editor Ann Chadeau, 1995). However, they can also be used to measure parts of the NOE that should be included in the national accounts. In particular they can provide insight into the size and structure of household production for own use, as further elaborated in Chapter 11.

4.52.   If used in the context of the national accounts, special care must be taken in classification of the relevant activities. For a number of activities, additional questions are necessary. For example, it must be possible to distinguish between time spent on working as an employee in an enterprise and time spent as an own account worker. If respondents acknowledge that time is spent working on own account, they should be asked some additional questions to enable a classification of their work by branch and an estimate of the turnover and the amount of income earned. If the latter information cannot be obtained, questions on the living conditions and the wealth of the responding household, which can be part of the block containing general questions to classify the household, may provide an indication of the profits earned.

4.53.   Similar information can be collected in a regular labour force survey. However, the advantage of the time use approach is that the questionnaires require respondents to account fully for their time. This improves the reliability of the results if everything else (geographic coverage, sample size, response rates, etc.) is equal.

Surveys of the informal sector and household production for own use

4.54.   Surveys specifically designed to measure the informal sector or household production for own use can shed light on the extent of activities in these NOE problem areas. As with surveys of time use, they have to be carefully designed so that the results they provide regarding the extent of the NOE can be blended with the results of other surveys in the sense that there is no overlap between them, or, if there is overlap, it is known. These surveys are discussed in detail in Chapters 10 and 11.

Qualitative surveys

4.55.   Qualitative surveys of enterprises and of households can also provide information about non-observed activities. They have a number of advantages relative to quantitative surveys. They are quicker and easy to answer. They can be easily changed or supplemented to deal with new circumstances. They can also address questions regarding the causes as well as prevalence of non-observed activities. They can be addressed to very senior staff in surveys of large enterprises but are equally effective with very small enterprises. They can be designed to be less threatening than quantitative surveys by using questions referring to an industry or population group rather than the particular respondent. For example in place of asking a business respondent whether they accept "under the table" payments, the question can be phrased along the lines "What proportion of payments do you think are made in cash in your industry?"

4.56.   Whilst qualitative surveys do not often lead directly to quantitative values that can be directly incorporated into national accounts estimates, they can provide impressions of the size of specific types of NOE activities. For example, approximate ratios of observed to concealed production can be obtained for each of the various branches of industry. They can also provide guidance in assigning priorities for subsequent more precise quantitative assessment.

4.57.   The Russian Federation Centre for Economic Analysis (2000) describes opinion surveys of businesses in retail, construction and manufacturing conducted on an experimental basis in the Russian Federation. In a study of the underground economy as viewed by households, the Hungarian Central Statistical Office (1998) included some qualitative questions aimed at collecting citizens' views. Further details are provided in Chapter 8.

Analyses of tax audit data

4.58.   Quantitative surveys of tax evasion are unlikely to yield reliable results because of the delicate nature of the subject, even if anonymity is guaranteed. Tax audits by their very nature are more compelling than surveys. The "respondents" are obliged to provide their complete accounts, not simply information derived from them. However, because they are designed for tax auditing not statistical purposes, tax audit samples have limitations for estimating undercoverage of the GDP, typically including the following:

- the definitions they use may not be consistent with 1993 SNA;
- they do not include all undeclared income, only what the auditors can find based on their examination of the accounts;
- they refer only to small enterprises;
- they are usually clustered in certain activity sectors and/or geographic areas;
- they are rarely selected on a probability basis.

4.59.   Nevertheless, in the absence of any better source, tax audit samples can provide useful information on some types of non-observed activities, in particular those associated with underreporting. This is illustrated in Section 5.2.5 in the description of the procedures used by INSEE to derive adjustments for underreporting.

4.5.   IMF Data Quality Assessment Framework

4.60.   Exhaustiveness must also be seen within a broader context, namely that of the overall quality of the national accounts. A tool that provides a structure and a common language for assessing data quality in general, including that of the national accounts, is being developed by the International Monetary Fund (IMF). Referred to as the Data Quality Assessment Framework (DQAF), it complements the quality dimension of the IMF's Special Data Dissemination Standard (SDDS)[1] and General Data Dissemination System (GDDS). It also aims to assess even-handedly the quality of the data covered by the IMF Reports on the Observance of Standards and Codes.[2] Its construction and general structure are summarised in the following paragraphs.

4.61.   As noted by Carson (2001), a data quality assessment framework should be:

- comprehensive as regards the dimensions of quality and the elements (indicators) that might represent quality;
- balanced between the rigor desired by an expert and the bird's-eye view desired by a general data user;
- structured but flexible enough to be applicable across a broad range of stages of statistical development;
- structured but flexible enough to be applicable (at least) to the major macroeconomic datasets;
- designed to lead to transparent results; and
- arrived at by drawing on best practices of national statisticians.

4.62.   Consideration of these criteria leads to a five level hierarchical structure, in two parts, going from the general to the specific, as shown in Figure 4.1. First, recognising that data quality, in the sense of fitness for use and meeting users' needs, is multidimensional, there is a general purpose set of *dimensions of quality* which are broken down into *elements* and *indicators* that constitute *pointers to quality*. These three levels are collectively termed the *generic framework*. A full copy of the generic framework is reproduced in Annex 5. The generic framework embodies internationally accepted core principles for official statistics. It provides the basis for the fourth and fifth levels of the DQAF, which contain more detailed and concrete sets of pointers termed *focal issues* and *key points*. These are collectively referred to as the *data specific framework* and vary according to the type of data being assessed. There are data specific frameworks for national accounts, balance of payments, monetary, government finance, price, and employment statistics, etc. For the purposes of this Handbook, the framework of most interest is that for the national accounts.

4.63.   The first level of the DQAF defines five *dimensions* of quality: integrity, methodological soundness, accuracy and reliability, serviceability, and accessibility, as well as a set of prerequisites, or institutional preconditions,[3] for quality. They are described in more detail in the paragraphs below. For each dimension, element, and indicator, the generic framework presents a brief statement of good practice. The data-specific frameworks provide more detail in the form of focal issues for each indicator that are tailored to the dataset in question. Further, the bullet points below for each focal issue are the key points that describe quality features that may be considered in connection with the focal issues. Although they are considerably more specific than the generic framework, the data-specific frameworks cannot, and indeed are not meant to cover all quality issues exclusively.

4.64.   Using *accuracy and reliability* as the example of a quality dimension, Figure 4.1 shows how the framework identifies five elements that point towards quality. Within the *source data* element, the framework identifies three indicators. Within the *comprehensive data collection program* indicator there are seven focal issues, which are dataset specific. For the *regular comprehensive annual business statistics* focal issue, quality is assessed by considering four key points.

Prerequisites of quality

4.65.   The quality of an individual dataset is intrinsically bound together with that of the institution producing it. The legal framework should be supportive of statistics; resources should be commensurate with the needs of statistical programmes; and quality should be recognised as a cornerstone of statistical

---

1. For a description of the SDDS, see *http://dsbb.imf.org/sddsindex.htm*.
2. Materials on the reports can be found on *www.imf.org/external/np/rosc/index.htm*.
3. The DQAF recognises that the quality of a dataset is intrinsically linked with that of the institution producing it. Thus, it also includes some elements and indicators that, although not constituting a quality dimension in themselves, have an important role as pointers to quality. They generally refer to desirable attributes of the agencies of the statistical system.

Figure 4.1.   **Example of structure of data quality assessment framework for national accounts estimates**

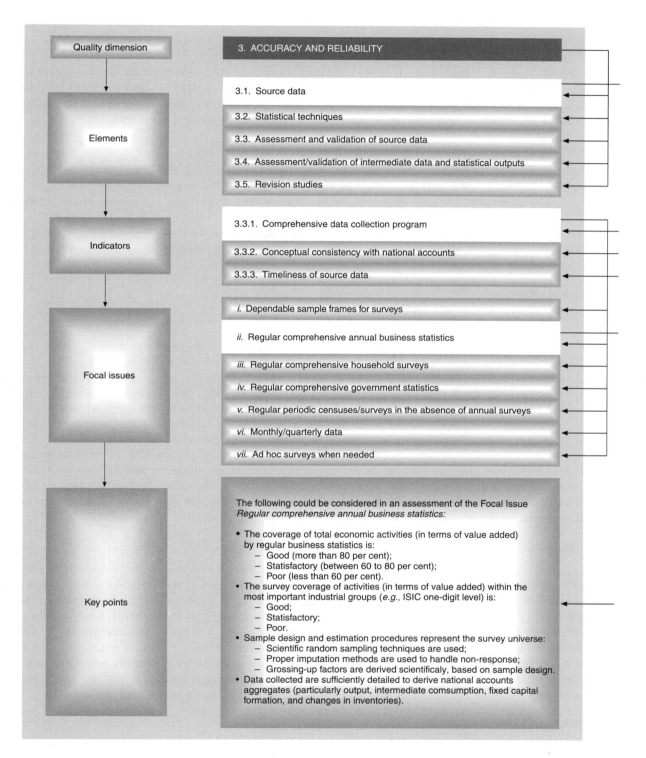

work. For example, one element of institutional preconditions is whether the responsibility for compiling national accounts is clearly delineated, while another element is whether there exist mechanisms to co-ordinate the exchange of information between data producing agencies.

Integrity

4.66.   This dimension is intended to capture the notion that statistical systems should be based on firm adherence to the principle of objectivity in the collection, compilation, and dissemination of statistics. The dimension encompasses the institutional foundations that are in place to ensure professionalism in statistical policies and practices, transparency, and ethical standards.

Methodological soundness

4.67.   This dimension of quality covers the idea that the methodological basis for the production of statistics should be sound and that this can be attained by following international standards, guidelines, and generally accepted practices. In application, this dimension will necessarily be data-specific, reflecting differing methodologies for different datasets. For example, the 1993 SNA or ESA 1995 provide the yardstick for the overall methodological soundness of the national accounts. Specifically, the principles of these manuals are used to assess the coverage of the constituent units of an economy, and to determine the production and asset boundaries.

Accuracy and reliability

4.68.   For most users, accuracy and reliability are among the most sought-after attributes of data. We are all concerned that the data we use sufficiently portray reality at all stages of dissemination, from first (or "flash") estimates to "final" estimates. Thus, this dimension relates to the notion that source data and compilation techniques must be sound if data are to meet users' needs. For national accounts, the coverage and comprehensiveness of data sources used in their compilation are evaluated. Elements on the statistical techniques cover the level of industrial detail at which the output and intermediate consumption estimates are compiled, the size of the economy that is covered by regular national accounts compilation, degree of reliance on fixed ratios derived from outdated benchmarks, the techniques used to address specific issues of GDP compilation, and the procedures for compiling volume measures of GDP according to the production approach. The measures of the accuracy of source data are tracked on the basis of different types of errors and the extent to which estimates are underpinned by observed data either from surveys/censuses, or from appropriate administrative records. One way of testing the reliability of the national accounts estimates is by analysing the magnitude and causes of revisions. The framework contains indicators on whether such studies are made routinely.

Serviceability

4.69.   Another area of concern for users is whether the data that are produced and disseminated are actually useful. This dimension of quality relates to the need to ensure that data are produced and disseminated in a timely fashion, with an appropriate periodicity, provide relevant information on the subject field, are consistent both internally and with other related datasets, and follow a predictable revision policy. Timeliness and periodicity are addressed within the context of the requirements of the IMF dissemination standards. The consistency indicators are tracked on the basis of specific measures, such as availability of consistent time series, consistency between annual and quarterly accounts, and consistency with balance of payments statistics and other related datasets. The revision issue is addressed in terms of the transparency of the revision process, and in terms of release and timing of adequate documentation.

Accessibility

4.70.   Users want understandable, clearly presented data and need to know how data are put together as well as be able to count on prompt and knowledgeable support from data producers for their questions. Thus, this quality dimension relates to the need to ensure that clear data and information on the sources and methods used to compile them are easily available, and that assistance to users of data is adequate.

Implications for NOE measurement

4.71.   NOE measurement can thus be seen to have a place within the broader context of quality assessment over five dimensions of (plus prerequisites for) quality. From the NOE perspective, the key points, focal issues, and indicators associated with the *accuracy and reliability* dimension are of particular relevance.

4.6.   Eurostat National Accounts Process Table

4.72.   Another general-purpose national accounts measurement tool, termed the National Accounts Process Table (NAPT), is being developed and pilot tested by Eurostat (2001) in co-operation with the statistical offices of European Union (EU) Member States. It arises from the need for an objective assessment of the quality and comparability of the national accounts estimates of EU Members. This is especially important given that EU Member contributions depend upon gross national income (GNI), which is obtained by transition from GDP.

4.73.   Member States provide Eurostat with detailed sources and methods metadata, a considerable amount of which will soon be available on the Eurostat website. These metadata follow a common structure and enable well-founded *qualitative* judgements of the reliability, comparability, and exhaustiveness of Members' national accounts. The NAPT is an attempt to provide the basis for a *quantitative* assessment. Although developed independently of the IMF's DQAF, it provides, in fact, a rather detailed elaboration of the DQAF accuracy and reliability dimension.

4.74.   The NAPT embodies a condensed and structured quantitative description of the GNI compilation process. It is stylised to highlight the main successive stages by which national accountants make adjustments to basic data to arrive at final estimates. The table consists of three layers: a top layer containing numbers; a second layer with references to the appropriate sections in the sources and methods metadata; and a third layer with questions that summarise specific points relating to the compilation stages. For NOE measurement, the first layer, illustrated in Table 4.5, is of special interest.

4.75.   The columns of Table 4.5 reflect the different stages in compiling the national accounts aggregates that are specified on the rows. Three blocks of columns are distinguished. A first block deals with the *primary data sources*, which can be from surveys or censuses or administrative files (*i.e.*, *basic data* in the nomenclature of this Handbook), or extrapolation models, or other sources. Here, *other sources* refers to data taken directly from other statistical accounting systems, such as the balance of payments, also to the results of special one-time investigations. The primary data sources also include *extrapolation models*, examples of which are those used for imputing rents for owner-occupied housing, for consumption of fixed capital, and for extrapolation from benchmark years.

4.76.   The second block shows the adjustments made to the primary data sources. They are broken down into data validation adjustments, conceptual adjustments, adjustments for exhaustiveness and balancing adjustments. Data validation adjustments are corrections to the data sources that are uncovered because the various data sources used in the national accounts compilation process contradict each other. Conceptual adjustments are changes made to the data to bring them in line with the ESA 1995 definitions. Exhaustiveness adjustments include adjustments for non-observed activities that are not included in the primary data sources. Balancing adjustments are adjustments made for no other reason than to satisfy national accounting identities. The sum of all columns should equal the final estimates, which are in the third block.

4.77.   The rows in the table show the three different approaches to the calculation of GDP and the transition to GNI. The classifications used and the degree of detail are indicated in the second column of the table.

4.78.   The table does not provide quantitative estimates of the accuracy or reliability of the national accounts estimates. It does, however, show the extent to which these aggregates are based upon real data and the extent to which these data are modified and adjusted. Together with methods and sources metadata, comparisons over time and between countries can be expected to uncover the relative strengths and weaknesses of the various methods.

Table 4.5. **Eurostat national accounts process table, layer 1: Quantitative overview**

	Level of detail	Basis for NA Figures					Adjustments				Final estimate
		Surveys + censuses	Administrative data	Extrapolation + models	Other	Total	Data validation adjustments	Conceptual adjustments	Explicit exhaustiveness adjustments	Balancing adjustments	
Production approach											
Output of goods and services (basic prices)	17 (NACE)										
Intermediate consumption (purchasers' prices)	17 (NACE)										
Gross value added (basic prices)	17 (NACE)										
Taxes on products											
Value added type taxes											
Other taxes on products											
Subsidies on products											
Residual item											
Gross domestic product											
Expenditure approach											
Total final expenditure											
Household final consumption	COICOP 2-digit										
NPISH final consumption											
General government final consumption											
Gross capital formation											
Gross fixed capital formation											
Changes in inventories											
Acquisition less disposals of valuables											
Exports of goods and services											
Goods											
Services											
Imports of goods and services											
Goods											
Services											
Residual item											
Gross domestic product											
Income approach											
Compensation of employees											
Gross operating surplus and mixed income											
Taxes on production and imports											
Subsidies											
Residual item											
Gross domestic product											
Compensation of employees received from Rest of world (ROW)											
Compensation of employees paid to ROW											
Property income received from ROW											
Property income paid to ROW											
Taxes on production and imports subsidies											
Gross national income											

Chapter 5

NATIONAL ACCOUNTS METHODS TO ACHIEVE EXHAUSTIVENESS

5. NATIONAL ACCOUNTS METHODS TO ACHIEVE EXHAUSTIVENESS

5.1. Introduction

5.1. This chapter supports the third line of action in the NOE measurement strategy, namely identifying improvements in the national accounts compilation procedures that will ensure that GDP estimates are exhaustive. Ideally, the NOE should be addressed through the improvement of the basic data collection programme. This is the fourth line of action and is discussed in Chapter 6. However, such efforts may take a long time and, even then, the basic data can never be expected to cover all production falling within the 1993 SNA boundary. There will always some productive activities that cannot be directly observed. Thus, this chapter describes *indirect methods* for compiling the national accounts that can be used where the basic data are insufficient but measurements (*adjustments for the* NOE) can be derived on the basis of indicator series or estimates from other parts of the accounts.

5.2. The focus is on methods for measuring productive activities that are non-observed because they are underground, informal sector, undertaken by households for their own final use, or missed due to deficiencies in the basic data collection programme. Measurement of illegal production poses different challenges and is not explicitly covered in this chapter, though several of the compilation methods described may actually include illegal productive activities without separately identifying them as such. Specific methods for dealing with illegal production are suggested in Chapter 9.

5.3. The compilation methods for covering non-observed activities rely on *indicators* of these activities that have been captured in existing data. The prime objective is to use available data to produce an exhaustive measure of GDP while avoiding double counting. Based on an assessment of the incidence, extent, and nature of the NOE (by the methods described in Chapter 4) a broad range of available data should be analysed to determine if and how they could be used as indicators for measurement of non-observed activities. In this context there are a number of considerations to be taken into account, as follows.

5.4. *Coverage is often partial.* Each data collection has its own reference population. Some sources represent total activity, such as a nation-wide household budget survey or a household labour force survey. However, many sources have a specific reference population. Therefore, indirect indicators of production derived from existing sources may still be incomplete, particularly where household unincorporated enterprises prevail. Thus, it is important to identify activities that are not represented in the existing data.

5.5. *Deficiencies in coverage and content.* Existing data collections may be deficient due to problems in the coverage of units, in data reporting, and in survey design and operation. If there are biases in the data, they should be corrected to the extent possible. The information and ratios used to make adjustments for the NOE should be based on corrected survey data, otherwise biases in these data will distort the adjustments.

5.6. *Overlap in coverage.* The existing data sources may have overlaps in coverage. If sources with overlapping coverage are used, care should be taken to avoid double counting. It is important to note that some activities are usually not covered by any survey while other surveys provide overlapping coverage. For example, a manufacturing establishment survey covering establishments with five or more employees and an urban household non-agricultural production survey may have overlaps in coverage (household manufacturing enterprises with five or more employees) but exclude household manufacturing activity in rural areas.

5.7.   *Classifications used in various sources may differ.* The classifications used in the various sources may differ from each other and from those used in the national accounts. Often the breakdowns of the income and expenditure items in source data lack details for estimating intermediate consumption, value added, or capital formation. For example, the data may contain an item "other costs", which could include transactions that should be classified as intermediate consumption, components of value added, capital formation, or other flows.

5.8.   *Concepts and accounting rules may differ.* Source data may use concepts, definitions and accounting rules that differ from the national accounts. For example, wages in-kind in the business accounts may have been recorded as expenses on materials rather than compensation of employees. Information gathered in data collections may not always be on an accrual basis. The collection reference period may not coincide with the accounting period used in the national accounts. Accounting conventions could also differ. For example, business accounts generally use historic cost for inventories and capital stock, whereas national accounts use current replacement cost.

5.9.   *Indicators are often by-products.* It is important to determine whether an indicator of production is collected as a *primary data item* or as a *by-product.* For instance, labour force information in a household labour survey or data on the stock of dwellings in a housing census are collected as primary data. In contrast, information on employment in a household budget survey or data on economic activities in a population census are usually collected as a by-product. Data collected as a by-product may have several shortcomings because the survey procedures are not primarily designed for them. Most of the indicators of production obtained from administrative sources can be considered as by-products of an official record-keeping function, and may suffer from problems relating to coverage, time of recording, valuation, and consistency over time.

5.10.   *Information is partial.* Compilation of value added by economic activity requires data on output and intermediate consumption (current values and volume measures). Any single indicator of production (such as labour inputs, other inputs, demand for products) provides only a limited part of the information needed to estimate value added at current prices and in volume terms. Thus, even if a good indicator of output is available, appropriate procedures and supplementary data are needed to prepare the value added estimates. In some cases, ad-hoc supplementary surveys or investigations may be useful or needed to make efficient use of existing source data.

5.11.   *Information is irregular or infrequent.* While some sources are available on a regular basis, others may be available only infrequently. While infrequent sources are valuable in establishing benchmark estimates, appropriate procedures need to be designed for regular compilation of annual or quarterly GDP estimates.

5.12.   In summary, the chapter presents data sources and methods for including non-observed activities in GDP estimates compiled by production and expenditure approaches, and it describes a supply and use framework for ensuring GDP figures are comprehensive and consistent through reconciliation of the estimates derived using the different approaches. Sections 5.2-5.5 refer to the production approach, describing general methods (including the labour input method), industry specific methods, compilation issues, and the Italian approach, respectively. Section 5.6 deals with expenditure approach methods and Section 5.7 describes the set-up and use of supply and use tables.

5.2.   Production Approach: General Methods

5.2.1. Introduction

5.13.   This section describes *general* methods, *i.e.*, compilation procedures that, in principle, can be applied to any branch of economic activity, provided that the required data are available. The choice of an appropriate method depends on the availability and quality of the data that can be used to derive indicators of production. Such indicators may refer to uses in production or other uses. They may refer to:

- total production including non-observed production, for example total labour input, total capital stock, etc.; or
- a part of total production including a part of non-observed production, for example household purchases of various types of personal services; or
- a part of non-observed production, for example building permits for private residential construction, taxes collected from entrepreneurs, etc.

5.14.   The process of incorporating non-observed production in GDP estimates involves complex procedures. The following points should be taken into account.

- Some procedures yield estimates of total production for a specific activity without separately identifying various types of non-observed activities.
- *Ad-hoc* supplementary data are often required to make efficient use of existing sources; for example, value added estimates can be derived from output estimates obtained from a commodity flow method using a value added/output ratio calculated from an ad-hoc study.
- The compilation should be based on detailed and specific adjustments using specific sources and known linkages and relationships.
- Where possible, alternative estimates should be derived, compared, and assessed for plausibility of the results. Data relating to similar topics but from different sources should be compared and analysed to identify errors or remaining gaps.
- The assumptions underlying the estimation procedures should be made explicit in the calculations and reviewed regularly for their plausibility.

5.15.   General indirect compilation methods that can be used to include the NOE in GDP estimates compiled by the production approach may be divided by type into *supply based* approaches, including the *labour input* approach, *demand based* approaches, *income based* approaches, and *commodity flow* approaches. These are described in the following subsection.

5.2.2. *Supply Based Methods*

5.16.   Supply based methods rely on data about the supply of inputs that are used in producing goods and services. Inputs may include a number of primary raw materials, just one major raw material, labour, land, fixed capital stock, etc. If data on the supply of one or several inputs used in a given production activity are available, the total production of the activity that uses these inputs can be estimated.

5.17.   Input/output and input/value added ratios are needed to calculate output and value added estimates from the input data. Preferably, these ratios should be obtained through ad-hoc surveys for the current period because productivity or relative prices of inputs and outputs may be changing. If ratios from the past are used, it is recommended that volume (constant price) measures of output and value added are derived first and current values obtained by using appropriate price indicators. Fixed ratios from previous periods can be used if a fixed technology assumption is valid, but should not be applied to current values in a later period if there have been changes in relative prices.

5.18.   In making supply based adjustments factors to consider include:

- changes in productivity;
- changes in capital utilisation;
- the uses of certain inputs for purposes other than production;
- valuation differences between supply (time and place) and use (time and place);
- creation and updating of comprehensive benchmark estimates; and
- supplementary information to derive output and value added estimates from input indicators.

5.19.   The particulars of using supply based methods depend on circumstances, as illustrated by the following examples for agricultural production and housing construction. In the Russian Federation adjustments for the production of cereal and other crops by agricultural enterprises are made on the basis of quantities of seeds required per hectare. First, an estimate of the unrecorded cultivated area is determined using data on consumption of seeds reported by enterprises and the average standard quantity of seeds per hectare in various regions. Total production is then derived by multiplying the estimated total area under a crop by the estimated average yield per hectare. Adjustments for livestock products are made on the basis of the average quantity of meat produced per tonne of forage consumed. The reported data on the quantities of forage consumption are considered reliable. Average production per tonne of forage is determined from rural household surveys and expert judgement. (See Goskomstat of Russia, 1998, pp. 91-92.)

5.20.   In many countries, the output of the construction industry is calculated using data on supply of construction materials. For example, in India the output of *pucca construction*, defined as construction using modern manufactured construction materials, is calculated using the estimated supply of basic construction materials in the domestic market. The available commodities are evaluated at the prices at the building site using information on retail prices, dealers' margins, transport costs, and taxes on products. The ratio of the cost of basic materials to output is derived from research studies on various categories of construction (Central Statistical Organisation, Government of India, 1989 pp. 99-104).

5.2.3.   *Labour Input Method*

5.21.   The most significant supply based procedure is the labour input method. It was pioneered by Istat during the 1980s and is sufficiently widely applied to merit a section of its own. At the core of the method are three basic steps:

- obtain estimates of the supply of labour input to GDP, for selected economic activity and size of enterprise, from a household labour force survey and/or other demographic sources;
- obtain estimates of output per unit of labour input and value added per unit of labour input for the same activity and size breakdown from regular or special purpose enterprise survey; and
- multiply the labour input estimates by the per unit ratios to get output and value added for the activity and size categories.

5.22.   In effect, in each economic activity by size category, the labour input estimates are providing the weighting factors by which to inflate enterprise survey based estimates of output and value added to totals. This procedure can be expected to give a more exhaustive coverage of production if the household survey data give more complete coverage of labour input to GDP than do the enterprise survey data. There are two reasons to suppose that this is likely.

- Household based surveys pick up labour inputs to enterprises that are not included in enterprise surveys, for example because these enterprises are too small to be registered in the files from which the survey frames are constructed or because they are too small to be included within the survey.
- Individuals may report their labour inputs to household surveys whereas enterprises may conceal those same inputs in order to evade taxes or administrative regulations.

5.23.   The method depends upon reliable estimates of labour input and per unit ratios at a detailed level of economic activity and size breakdown. It can be applied only for those branches of the economy for which these data are available. Typically the level of detail available is limited by the labour force survey. Thus, broad application of the method implies the need for a very strong labour force survey. The method can be used to estimate production in total within an economic activity branch, or just that part of production that is non-observed through enterprise surveys. In more detail, the elements of the method are as follows.

5.24.   *Estimation of labour input to production based on data from households*. Data are obtained from a household labour force survey, supplemented with any other relevant information from demographic and administrative sources on labour participation. The household survey must include questions about kind of activity, hours worked, and size of employing enterprise(s). These questions provide the basis for an activity by size breakdown and for converting employment data into standard labour input units, such as hours worked or full-time equivalent employment. Together with the sample size and response rates, the questions also determine the level of breakdown at which the data can be considered reliable.

5.25.   *Estimation of labour input to production based on data from enterprises.* Data should be broken down by activity and size of enterprise to at least the level of detail supported by the household surveys. They must also provide sufficient information to be able to convert data about employees into standard labour input units.

5.26.   *Standardisation of labour input estimates.* Data from household surveys are usually in terms of employment. Data from enterprises are usually in terms of jobs. A person can have more than one job. Thus, in order that data from the two sources can be meaningfully compared, they must be converted to the same standard units of labour input, either hours worked or fulltime equivalent employment. In addition any differences in reference period or geographic coverage between the two sources must be taken into account.

5.27.   *Comparison of the sets of estimates.* Enterprise based and household based estimates of labour input are compared. The discrepancies are analysed, taking into account the quality characteristics of the different sources. As noted above, the household surveys can be expected to provide greater coverage and are thus regarded as the primary source. However, account must be taken of the fact that the enterprise based data can be considered to provide a more reliable activity by size breakdown.

5.28.   *Identification of labour input missing from enterprise surveys.* An excess of the household based estimates over the enterprise based estimates is a measure of production (in labour input units) that is non-observed by the enterprise surveys. It is a lower bound as some labour input could be missing from both sources.

5.29.   *Estimation of output and value added per unit of labour input ratios.* These ratios are required at the same level of activity by size breakdown as that for which the labour inputs are computed. Ideally these ratios are obtained using special purpose surveys or studies. If this is not feasible, data from enterprise surveys and administrative files can be used. The need to adjust for underreporting of output should be considered.

5.30.   *Estimation of contribution to GDP as product of labour input and ratios.* The final step is to compute, output and value added for the selected economic activities and size groups.

5.31.   An example of an application of the labour input method is contained within the exercise prescribed by the European Commission for the EU Member States to assess exhaustiveness. As was outlined in Section 4.2 in context of assessment methods, and as detailed by Hayes and Lozano (1998), this exercise includes the use of the labour input method for assessment and possible adjustment. The labour input underlying GDP estimates compiled by any other means are compared with those generated by labour input method. A larger value of the latter suggests that there is non-measured production that should be compensated for. In computing the adjustments it is proposed that:

- for each branch, the value added per unit of labour input for non-observed production may be assumed to equal that for which production is actually measured;

- allowance is made for the likely differences in sizes of the enterprises to which extra labour input has been provided, and for any other significant characteristics;

- the resulting adjustments do not duplicate the effects of other calculations or adjustments made in the accounts.

5.32.   Another application of the method is within the framework of the Italian Approach to compilation of GDP as described later, in Section 5.4

5.2.4. Demand Based Methods

5.33.   Demand based methods aim at determining production by using indicator data on specific uses of goods and services. These indicators can be any use of goods and services that sufficiently describe their production. They could be household final consumption expenditures of a certain commodity (*e.g.* health and personal services), uses of major products as raw materials (*e.g.* processing of agricultural products), exports (*e.g.* major export commodities), or administrative data indicating demand for a product (*e.g.* motor vehicle registrations and building permits). After a measure of output has been obtained, value added estimates can be derived using output/value added ratios, as for supply-based methods.

5.34.   Demand indicators are usually incomplete. In most cases, only data on one or a limited number of major uses are available. For instance, the export value of a commodity that is mainly exported does not cover domestic uses of that commodity. Likewise, household consumption of personal services does not cover other uses, such as uses by producers, or exports, but it may include imports, *i.e.*, expenditures abroad by resident households. Therefore, all the possible uses of a given product must be considered. Demand-based methods work best when a product has one major use for which a comprehensive estimate can be prepared. There are also differences between valuation of uses and output. All uses are to be valued at purchasers' prices, while outputs are to be valued at basic or producers' prices (see 1993 SNA: 6.204 – 6.217).

5.35.   Specific applications of demand-based methods vary from country to country. For example, in Ghana the output of building repair and maintenance is calculated as one month's rental value, thus relating its measure to the stock of buildings. (For details see AFRIstat (1997).) In Nepal, output for motor vehicle repair services is derived on the basis of number of vehicles by types and average repair and maintenance expenses (Central Bureau of Statistics Nepal, 1994).

5.2.5. Income Based Methods

5.36.   Data on some categories of income are available from administrative sources and can be used to obtain an indication of production covered by the administrative system. Information on income taxes or social security contributions paid by self-employed persons (or private entrepreneurs) are often readily available. However, adjustments are usually necessary to account for activities not covered by tax laws and for underreporting of incomes for tax purposes.

5.37.   Calzaroni and Madelin (2000) describe how adjustment coefficients for output and value added are calculated by Institut national de la statistique et des études économiques (INSEE) in France using data from tax audits conducted by the French taxation authorities. The data are transmitted without enterprise identification details to INSEE. The adjustment procedures vary according to the tax system applicable to the enterprise. The data are stratified by legal form, sector of activity, and size of enterprise. The statements of position before and after the audit and the reason for changes are examined. Only upward adjustments resulting from the concealment or omission of receipts are considered. Based on these data, adjustment coefficients are computed separately for corporate enterprises and unincorporated enterprises by sector.

5.38.   In many countries, the output estimates for certain professional business services, such as accounting and legal services, and personal services, such as private health practitioners' services, are made on the basis of average income per practitioner obtained from tax records, from market studies, or though consultations with a few practitioners.

5.2.6. Commodity Flow Method

5.39.   The commodity flow method involves balancing total supplies and uses of individual products. It is used to estimate the output of a commodity by balancing the supply and use of that commodity, using the following equation:

> output = the sum of all intermediate consumption, final consumption, changes (positive or negative) in inventories, gross fixed capital formation, acquisition less disposals of valuables, and exports *minus* imports.

5.40.   This method is effective if a product is primarily used for one or a limited number of uses, and if accurate data on these uses are available. Also, output prices (basic or producers' prices) differ from the prices paid by purchasers so that allowances should be made for the price differences when output of a product is derived using the commodity flow method. The method may be useful for analysing the prices paid by final purchasers of a good and the prices received by the producers as well as for assessing the accuracy of distribution margins.

5.41.   A specific application of a commodity flow method is to derive the output of retail trade from the supply of commodities. Often data on supply of commodities are compiled at a detailed level (usually separately for agricultural products, domestic manufacturing products, and imported goods). Information on shares of the product flows passing through retail trade, and on margin rates, are obtained from benchmark surveys, spot checks, and interviews. These data can then be combined with the data on supply of commodities to estimate the output of retail trade.

5.3.   Production Approach: Industry Specific Methods

5.42.   In addition to the general compilation methods described in Section 5.2, there are methods appropriate for specific industries. These methods can be used to cover all production within an industry, or to provide a complementary estimate if there are gaps in the coverage of the regular statistics. Such gaps are most likely to concern small-scale activities undertaken by household unincorporated enterprises. Large or medium size business enterprises may also be not covered through regular collections. As emphasised earlier, using complementary sources and methods may result in overlaps and gaps, which need to be identified and eliminated.

5.43.   Examples of the sort of administrative and survey data that may be available are listed in Annex 3. However, the actual situation in a country may be quite different. Various types of data sources and compilation methods that are commonly used in different industries are described below.

Agriculture

5.44.   Agriculture is an activity in which small-scale household production is pre-eminent. If no regular data are available covering agricultural output, intermediate consumption, and value added, estimates can be based on data on areas under cultivation, yields, and costs. Data on areas under cultivation and average yield rates are often used to estimate the quantity of crop production. If there is a regular system of crop statistics, up to date information on areas under cultivation are usually available. Data on land use patterns obtained from agriculture censuses and/or land resource maps based on an aerial survey or a cadastral survey may be used to estimate areas under cultivation. Average yield rates are best established through crop-cutting surveys. Agricultural surveys, farm management surveys, or studies on crop cultivation may also provide yield rates. These sources often also provide data on the cost structure, which can be used to derive value added estimates. Typically these sources and methods provide estimates for total agricultural production. Care should be taken to account for the fact that such crop-based estimates may overlap with data from other industries that have agriculture as a secondary activity.

5.45.   Nutritional statistics may also be useful. For major cereal products, government bodies may have prepared food balance estimates. The sources and assumptions used to prepare food balances may provide useful supplementary information.

5.46.   Annual data on number of livestock, if available, are a good source for estimating the contribution of animal husbandry. If they are available only infrequently, the annual change may be extrapolated from the benchmark estimates using reproduction and slaughter rates, with adjustments for exports and imports as necessary.

5.47.   Data on major inputs, such as seeds and fertilisers, may be applicable if data on distribution of such inputs are available, for example, when seeds are distributed through a central channel. Industrial purchases of outputs (such as sugar cane, animal hides, and wool) may be used as indicators if a substantial portion of output is processed in manufacturing industries. Data on sales to marketing boards or exports may also be of use.

5.48.   Household surveys of income and expenditure may provide data on household production for own final use as well as for markets.

Mining and quarrying

5.49.   Mining and quarrying are usually capital-intensive activities performed by large enterprises that are comprehensively covered in regular statistics. Nevertheless, some small-scale activity may not be covered. Data on mining and quarrying activities undertaken by households are usually lacking. It may be possible to use information from the licensing system on production or employment. If employment data are available, average revenue per establishment is needed, which can be established through ad-hoc studies. Alternatively, reasonably comprehensive estimates for certain mining and quarrying products may be made on the basis of data on intermediate consumption of these products by manufacturing and construction (duly adjusted for exports and imports).

Manufacturing

5.50.   Manufacturing, although often capital-intensive, is an activity in which households also engage, usually employing less capital-intensive technology. Surveys of manufacturing activity are usually conducted on a regular basis, but cover only enterprises above a certain cut-off size. This necessitates complementary estimates for small-scale production. Comprehensive benchmarks may be available from periodic manufacturing censuses if these also cover small-scale operators. Data on employment, exports of manufactured products, imports of raw materials, and taxes may be used, where relevant, in combination with the benchmarks to derive estimates for current periods. Household manufacturing activity, particularly for own consumption, is difficult to capture. However, data on household manufacturing activity may be obtained from household income and expenditure surveys or occasional surveys of cottage industries.

Construction

5.51.   Construction of private residential dwellings is often left out of regular data collections. However, infrequent or one-time survey data are often available. Building permits or projections of housing demand can be used as an indication of housing construction. Additional details may be obtained from housing or population censuses.

5.52.   In many cases, construction activity as a whole is measured through an indirect approach. In such an approach the value of construction output is estimated by the commodity flow method, from which an estimate of the supply of construction materials going into construction activity is first derived. This estimate of the net supply of materials is then used with input/output ratios obtained from benchmark or other comprehensive source data to estimate the volume of output. It should be emphasised that changes in the mixture of various types of construction affect the input/output ratios needed to derive output measures. Care should also be taken to avoid duplication as enterprises not in the construction industry may be involved in construction as a secondary activity and may include this in reporting their total output.

5.53.   Building permits, data on building starts or various construction stages may also provide a basis for measuring construction activity. Separate data on repairs and maintenance, particularly related to dwellings, are usually not available. Data on housing stock together with some estimates for average dwelling maintenance cost can be used.

Trade

5.54.   Trade is an activity in which small-scale operators are usually pre-eminent (at least, in numbers). If direct information on small-scale retailing activity is lacking (which is often the case) it may be possible to combine estimates of the supply of groups of products with information on the proportion of the total supply distributed through retail channels to derive retail turnover. Gross retail trading margin rates are needed to derive output estimates. Such margin rates are best established by conducting ad-hoc spot check surveys. The comprehensiveness of estimates obtained through such a commodity flow method depends on the coverage of the supply statistics. It is often the case that import statistics do not properly include shuttle trade imports. Comprehensive supply data can also be used to validate and adjust retail trade survey data.

5.55.   It should be emphasised that using such indirect sources can result in double counting because trade is often performed as a secondary activity, which may thus be included in the estimates for other industries.

5.56.   Data on purchases of goods by households collected in household expenditure surveys may also be used to derive retail turnover. However, allowances should be made for retail purchases by other users (industries, governments, tourists, etc.).

5.57.   Revenues from trading activity that is not covered in regular trade surveys may be captured through data on employment, if available. Tax administration systems and local government bodies may also provide useful information, for example, on the number of small traders filing tax documents or registered with tax authorities. An estimate of trade margins can also be derived from the use table within a supply and use framework by applying estimated trade margin rates to various uses flows.

Restaurants and hotels

5.58.   Information may be lacking for small restaurants, bars, cafés, other eating places, and for lodging and boarding houses. Employment or taxes paid by producers or registration records maintained by local bodies or business associations may be used as a basis for estimating value added. Household expenditure surveys can be used to estimate data on restaurants and hotel services consumed by households. However, adjustments should be made for other domestic uses, such as intermediate consumption (purchases of restaurant or lodging services by enterprises), exports (purchases of these services by non-residents) and imports (purchases abroad by resident households).

5.59.   Information from value added tax systems may cover a sizeable portion of hotel activity. Indicators from tourism statistics, such as tourist arrivals, hotel bed-nights, length of stay, average expenses (often available by type of tourists) can also be used. Tipping may be an important part of output and value added for the hotel and restaurant industry in many countries, but may not be captured even in surveys of the hotel industry. Thus special studies may be necessary. Employment in the industry can be used as an indicator for measuring the amount of tipping.

Transportation and communication services

5.60.   Data on road transport by taxis, mini-buses and trucks are unavailable in many countries. Information on vehicle registrations and traffic statistics are possible indirect sources. The information on revenues and expenses per transport unit (e.g. freight-tonne kilometre or taxi journey) can be collected from ad-hoc surveys. An estimate of total demand may be available for certain types of transportation. For example, freight data may be derived from foreign trade statistics.

5.61.   Private communication services on a small-scale such as provision of e-mail, fax, and telephone services are becoming important in many countries. Registration records from government bodies or business associations may provide information on the number of business units.

5.62.   It is useful to cross-check the output estimates of transportation and communication services against data on the use of such services, which can be obtained from household expenditure surveys, business statistics, government data, and balance of payments.

5.63.   An estimate of transport margins can also be derived from the use table within a supply and use framework by applying estimated transport margin rates to various uses flows.

Business, professional, and technical services

5.64.   Information on the numbers of professionals involved in providing various business, professional, and technical services may be obtained from licenses issued by regulatory bodies or from professional associations. Population censuses or household labour force surveys may also provide information on the number of persons engaged in these activities. Income tax data on the gross receipts of units or professionals involved in these activities can also be used to determine output, with adjustments made for underreporting of incomes in tax declarations.

Education, health, and personal services

5.65.   Data on private education, health, and personal services (where small-scale operators are often important) are not available in many countries. Several indicators may exist that can be used to prepare the estimates, to supplement the survey data, or to validate the estimates derived using a particular method. Various physical indicators of education and health services may be available from administrative sources. The number of establishments or professionals can be obtained from administrative registrations, issue of licenses, and professional associations. Population censuses or household labour force surveys may also provide information on the number of persons engaged in these activities. Similarly, tax records may provide a basis for output estimates. Household expenditure surveys often supply data on consumption of these services by households, but these surveys may not be comprehensive in this respect because they will not capture the use of these services that is covered through insurance schemes.

Domestic services

5.66.   Domestic services are usually small-scale, although sometimes provided by enterprises. It may be possible to cover small-scale activities in this area through population censuses and household labour surveys, which often include data on the total number of persons employed in domestic services. Average income per employee may be estimated from small-scale ad-hoc surveys. It may also be possible to use household expenditure surveys to calculate average incomes of domestic employees.

Owner-occupied dwelling services

5.67.   Estimates of the value of owner-occupied dwelling services cannot be based on direct observations since there are no market transactions for these services. A common procedure is to estimate the number of owner-occupied dwellings from housing or population censuses and to estimate the value of owner-occupied dwelling services from rents paid for comparable dwellings which may be derived from housing censuses or real estate agents.

5.68.   An alternative method is imputation of rents by reference to *opportunity costs*. In this method, net value added is derived by applying some interest rate to the estimated value of the stock of owner-occupied dwellings. The consumption of fixed capital and intermediate consumption is then added to obtain the gross output of owner-occupied dwelling services. It should be noted that this method might cause erratic movements in production and consumption of these services due to the volatility of interest rates. Furthermore, in areas with a relatively undeveloped financial system, such as rural areas in developing countries, interest rates can be uncharacteristically high.

5.69.   Estimates of owner-occupied dwelling services are usually prepared from benchmark estimates for a year for which detailed data are available, supplemented by other indicators such as price indices (*e.g.* rent index within the consumer price index) for later years. Construction statistics and statistics of building permits are often used to update the estimated stock of housing, particularly in the case of urban areas where building construction is regulated. Usually the benchmarks are prepared with an urban/rural or some other regional breakdown. The benchmark estimates should be updated periodically, and the indicators and assumptions used in the estimation should be reviewed regularly.

5.4.   Production Approach: The Italian Approach

5.70.   This section summarises the Italian Approach to GDP estimation by the production approach. It was developed by Istat during the 1980s to deal with the particular characteristics of the Italian economy. Whilst a hallmark of the approach is the use of labour input method, this is not its only distinguishing characteristic. It also involves a substantial correction for underreporting. It is more than simply an application of labour input method. It is a complete approach to GDP estimation that has been designed for Italy but can be applied in any other country with similar features, namely:

- many small enterprises, which may be missing from, or misclassified in, the business register because they are unregistered or because of their high turnover rate;
- high volume of irregular, *i.e.*, unregistered, labour;
- considerable underreporting of production by enterprises; and
- strong labour force survey.

5.71.   The Italian Approach is specifically designed to deal with the NOE, which is why it is being discussed here. The following outline has been extracted from detailed descriptions by Istat (1993) and Calzaroni (2000).

General approach for estimating GDP

5.72.   Estimation procedures are divided into groups by economic activity according to the data available:

- branches for which estimates are based on quantity times price – including agriculture, energy and part of construction;
- branches for which estimates are based on expenditure data – part of construction, rents and private services for education, research, health, entertainment and leisure;
- branches for which estimates are based on costs and earnings directly from balance sheets – credit, insurance, some branches belonging to public enterprises;
- branches for which estimates are based on distributed incomes – non-market services;
- branches for which estimates are based on the labour input method.

5.73.   Some such division is typical of estimation by production approach. What characterises the Italian Approach is that 70% of production is estimated using labour input method.

5.74.   The procedure for estimating output, value added (and other national accounts aggregates) by branch of economic activity is summarised in the following formula:

$$Y = \sum_{i=1}^{m} \sum_{j=1}^{J} X_{ij} * U_{ij} + \sum_{i=m+1}^{M} Y_i$$

where: Y = overall estimate of the aggregate

i = indicator of the branch of economic activity

M = number of branches (101 in the case of Italy)

j = indicator of the size of the establishment

J = number of size groups (J = 8 for Italy: 1-5, 6-9, 10-19, 20-49, 50-99, 100-249, 250+)

X = average per capita value of the aggregate

U = fulltime equivalent employment

$\sum_{i=m+1}^{M} Y_i$ = part of the aggregate not estimated using labour input method

Application of labour input method

5.75.   Estimation of GDP using the labour input method is along the lines described in Section 5.2.3. The steps are illustrated in Figure 5.1. The following paragraphs describe some particular features of the application in Italy.

- *Adjustment of incoming data.* This involves temporal and territorial harmonisation, and conceptual harmonisation to national accounts definitions.

79

Figure 5.1. **Estimation of GDP by input of labour method (Italian approach)**

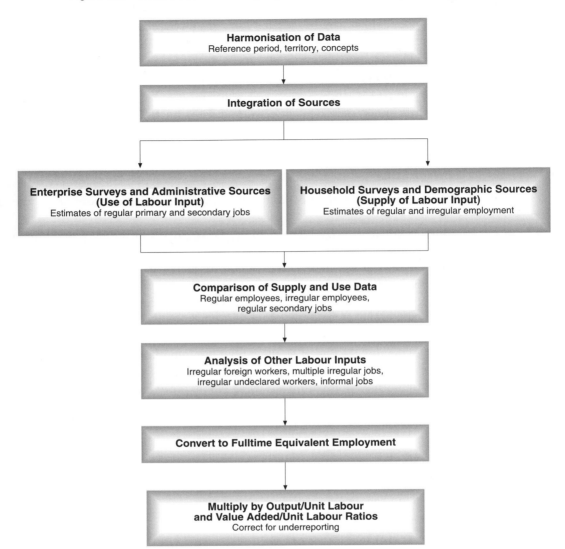

- *Integration of enterprise data*. Labour input data are obtained through enterprise surveys and administrative sources. A comprehensive business register is lynchpin of the enterprise survey programme. The aim is to produce exhaustive estimates of the registered employment covering primary and secondary regular jobs.

- *Integration of household data*. This involves a micro-level comparison of records from the labour force survey and the annual population census. The objective is to obtain as precise an indication of employment status as possible. The same status according to both sources is a confirmation. In the case of conflicting status indicators, it is assumed that a person employed according to the labour force survey is actually employed, and that employed according to the census but not the labour force survey may be indicative of irregular employment. In the later case the conflicting information is resolved by assigning the person in question the status of a "donor" person within the database for which the employment status has been confirmed. The donor is chosen on the basis of the minimum distance between the person and all possible donors, where distance is defined in terms of characteristics available in the original data sources.

- *Comparison of supply and use of labour inputs.* Comparisons of numbers of jobs are made at a detailed level of economic activity by region, separately for employees, self-employed and unpaid family workers. Three cases are distinguished:
  - regulars, for which the number of employed people equals the number of jobs;
  - fulltime irregulars, for which the number of employed people exceeds the number of jobs;
  - regulars with multiple jobs, for which the number of jobs exceeds the number of employed people.
- *Other components of labour input.* The household and enterprise survey sources account for about 90% of the total labour input. Other sources are used to estimate for the remainder. Expenditure side data are used to give estimates for irregular multiple jobs. Data from the Ministry of Internal Affairs provide data on non-resident foreign workers. Informal jobs are estimated through special purpose surveys.
- *Computation of full-time equivalent employment.* Jobs are converted to full-time equivalent employment. Two situations are distinguished:
  - where (regular or irregular) employment is on a less than full time basis, *e.g.* secondary and part-time jobs;
  - where employment is on a full-time basis but the quantity of work delivered is reduced, *e.g.* as a result of hours unworked due to lack of orders.
- *Compilation of output and value added.* Ratios of output per unit of labour input and value added per unit are estimated on the basis of annual surveys of enterprise budgets, with adjustments for underreporting as described below.

Adjustment for underreporting

5.76.   Output and value added ratios are adjusted to compensate for underreporting of turnover. The hypothesis underlying such corrections is that the income of a self-employed worker of an enterprise should at least equal the average wage of the regular employees. The income of self-employed workers is obtained by taking the value added reported by the enterprise and subtracting the compensations of employees, the capital consumption and other components in accordance with the 1993 SNA. When income thus computed is less than the average wage of employees, it is adjusted upwards to be the same as the average wage. This adjustment carries through to the calculation of the ratios and hence to output and value added.

5.5.   Production Approach: Compilation Issues

5.77.   This section deals with some specific compilation issues involved in measuring the NOE through the production approach. As described in the Sections 5.2, 5.3 and 5.4, NOE adjustments are based on indirect indicators of production obtained from various data sources. The national accounts estimates (output, intermediate consumption, and value added) are calculated by means of certain ratios based on assumptions regarding the relationship between the variable to be estimated and the indicator. The indicators may refer to output or intermediate consumption or other inputs. Furthermore, they may be in volume terms (such as dwelling floor areas or number of full-time equivalent employment), or in current price values (such as exports or taxes). However, compilation of GDP by the production approach involves calculating output, intermediate consumption, and value added at current prices as well as in volume terms. Because of definitional relationships, data can be considered effectively complete if two items out of output, intermediate consumption, and value added are available; and if two items out of values, volumes, and prices are available. Therefore, even if an appropriate indicator of production can be obtained, the national accountants still have to use appropriate compilation techniques to derive value added estimates both at current prices and in volume terms. The major compilation issues that have to be considered in this context are described in the following paragraphs.

Explicit calculation of all items of the production account

5.78.   Explicit calculation of all items of the production account (output, intermediate consumption, and value added) is needed because attempting to estimating value added directly suffers from severe disadvantages. The most important disadvantage is that value added does not itself have observable volume and price dimensions, which makes it impossible to derive proper volume measures from current price data or *vice versa*. To get around this problem, output or input prices are often used to deflate current price value added or to inflate volume measures of value added. The implicit assumption of this procedure is that input and output prices develop in parallel, which is not always the case. The direct calculation of value added alone involves implicit assumptions about input/output ratios that cannot be verified. Also, applying a fixed input/output ratio to current value estimates may result in implicit deflators that are implausible. A further problem in estimating value added directly is that the estimates cannot be incorporated into a supply and use framework because such a framework requires separate data on supply (output) and use (intermediate consumption) as well as value added.

Supplementary information and fixed ratios

5.79.   Where possible, attempts should be made to gather supplementary information to derive ratios for the current period (such as input/output ratios, ratios of output per self-employed person, and cost per square unit of dwelling construction). *ad hoc* supplementary data increase the efficiency of the existing sources. For example, output can be derived by commodity flow method and the value added/output ratio can be calculated from an *ad hoc* study. In cases where single indicators are used in combination with ratios from past periods, volume measures should be derived first. Using fixed ratios assumes unchanged technology, which seems reasonable for the medium-term. However, using fixed ratios with current price data implies the additional assumption of parallel price movements of input and output prices, which, as previously mentioned, is often not the case. Once volume measures have been estimated, current value estimates can be obtained through the use of price indices.

Techniques for deflation or inflation

5.80.   Appropriate techniques should be used to derive volume measures from current values (deflation) and current values from volume measures (inflation). If indicators are available for both output and intermediate consumption, the double indicator method should be used to calculate the volume measure of value added (as the volume measure of output less the volume measure of intermediate consumption). As mentioned above, if a single indicator is used in combination with a fixed ratio it is always desirable to calculate explicitly the volume measures of output and intermediate consumption, and to multiply them separately with relevant price indicators to obtain current price values.

5.81.   Attempts should be made to match indicators with the concepts. For example, for output of personal services, the consumer price index for these items is more appropriate than the overall consumer price index.

Single or composite indicators

5.82.   A composite indicator of production combines several indicators, often inputs to production. For example, a composite indicator of construction output may include all major raw materials and labour inputs. In contrast a single indicator may be one major raw material (such as cement) or labour. The appropriate choice of indicators depends on the quality of the data and the correlation between the indicators and production. Composite indicators reduce the risk of bias that may result from use of a single indicator.

Benchmark estimates and regular compilations

5.83.   Comprehensive and detailed data may be available only infrequently, for example at five or ten year intervals, or on an *ad hoc* basis. Similarly, data may only be available for certain types of non-observed production activities. Thus a combination of benchmarks and indicators is required in compiling the national accounts generally and in adjusting for non-observed activities in particular.

5.84.   The benchmarks provide an estimate for a certain period as well as a basis (*i.e.*, benchmark levels and the ratios derived from them) for regular compilations. The assumptions for benchmark-indicator adjustments should be made explicit and their suitability reviewed regularly. One way of assessing an indicator is to gather information about its coverage and definitions and identify its major differences from the benchmark. If benchmarks for more than one year are available, the change shown by the indicator over the period can be compared with the change in the benchmark series over the same period. The difference is a measure of the indicator bias. This kind of review may suggest how the indicator could be improved.

5.85.   The benchmark-indicator relationships may change over time due to several factors. When subsequent benchmarks show different benchmark/indicator ratios, the difference should be allocated over the period between benchmarks.

5.6.   Expenditure Approach: Sources and Methods

5.86.   The estimates of GDP by expenditure categories show the final demand for goods and services. Estimates of final expenditures on GDP are particularly useful for policy purposes, but in many countries the expenditure approach is less developed than the production approach. The main causes might be the traditional focus on production statistics and problems in the availability of expenditure source data. In many cases, independent estimates of GDP from the expenditure approach are not compiled. Instead, GDP by type of expenditure is estimated for available components such as gross fixed capital formation, government final consumption, exports and imports, while the missing items (for example, household final consumption and/or changes in inventories) are derived as residuals by subtracting the available components from the GDP estimate compiled from the production approach. Such practices attribute errors in the estimates for all other aggregates to the item(s) derived as a residual. Furthermore, such expenditure estimates can not provide an independent check on the production estimates.

5.87.   Comprehensive basic data on expenditures are usually not available. Thus indirect compilation methods are used. They depend on the availability of source data, which vary between countries and within a country over time. Selection of the appropriate approach requires investigation of the various possible alternatives. This Handbook suggests that compilation methods that derive estimates at an aggregated level (such as household final consumption expenditure) as a residual should be avoided. Instead, the compilation should be based on detailed and specific adjustments using specific sources and known relationships. Such an approach also allows the full use of available data and an assessment of the plausibility of the methods and results. For example, derivation of household final consumption expenditure as a residual does not take advantage of several data sources, in particular production of goods and services primarily used for final consumption, imports and exports of consumer goods, and household production for own consumption. These are available in most countries and can be used to estimate components of household consumption expenditure.

5.88.   This section identifies typical sources and methods that can be used to prepare exhaustive estimates of the expenditure categories of GDP. The expenditure categories are household final consumption expenditure, government final consumption expenditure, final consumption expenditure of non-profit institutions serving households, gross fixed capital formation, changes in inventories, acquisition less disposals of valuables, and exports and imports of goods and services. Within each of these categories, the presentation below describes sources and compilation methods for items that have data shortcomings.

5.6.1. *Household Final Consumption Expenditure*

5.89. A comprehensive estimate of household consumption requires a combination of different sources and methods that are best suited to measuring a certain set of consumer items. Households obtain consumer goods and services through various channels and means. No one single source can be considered adequate, and data on household consumption should be gathered from different sources. Multiple sources may be available for some expenditure items. Estimation procedures and adjustments depend on the nature and quality of data sources, and more than one method may be applicable. A set of categories of household consumption that is helpful in assessing and achieving comprehensive coverage is the following:

- purchases of goods and services;
- consumption of goods from own production;
- services of owner-occupied dwellings;
- services produced by paid domestic employees;
- goods and services received as income in kind;
- financial intermediation services;
- insurance and pension fund services; and
- payments for licenses and fees.

Data sources

5.90. The main sources of data are household expenditure surveys, retail trade statistics, production statistics, administrative data, reports of individual companies, socio-demographic data, and international trade statistics. (Annexes 3.4 and 3.5 provide typical lists.)

5.91. A household expenditure survey (HES) usually provides detailed information, facilitating a systematic classification of consumption expenditure using a classification such as the *Classification of Individual Consumption by Purpose* (COICOP). A HES can furnish data on many types of household consumption, typically including all the items listed above except financial intermediation and insurance and pension fund services. A HES measures the flow of goods and services at the time of purchase at purchaser's prices and this is consistent with the time of recording and the valuation required by the 1993 SNA. Furthermore, a HES may ensure a better coverage of purchases from small scale retailers and service providers than the data on sales collected directly from the sellers, because purchasers are less likely than sellers to understate expenditure. The HES may also provide information on payments for domestic servants, goods and services received as income in kind, and payments for licenses and fees.

5.92. A HES usually has certain limitations as a data source for comprehensive estimates of the household consumption expenditure. It may not cover the whole population, often excluding persons living in hospitals, prisons, and other institutions. HES sample sizes are usually relatively small, which may adversely affect the representativeness of items that are purchased by particular groups of the population or the population in particular geographic areas. Seasonally purchased items may not be properly covered. Data on items that are infrequently purchased (such as consumer durables) or that are socially sensitive (such as alcohol and tobacco) are also less reliable. Furthermore, some goods and services may be used for business purposes as well as for household consumption, and households owning unincorporated enterprises may not report items purchased for the different uses separately.

5.93. For consumption of goods from own production, a HES may have three major shortcomings:

- own account producers may not be adequately represented;
- production retained for own consumption may be difficult to separate from other uses; and
- valuation of output for own consumption may be inappropriate.

Also, imputed values of owner-occupied dwelling services and imputed services charges for casualty and life insurance can not readily be estimated by respondents to a HES. Thus they must be estimated by national accounts compilers using other data sources.

5.94.   Retail trade data constitute an important source of information on household consumption, particularly for goods that are mainly distributed through retail channels. Many types of retail providers are fairly specialised but some stores sell a wide range of goods, which require additional information on product breakdowns. Retail trade data include sales to users other than households. Such products should be identified and should not be attributed to household consumption. On the other hand, households may acquire products directly from manufacturers, wholesalers, and farmers. Retail trade surveys may also suffer from undercoverage, particularly regarding small-scale trade by household unincorporated enterprises. In most cases, therefore, the retail trade statistics require adjustments based on information from other sources.

5.95.   Retail turnover data are most appropriate when the product group in question is mainly distributed through retail trade, the retail trade survey has an adequate representation of the retail outlets, and there is a clear link between the commodity groups distinguished in trade data and other sources (such as a HES, production statistics, tax records, and international trade statistics). Linking the data on the commodity groups from various sources provides a basis for adjustment to the retail turnover data, if necessary.

5.96.   Production statistics can be used to estimate household consumption of particular commodities that are mainly used for household consumption, provided comprehensive data on their production are available. Data on production of farm products consumed by the farm households may be available from agricultural surveys. Household production or income surveys may also provide data on production of goods (agricultural as well as non-agricultural) by households for their own consumption. If surveys ask for total production only, additional information is needed on the allocation of production between final consumption and other uses, *e.g.* intermediate consumption as seeds.

5.97.   Surveys of enterprises providing consumer services can be used for estimating household consumption of these services. In such cases, the main difficulty may be the allocation of the total production between household consumption and other uses. Such allocation ratios may be derived by analysing uses of these services in production by industries and by government, or they may come from data on balance of payments, or from household expenditure survey data. For some services, particularly owner-occupied dwelling services and domestic services produced by paid employees, the consumption estimates should be identical to the output estimates from the production approach. Thus, household consumption can be taken directly from the output estimates (see Section 5.3).

5.98.   For consumer goods that are usually exported and/or imported, the production statistics should be used in combination with international trade statistics, which are further discussed in Section 5.6.7.

5.99.   Administrative data can be used in cases where a regulatory system provides indicators of household consumption. For example, government administrative records can provide information on excise or other special taxes on sales of tobacco and alcohol. Other examples of administrative data that can be used to estimate particular components of household expenditure are:

- number of private vehicle registrations (to estimate vehicle purchases);
- stock of vehicles (to estimate expenditure on car repairs);
- number of marriages or other social and vital events (to estimate expenditures on religious ceremonies and funerals);
- number of providers of certain services such as child care centres and retirement homes (to estimate expenditures on these services); and
- several indicators for health and education.

5.100. Government records provide information on fees and licenses, but additional information is needed to separate payments by households from payments by producers.

5.101. The accounts and records of major producers can be used where a small number of large producers supply the bulk of a particular item. Examples include sales to households of electricity, gas, water, telecommunication, and postal services. Distribution of some goods (such as petroleum products, certain food products) may be regulated centrally, in which case the data from the regulatory bodies can be used. Data may not always refer to sales to households, and adjustments should be made using additional information. Reports of financial institutions, insurance companies, and pension funds are important sources for calculating consumption of financial and insurance services.

5.102. Socio-demographic data may also provide useful information for estimating particular items of household consumption. Nutrition statistics can be combined with data on population to derive food consumption. Statistics on living conditions and housing can provide several indicators of consumption such as ownership of dwellings, private vehicles, and access to facilities. Health and education statistics may also be useful for estimating consumption expenditures on these types of services.

Compilation methods

5.103. Selection of an appropriate compilation method depends on a particular data situation. Four types of compilation methods can be distinguished: direct observation methods; commodity flow methods; benchmark-to-indicator methods; and consumption indicator methods.

5.104. *Direct observation* methods use information on consumption obtained from households, the consumer units, through a HES. As explained above, the comprehensiveness and accuracy of estimates depend on the quality of HES data, and adjustments are needed in many cases.

5.105. *Commodity flow* methods use information about the supplies of goods and services from domestic production and imports, and information on the uses of these supplies in activities other than household consumption. Compilation methods that use retail trade turnover, production statistics, international trade statistics, and reports of producers/suppliers are variants of a commodity flow approach. The commodity flow methods give best results if a product is entirely or predominantly used for household consumption. Furthermore, the commodity flow methods require that:

- comprehensive data on supply are available;
- information on any uses other than household consumption is available or can be calculated;
- information on taxes and distribution margins can be estimated to convert values at supply point (basic prices, producers' prices, c.i.f. values) to values at purchasers' prices; and
- estimates can be made for direct purchases abroad by resident households and for direct purchases in the domestic market by non-resident households.

5.106. Because international trade statistics do not cover expenditures of residents abroad and of non-residents in the domestic economy, commodity flow methods result in estimates of household consumption expenditure in the domestic market. Therefore, purchases abroad by residents should be added and purchases in the domestic markets by non-residents should be deducted to calculate final consumption expenditure of resident households.

5.107. *Benchmark-to-indicator* methods imply that comprehensive and detailed estimates of household consumption expenditure (*benchmarks*) are made only at some intervals (say three or five years, or annually in the case of quarterly estimates) and the regular estimates are prepared using *indicators* to extrapolate the benchmark estimates. The benchmarks for an item or group of consumer products should be based on the most appropriate data source with adjustments as necessary to ensure comprehensive coverage. The indicators may be obtained from the sources described above and others. They can be in value terms (*e.g.* sales and excise taxes) or in volume terms (*e.g.* stock of cars, dwelling area, and number of households). The benchmark-indicator relationship should be reviewed regularly for assessing the suitability of the indicators. Subsequent benchmarks may indicate a shift in the benchmark-indicator ratios. These changes should be allocated over the period between benchmarks because they reflect changes that must have occurred over the period between the benchmarks. If no adjustment is made, it causes a step problem in the series by allocating the entire difference to a single period when the new data are introduced. When indicators are poor, the different estimates obtained using alternative indicators may be large. In such cases, the causes of indicator bias should be investigated and an indicator that reflects as closely as possible the behaviour of the target variable should be used. (Bloem *et al.* (2001) provides more information on benchmark-indicator techniques.)

5.108. *Consumption indicator* methods use information that may be linked to household consumption of certain products. Examples include the use of administrative and socio-demographic data to estimate household consumption expenditure. For example, nutrition data can be used to estimate consumption of food products. Similarly, the numbers of students by grades may be an indicator for school fees and other educational expenses.

5.6.2. *Government Final Consumption Expenditure*

5.109. The estimates of output and final consumption expenditure of government are closely related and should be calculated in conjunction with each other. For conceptually correct estimates of government final consumption, separate estimates of output should be prepared for market output, fixed capital formation on own-account, and other non-market output produced by government.[1] Information is also needed on receipts from sales of non-market services and purchases by government of goods and services that are provided to households free or at prices that are not economically significant.

5.110. Data for preparing the estimates described in the previous paragraph are usually available from budget reports and other government accounts. There are, however, a number of issues that need to be examined before information obtained from these sources can be used for compilation purposes. These include:

- Data may be lacking for provincial or local government, extra-budgetary funds, and defence related expenses. In such cases, methods that rely on indicators relating to current activity levels could be used, for example, wages paid by government and central government payments (when they constitute a major source of funds).
- Data on consumption of fixed capital are usually not available from the government accounts. In this case the data should be calculated on the basis of the stock of fixed capital owned by the government valued at current prices.
- Government accounts are traditionally prepared on a cash basis, which may differ significantly from the accrual basis needed for national accounts. Therefore, additional data should be used to adjust data recorded on a cash basis to approximate accrual accounting.

5.6.3. *Final Consumption Expenditure of* NPISH

5.111. Data for larger NPISH may be available from their published reports as submitted to the tax or regulatory authorities. Government may be a good source of statistical indicators if it monitors, regulates, or provides funding. However, data may not be available for smaller organisations. A small-scale survey may be a good choice if registers or listings of NPISH are available as a survey frame. Data on foreign transfers to NPISH may also be an important indicator in countries where foreign aid is a major source of funding for NPISH.

5.6.4. *Gross Fixed Capital Formation*

5.112. The main approaches used for compiling capital formation are direct observation of capital expenditures and various indirect techniques relying on commodity flow analysis or other data on supply of, or demand for, capital goods.

5.113. Surveys of capital expenditure by enterprises is the preferred source for estimating capital formation. However, they are very sensitive to coverage problems. In particular, new enterprises, which may not yet be in production or recorded in the statistical office business register, are particularly likely

---

1. The government final consumption expenditure is equal to government non-market output (excluding own account fixed capital formation) less receipts from sales of non-market output plus purchases of goods and services provided to households free or at economically insignificant prices.

to have higher rates of capital formation than established businesses. On the other hand, many existing enterprises may have little or no capital formation in a given period.

5.114. Data on the acquisition of fixed assets are usually available for government, public corporations and large companies and for large investment projects funded from abroad. Such data may also be available for other types of producers from capital expenditure surveys or when information on fixed assets acquired is collected in production surveys. Data on acquisition of fixed assets and own account capital formation by small and household unincorporated enterprises are usually not available.

5.115. Where a value added tax system is in place that requires capital and current purchases to be split, this can provide a useful indicator. However, value added tax statistics often do not provide a breakdown by type of product and they usually exclude own account capital formation.

5.116. Commodity flow methods are widely used to derive total fixed capital formation. They yield a classification by type of assets, but not a classification by kind of activity or institutional sectors. They can be more easily used for machinery and equipment as data on their supply are readily available and their coverage is usually satisfactory. Adjustments to supply data should be made to include taxes, distribution margins, and installation costs. Deductions should be made for goods that are used for intermediate consumption (*e.g.* parts for repairs), household final consumption (*e.g.* computers, cars used by households), or inventories, and net sales of capital goods (*e.g.* enterprises selling second-hand cars to households or non-residents).

5.117. Commodity flow methods can also be used to estimate construction, in which case the estimates of capital formation are closely related to the output estimates for construction. (See Section 5.3.) The main differences between construction output and capital formation in construction for which adjustments should be made are the following:

- construction output includes current maintenance, which is not capital formation;
- speculative construction (construction for which a purchaser is not identified and that continues to belong to the builder) is part of construction output, which should be classified as inventories but not as fixed capital formation until it is finished and sold; and
- ownership transfer costs are part of capital formation.

5.118. In addition to construction and equipment (which constitute the largest share), gross fixed capital formation includes cultivated assets (such as livestock and trees), intangible fixed assets (such as mineral exploration, computer software, and literary, entertainment, and artistic originals), and additions to the value of non-produced assets (such as land reclamation). Indicators for these assets are less commonly available. They may include the following.

- For cultivated assets, livestock statistics and agricultural censuses/surveys can be used.
- For software, estimates can be made from the supply side (*i.e.*, manufacture of standard or off-the-shelf software plus in-house development of software by government and enterprises plus imports less exports), or from the demand side (*i.e.*, expenditure on software). Supply data have the advantage that a relatively smaller number of businesses are involved in manufacturing standard software but have the disadvantages that a substantial proportion of off-the-shelf software is for household consumption and that many enterprises and government departments develop their own software in-house. A further problem is that some software is sold in conjunction with hardware and this may lead to double counting.
- For mineral exploration, administrative requirements for mining exploration permits may provide useful indicators. However, there are timing differences between the granting of permission and when the actual exploration takes place.

5.119. As described above, the data on expenditures by purchasers on the acquisition of fixed assets usually have partial coverage. On the other hand, commodity flow methods can provide only a total estimate for a class of fixed assets. Special care is needed to avoid duplication and omissions when combining different sources and methods, which is the approach usually followed.

5.6.5. Changes in Inventories

5.120. All countries have difficulties in estimating changes in inventories and several countries derive their estimates mainly as the difference between GDP estimates derived from the production and expenditure sides. This is obviously unsatisfactory and can be seriously misleading at turning points in the business cycle when inventory changes may move rapidly from negative to positive and *vice versa*.

5.121. Enterprise surveys provide data on inventories for establishments covered in those surveys. Administrative data on stocks of inventories held by government agencies supplying or regulating the supply of important products are an additional source. Information on inventories can also be obtained from agricultural and livestock statistics, food and energy balances, and reports of marketing boards. Generally, it can be expected that the NOE does not contribute significantly to inventories. Inventories associated with the NOE are mostly related to agriculture, trade, and manufacturing, and are probably concentrated in a limited number of goods.

5.122. Changes in inventories present specific difficulties with respect to valuation. Commercial enterprises use several different valuation methods, most of which are not consistent with the current-cost valuation required for national accounts (1993 SNA: 6.57–83). Adjustments are required to remove holding gains/losses on inventories. Bloem et al (1996) provide a description of some methods. Estimates of changes in inventories should be consistent with the treatment of inventories for deriving gross output and intermediate consumption in the production account.

5.6.6. Acquisitions Less Disposals of Valuables

5.123. The 1993 SNA classifies valuables (such as jewellery, works of arts, antiques, precious stones and metals) as a separate category of capital expenditure. In many countries, purchase of valuables by households may be important. Estimates for valuables may be prepared using data from producers (production statistics), imports, retailers, or purchasers (household surveys).

5.6.7. Imports and Exports of Goods and Services

5.124. The international trade statistics constitute the main sources of data about imports and exports of goods. Usually data on merchandise exports and imports are compiled from customs declarations, but some countries use reports of enterprises specialising in international trade. Customs records do not cover services. An additional problem is that the timing of recording may not match the national accounts concept. In many countries the data suffer from undercoverage and estimates must be made for missing items. Direct imports by government, particularly military goods, and foreign aid in-kind may not be recorded. In some countries, smuggling is a serious problem. There might be a substantial amount of border trade, particularly in cattle, crops, and food and other consumer products. Exports and imports of oil and natural gas, especially by pipeline, may be outside the customs statistics. Gifts and parcel post are often below the threshold value for inclusion in the data. Details regarding the concepts and methodology for compiling international merchandise trade statistics are provided by United Nations (1998).

5.125. In many transition countries, *shuttle trade* has grown rapidly. Shuttle trade refers to imports and exports by individuals who travel to neighbouring countries to purchase goods for resale in street markets or small shops. Shuttle trade is often excluded from customs record. The best approach is to conduct surveys of shuttle traders. Some countries have used data from small samples of traders on the total numbers of shuttle trade journeys and the average values of goods imported or exported.

5.7. Supply and Use Framework

5.7.1. Introduction

5.126. Use of a supply and use framework as a statistical tool in compiling GDP estimates has been increasing in recent years. It provides a basis for comprehensive, systematic, and consistent adjustments to obtain exhaustive measures of GDP, even if non-observed activities have been estimated using the adjustment methods described in the previous sections. In particular, it facilitates:

- identifying gaps and inconsistencies in the basic data sources;
- filling gaps by calculating estimates for missing supply or use as a residual;
- cross-checking and reconciling as well as improving the consistency, plausibility, and completeness of the estimates of supply and uses; and
- calculating estimates for periods for which less detailed and/or less reliable data are available by using coefficients and other information from benchmark tables.

5.127. The supply and use framework provides a detailed basis for analysing industries and products through a detailed and systematic breakdown of:

- the *goods and services account*, showing the total supply of goods and services (output and imports) and their use (intermediate consumption, final consumption, changes in inventories, gross fixed capital formation, acquisition less disposals of valuables, and exports);
- the *production account*, showing output, intermediate use of goods and services, and value added; and
- the *generation of income account*, showing value added and its component primary incomes generated in the process of production.

5.128. The supply and use tables show two types of balances:

- for each *industry*, output equals intermediate consumption plus value added; and
- for each *product*, total supply equals total use.

5.129. Supply and use tables can be seen as a comprehensive, systematic, and economy-wide application of the commodity flow method. Discrepancies between supply-use balances indicate missing items or other weaknesses. These discrepancies and the analysis of their causes lead to imputation of missing items or adjustments to items with poor estimates. These adjustment factors can also be used in the national accounts compilation during the period following the compilation of the latest supply and use tables. However, the effectiveness of such methods of estimation depends on the extent to which corrections can be and have been made to the source data for underreporting, non-response, and bias. Moreover, commodity flow methods do not capture aspects of economic activity that are not recorded in either supply or use. The 1993 SNA (Paragraphs 15.54-119) elaborates the concepts and methodology, and more details are presented in United Nations (1999).

5.7.2. *Basic Structure of Supply and Use Framework*

5.130. In order to produce supply and use tables the following eight building blocks are required.

- Definition of the products to be distinguished in the supply and use tables in terms of product classifications. The 1993 SNA recommends the Central Product Classification (CPC), but other classification systems, such as the Harmonised System (HS), may also be considered.
- A key linking the classifications used for domestic production statistics and international trade statistics and the product groups used in the supply and use table.
- A breakdown of total output or sales by product for most of the goods producing industries and, to the extent possible, for services as well.
- International trade statistics for goods and records for exports and imports for services. The latter usually come from balance of payments statistics and are at a high level of aggregation.
- Conversion keys between output from activities not covered by product statistics and the product groups used in the commodity flow system. This may often be necessary for service activities. The default option is to define service groups by ISIC classes.
- Estimates of the ratios of intermediate consumption to output for various industries. In some countries these data are collected in special surveys of production costs.

- Cost structure surveys giving the total intermediate consumption by product, ideally in at least as much detail as the product groups defined for the supply and use table. The minimum requirement is a survey on intermediate consumption for manufacturing industries for the benchmark year.

- Sources giving final household consumption expenditure, gross fixed capital formation, and changes in inventories by product groups. Preferably these should be available annually; failing this results from a household budget survey for a benchmark year are the minimum requirement.

5.131. In setting up a supply and use table by means of the commodity flow method, the third and fourth items are indispensable, since the whole idea is to combine domestic production statistics and imports in order to determine the total supply of each product available for domestic uses. Ideally, the other items mentioned should be available with comprehensive coverage annually, but in practice, some of these items may only be covered partially or at intervals of several years. The commodity flow method can also be used when basic statistical sources are scarce by exploiting benchmark information to estimate data for other years.

5.132. The introduction of supply and use tables and application of the commodity flow method should not be seen as a procedure that is applicable only when an abundance of data is available so that each cell in the tables can be directly filled. On the contrary, the supply and use framework is a method to make the maximum use of available information, no matter how limited it is. A very basic principle is to avoid the loss of any information that is potentially useful in compiling the national accounts.

5.133. The following two scenarios show the usefulness of a supply and use framework even if applied on a very limited scale.

Scenario one: mainly supply side data available

5.134. In most countries, it is possible to establish the supply for the domestic market (as domestic output *plus* imports *minus* exports) at a fairly detailed level, as international trade statistics are usually compiled at a detailed level and industrial output is also usually available at a rather detailed level. For services, it is usually necessary to accept a more aggregated classification, perhaps related to the ISIC Rev. 3 classification. In spite of these shortcomings, the establishment of fairly detailed statistics on the supply of products to the domestic market enables national accountants to make some sensible judgements about the uses of the products based on their type and other characteristics. The main distinction is between intermediate consumption and final uses, and, for final uses, the nature of the product often indicates whether it is for consumption or fixed capital formation. A rough exercise of this kind helps to identify major flaws and inconsistencies in the accounts, even though it does not take full account of finer details.

Scenario two: macro balancing except for a few major products

5.135. The goods and services account for the total economy can be seen as a highly aggregated supply and use table, containing just one product group and showing no breakdown of intermediate consumption by industry. If this is all that is initially available, one way to proceed is to apply the commodity flow method "top down" by separating out a single, well-defined product and assessing whether the existing detailed information for this product is consistent with the aggregated goods and services account. The product chosen should be one of major importance for the economy (energy products, grain, steel or metals, fish, cement, etc.), for which, because of its importance, detailed information may be available from several sources. This may have repercussions for the residual "aggregate product", *i.e.*, all other products for which a more detailed supply-use balance cannot be derived. In the same way, it may be possible to separate the intermediate consumption for a strategic industry from the total. This breakdown on the supply and use side could be continued to embrace more products and industries. The strength of this partial approach is that it may reveal counterbalancing statistical discrepancies that were previously concealed.

5.136. The underlying message is that organising all available data into a supply and use framework makes it possible to combine information on the characteristics of the various products with the accounting rules of the system to fill in empty cells for which no direct information is available.

5.7.3. *Choice of Product, Industry, and Final Use Classifications*

5.137. The choice of product and industry classifications is a crucial step in setting up a supply and use system. Once these classifications are fixed, they determine the main characteristics of the system, and all data entering into the system have to be adjusted and classified accordingly. The main issues to be considered in this connection are:

- The supply and use tables cannot have a more detailed industrial breakdown than the basic statistics. The product grouping is usually decided by the level of detail existing in statistics on domestic output as international trade statistics typically have much greater detail. For services a special approach may be needed, as *product* statistics do not usually exist. Consequently service products may have to be defined in accordance with an *industrial* classification such as ISIC Rev 3.

- Aggregation means a loss of information and so the supply and use system should be as detailed as possible. Having more detail does not necessarily require substantial additional work. Some limitations which compilers had to face in the past due to limited capacity of computing capacity are no longer relevant.

- When defining the industries and product groups, certain technical properties should be taken into account, such as distinguishing separately products that have only one use, or one predominant use. For practical reasons and to meet users' need, it is advisable to choose an industrial classification at least as detailed as the ISIC two-digit level.

- Exports and imports can be shown with finer product detail than for domestic production. This can help in the process of balancing supply and uses.

5.138. In the choice of product classification and the level of detail, the classifications for which price indices are collected should also be taken into account. Price indices are required for product groups in the calculation of volume measures based on the balanced supply and use table. For final expenditures, exports usually appear in only one column and thus represent no classification problem. For analytical reasons as well as for compilation reasons, it may desirable to have a sub-classification of exports. Gross fixed capital formation can be classified according to both the type of capital goods (indispensable) and according to the kind of activity of the producer acquiring the asset. Changes in inventories raise special problems in relation to estimates by detailed products. Usually the product specification for inventories is determined taking into account the assumptions about the product composition for either finished products or raw materials in the individual branches for which information about changes in inventories may exist.

5.7.4. *Entering the Data*

5.139. Defining the classifications determines the framework. Once the framework is determined, it is possible to enter all existing data into the tables. Data on supply and use of products that are available from international trade statistics and production statistics should be entered into the system at the maximum level of detail. Some sources provide complete or partial data on both supply and use of products. For example, supply and use of electricity, at least by main categories of use, may be available from producers or distributors of electricity. Detailed product classifications may provide the potential to fill in the cells for the supply and uses of certain products having a close link, or even a one-to-one correspondence, between product types and uses, although valuation of demand and supply may differ due to trade and transport margins and taxes and subsidies on products. For example, imports of aircraft will almost always be shown as fixed capital formation.

5.140. Obviously, not all cells in the supply and use tables can be completed directly using existing sources. Particularly when the system is first established, the greatest challenge is the establishment of the initial input structures and the structure of final expenditures by product. Before these structures can be established, estimates have to be made for all the important totals and sub-totals, namely, total gross output and total intermediate input for all industries. Furthermore, estimates for all categories of final expenditures are needed. If national accounts statistics are compiled at a detailed level, most of these aggregates (many of which may have been estimated using indirect compilation methods presented in the previous sections), should be available. The initial estimates of supply and use tables do not necessarily need to show a balance between supply and use.

5.141. Preferably, as soon as the dimensions of the supply and use framework have been decided, a software system should be designed to conduct consistency checks.

5.7.5. Balancing

5.142. After all available data and estimates have been entered in the system, inconsistencies appear that need to be removed. This process is known as *balancing*. It is necessary to distinguish between the balancing for the *benchmark year* (for which the source data are usually more comprehensive) and for *current years* outside the benchmark year where less comprehensive data are available. Balancing the benchmark year requires more human resources and time than non-benchmark years because the benchmark year has to be built from the beginning whereas for the following years the point of departure is a balanced system for the preceding year. This is, in particular, the case for the use table. The supply table is more likely to be covered by current data.

5.143. Even though the system takes advantage of the fact that supply and use for each individual product group must balance, this does not necessarily imply that the way to proceed is to balance all products one by one. In fact, to follow such a procedure would make the balancing work overwhelming and impossible to handle in practice. The balancing procedures must simultaneously take into account many restrictions imposed on the system by other commodity balances and the initial estimates for the aggregates and sub-aggregates of the system. This is exactly what makes the balancing efficient, and, therefore, also underlines the need for a relatively complicated computerised balancing system. For non-benchmark years, balancing usually uses more implicit assumptions than for the benchmark year, based on relations established for the base year (such as input/output ratios). This does not, however, mean that these relations are also maintained in the results for the current years, only that they are taken as the point of departure and subsequently adjusted as needed to obtain balance for the current year.

5.144. It is usually possible and advisable to establish, a priori, balanced sub-systems for important products such as energy products, some agricultural products and minerals.

5.7.6. Calculations of Volume Measures

5.145. For the conversion of current price estimates to constant prices, the most detailed price information available from the consumer price index, the producer price index, and import and export price or unit value indices should be used. In practice, each product balance is associated with one or more price indices depending on whether there are price indices available for specific sources of supply or specific kinds of uses. Thus, imports are usually deflated separately using either proper price or unit value indices, while domestic output can be deflated with prices from the consumer or producer price indices.

5.146. A similar situation prevails for final uses such as household consumption and fixed capital formation. For the items in the product balance that cannot be associated with a separate price index, a residual price index can be calculated in such a way that the product group will also be balanced in volume terms. Ideally, compilation of supply and use tables at current prices should be done together with the compilation of supply and use tables in volume terms, because these two dimensions, combined with the price dimension, can provide useful plausibility checks on the data through the implicit growth rates.

Chapter 6

ASSESSMENT AND IMPROVEMENT OF DATA COLLECTION PROGRAMME

6. ASSESSMENT AND IMPROVEMENT OF DATA COLLECTION PROGRAMME

6.1. Introduction

6.1. This chapter deals with the fourth line of action in the NOE measurement strategy, namely improvement of the basic data collection programme so as to reduce the amount of production that is non-observed. Assessment of non-observed activities and their indirect measurement during compilation of the national accounts (as described in Chapters 4 and 5) will almost certainly reveal weaknesses in the basic data. Addressing these weaknesses is the basis for long-term improvement in NOE measurement. Thus the objective of this chapter is to provide an *assessment template* for systematic review of the basic data collection programme and identification of potential improvements. The template comprises a description of the desirable components and characteristics of the programme, accompanied by a list of *review points*. Whereas the presentation in Chapters 4 and 5 are from a national accountant's perspective, in this chapter the discussion is aimed primarily at the survey statisticians responsible for data collection.

6.2. Exhaustive coverage of activities within the production boundary is just one aspect – admittedly a very important aspect – of data quality. Thus, NOE measurement cannot be handled independently of other quality assessment and improvement initiatives. It must be harmonised with them. There is a wide range of survey design and quality management documentation available, including the new IMF Data Quality Assessment Framework summarised in Chapter 4. However, such material covers a much broader range of quality issues than simply exhaustive coverage. Thus, the aim of this chapter is to extract the essentials that have some bearing, directly or indirectly, on NOE measurement and to present them within a comprehensive assessment template that takes account of other quality improvement considerations.

6.3. The assessment template covers the following points:

- *Statistical data requirements*. Identifying the data requirements of major users is the starting point for defining programme content. Inadequate understanding of user needs may result in misallocation of resources and outputs that do not match user expectations. In a nutshell, how much do users care about the NOE and are their data needs being met?

- *Institutional framework*. The legislative framework, organisational structure, planning and quality management practices all affect the ability of a programme to meet its user needs efficiently and to deal with problems such as the NOE. In short, will the institutional framework support efforts to improve NOE measurements and, if not, how can it be changed to do so?

- *Conceptual framework*. Identification and use of appropriate standards is vital for integration of data from the usual wide range of data sources. Does the programme make use of the international standards?

- *Data collection mechanisms*. Choices have to be made in the selection of administrative and survey data sources. Have the right choices been made from the NOE perspective?

- *Survey frames*. The quality of the business register is the main determinant of the coverage of enterprise surveys and the extent to which the data they produce are consistent with one another. A general-purpose household area frame provides an operational integrating framework for household surveys and determines their coverage. Are improved survey frames likely to be a source of significant improvements in dealing with the NOE?

- *Survey design principles and practices.* Good survey design is vital in addressing coverage, response and reporting problems whether or not they are NOE related. Are there improvements in survey design practices that could address NOE problems?

- *Enhancing programme content.* Assessment of the extent to which the basic programme provides the exhaustive coverage required for the national accounts was discussed in Chapter 5. Having done everything possible to improve existing surveys and data from administrative sources, what new data collections should be added?

- *Relationship with* NOE *analytical framework.* The final section relates the assessment back to the analytical framework.

6.2. Statistical Data Requirements

6.4. The starting point for the review of the data collection programme is the set of economic statistics required by the users and the uses to which these statistics are put. Users and uses define the data requirements that the programme has to address. Given that there are many diverse users and uses, it is helpful to classify them into broad categories. The significance of the various components of the NOE on the statistical outputs can then be more easily assessed in terms of their effects on the major types of use and users.

6.5. As an example, the major uses to which users put the data can be classified as macro-economic analysis (structural and short term), micro-economic analysis (short term, industry based, activity based, and business dynamics), and regional analysis. Users can be grouped into seven broad headings:

- internal statistical office users, specifically including the national accounts area;
- national government – the national bank, and the ministries dealing with economic affairs, finance, treasury, industry, trade, employment, environment;
- regional and local governments;
- business community – individual large businesses and business associations;
- trade unions and non-governmental organisations;
- academia – universities, colleges, schools, research institutes, etc.;
- media – newspapers, radio and TV stations, magazines, etc.;
- general public;
- international organisations.

6.6. The table in Annex 3.1 indicates how, based on broad use and user categories, data requirements may be summarised. This table should be regarded as illustrative only. In fact, there is no international standard stipulating exactly what statistics a national statistical office should produce, although the Special Data Dissemination Standard (SDDS) and the General Data Dissemination Standard (GDDS), created and maintained by the International Monetary Fund (2002*a*, 2002*b*), and the Eurostat (1998) statistical requirements compendium go part way in this direction.

6.7. From the perspective of exhaustive measurement of the GDP the most important data requirements are those associated with GDP compilation. However, although the 1993 SNA defines precisely the structure of the national accounts and the corresponding data components, it does not specify how or at what level of detail these data should be obtained. The table in Annex 3.2, prepared by the Interstate Statistical Committee of the Commonwealth of Independent States, is an example of how the basic data requirements may be more explicitly identified. The first column of the table summarises the minimum data needed for compilation of the production account, the generation of income account (compiled for industries or economy as a whole) and the goods and services account. With these data, GDP can be estimated by the three methods. Annex 3.3 indicates the minimal data for compilation of sector accounts.

6.3. Institutional Framework

6.3.1. *Legislation*

6.8.   Satisfying data requirements requires an institutional framework within which to collect, process and disseminate the data. An important element of this framework is the legislation within which the statistical office operates. Typically it is proclaimed in one or more *statistics acts* and in accompanying or supplementary government regulations, which should include:

- the right to collect data;
- the obligation to ensure that the data collected are used only for statistical purposes except with the express permission of respondents and except for certain types of data that are in any case publicly available;
- the right to access for statistical purposes data that have been collected for government administrative purposes;
- the obligation to ensure that no individual data are released either consciously or unwittingly;
- freedom from political interference in the timing or content of data releases, *i.e.*, independence of the statistical office from political pressure;
- designation of an agency responsible for overall co-ordination of official statistics within the country; and
- arrangements for appointment and removal of the chief statistician of that agency that do not depend upon political whim.

6.9.   Without such safeguards it is difficult to address data problems. Eurostat (1999a) presents a generic statistics act that can be used as a starting point for development of a statistics act tailored to a specific country.

6.3.2. *Organisational Structure*

6.10.   Another aspect of the institutional framework is the organisational structure of the national statistical office. Typically it comprises the following functions:

- economic data collection, processing and analysis – comprising *subject matter area*s concerned with the collection of economic data by surveys and from administrative sources and the processing and analysis of these data;

- social data collection, processing and analysis – comprising subject matter areas, concerned with social data;

- national accounts, balance of payments and economic analysis – areas concerned with integration and analysis of data from surveys and administrative sources;

- marketing and dissemination – assessing user requirements, segmenting users into groups, managing output;

- concepts, standards and methods – developing, promoting, and monitoring use of a common conceptual framework, survey best practice, and quality management;

- information technology – developing and promoting effective use of data processing, data and metadata management, and communications technology;

- management and services – budgeting, planning, personnel, pay, training, etc. – required in any organisation, not just a statistical agency.

6.11.   These functions may be combined or split in a variety of different ways. For example, the economic and social subject matter areas may not be separated and instead there may be a split into business register, data collection and capture, and data analysis functions. The functions may be divided between central and regional offices. Furthermore, they may be divided among several agencies, hence the need to distinguish the *national statistical office* – the lead statistical agency – from the *national statistical system*. However, regardless of the particular arrangements, all the functions should be present. The fundamental principles of offical statistics (United Nations Statistical Commission, 1994) provide guidance.

Review points

- *Does the statistical office recognise and attach appropriate importance to these functions in its structure? Is the present structure out of date? Does it enable communication within and between functions, in particular between data collection and national accounts areas?*

- *Does the structure unnecessarily constrain conception and implementation of improvements in NOE measurement?*

6.3.3. *Planning Framework*

6.12.   The national statistical office should have a strategic master plan that outlines the major initiatives and statistical outputs envisaged over the next five years or so. It should be accompanied by a multi-year plan that indicates the provisional allocation of resources by project and function over the next, say, three years, and by a definitive allocation of the budget for the current year. The multi-year plan and budget allocations should be updated on an annual cycle. They provide the basis for and expression of priority setting amongst the many ongoing programmes and development initiatives that are competing for resources. The Multi-annual Integrated Statistical Programme (MISP) framework developed by Eurostat (1999*b*) indicates the sort of information that needs to be developed and maintained.

Review points
- *Does the statistical office have a multi year plan? if not, this is a priority.*
- *Are there procedures for involving external and internal data users in the planning process?*
- *How can NOE related initiatives best be included within the planning framework?*

6.3.4. *Quality Consciousness and Organisational Culture*

6.13.   The performance of an organisation is often thought of in terms of two aspects – effectiveness (the organisation is doing the right thing) and efficiency (the organisation is doing the thing right). To ensure effective and efficient operations a statistical office should have a quality programme. Measurement of the NOE should be seen as just one, albeit very important, factor in the quality programme. The quality programme should be based on the sort of principles that have been popularised in the total quality management literature over the last two decades, including (see Colledge and March, 1993):

- Customer (user) focus: user satisfaction is a paramount goal; establish partnerships with users; define quality of statistical products in terms of fitness for use.
- Supplier (respondent) focus: establish a partnership relationship with respondents by ensuring that the reporting characteristics of respondents are well understood, that respondents are motivated to report, and that the burden on them is minimised.
- Internal partnerships: improve the quality of the data collection processing and dissemination process by considering it to be a chain of customer-supplier interfaces.
- Continuous improvement: define quality and encourage small scale initiatives to improve it, develop and use quality measures.
- Reengineering: start from scratch in large scale redesign initiatives.
- Total employee involvement: value all staff members, promote their involvement, give them responsibility and resources to make improvements, and recognise their achievements.
- Quality management programme: the programme does not necessarily involve a "quality unit", but it does require quality to be championed and budgeted by a very senior staff member or committee so that it is high on the organisation's agenda and permeates the organisation's culture.

6.14.   At the core of a quality programme is the definition of *data output quality*. Here quality is interpreted broadly in terms of fitness for use, not just accuracy. As elaborated by Eurostat (1999*d*), Brackstone (1999), Carson (2001) and others, the dimensions of quality typically include:

- relevance: the data serve well the identified needs;
- accuracy: the data are sufficiently accurate for the purposes to which they are targeted and their limitations in respect of accuracy are made known;
- timeliness: the data are produced sufficiently early to be useful;
- presentation: the data are well publicised, easy to access and easy to understand;
- consistency: the data are not subject to major revisions or to differences across the various media in which they are disseminated; and
- coherence: the data can be analysed meaningfully in conjunction with previous data from the same survey or other related data.

6.15.   Data output quality is a measure of the effectiveness of a statistical office's performance. The efficiency aspect is reflected in the quality of the organisation's internal organisation and processes. Aspects of this are as follows.

- The statistical office is a *learning organisation* where creative ideas are encouraged and nurtured, where problems can be openly discussed and not underground for fear of repercussions.
- There is communication, co-operation and data sharing between staff in all areas, and at all staff levels, from the highest levels of management down. Staff are aware of data and developments in other areas that might help them in their own work.
- Staff in data collection areas go beyond their traditional data gathering and processing role and assess the quality of their statistical outputs. Where possible, they cross check their outputs with data from other areas in the agency, knowing the degree of consistency they should expect to find.
- Staff are open to new ideas. They do not have a tendency to defend existing methodologies simply because of workload pressures and the need to meet tight deadlines.
- Senior management play a leadership role in developing an environment where critical assessment of existing methodologies is encouraged, together with a willingness to accept/ adopt changes required to resolve identified short-comings in the basic data collection programme.

6.16.   Fellegi (1996) elaborates the characteristics of a well-run statistical agency and Fellegi and Ryten (2001) describe an assessment of a national statistical office in these terms.

Review points
- *Are the survey statisticians responsible for analysing and validating the statistical outputs they produce?*
- *Are the survey statisticians and national accounts in open and regular two-way communication, sharing data, problems and ideas? In particular are survey staff aware of and involved in addressing NOE problems?*
- *Is open expression of problems possible? Are creative ideas encouraged and followed up?*
- *Are senior managers fully supportive of quality management in general and are they funding initiatives to improve measurement of the NOE in particular?*
- *Do senior managers deal effectively with critical comment from users about the quality of the statistics produced by the agency, in particular with criticisms that the NOE is not being measured?*
- *Is staff adequately trained in survey design and operations? Are survey and questionnaire design guidelines and manuals readily available?*

6.3.5. **Data and Metadata Management**

6.17.   Data acquired from individual surveys and administrative sources are typically processed and analysed in separate organisational units each focusing on a particular subject matter area. To ensure appropriate communications between these staff and with the final users, all the *metadata* – *i.e.*, the information about the definitions, sources and methods required for accessing, combining, interpreting and using the data – should be stored in a commonly accessible *metadata repository*. Furthermore, to ensure that the resulting statistical outputs may be readily combined and viewed collectively, they should be brought together in an *output database* that can be accessed by all staff and, with appropriate security and possibly payment, by external users. This database may physically contain the data. Alternatively, it may be a conceptual store that appears to be a single integrated repository but that actually interfaces seamlessly with data physically stored in a number of separate databases. An integrated output database facilitates *horizontal* confrontation of data from different sources and encourages survey staff to go beyond the purely *vertical* data flows within individual organisational units.

Papers by Sundgren (1997) and Colledge (1999) provide further details and there is more documentation available in a Eurostat (1999*c*) handbook on information technology, also from the Statistical Output Database Seminar Series (Statistics Canada, 2001) and the UN/ECE Work Sessions on Statistical Metadata (UN/ECE, 2002).

Review points

- Are the definitions, sources and methods metadata required to identify and analyse NOE problems readily available?
- Are the data required to identify and analyse NOE problems readily available and easy to combine and analyse?

6.4. Conceptual Framework

6.4.1. *Introduction*

6.18.   The effective integration of data from a broad range of administrative sources and statistical surveys depends upon the definition and use by a statistical office of a common conceptual framework for its data collection programme. This framework should be based on the relevant international standards, supplemented as necessary by country specific standards and operational practices.

6.19.   International standards alone are not sufficient. For example, the 1993 SNA defines the data items required to compile GDP, but it does not specify how they are to be obtained from the data actually available in business records, which are based on country specific legislation and accounting standards. It indicates the need for a breakdown of large enterprises into smaller producing units, but it does not specify how these units should be derived. It designates Resolution II of the Fifteenth (1993) International Conference of Labour Statisticians as the basis for defining the informal sector, but does not specify a precise operational definition. It stipulates the use of ISIC Rev 3 for classification by industrial activity but provides no standards for classification by geography or size, which are also needed for sampling and analytic purposes. In summary, the international standards need to be extended along the lines described in the following paragraphs.

6.4.2. *Statistical Units*

6.20.   As noted in Section 2.3.2, the 1993 SNA and ISIC Rev 3 suggest that an enterprise engaged in a range of different activities and/or at a number of different locations be divided into smaller, more homogeneous producing units that can be more precisely classified and that collectively represent the enterprise as a whole. Partitioning an enterprise by reference to its activities results in one or more *kind of activity* units. Partitioning an enterprise by reference to its various locations results in one or more *local units*. Using both methods of partitioning simultaneously results in one or more *establishments*. The 1993 SNA does not specify the operational procedures by which these statistical units should be delineated nor in what circumstances they should actually be used, although the European Council Regulation on Statistical Units (European Commission, 1993) provides some additional guidance.

6.21.   The simplest arrangement of all is to have no breakdown of enterprises at all and, for better partitioning of the data, to request each enterprise to report its data broken down by kind of activity and location. However, this is in effect asking each enterprise to make its own division without providing guidance on how to identify the units into which the enterprise's activities should be subdivided. It does not work well, as an enterprise cannot be expected to understand the breakdown that is required.

6.22.   On the other hand, dividing enterprises into kind of activity units, local units and establishments is heavily resource intensive in terms of both the investigations required and the computer systems. So the benefits of maintaining four different types of *standard statistical unit* may not justify the costs. There is no "right" set of statistical units, *i.e.*, *standard statistical units model*. In practice, a national statistical office must identify the standard statistical units that it intends to maintain, based on the enterprise structures that are typically found in the country and the size of the statistical office budget. It is even possible that an additional standard unit should be defined for statistical purposes, comprising groups of enterprises that are linked by ownership and control. This occurs when there are groups of enterprises that are, in effect, operating like single enterprises and need to be treated as such. In summary, the key principle in the choice of the statistical units model is that it should be as simple as possible whilst providing detail sufficient to meet user needs.

6.23. The practical process of dividing enterprises into smaller producer units (or combining them) in accordance with a statistical units model is referred to as *profiling*. Profiling procedures include the specifications for handing births, deaths, mergers and other changes of enterprises and any associated producing units, as discussed later.

6.4.4. Classification by Industry

6.24. ISIC Rev 3 provides the international standard classification by industry. It has four levels, which going beginning with the most detailed, are *Class*, *Group*, *Division*, and *Section* (*Tabulation Category*). Additional breakdown of some industry classes may be appropriate, depending upon the circumstances in the country.

6.4.5. Classification by Geography

6.25. As countries are quite different in shape and size, there is no international standard for geographical classification, although the EU provides guidance for its Member States. The statistical office should design and promote a national standard. The factors to be taken into account are:

- user needs for geographic breakdown;

- the area boundaries that are of most utility for sample stratification and data collection; and

- existing administrative boundaries – in addition to the fact that users may require data for administrative areas, it is cheaper for the statistical office if another organisation is responsible for defining and maintaining the geographical descriptions.

6.4.6. Classification by Size

6.26. In comparison with people, or even households, enterprises are very heterogeneous. In particular they can vary enormously in size and hence have very different impacts upon the statistical aggregates to which they contribute. Thus classification by size is vital for sampling and data collection purposes, and useful for analysis. The European Community Council Recommendation on structural business statistics (European Commission, 1997) specifies a classification by size, but there is no international standard. Experience suggests that, for most data collection purposes, a classification of producing units into four basic size groups based on number of employees along the following lines is useful:

- Large: more than X employees – typically X is in the range 50-200;

- Medium: less than X but more than Y employees – typically Y is in the range 20-100;

- Small: between Y and Z employees – typically Z is in the range 1-5;

- Micro: 0 employees.

6.27. Sometimes no distinction is made between small and micro and/or between medium and large. Sometimes the micro group is split into *market producers* and *producers for own final use*, in accordance with 1993 SNA (Para 6.52). All boundaries, X, Y, and Z, may be varied according to the industrial division of the units being classified in order that the producing units within the large (or large and medium) categories account for a specified percentage of the total production within each division.

Review Points

- *Are survey staff familiar with all aspects of the conceptual framework that are important in terms of NOE definition and analysis?*
- *Has a standard model for statistical units been defined? Is it too simple to provide adequate industrial and geographical breakdown of data? Is it too complex to be implemented in practice?*
- *Are classifications by industry, geography and size based on international and national standards? Does misclassification result in a significant undercoverage of enterprises?*
- *Have the procedures for transforming from business to national accounting concepts been defined and fully understood by survey and national accounts staff?*

6.5.   Data Collection Mechanisms

6.5.1. Introduction

6.28.   To produce the data outputs required, a statistical office collects and transforms basic data from the institutional units – corporations, government units, households and non-profit institutions serving households – in their roles as producers, consumers and investors, income earners, etc. There are two basic mechanisms for collecting economic data. They are, access to data already being collected for administrative purposes, and direct survey by the statistical office. The relative merits of these two mechanisms, and the basis for choosing between them, are discussed in the following paragraphs. In either case, however, the original providers of the data are the same, namely the institutional units, and the original sources of the data are the same, namely the records kept by these units. Typically, these records are set up by the units in response to legislated administrative requirements or simply for internal purposes to assist the units in managing their operations. In the case of corporations, for example, corporate law requires certain accounting reports, tax laws require income tax returns, and payroll deductions records for employees. Only a very few data items, for example opinions asked by business tendency surveys, do not depend upon such records. Where appropriate records are not maintained by the units being queried, the statistical office may persuade the respondents to set up special records for reporting purposes, for example to collect data on household spending patterns, but this is a difficult and expensive process. Thus, the records kept by enterprise and household units typically set a limit to the data that can actually be obtained from these unit, whatever the user requirements.

6.5.2. Administrative Sources

6.29.   Administrative processes are set up in response to legislation and regulation. Each regulation (or related group of regulations) results in a register of the institutional units – enterprises, persons, etc. – bound by that regulation and in data resulting from application of the regulation. Typically the register and data are referred to collectively by the statistical office as an *administrative source*. Administrative sources thus produce two types of data that can be used by the statistical office for statistical purposes:

- *registration data*, describing the institutional units that are required to register under the legislation – useful in building and maintaining lists of units as the starting points for surveys; and
- *transaction data*, describing the transactions administered under the legislation – useful to supplement or replace surveys.

6.30.   Each administrative register of enterprises is potentially usable by the statistical office to create and maintain a single statistical register as the starting point for data collection from enterprises. As elaborated later in this chapter, such a statistical register is commonly termed the *business register* and contains a list and details of enterprises (and other statistical units) on the basis of which survey samples are selected.

6.31.   Administrative data have some significant advantages relative to survey data. It is invariably cheaper for the statistical office to acquire data from an administrative source than to conduct a survey. Furthermore, administrative sources provide complete coverage of the population to which the administrative process applies and generally have very high response rates.

6.32.   On the other hand, the fact that the administrative processes are not under statistical office control limits their data coverage, content, quality, and consistency, and hence their use. An administrative process such as employer registration almost inevitably does not use the standard statistical definitions of the corresponding units and data items. It does not cover enterprises that are not employers. The administrative data referring to numbers of employees and wages and salaries will not be sufficient for all statistical purposes. The classifications of the data, for example by industry, are unlikely to be in exact accordance with statistical standards and may be not be based on coding procedures that are sufficiently reliable for statistical purposes. Furthermore, administrative processes are subject to change in response to new legislation without much (or any) regard for the impact on the statistical series.

6.5.3. *Statistical Surveys*

6.33.   Administrative data alone are not sufficient to meet all the needs of the basic programme. Thus they must be supplemented by statistical *surveys*,[1] *i.e.*, direct collections by the statistical office of data for statistical purposes. Conducting surveys is the main activity of the statistical office.

6.34.   The advantages of surveys over data from administrative sources are that the data items to be collected and the collection and processing procedures are under statistical office control. Also, in principle, respondents have less reason to deliberately misreport as the statistical office guarantees that the data it collects are strictly confidential and that they will not be used for administrative purposes. The disadvantages of surveys are higher costs, higher non-response rates, and additional respondent burden. Another problem is that in practice respondents may not trust the confidentiality clause.

6.35.   Given its budget, an NSO has to choose what surveys to conduct as part of its regular programme, and of what type these surveys should be. Surveys may be divided into five general types according to the units sampled and/or contacted: *enterprise surveys*; *household surveys*; *mixed household-enterprise surveys*; *indirect enterprise surveys*; and *price surveys*.

6.36.   *Enterprise surveys* are those in which enterprises (or statistical units belonging to these enterprises) constitute the sampled units, the reporting units from which data are obtained, and the observation units about which data are obtained. By contrast, in *household surveys* the sampled, reporting and observation units are households. In *mixed household-enterprise surveys* the sampled units and initial reporting units are households but the final observation units are enterprises. In *indirect enterprise surveys*, the reporting enterprises are asked for data about a different set of enterprises, *i.e.*, the observation units do not belong to the reporting units. An example would be a survey of city markets in which the market administrators are asked about the numbers and turnover of the market traders. *Price surveys* are those used to obtain data on prices, which may involve collection from enterprises or households, or direct observation of prices in the market.

6.37.   Surveys may also be classified as *list based* or *area based* depending upon the source of the list of enterprises or households from which the survey sample is drawn. In a list based survey, the initial sample is selected from a pre-existing list of enterprises or households. In an area based survey, the initial sampling units are a set of geographical areas. After one or more stages of selection, a sample of areas is identified within which enterprises or households are directly listed. From this list, the sample is drawn and data obtained.

---

1. Here, the term survey is assumed to include a census as a particular type of survey in which all units are in the sample.

6.38.   Each type of survey has its own particular characteristics and appropriate uses, as described in the following paragraphs.

Enterprise surveys

6.39.   In a list based enterprise survey, the initial sample is selected from a pre-existing list of enterprises. Typically the list is supplied from the business register (described later) that is maintained by the statistical office to support a range of surveys. Sometimes the survey list is derived from another administrative register. In an area based enterprise survey, a sample of areas is selected, within each of which enterprises are enumerated and then sampled. List based enterprise surveys are generally preferred to area based surveys for the following reasons:

- A list-based survey is more efficient from a sampling perspective. Because the area based approach involves cluster sampling, a larger sample is required to achieve a given level of precision than in the case of list based survey.
- It may be difficult to enumerate the enterprises within an area. While retail enterprises are likely to be readily visible, service enterprises that carry out their work in other locations are usually difficult to identify.
- Maintenance of a list of enterprises via a general purpose business register is cheaper than maintenance of an area based list, except for very small enterprises;
- Area based sampling is inappropriate for large or medium sized enterprises that operate in several areas because of the difficulty of collecting data from just those parts of the enterprises that lie within the areas actually selected. Furthermore, in order to avoid inadvertently missing parts of the enterprise, it is usually considered preferable to collect data from the whole of an enterprise not just a part of it.

6.40.   Thus, area based enterprise surveys are typically only used for collection of data from small enterprises (particularly agricultural smallholdings) and then only when no adequate list exists. Even in these circumstances, a mixed household-enterprise survey (described below) may be preferable. Those area based enterprise surveys that do exist are usually supplementary to a list based survey. An example is the long-standing area frame component of US Bureau of the Census Retail Trade Survey (Monsour, 1976).

Household surveys

6.41.   Household surveys are valuable in providing coverage of production by household enterprises that are too small to be recorded in any readily usable administrative list of enterprises. As household surveys exist for the purposes of collecting labour force and household expenditure data, additional questions related to production activities can be added at relatively little extra cost. This makes the use of a household survey generally cheaper than conducting an area based enterprise survey for the same purpose. However, the responding unit is a person in a household, not an enterprise, thus the data that can be collected about the activities of the enterprise may be correspondingly more limited.

6.42.   Some statistical offices maintain, or can access, population or household registers, at least for urban areas, and thus can conduct list-based household surveys. However, there are few such registers, so most household surveys are area-based.

Mixed household-enterprise surveys

6.43.   In a mixed household-enterprise survey, a sample of households is selected and each household is asked whether any of its members is an *entrepreneur, i.e.,* the sole proprietor of, or a partner in, an unincorporated enterprise. Data for all the enterprises thereby identified (or for a sub-sample of them) are then collected – either immediately from the respondent reporting on behalf of the enterprise or in a subsequent stage of data collection. Thus the feature of a mixed household-enterprise survey that distinguishes it from a household survey is that it collects information about enterprises *per se*, whereas a household survey collects information about the persons in a household, including possibly their personal contributions to enterprises.

107|

6.44.   Mixed household-enterprise surveys can thus provide coverage of small enterprises that are not included in list based enterprise surveys. However, they suffer from similar disadvantages to area based enterprise surveys, namely the inefficiency of the sample design and the difficulty of handling enterprises with production units in more than one location.

6.45.   In addition, an enterprise that is a partnership may be reported by each of its partners who may be in different households. The duplication of coverage that this implies has to be allowed for in the survey estimation system. This is the feature that distinguishes a mixed household-enterprise survey from an area based enterprise survey, as, in the latter case, enterprises are directly identified and listed (hopefully) without duplication. The process of producing an unduplicated list is the reason why area based enterprise surveys are generally more expensive than mixed household-enterprise surveys.

6.46.   In summary, mixed household-enterprise surveys are sometimes preferred to household surveys or area based enterprise surveys for estimating the production of small units that are excluded from list based enterprise surveys.

Indirect enterprise surveys

6.47.   An example of an indirect survey is where the enterprises that administer city markets are asked for data about the holders of the market stalls. This sort of survey provides only limited data about the observation units and often only in aggregate form.

Price Surveys

6.48.   Producer and consumer prices are usually collected by entirely separate surveys from those used to measure production or expenditure. With few exceptions, the survey samples are not probability samples – as the items selected for pricing and the enterprises from which the prices are collected are chosen purposively. Thus exhaustive coverage is not a goal.

Choice of survey type

6.49.   Table 6.1 illustrates how registration, sampling and surveying mechanisms could vary according to size of enterprise.

Table 6.1.   **Survey registration and collection characteristics by size of enterprise**

Registration and collection characteristics	Size of enterprise		
	Small and micro	Medium	Large
Sector	Household/corporate	Corporate	Corporate
Registered	No/yes	Yes	Yes
In business register	No/yes	Yes	Yes
Need for profiling	No	No	Yes
Survey type	Household/enterprise/mixed	Enterprise	Enterprise
Survey frame	Area/list	List	List
Sample unit	Household/enterprise	Enterprise	Enterprise/establishment
Reporting unit	Household/enterprise	Enterprise	Enterprise/establishment
Observation unit	Enterprise	enterprise	Establishment
Collection vehicle	Interview/self completion short form	Self completion long form	Self completion long form

Review Points

- *Have all administrative data sources been thoroughly examined to determine to what extent the data they contain can be used to support the statistical programme? Are there unused administrative sources that would help address NOE coverage and misreporting problems?*
- *Is there scope for partnerships with administrative agencies with a view to enhancing administrative sources to better satisfy statistical office data needs, in particular to address NOE coverage problems?*
- *Are the existing surveys the most appropriate type for the size of enterprise being contacted?*
- *Is there any way in which the present set of surveys can be combined or split thus releasing resources that could be applied to better NOE measurement?*
- *Are there any surveys in the present programme that can be eliminated totally, thus releasing resources that could be applied to better NOE measurement?*

6.6. Survey Frames and Business Register

6.6.1. *Survey Frame Requirements and Characteristics*

6.50.   The starting point for every survey is the *survey frame, i.e.,* the set of units subject to sampling and the details about those units required for stratification, sampling and contact purposes. The set of units and data are collectively referred to as *frame data*. The survey frame has more influence than any other aspect of survey design upon the coverage of the survey and hence on measurement of the NOE.

6.51.   Ideally the frame for a survey should contain all the units that are in the survey target population, without duplication or superfluous units. Associated with each unit should be all the data items required for efficient stratification and sample selection, for example, industrial, geographical and size codes, and these data should be accurate and up to date. Also associated with each unit should be the contact information – name, address and description of the unit, telephone and preferably a contact name and this should all be accurate and up to date. The extent to which survey frames in practice fall short of these requirements determines to a considerable extent the size of the NOE statistical deficiency problem area.

6.6.2. *Need for Business Register*

6.52.   The frame for (almost) every list-based enterprise survey belonging to the basic programme should be derived from a single general purpose, *business register* maintained by the statistical office.[2] There are two basic reasons for using a single business register. First, and most importantly, the business register operationalises the selected model of statistical units and facilitates classification of units according to the agreed conceptual standards for all surveys. If survey frames are independently created and maintained, there is no means of guaranteeing that the surveys are properly co-ordinated with respect to the coverage they provide. For example, there may be unintentional duplication of coverage by surveys that are supposed to have mutually exclusive target populations; some enterprises may fall between the cracks and not be covered by any survey. Second, it is more efficient for a single organisational unit within the statistical office to be responsible for frame maintenance than for each survey unit to create the frames for each of its surveys.

6.53.   In some countries, enterprise survey frames are derived from lists created during periodic enterprise censuses or from a specially maintained area frame. This is not an ideal arrangement. At the very least there should be a permanent business register containing the very large enterprises in view of the special treatment that these must be accorded on account of their geographic or industrial diversity.

---

2.   More precisely this should be referred to as a statistical business register to distinguish it from other (administrative) business registers, but when the context is clear the qualifier statistical is usually omitted.

6.54.   The only surveys that need not be based on a business register are those where the frame is derived from a well-defined administrative process and for which there is no requirement for co-ordination with other surveys. An example might be a survey of registered banking organisations that collects financial information specific only to the banking industry.

6.6.3. *Construction of Business Register*

6.55.   In principle, a business register can be built from scratch and maintained by the statistical office by enumerating all the enterprises within the country. However, this is an impossibly expensive process. Thus, the starting point for a business register is invariably one or more *administrative (business) registers*, that is registers of enterprises that are created and maintained to support the administration of regulations. The ideal administrative register would be one that provided complete, up to date coverage of all enterprises within the 1993 SNA production boundary without duplication or inclusion of defunct units, and that contained all the appropriate frame data, *i.e.*, classification and contact items required for sampling and data collection. However, given the broad range of enterprises within the production boundary, including household enterprises, even those with no market output, there is no such perfect source. Thus the choice of administrative registers on which to base the business register is a compromise.

6.56.   In some countries (for example France) the administrative register used by the statistical office to underpin the business register results from a regulation that specifically takes account of statistical needs and that is actually administered by the statistical office. In this case coverage and content are likely to be very good, though not perfect. In most countries, however, use is made of an administrative register maintained for another purpose, for example, value added tax in New Zealand and pay-as-you-earn income tax deductions in Australia. The resulting business register is inevitably deficient in coverage and content. The greater the difference between the set of enterprises defined within the 1993 SNA production boundary and the administrative register underlying the business register the greater the risk of non-observed production.

6.57.   The coverage and content of a business register can be improved by incorporating data from several administrative sources. This is illustrated by the following examples from Canada and Ukraine.

6.58.   Until June 1997 the Statistics Canada business register was based on one primary administrative source, namely payroll deduction accounts maintained by Revenue Canada. Thus it included only enterprises with employees. Since 1997 the business register has been using three additional sources maintained by Revenue Canada, namely incorporated tax accounts, goods and services tax accounts and import/export accounts. Blending these data was made possible by the introduction of a single business number for all enterprises. Castonguay and Monty (2000) provide more details.

6.59.   The State Statistics Committee of Ukraine maintains a business register for administrative and statistical purposes, known as the Unified State Register of Enterprises and Organisations of Ukraine. As described in World Bank (2001), the register is based on essentially three groups of administrative sources, but the Statistics Committee has responsibility for assigning the enterprise identification numbers.

- Most enterprises are registered under national legislation by the district or regional administration in their locality. Registration is a prerequisite for obtaining appropriate permissions, including being able to open a bank account. An enterprise may be registered as a legal person or may operate as an entrepreneurship under the legal framework of one or more natural persons. A legal person may also register a geographically separate part of itself (division, affiliate, etc.) as a local unit. The business register records all legal persons and local units thus registered.

- Enterprises engaged in certain regulated types of activity (*e.g.* banking, stock exchange) and other legal persons are registered by the bodies that administer the legislation under which they exist, *e.g.* Ministry of Justice, State Tax Administration, Ministry for Foreign Economic Relations and Trade, the State Committee for Religious Affairs Commission for Securities and the Stock Market. These are also recorded in the business register.

- Other enterprises, including government budgeted organisations, professional associations, non-market co-operatives and associations of apartment owners are not required to register formally their economic activities. However, these enterprises are required to complete a registration card for statistical purposes and they are recorded in the business register.

6.60. The key feature of both of these examples is a common enterprise identification coding system. In fact, use of multiple administrative sources is practical only if they are known to contain mutually exclusive sets of enterprises or if they share a common identification coding system that allows records for the same enterprise to be brought together. Experience has shown that trying to identify units across registers in the absence of a common identifier is impossibly expensive unless one of the registers is very small.

6.61. Even in the event of a common identification coding system, the use of multiple administrative sources should be undertaken with care. The gain in coverage resulting from the incorporation of data from an additional administrative source may not justify the increase in cost, particularly if the additional source is of poor quality. To take a specific example, based on the Ukrainian case described above. Suppose that the primary source for a business register is an administrative source based on legislation that requires all enterprises other than those in the household sector to register. Suppose, furthermore, that all individuals operating a household enterprise are required to file a personal tax return reporting their business earnings under personal tax legislation and that the resulting list of personal tax returns is made available to the statistical office. Should it be used as a second source? The benefit is that the tax returns provide coverage of household enterprises that are not covered by the primary source. Furthermore, there is no duplication, as no business will be registered to pay tax twice. However there are some quality problems to consider. Firstly there are likely to be a very large number of household enterprises of which quite a large proportion will go out of business each year. Thus the tax list contains many records that refer to inactive or dead businesses. Secondly, the industrial activity codes associated with the tax records are likely to be unreliable. Finally, there are a significant number of duplicates in the tax list because each of the business partners in joint proprietorship files a tax return. These quality problems have to be addressed if the tax list is to be incorporated in the business register and used for sampling purposes. The question to be answered is whether the additional coverage that the tax list provides justifies the costs of dealing with the problems that it brings. The alternative, and quite possibly better, approach is to obtain coverage of household enterprises through an entirely different mechanism such as an area frame household based survey.

6.62. The administrative register usually provides a list of legal entities, or some breakdown of these entities, to suit the administrative purpose for which it is designed. Typically it does not provide a list of enterprises broken down into establishments (or other statistical units) according to the statistical office units model and classified by activity. The information to support such a breakdown is gathered by business register staff using a form of register survey commonly referred to as *profiling*. Profiling procedures include all the rules for identifying the enterprises and other units defined in the statistical unit's model.

6.63. Profiling of enterprises often requires personal visits by statistical office staff and tends to be expensive and resource intensive. Thus typically it is restricted to large enterprises. It is rarely worthwhile subdividing medium or smaller enterprises, even if they are engaged in a variety of activities. First, the enterprise may not actually be able to report data for subdivisions of itself. Second, the loss of information by not subdividing is usually statistically insignificant and less than the errors in trying to obtain a subdivision.

6.64. In summary, the development of a business register can be seen along a continuum of gradually expanding scope and complexity:

- at a minimum, comprising a list of large enterprises divided into establishments;
- including medium and small sized enterprises derived from a single primary administrative source;
- including additional enterprises and data from supplementary administrative sources.

6.6.4. *Register Maintenance*: *Dealing with Enterprise Dynamics*

6.65.   Enterprises do not remain the same over time. The institutional units that own them may merge or amalgamate; they may split up or go out of business; they may change production activities, they may move location; and so on. New enterprises may be created (*births*), existing enterprises may cease to exist (*deaths*), and ongoing enterprises may change activity. Births, deaths, and changes of classification of enterprises must all be fully defined, and the corresponding business register procedures must be articulated. For example, it must be clearly stated whether an enterprise can be deemed to continue existence through a change of ownership, or whether a change of ownership inevitably means the death of an enterprise and the birth of another. For practical reasons, these procedures depend upon the sources of information for updating the business register. There are three basic sources, namely administrative sources, feedback from enterprise surveys, and business register surveys, as further described below.

Administrative Sources

6.66.   Given the large number of small enterprises in any market economy, it is vital that maintenance of the business register is automated to the maximum extent possible. This means that the frame data for small enterprises is maintained essentially by updating the register from administrative sources. Updating must be substantially automated as there are neither the time nor resources for register staff to verify all the frame data received from each source. Staff effort should be focussed on collecting and verifying frame data for the medium and larger enterprises that cannot be automatically updated.

6.67.   Administrative registers are notorious for containing inactive units. Thus, it is vital to make use of any information from administrative sources that can indicate whether the enterprise is active or not. For example, if the administrative source contains information about enterprises required to make payroll deductions on behalf of employees, then the date of the last recorded deduction and the total size of the deductions over the preceding year and a half are good indicators of enterprise activity. No deductions suggest that the enterprise is inactive, at least as an employer. This information can used to reduce the number of inactive enterprises.

6.68.   Notwithstanding comprehensive use of all the administrative sources available, the data obtained will be somewhat deficient in terms of activity classification, of contact information, and of the ability to track an unincorporated enterprise through a change of owners. The sale of an enterprise may well appear in the business register as the death of an enterprise and the birth of another, in line with the changes recorded in the underlying administrative register.

Feedback from enterprise surveys

6.69.   Feedback from enterprise surveys is a vital source for maintaining the business register as regards medium and large enterprises. However, for small enterprises that are sampled with probability less than one in repeating surveys, updating information has to be carefully applied so as not to cause bias in future survey samples. For example, suppose that when a particular quarterly survey is first conducted, the sample is found to contain 30% dead enterprises. (This is not an improbable figure.) Furthermore, suppose that, based on this sample information, the dead enterprises are removed from the business register, and that the survey sample for the next quarter comprises the 70% live units from the previous sample plus a replacement of the 30% drawn afresh from the register. This new sample contains about 9% (30% of 30%) dead units. Thus it is no longer representative of the population of dead enterprises on the register which is still nearly 30%, assuming that the survey sample is a relatively small proportion of the population. There are proportionally too many live enterprises in the sample. If the weighting procedures do not take this into account by, in effect, including the dead enterprises that were found in the samples, the result will be an upward bias in the estimates. Furthermore, the bias will get increasingly worse with each survey repetition.

Business register surveys and profiling

6.70.   Register updating information that cannot be obtained from the administrative source on which the register is based, or from survey feedback, has to be obtained by *business register surveys* (sometimes termed *nature of business surveys*) and profiling operations conducted by business register staff. Re-profiling large enterprises is a resource intensive activity but vital to keep the register up to date when institutional units owning large enterprises go through complicated changes like mergers, amalgamations, split-offs, etc.

6.6.5. *Area Frames for Household and Enterprise Surveys*

6.71.   For household surveys, the direct equivalent of the business register is a household register. However, in most countries there is no administrative source on the basis of which a household register can be readily constructed and maintained. Thus an area frame is commonly used as the starting point for household surveys, in particular for labour force and household budget surveys that are likely to form part of the basic programme.

6.72.   Construction and maintenance of a household area frame involves:

- division of the country into area segments, using information about the numbers of households in each segment obtained from the population and housing census;
- selection of a representative sample of segments;
- a two, three, or even four stage design – typically involving different treatment of urban and rural areas – the penultimate stage being enumeration of all households within the areas selected and the final stage being selection of a sample of these households;
- systematic maintenance of the selected areas and enumerated households;
- replacement of the frame following the next census when new information on the numbers of households in each area is available.

Review Points

- *Is there a single, general-purpose business register? At the minimum there should be a business register containing large, multi industry and/or multi region enterprises that require profiling.*
- *Is the business register based on the most suitable administrative sources? What enterprises within the 1993 SNA production boundary are not covered?*
- *What is the time lag between the birth of an enterprise and its appearance on the business register? Is this a serious source of undercoverage?*
- *What is the quality of industrial and size classification of the units in the business register? Is misclassification likely to be a source of NOE and if so how can it be addressed?*
- *What are the proportions of duplicate and inactive and dead units in the business register? Are they so large as to prevent efficient surveying of small enterprises?*
- *What are the proportions of units in the business register with wrong or missing contact details? Are they so large as to prevent efficient surveying of small enterprises?*
- *Are large units with multiple activities in more than one region profiled in accordance with the units model?*
- *Is the business register actually used as the source of survey frames for enterprise surveys, or do some surveys use other sources, thus risking duplication or omission in coverage?*
- *Is the information about enterprises obtained by surveys fed back to the register? If so, is it fed back in such a way as to avoid survey bias?*
- *Are area frame maintenance procedures adequate? Is the frame kept current or is there a risk that some areas that may be important from the NOE perspective are not properly represented?*

6.73.   Similar design principles are used for area based enterprise surveys as for area based household surveys. However, as the ultimate object is to enumerate enterprises, the size criterion used in delineating the areas is the number of enterprises rather than the number of households.

6.7.   Survey Design Principles and Practices

6.7.1. Introduction

6.74.   An important part of the statistical office infrastructure is a set of standards and best practices for survey design, data collection, processing and dissemination, and for the use of data from administrative sources. Application of internationally or nationally accepted methodology not only ensures that good practices are incorporated, it speeds up the process of survey design and it facilitates the use of standard computer software. However, although there are international regulations, standards, and guidelines providing a solid conceptual framework, as discussed in Chapter 2, there are relatively few that provide up to date guidance on survey design methodology and even fewer that deal with the use of administrative data. The survey design handbook by Eurostat (1998) is a good starting point. It references the relevant European Commission regulations, directives, and recommendations and other manuals. Beyond this, each statistical office must develop its own best practices. There are a number of documents produced by individual statistical offices that are useful. For example, "Quality Guidelines" (Statistics Canada, 1998) and "Statistical Quality Checklist" (Office of National Statistics, 1998) provide good design and planning checklists for surveys and administrative collections. There are also many textbooks on sample and survey design, of which Cochran (1977) is probably the best known. The following paragraphs provide a summary and review points applicable to each individual survey, with particular reference to the NOE measurement problems of undercoverage, non-response and misreporting.

6.7.2. Survey Objectives, Users and Uses

6.75.   The starting point for design of each survey within the programme is identification of the primary groups envisaged as users of the data and the basic uses that they make of the data. These uses are interpreted concretely in the form of the main statistical output tables that are required and the frequencies with which they are needed. The outputs are then expressed in terms of the input data to be requested from enterprises or households that will report to the survey.

6.76.   The target population, *i.e.*, the set of enterprises (or establishments), or households, about which the data are required, must be established. In particular, for enterprise surveys it must be decided if the estimates are to include small and micro enterprises. Typically this decision will depend on the balance between the extent of the deficiencies in the estimates caused by their omission and the costs of their inclusion. If they are excluded they become part of the NOE.

6.77.   The possible sources of the required data within the enterprises or households are identified and the feasibility of data acquisition thereby determined. Target response rates are specified, as should the maximum allowable response burden, particularly in the case of enterprise surveys. The resource and operational constraints within which the survey must operate have to be articulated as they influence all aspects of the design.

Review points
- *Can the target population be increased to provide better coverage of activities inside the 1993 SNA production boundary? If so, can the costs associated with providing the additional coverage be justified?*
- *Are the data items consistent with the 1993 SNA framework?*

6.7.3. Collection Vehicles and Questionnaire Design

6.78. For many enterprise surveys, *mail out mail back* of self-completion questionnaires is the most efficient collection method. Both the mail out and mail back may be by regular mail, telefax or e-mail depending on the respondents' preferences. For enterprise surveys covering a limited set of variables, collection by telephone may be possible and quicker, though usually more costly. In industrialised countries, personal interviews are usually inappropriate although they may be used in the collection of complex information, for example in conjunction with profiling very large enterprises to establish data supply procedures or to solve data supply problems. In developing countries on the other hand, labour costs are generally low enough to justify personal interviews particularly where literacy rates are low and enterprise accounting is not well developed. Rapid progress in electronic processing and communications technology means that the ultimate goal of automated data collection, direct from enterprise computer to statistical office computer, may soon become feasible.

6.79. For household surveys, personal or telephone interview is more frequently appropriate than mail questionnaires.

6.80. The design of questionnaires has a significant impact on response rates and incidence of misreporting. Questionnaire design is a specialised craft, involving knowledge of accounting practices (how enterprises or households keep their records), of the cognitive reactions of respondents (how they interpret questions), of subsequent data capture procedures (how easily statistical office staff are able to convert the responses into electronic form), and of the underlying data requirements (how data are to be transformed to 1993 SNA concepts). In a nutshell, the questionnaire must:

- indicate the purposes for which the data are being collected and the confidentiality provisions;
- motivate the recipient to respond, for example by explaining briefly the uses of the data; and the confidentiality provisions;
- be concise yet clear, with adequate but not too many instructions and an attractive layout; and
- ask only for data that are needed and that can reasonably be provided without undue respondent burden.

6.81. Questionnaire testing prior to its use, and evaluation after its use, are an essential part of the survey design process.

Revi12 0ew Points

- *Is every question on the questionnaire essential? Are there questions for which the responses are never captured or captured but never used, thus contributing to unnecessary respondent burden and increased risk of non-response?*
- *Could a questionnaire with a reduced set of questions be used for small enterprises, thus reducing the risk of non-response?*
- *Is the layout of the questionnaire attractive or does it contribute to non-response and misreporting?*
- *Does the questionnaire emphasise the confidentiality of the results?*
- *Does the questionnaire contain clear instructions? Do respondents understand the questions? Has their comprehension of the questions ever been assessed?*
- *Are answers to the questions readily available from the records maintained by enterprises?*

6.7.4. Sampling and Estimation

6.82. Typically the sample design for an enterprise survey has the following characteristics:

- identification of the set of enterprises in the business register that are in scope for the survey;
- stratification by size to improve sample efficiency, with not more than 4 strata recommended, unless the size measures on the business register are known to be very accurate;

- stratification by geographical area, primarily to meet user needs;
- stratification by industrial activity, primarily to meet user needs;
- identification of a *design data item* (usually the most important single item) on which to base the size of the sample and allocation across strata;
- sampling enterprises in the largest size strata with certainty (as data from these units are vital);
- sampling enterprises in the other size strata with probability depending upon size in such a way that, after weighting, the sampled units in different strata each tend to make roughly the same contribution to the total value of the design data item;
- control of sample overlap between successive occasions of repeated surveys, in particular, controlled rotation of the sample;
- control of sample overlap between separate surveys, for example by assignment of a random number to each enterprise used by all surveys for selection purposes.

6.83. In extracting the frame for an enterprise survey from the business register, it may be desirable to have a size cut-off, *i.e.*, not to include enterprises beneath a certain size because of the absence or unreliability of their frame data or the insignificance of the economic activity they represent. If significant economic activity is thus missed, an area-based survey can be used to provide complementary coverage. The choice of whether to provide complete coverage of all enterprises in the business register or to omit the small enterprises and carry out an additional area based survey, is based on the relative costs. The complete coverage option may involve sampling and collecting data from enterprises in a poorly defined list frame. The alternative option means having to create and maintain an area frame and separate survey.

6.84. For a household survey, the design features typically include:

- use of a general purpose household area frame;
- a two, three, or four stage design – typically involving different treatment of urban and rural areas, with the last stage being selection of households enumerated within selected areas;
- systematic rotation of samples.

Review Points
- *Could a census be replaced by a sample survey?*
- *Is the sample design appropriate?*
- *Are there procedures to control the number of questionnaires received by any one enterprise?*
- *What is the coverage of small enterprises? Is there scope for increasing coverage?*

6.7.5. *Respondent Interface: Data Collection, Capture, and Follow-up*

6.85. Effort should be made at every design stage to minimise response burden. For enterprises, the costs incurred in responding to surveys are every bit as real as the costs to the statistical office of collecting data. While households might not calculate the costs, a high response burden due to long and complicated questionnaires will negatively affect response rates. Response burden can be kept to a minimum by efficient sample design, clarity of questionnaires and flexibility in the time when interviews take place and in how respondents may supply information.

6.86. Before a respondent receives a questionnaire for the first time, especially one that is to be repeated, there should be some form of initial contact in which the purpose of the survey and the reporting arrangements are explained. Ideally enterprise respondents should be presented with a variety of response options, for example mail back, fax, telephone, from which they can choose the one that suits them best. This is more trouble for the statistical office but raises response rates. Likewise household respondents should have a choice of types and times of interview. Data capture procedures must be decided well in advance. There must be a well-defined, follow-up strategy, without which response rates are unlikely to be acceptable.

Review points

- *What is the current response rate? Should it be improved by introducing more rigorous follow up procedures?*
- *Are efforts being made to establish a good rapport with the enterprises in the sample?*
- *Have the procedures for handling non-response been articulated? Are non-responding enterprises all assumed to be inactive and imputed as zero thus contributing to the NOE?*

6.7.6. Editing, Imputation and Estimation

6.87.   The aims of editing are the detection and elimination of errors. Whilst editing is essential in assuring quality, there has to be a balance between the resources applied to editing and those invested elsewhere. For example it is better to spend effort in eliminating poorly phrased questions on a questionnaire than in trying to correct the wrong responses received as a result of the poor questions. In quality management terms, the focus should be on *upstream quality assurance* not on trying to "inspect the quality" into the data by editing.

6.88.   Large random errors by respondents can usually be picked up through plausibility checks on the data, for example by comparing the data reported with previous values, or the ratios of data reported with reasonable bounds for the types of enterprise. However, small random errors cannot be detected by these means. Neither can sustained, systematic errors, such as under-reporting incomes or exaggerating costs such as are associated with the NOE.

6.89.   It is impossible to eliminate all errors, nor is it necessary to do so as some errors have negligible effect on the estimates. Thus in enterprise surveys, editing effort should be focused on those particular data item responses, often termed *influential observations*, that will have the most significant impact upon the main estimates. In particular, very large enterprises are usually a source of influential observations and their data should be individually checked.

6.90.   *Outliers* are a particular category of influential observations for enterprise surveys. They are observations that are correct but that are *unusual* in the sense that they do not represent the population from which they have been sampled and hence will tend to distort the estimates. A typical example would be the response from a large retail supermarket that was by mistake included in the smallest size stratum and thus sampled as if it were a small store. The simplest treatment for outliers is to reduce their sampling weight to one so that they can only (and correctly) represent themselves. This requires reweighting of the rest of the sample appropriately to make up for the loss.

6.91.   The values of individual data items that are missing from the original response or believed to be in error should not be automatically interpreted as zeroes. They should be imputed by one of the following types of methods:

- (for monthly or quarterly repeating) carry forward the value for the enterprise from the previous survey occasion, possibly adjusting the value to reflect the average increase (decrease) of the data item reported by other respondents in the stratum;
- (for monthly or quarterly repeating) carry forward the value for the enterprise from the same survey occasion in the previous year, adjusted to reflect the average increase (decrease) of the data item in the stratum;

- if no previous data for the enterprise is available, impute the value from a responding enterprise that is judged to be similar, or impute the stratum mean.

6.92.   Preferably imputation should be automated, not only to save time but also to ensure consistency of treatment.

6.93.   Total non-response from an enterprise or household that has never responded is not usually dealt with by imputation but rather by re-weighting the sample to include only the respondents. This approach can also be used to deal with missing individual data items but is not commonly used, as it requires different weights for different data items on an individual record. It is essential that the weights be revised to reflect the absence of non-respondents and the reweighting of outliers. If not, estimates will be biased towards zero, contributing towards the NOE.

Review Points
- *Are influential observations identified and dealt with?*
- *Are item non-responses being inappropriately imputed as zeros thus contributing to the NOE?*
- *Are the data being appropriately reweighted to allow for non-response?*

6.7.7. *Analysis, Dissemination, Revision, and Evaluation*

6.94.   One of the best ways of finding the strengths and deficiencies of data is to use them in a wide range of analyses. Comparisons with data from other sources are invaluable in checking the quality and coherence of the data and identifying possible problems. The national accounts provide a very good framework for confrontation of data from different sources.

6.95.   Dissemination is an important aspect of quality defined in the broad sense. Unless users are aware the data exist, are able to access them and to understand them, then the survey might just as well not have taken place. User needs regarding format, media and style should be identified and taken into account in building the dissemination mechanisms. Confidentiality of data for individual enterprises or households must be preserved or respondents will fail to report or will misreport. Data items should be accompanied by metadata defining them and explaining how they have been produced, thus enabling users to determine how suitable the data are for their purposes.

6.96.   The revision policy for each series has to be articulated in accordance with user needs. Too many large revisions suggest that timeliness should be reduced to improve accuracy. No revisions suggest timeliness could be improved.

6.97.   Evaluation completes the survey design cycle. The outputs are evaluated in terms of user requirements, respondent burden and resources available. Possible improvements are identified, prioritised and implemented for subsequent survey repetitions.

Review Points
- *Are the data weaknesses encountered during national accounts compilation being fed back and discussed with survey staff?*
- *Are adequate metadata made available to users? Can users readily see the scope for NOE?*
- *Are NOE problems being articulated and considered during the evaluation process?*
- *Are contact points for further information publicised?*

6.7.8. Data from Administrative Sources

6.98. With the possible exception of sampling, the design principles for surveys have their counterpart in relation to the collection of data from administrative sources. Even sample design is appropriate in cases where data from an administrative source are actually sampled. The main challenge is to persuade the administrative authorities to take account of the statistical needs and to apply appropriate design principles. Thus, for each particular source used, the statistical office should establish an agreement with the corresponding administrative agency. The agreement should specify the content and quality of the data to be provided, the mechanism for transfer of the data from the administrative source to the statistical office, and the procedures for introducing changes to the administrative processes in such a way as to minimise the impact upon the statistical office. If possible, the statistical office should influence the legislation itself in order to secure the best possible supply of data.

Review Point

  • Are NOE *related data problems being discussed with administrative authorities?*

6.8. Additional Surveys and Administrative Data Collections

6.99. The previous sections in this chapter focus on potential improvements that can be brought about through better organisation of the existing data collection infrastructure and programme. This section considers enhancements through additions to the programme, either new surveys or use of different administrative sources. Such additions can be conducted on a regular or occasional basis. Additional regular surveys augment the basic data output and may thus contribute to reduction in the incidence of non-observed activities. Occasional surveys may contribute to better understanding and measurement of non-observed activities in compiling the national accounts, *i.e.*, reduction of non-measured activities. The decision whether a new survey or administrative collection should be regular or occasional will vary according to the particular situation of the national statistical office.

Additional Regular and Occasional Surveys

6.100. The existing programme of regular surveys should be examined to determine what (if any) additional surveys should be conducted to fill the data gaps. Annex 3.4 gives an indication of the sort of regular surveys included in the basic programme of a national statistical office in a developed country. The appropriate choice will depend upon the size and nature of the NOE related data problems, the options for using administrative sources, the potential respondent burden involved, and the resources available. Some examples of surveys that can be introduced on a regular or occasional basis are as follows:

  • City market surveys to measure retail trade in small enterprises. Booleman (1998) provides an example.

  • Surveys of services to measure turnover by small enterprises. Masakova (2000) provides an example of a sample survey for small enterprises.

  • Agricultural production surveys to measure informal sector and household production of specific commodities for own use. Masakova (2000) provides examples.

  • Informal sector surveys. Specialised surveys of the informal sector conducted occasionally or regularly may also serve to improve the information base for the national accounts. These are described in detail in Chapter 10.

119

• Qualitative surveys. Opinion surveys can be used to monitor incidence and causes of non-observed production, typically asking respondents for their impressions of the industry as a whole rather than their personal involvement in the underground or illegal activities. Examples were given in Chapter 4 and are further discussed in Chapter 8 in connection with underground production.

Additional Administrative Sources

6.101. It is also appropriate to evaluate administrative data sources not currently being accessed by the statistical office and to determine to what extent the data they contain could be accessed and used to support the basic data collection programme in general and to reduce NOE in particular. Annex 3.5 gives an indication of the sort of administrative sources included in the basic programme of a developed western national statistical system. The appropriate choice will depend upon the size and nature of the data problems relating to the NOE, the availability, accessibility, content and coverage of the administrative sources, the options for direct survey, and the resources available.

6.9.   Relationship to NOE Analytical Framework

6.102. In concluding this chapter, it is worthwhile reiterating what the basic programme can be expected to measure and its inherent limitations in terms of the NOE problem areas and the types of statistical deficiency.

Undercoverage of enterprises

6.103. Although it is undoubtedly possible to make improvements, the basic data collection programme cannot be expected to deal completely with undercoverage of enterprises. The business register can only provide coverage of those small enterprises that are included in the administrative sources on which it is based. Whilst it may be possible to mount an occasional large-scale household survey to cover the missing small enterprises, including those involved in production for own final use, it is unlikely that this is affordable as a regular part of the basic programme. Adjustments must be made within the national accounts to compensate for undercoverage of the basic programme, as described in Chapter 5.

Underreporting by enterprises

6.104. Likewise, although editing and plausibility checks can pick up many reporting errors, the basic programme cannot provide a mechanism for detecting sustained, deliberate, and widespread underreporting by enterprises of their activities. Again these require special investigations and adjustments within the national accounts.

Non-response by enterprises

6.105. On the other hand, non-response problems should be fully addressed within the basic programme. Entries missing from returned questionnaires should be appropriately imputed and the data re-weighted to allow for questionnaires that have not been returned. Thus non-response should not be a source of non-observed activities for which corrections have to be made during the national accounts compilation.

6.106. In summary, improvements to the basic programme are the appropriate way to tackle all NOE problems due to statistical deficiencies. There is also scope to address, in part at least, the coverage problems that arise because of the small size and lack of registration of enterprises that are in the informal sector or involved in household production for own final use. However, special surveys and adjustments within the national accounts are needed to deal with most underground and illegal activities.

6.107. Prioritisation and choice of options for improvement depend upon the particular situation of the national statistical system, including the current state of its basic programme, the likely magnitudes of the improvements in terms of reduction of non-observed activities, the resource implications, and the resources available. This is further discussed in the following chapter. Furthermore, as previously noted, the NOE measurement programme must be blended with, and considered a part of, the statistical office strategic objectives and quality improvement framework as a whole.

Chapter 7

IMPLEMENTATION STRATEGY

7. IMPLEMENTATION STRATEGY

7.1. Introduction

7.1.   This is the last chapter in the sequence describing the five lines of action for achieving exhaustive estimates of GDP by better measurement of the NOE. Chapter 3 defined the NOE problem areas and illustrated how they could be examined through the use of an analytical framework. Chapter 4 summarised techniques for assessing the national accounts from the perspective of non-observed and non-measured activities. Chapter 5 described national accounts compilation methods aimed at eliminating non-measured activities. Chapter 6 showed how the basic data collection programme could be improved to reduce non-observed activities. Whereas these chapters dealt with NOE measurement from a conceptual viewpoint, this chapter is concerned with operational considerations. Its intention is to help survey statisticians and national accountants set priorities and develop action plans to deal with the NOE in their particular circumstances. It outlines the elements of a comprehensive NOE measurement strategy, through the systematic formulation of short and long term initiatives across the national statistical system.

7.2.   Since the mid-1970s numerous attempts have been made to improve measurement of the NOE, both in the context of compiling exhaustive national accounts and in obtaining stand-alone estimates of specific NOE problem areas such as underground or informal sector production. Review of the vast body of literature indicates that the results of NOE measurement programmes are varied and difficult to compare, either between countries or even within the same country over time. However, there are certainly some lessons to be learned, for example those described by the Organisation for Economic co-operation and Development (1997) in relation to countries in transition. Common problems with NOE measurement programmes include the following:

- *Lack of consultation with major external users*. Major data users are not brought into the process through consultation on their concerns and priority needs with respect to NOE measurement.

- *Inadequate statement of objectives*. The aims of the programmes are unclear. For example, are they focused solely on exhaustiveness of the national accounts, or are stand-alone estimates of the NOE problem areas also an objective? Are the additional data collected going to be built into the basic data collection program or are they intended simply to adjust the national accounts? Are the measurement procedures a one-off exercise or are they going to be repeated?

- *Inadequate statement of responsibilities*. The roles of the organisational units within the statistical system are not well defined or communicated. It is not clear which responsibilities reside with national accountants and which with the survey statisticians. Regional office staff who conduct the actual data collection are often left entirely in the dark.

- *Narrow focus*. Programmes focus solely on measuring the NOE through indirect methods rather than tackling the underlying problems in the existing basic data collection program, *i.e.*, they exclude long term objectives aimed at building improvements into ongoing data collection.

- *Lack of integration*. Attempts to improve measurement are not carried out within an overall framework of short and long-term initiatives such that the development of new data collections and compilation techniques is blended into the ongoing statistical programme. The result is the production of various NOE measurements that cannot be integrated or combined with other data compiled by the statistical office. National accounts estimates may become out of step with other macro-economic statistics. Furthermore, the absence of an overall framework makes it almost impossible to monitor progress over time or to identify and change priorities.

7.3.   While the aim of this chapter is to outline the essential ingredients of an NOE implementation strategy, it must be emphasised from the outset that there is no "magic bullet" or formula for an NOE programme. Improved measurement is most likely to result from a number of incremental steps undertaken within the context of an overall framework that links them in some way. What is important is that the statistical office adopts an implementation strategy that is systematic, comprehensive, and tuned to local circumstances. The strategy should, as a minimum, contain the following elements:

- a comprehensive programme of consultation with internal and external users on their needs and priorities with respect to the measurement of the NOE;
- a set of clear, realistic, broad objectives indicating what the statistical office is trying to achieve in terms of NOE measurement and how this will address the needs of major data users;
- a well defined conceptual and analytical framework appropriate for NOE measurement;
- an assessment of the sources and outputs of the existing basic data collection programme and the national accounts compilation procedures with the aim of identifying NOE related problems and their magnitudes;
- a prioritised set of possible short and long short term initiatives for improving the statistical infrastructure and outputs of the existing basic data collection programme, and for improving the national accounts compilation processes;
- an implementation plan providing clear targets, milestones and an allocation of responsibilities and expectations for all the various players in the national statistical system;
- a data revision strategy for preventing breaks in macro-economic data outputs resulting from NOE related improvements;
- documentation procedures that ensure proper recording of: the results of the NOE assessment; estimates of the magnitude of the NOE activities by type; and the existing and planned data sources and compilation procedures;
- documentation and evaluation of the NOE measurement programme.

7.4.   These elements and their relationships are shown in Figure 7.1 and further elaborated in Section 7.2. Figure 7.1 emphasises the fact that obtaining exhaustive measures of GDP is not a set of disparate activities. Rather it is an on-going process of co-ordinated and clearly linked procedures undertaken by staff throughout the national statistical system. It also indicates the separation of improvements into those that involve basic data collection and those that refer to compilation of the national accounts. This highlights the need for a clear definition of roles and responsibilities across the organisation to avoid duplication of effort and double counting of NOE measures by survey statisticians and national accountants.

7.2.   Elements of Implementation Strategy

7.2.1.   *Formulation of Broad Objectives and User Consultation*

7.5.   The first element of the implementation strategy is development and dissemination of a clear and unambiguous understanding of what the statistical office is aiming to do with respect to NOE measurement. The primary objective is to improve the exhaustiveness of GDP estimates. Other objectives may include production of individual measures of the informal sector, or underground or illegal production. Whatever it decides to do, the statistical office must be realistic in determining what is feasible. Furthermore, the NOE measurement programme should be viewed as part – albeit a very important part – of any overall quality management strategy. The statistical office must articulate the broad objectives to staff so they have a good understanding of their roles.

Figure 7.1. **Elements of NOE measurement implementation strategy**

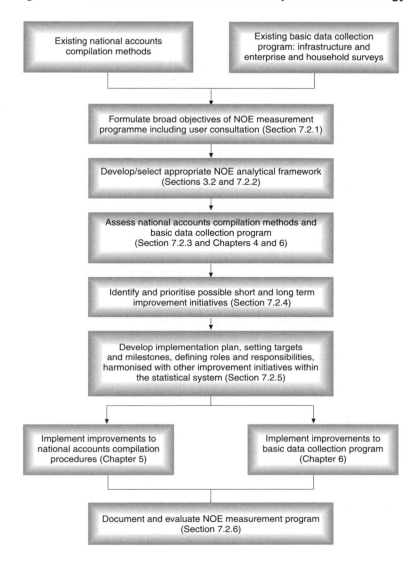

7.6. Formulation of objectives involves consultation with internal and external data users to determine their needs and priorities. Ideally, such consultation should be conducted at regular intervals, preferably at least once a year, with major users. The aims of user consultation include:

- obtaining advice and feedback regarding the NOE measurement strategy and implementation plan;
- educating users regarding the principal reasons for the NOE and the limitations of the measurement methods; conveying a realistic appreciation of what the problems are, what can be achieved with the resources currently available, and what could be achieved if the programme were given higher priority;
- marketing the results of improvements in NOE measurement.

7.7. The process of user consultation should be as open and transparent as possible. Mechanisms for achieving this include dissemination of the NOE measurement strategy, initially perhaps in the form of a draft document inviting user input and suggestions, meetings with individual users and groups of users, and provision of regular feedback on progress in implementing the plan.

7.2.2. *Selection of an Analytical Framework*

7.8.   A prerequisite for assessment and documentation of the NOE related problems and potential improvements is the selection and use of an analytical framework tuned to the particularities of the national statistical system. The Eurostat Tabular Framework is a possible starting point. The breakdown of non-observed activities by type may need to be elaborated, or some types combined, depending on local circumstances. The tables in which the current adjustment descriptions and magnitudes are recorded may also prove to involve too much or too little detail, depending upon the scale of the NOE measurement programme.

7.2.3. *Assessment of National Accounts and Basic Data Collection Programme*

7.9.   The assessment should start with national accounts compilation methods and work backwards to the data sources and data collection infrastructure. The assessment techniques can be selected from amongst those described in Chapters 4 and 6. The objective is to identify every possible type of non-observed activity, to estimate its magnitude, and to document the adjustment (if any) that is presently made for it. For example, if the Eurostat Tabular Framework were being used for NOE analysis, the aim would be to complete every cell of the accompanying tables (shown in Annex 4.1).

7.2.4. *Identification and Prioritisation of NOE Improvement Initiatives*

7.10.   Hand in hand with assessment of the national accounts and the basic data collection programme, possible improvements in NOE measurement can be identified based on the description of best practices in Chapters 5 and 6. Because the NOE has many facets, it is likely that many potential improvements will be identified, implementation of all of which would be beyond the resource capacity of the statistical office. Thus, they have to be prioritised and a corresponding set of short and longer-term improvement initiatives identified. The various options can be split into two basic groups – those, mostly short-term improvements that involve changes in the compilation of the national accounts and those, mostly longer-term improvements that imply modifications to the basic data collection programme.

7.11.   Working from short term to long term, the improvement possibilities include:

- introduction of low cost imputation techniques and model-based adjustments to the basic data prior to their use in compilation of the national accounts;
- introduction of new or improved imputation techniques and model-based adjustments during compilation of the national accounts;
- improving the statistical infrastructure, for example, the business register;
- improving (and where appropriate abandoning) existing statistical collections;
- introducing supplementary statistical collections, either on going or on an occasional basis, to provide regular or periodic benchmark estimates of various indicators that can help in improving NOE estimates.

7.12.   Improvements to national accounts compilation methods using small-scale supplementary investigations and model based adjustments provide relatively low cost, immediate solutions for dealing with non-observed production. The basic principles underlying such improvements are that there should be systematic analysis of all the problems and potential solutions; that full use should be made of all the data available; that preference should generally be given to direct estimates over model-based adjustments; and that the models actually used should be at as detailed a level as possible.

7.13.   In terms of long-term strategy, the first priority is to address deficiencies in the basic data collection programme. The theme is "upstream quality control". There is no point in continuing to use indirect compilation methods to patch up data problems that could be readily solved at the level of the basic data. Statistical co-ordination is an important aspect of the data collection programme. Consistency and utility are improved if all statistics are based on a common conceptual framework. The data collection programme is the place to deal with non-response. All missing observations should be imputed. Introduction or enhancement of a business register might increase coverage substantially. Misreporting should be addressed through editing and plausibility checks.

7.14.   Furthermore, as previously noted, the macro-economic outputs generated by the basic data collection programme are not simply inputs to the national accounts but are also important indicators in their own right. They should be consistent with the national accounts. Consistency can only be achieved by reducing the activities that are non-observed through improved data collection. Published outputs of the basic programme can reflect adjustments for non-observed activities made in the national accounts along a *continuum* reflecting the amount of time and effort involved, for example by:

- acknowledging the existence of non-observed production in the methodological descriptions accompanying the published basic data, *i.e.*, explaining why the basic data differ from national accounts estimates that include adjustments for non-observed production;

- publishing tables that are supplementary to the basic data and that include NOE adjustments;

- incorporating the adjustments in the basic data, *i.e.*, reducing the volume of production that is non-observed.

7.2.5. Implementation Plan

7.15.   The implementation plan should detail the improvement initiatives to be undertaken, the timeframe for each initiative, the outputs expected, the human, financial and systems resources involved and the allocation of responsibilities. It should be blended with, and considered part of, the strategic multi-year and quality management plans for the national statistical system.

Establishing responsibility for NOE measurements and improvements

7.16.   It is vital to establish the roles that national accountants and survey statisticians at central and regional offices should play. Traditionally, the national accounts areas take overall responsibility for an NOE measurement programme as the compilation of the accounts requires the systematic confrontation of data obtained from many different statistical sources and the national accountants are at the focal point. However, as previously emphasised, all areas of the statistical office must be involved.

7.17.   The normal process of data confrontation during compilation of the national accounts brings to light deficiencies and inconsistencies in the basic data, including those due to non-observed production. The traditional role of national accounts staff is to make adjustments to the data to compensate for inadequate coverage and errors and to allow for differences between 1993 SNA definitions and those used by enterprises and reflected in the basic data. Survey statisticians should play a crucial role in such adjustments because they are best placed to know the strengths and weaknesses of the data they produce. They can also be expected to have a good understanding of the types and scale of non-observed activities in their specific statistical subject matter area.

7.18.   Problems occur if the national accountants are unaware of the efforts made by survey statisticians to improve coverage. Thus, survey staff should:

- evaluate the methodology for each data collection in order to identify the likely extent of non-observed production; they should also validate the data by examining information from other sources;

- document existing practices in the form of methodological and definitional *metadata*; the process of metadata documentation itself often reveals deficiencies in methodologies that were hitherto unnoticed. Documentation also helps users to understand the extent to which NOE activities are included in the basic data;

- participate in the development of indirect compilation methods to overcome deficiencies in the basic data.

7.19.   Another reason for survey statisticians to play a prominent role in NOE measurement initiatives is that, as previously noted, the macro-economic data they produce are important indicators in their own right and should be consistent with the national accounts.

7.20.   National accounts staff have a responsibility to ensure that data collection statisticians are fully aware of the 1993 SNA concepts, definitions and classifications and adopt them in collecting data to the extent possible. Such considerations are particularly important when new collections are being developed or where the methodologies of existing collections are being modified.

7.21.   In countries where regional offices conduct most data collection, it is vital that regional office staff are involved as well as those in the central office. This is particularly true in the case of countries where regional office staff aggregate the data and central office statisticians work only with these regional aggregates.

Setting Priorities

7.22.   The causes and sizes of the NOE and the magnitudes of existing adjustments in the national accounts provide the basis for setting priorities in the allocation of resources to NOE measurement initiatives. Areas where non-observed production is relatively small are probably not worth much additional effort. Areas where non-observed production is large or where adjustments are based on weak assumptions or data sources merit more attention. For example, if big adjustments are being made to compensate for undercoverage of enterprises that should have been included in the business register, then effort should be focused on improvement of the business register and its use as a sampling frame. On the other hand, if undercoverage is associated with enterprises that are too small to be included in the business register, then improvement initiatives should be focused on adjustments in the national accounts, perhaps involving the use of supplementary surveys or the labour input approach.

NOE *programme outputs*

7.23.   The primary outputs envisaged from an NOE implementation plan might be expressed as:

- basic data that provide demonstrably better coverage of the economy, *i.e.*, the volume of production that is *non-observed* is reduced;
- improved procedures for compiling the national accounts that take into account the remaining deficiencies in the data, *i.e.*, the volume of production that is *non-measured* is reduced; and
- detailed documentation on how all the estimates and adjustments are derived.

7.2.6. *Documentation and Evaluation*

7.24.   Documentation is a key element of the implementation of the NOE measurement strategy. Documentation is essential to:

- help identify priority areas in basic statistics where further improvement in coverage of NOE activities is required;
- provide staff working on the national accounts with a systematic and complete picture of all information on the NOE that can be obtained from the available data sources;
- avoid duplication of work by staff working in the various areas;
- avoid double counting of NOE estimates by the national accountants and the data collection statisticians;
- ensure that previous work undertaken in estimating the NOE is incorporated where appropriate.

7.25.   Appropriate documentation also gives greater visibility to the relationship between the basic data currently produced by the survey statisticians and subsequent adjustments to these data by national accountants aimed at compensating for non-observed activities. Documentation facilitates revision of the estimates when more reliable information is available to make the adjustments. It also assists in the identification of priorities for new statistical collections and data sources, or modifications to methodologies used in existing collections.

7.26. Two types of documentation are required. First, there must be documentation of the methods used to compile and to improve measurements of GDP, in particular to deal with the NOE. Second the data obtained from the basic data collection programme and all the subsequent NOE related adjustments must be documented. Systematic completion of all the cells in the Eurostat Tabular Framework will produce good documentation.

7.27. Documentation is a resource consuming process often left to the end of improvement initiatives and then never completed. Thus there is a need to think through a strategy for preparing documentation, making it readily available, and ensuring it is updated.

7.28. As improvement of NOE measurement is an ongoing process likely to extend over many years, it is essential that evaluation processes be built into the NOE measurement strategy itself. These may be ongoing or periodic. Their aims are to:

- match actual achievements against planned performance;
- identify reasons for non-performance, under-performance, delays;
- identify and communicate processes that worked, achieved success; and
- provide input to ensuing rounds of user consultation.

7.3. Implementation Strategy for Countries in Transition

Special features

7.29. Whilst the general approach to NOE measurement should be the same for transition countries as for others, transition economies exhibit certain features that require special attention. These include a large volume of shuttle trade, a large informal sector, extensive use of garden plots to produce food for own consumption and, in some countries, large-scale illegal activities. In addition, economic processes, institutional structures and statistical methods are all changing rapidly. The following paragraphs highlight some of the key points to consider in developing an NOE measurement strategy in these circumstances.

Setting priorities

7.30. The first priority of the programme should be improvement in the coverage of value added by kind of activity and final expenditures in the GDP, through better measurement of underground activities, informal sector activities, and food production for own consumption. The basic data required to compile the estimates and the procedures for processing these data should be comprehensively reviewed and revised as necessary.

7.31. The second priority is to integrate estimates of the NOE into the sector accounts. This implies developing specific instructions for integration and reconciliation.

7.32. The last priority is to cover any significant illegal activities. This implies developing appropriate methods for measurement and inclusion of such activities in various accounts. As noted in Chapter 3, illegal activities may be divided into two groups – those that are productive, *i.e.*, that contribute to GDP, and those that are redistributive. Users may express a strong interest in measurement and analysis of both types. However, given the inevitable resource limitations and the need to set priorities, measurement efforts should be specifically focused on productive illegal activities.

Analytical framework

7.33. As also noted in Chapter 3, the NOE problem areas do not define mutually exclusive groups of activities. However, closely related mutually exclusive groups can be derived by selecting one of the

131

problem areas as the first group and defining subsequent groups to exclude any activities already included in the first group. Given the characteristics of the NOE in a transition economy and the measurement tools typically available, a suitable set of mutually exclusive groups based on this approach might be:

- informal sector production;
- household production for own final use that is not included in the informal sector;
- underground production that is not informal sector or household production for own final use;
- illegal production that is not underground, informal sector or household production for own final use;
- other productive activities that are non-observed due to deficiencies in the basic data collection programme.

7.34. Incorporating such groupings in place of the original NOE problem areas would also resolve any ambiguities in the boundaries between the NOE types when using the Eurostat Tabular Framework.

Introducing sampling methods

7.35. Statisticians in transition countries are likely to be very experienced in the use of censuses and administrative sources. Administrative sources should continue to be fully exploited, and this approach should be supported by ensuring that the national statistical office has the legal right to access tax records and other administrative data sources. However, in view of the vast increases in the numbers of enterprises, traditional sources alone are not sufficient and must be supplemented or replaced by sample surveys. Not only do sample surveys provide the only practical means for ensuring coverage of enterprises that are legal entities and that have been traditionally included in estimates, they are also the only means of covering household unincorporated enterprises.

Co-operation with other government agencies

7.36. Several government agencies, including taxation, finance, social security, customs, and police, are likely to have an interest in the NOE. Given the importance of using data from all possible sources, co-operation between these agencies and the national statistical office is vital. Estimates of the NOE may also be produced by independent research institutes. Whilst the experience of staff at such institutes may be useful in shedding light on NOE causes, the measurement methods they use are often not sufficiently rigorous for estimation of GDP as they do not have access to the full range of data available to national accountants. In particular, macro-model methods depending upon simplistic assumptions, as further described in Chapter 12, are not useful.

7.4. Implementation Strategy for Countries with Large Household Sector Production

Introduction

7.37. Countries with a large household sector production often have rather weak statistical systems. In such cases, although the general principles underlying the NOE strategy are still applicable, some of the methods proposed in Chapters 5 and 6 may be too resource intensive or may depend upon data that are available. For example, the introduction of a comprehensive suite of enterprise surveys may be prohibitively expensive. Thus, the objective of this section is to outline a simplified NOE strategy making full use of all pertinent economic and social data.

7.38. Estimates of the contribution of the household sector to GDP using traditional methods tend to result in rather low estimates. In sub-Saharan Africa for example, about 75% of the non-agricultural labour force work in the informal sector, but contribute only about 25% of the total GDP (Charmes, 2000a). Although many analysts conclude from these figures that the informal sector has very low productivity and income generation, the position taken in the Handbook is that inadequate measurement is another explanatory factor and that new methods of estimation should be considered.

In the 1968 SNA, household production for own final use was limited to subsistence agriculture, other primary production, processing of self produced primary products, paid domestic services and imputed rents. Inclusion of other goods for own final use within the 1993 SNA production boundary implies the need to develop new methods.

7.39.   Production in the corporate and government sectors is best covered through enterprise surveys, preferably based on a business register. For the household sector, there are various different types of production, as shown in Figure 7.2, and a variety of mechanisms is required. Household enterprises belonging to the formal sector are best covered by the same means as corporate enterprises. Household agriculture enterprises are best covered through agricultural surveys. Owner-occupied dwelling services can be estimated by the usual methods outlined in Section 5.3. Information on paid domestic services is often available from labour force surveys and household income-expenditure surveys. Informal sector enterprises can be handled through mixed household-enterprise surveys and/ or using the labour input method, and the remaining, non-market enterprises through time use surveys. In summary, and as further elaborated in the following subsections, the priority tasks are:

- introduction of a business register containing, at a minimum, all large and medium size incorporated and quasi-corporate enterprises;

- introduction of a mixed household-enterprise survey;

- application of the labour input method; and

- time use surveys.

Figure 7.2.   **Enterprises in household sector by type of production**

Household sector comprising all household unincorporated enterprises							
Market (1993 SNA) (all or most of output marketed)			Non market (1993 SNA)				
Producing at least some goods and services for market			Producing goods and services exclusively for own final use				
Non-Agricultural		Agricultural	Producing goods		Producing services		
Belonging to formal sector	Belonging to informal sector (ex agriculture)		Agriculture forestry fishing	Other kind of activities	Paid domestic services	Owner occupied dwelling services	

Business register and enterprise surveys

7.40.   A core part of the strategy for improvement of data collection is the introduction and use of a business register to provide the frames for enterprise surveys, at least for the large enterprises. In many countries with a large informal sector, the business register, if it exists at all, contains enterprises accounting for only a relatively small proportion of total production. In such cases, introducing and strengthening the business register is a priority.

7.41.   Ideally the business register should be based on data from an administrative register or registers, as outlined in Chapter 6. In the absence of a suitable administrative source, it can be constructed on the basis of an economic census, *i.e.*, door to door enumeration of all enterprises in the country. In this case it is essential that the census covers not only readily visible enterprises but also those that are conducting their activities within the owner's domestic premises or without fixed location.

7.42.   Small enterprises have a high rate of turnover. They are readily created, they frequently change activity and they often go out of business. Annual turnover rates of 20% can be considered quite normal. Thus, a business register based on an economic census is effective as a sampling frame only immediately after the census. Subsequently it can be used as the starting point for developing an area frame for micro-enterprise surveys, as described by Charmes (1999) in connection with a survey of micro-enterprises in Benin.

7.43. In summary, even though it is impossible to maintain a comprehensive register of all enterprises, there should be a business register containing, at the minimum, all large and medium size incorporated and quasi-corporate enterprises. It can be based on administrative data arising, for example, from the registration process for incorporated enterprises, or from social security systems. The register should be designed to contain all enterprises that are above a given size threshold and/or that are registered by the administrative source(s). The economic production of these enterprises should be measured by enterprise surveys, using the business register to provide the survey frames. The economic production of the market enterprises not covered by the enterprise surveys should be measured through mixed household-enterprise surveys or using the labour input method, as described in the following subsections.

Mixed household-enterprise surveys for informal sector

7.44. The ideal approach for measuring productive activities in the informal sector is to use a comprehensive, area frame based, mixed household-enterprise survey. Hussmanns (2000) notes that more than 20 countries with large informal sectors have already started to use this method. It is fully described in Chapter 10, together with other informal sector measurement methods.

7.45. There are unlikely to be the resources to conduct such a survey on an annual basis. However, provided the survey can be repeated, say five yearly, then data for intermediate years can be indirectly estimated. In particular, if there is an annual labour force survey then labour input data for the informal sector can be collected and used to extrapolate other informal sector characteristics such as output and value added for the intermediate years, as outlined in the following paragraphs.

Labour input method

7.46. According to Charmes (1999 and 2000a) a simplified form of the labour input method described in Chapter 5 has been applied in 15 countries with large informal sectors to provide informal sector estimates. The main features of the method are outlined in the following paragraphs.

7.47. Data on the supply of labour are obtained from a population census or labour force survey, or as a supplement to an income and expenditure, living standard, or other household survey. The survey must collect information that enables the enterprise for which a person works to be classified according to whether or not it belongs to the informal sector. For example, questions may be asked about the legal status of the enterprise (incorporated or not) and its size. The aim is to construct a table of employed persons cross-classified by informal/other sector, by kind of activity, by employment status (employers, own-account workers, family workers, and employees), by sex, and if possible by urban/rural area. It may be necessary to use data classified by occupation and to assume a fixed correspondence between occupation and kind of activity. From this table, agriculture should be extracted and treated separately. It is usually excluded from the informal sector.

7.48. Data on the use of labour may come from an economic census or survey, or from administrative sources, in particular from social security records. If the data are obtained from an economic census or survey, the first step is to check whether the information on the legal status of the enterprise has been collected. Where possible, outworkers (usually identified by questions about their place of work) should be treated as a separate category because they may require specific adjustments in the labour input matrix. In this context, it is useful to classify separately construction, transport, and domestic workers.

7.49. The next step is comparison of the numbers of employees and employers in the various categories on the supply side with those on the use side in order to arrive at a labour input matrix. If the employment associated with incorporated or quasi-incorporated firms can be eliminated from both sides, then the comparison can focus on the informal sector. Depending on the data available, the comparison can be broken down by sex and urban/rural area. Such a division is useful as output and value added per labour unit ratios may differ by sex and by urban/rural location.

7.50.   Once the labour input matrix has been constructed, output and value added per labour unit ratios are applied to arrive at output and value added totals. Ideally, these ratios are obtained from a comprehensive mixed household-enterprise survey, as noted above.

7.51.   There are likely to be a number of difficulties to overcome.

- There may not be a full set of data for the reference year. In this case it is necessary to use data spanning a number of years and to adjust as well as possible for differences in the reference periods.

- The supply side data may be available only for the main urban centres and require adjustment to include the whole country.

- The use side data may be incomplete and may have to be augmented to include, for example, public enterprises.

- In the absence of a comprehensive mixed household-enterprise survey, the output and value added per unit of labour input ratios may be based on a relatively small survey.

- Hours worked may have to be imputed from employment status and knowledge of whether the person was permanent, part-time or seasonal, or a multiple jobholder.

- Special attention should be given to multiple jobs of agricultural workers, seasonal or not, because according to Charmes (1989 and 1996), this is a major reason why production by women is underestimated in many countries.

Thus the accuracy of estimates obtained through the labour input method depends upon the quality and degree of harmonisation of the data sources used.

Time use surveys

7.52.   The extension of the production boundary in the 1993 SNA makes it easier to address gender bias in the measurement of production. Reasons why production by women, and therefore GDP, tend to be underestimated include:

- Women are frequently involved in multiple activities which tend to be overlooked;

- Production of women is concentrated in activities, particularly agriculture and trade, for which national accountants usually impute low output and income levels; and

- women not belonging to the household are often engaged in domestic activities from a young age but are only reimbursed by income in kind, in the form of food and lodging.

7.53.   These are some of the reasons for considering implementation of time-use surveys in countries with large household production for own final use. They may also provide information that is useful in evaluating the quality of labour force and informal sector survey data. Until recently, such surveys have been limited to developed countries. Among the findings from such surveys Charmes (2000*b*) notes that inclusion of non-market household production of goods for own use brings the hours worked by women to the same level as for men, and the share of women in the labour force to the same value as their share in the population.

7.54.   These results suggest that an adequate estimate of household production for own final use, at least of non-agricultural production, cannot be made without resort to time use surveys. They can be associated with other household surveys and thus incorporated in ongoing data collection programmes.

7.5.   Introducing Changes in the Estimates

7.55.   For many users a vital aspect of the national accounts and other major macro-economic data is the availability of extensive time series, allowing comparisons over time and analyses of growth rates. This feature is often as important, if not more important, than the accuracy of the level estimates. Evidently, improvements in measurement of the NOE by a statistical office will result in changes in the

135

data outputs. It is vital that these changes are not attributed by users to the economic phenomena being measured. This is a requirement associated with any changes to measurement or compilation methodology and not just those associated with the NOE programme. For example, changing GDP estimates as a result of more exhaustive coverage without taking proper measures to present these changes destroys the national accounts time series. Worse still, this may happen several years in a row, with each year bringing changes in estimates due to methods of measurement rather than actual movements in the economy. A revision strategy is needed that allows changes to be made to the national accounts and other macro-economic data without impairing their comparability over time.

7.56.　There are three options for introducing methodological improvements:

- The first option is to apply the new methodology to previous years. This is sometimes referred to as *backcasting* and is undoubtedly the preferred option. However, it is likely to be expensive, and the cost increases with the number of years for which the new methodology is projected backwards. The number of years is a matter of judgement. Costs can be reduced by fully applying the new methodology only for those parts of the accounts where the changes are greatest and for other parts of the accounts to make simple ratio adjustments based on a single year overlap between estimates using the old and new methodologies.

- The second option is to suppress the effects of the new methodology in the estimates until a sufficient number of years have elapsed, and then to introduce all the accumulated changes at once. What constitutes a sufficient number of years is again a matter of judgement.

- A third option, which is a compromise between the other two, is to continue publishing the level estimates according to the old methodology but to compute growth rates according to the new methodology.

7.57.　Whatever option is adopted, transparency is an important aspect of the revision strategy. Changes should be well documented and this documentation should be made available to the general public. To avoid any suspicion that political motives are determining the timing for the introduction of new estimates, forthcoming revisions should be announced well in advance.

UNDERGROUND PRODUCTION

8. UNDERGROUND PRODUCTION

8.1.   Introduction

8.1.   The first seven chapters of this Handbook focus on producing exhaustive estimates of GDP and its components, including methods for assessing and remedying deficiencies in the basic data collection programme and in the national accounts. This chapter and the three that follow are devoted to analysis and measurement of underground production, illegal production, informal sector production and household production undertaken for own final use. Each of these is viewed as being of intrinsic interest in its own right. None of them are reduced by better measurement of GDP.

8.2.   As previously noted, there can be overlap between these groups of productive activities – they are not mutually exclusive. In particular, production may be both informal sector and underground. This chapter deals with those production activities that are underground without consideration of whether or not they are informal sector. The breakdown of activities into formal, informal sector, and household production undertaken for own final use according to the type of enterprise responsible for them is another dimension that is discussed in Chapters 10 and 11.

8.3.   Up to this point in the Handbook, the term *underground economy* has been interpreted strictly in accordance with the definition provided by the 1993 SNA. However, the term has much broader application outside the context of the national accounts. It is in common use by sociologists, labour market analysts, lawmakers, the media and the public at large. The various meanings it is given depend upon the different perspectives and preoccupations of the users. Section 8.2 explores some of these meanings and their relationship to the 1993 SNA definition. It also refers to some of the other terms that are used as synonyms, or are closely related. Reference is made to some non-productive activities that are sometimes (but inappropriately) associated with the underground production to explain the sense in which they are not productive and how they can be viewed. Section 8.3 brings together various methods for measurement of the underground economy. Section 8.4 deals with the definition and measurement of some particular types of phenomena including tax evasion, cross border shopping and shuttle trade.

8.2.   Alternative Meanings, Synonyms and Closely Related Terms

Definition of underground production

8.4.   As previously noted in Chapter 3, the 1993 SNA defines the underground economy as all legal production activities that are deliberately concealed from public authorities for the following kinds of reasons:

- to avoid payment of income, value added or other taxes;
- to avoid payment of social security contributions;
- to avoid having to meet certain legal standards such as minimum wages, maximum hours, safety or health standards, etc;
- to avoid complying with certain administrative procedures, such as completing statistical questionnaires or other administrative forms.

8.5.　　It is important to recognise that this is not a definition that is commonly understood or strictly observed outside a fairly narrow circle of national accountants and economists. There are a variety of other different but valid meanings of the term, each reflecting the particular perspective of the users. Much confusion can arise because the various senses in which the term is used are not always recognised as being different. The following paragraphs outline some of the alternative definitions in common use, and the distinctions between them.

Inappropriate inclusion of non-productive activities

8.6.　　The first and most common cause of confusion in the meaning of underground economy occurs because it is sometimes presumed to include activities that are underground in the sense that they involve concealment from taxation or other authorities, but that are **not** productive. Examples are illegally exported capital or concealed interest income or capital gains. These activities may be underground in a loose sense of the word, but they should not be considered as underground *production* and thus part of the underground economy, given that the only broadly accepted notion of production is the one defined by the 1993 SNA. Not all monetary transactions are productive and conversely not all productive activities are monetary. It is important to recognise the distinction.

Inclusion/exclusion of illegal production

8.7.　　Another source of ambiguity in meaning is whether or not the underground production is deemed to include illegal activities. Of course, according to the 1993 SNA it does not. However, whilst the 1993 SNA is definitive in deciding what is production, it does not have a monopoly on the meaning of the term "underground". From the perspective of tax law enforcement, for example, the legality of the production activities is not the issue. The issue is the deliberate concealment of productive (and non-productive) activities that should be declared to the tax authorities. Thus, on occasions in the literature, the "underground economy" covers both legal and illegal concealed production without distinguishing between them. Whilst this is a source of confusion and better avoided, it is understandable.

8.8.　　If illegal production is separated from underground production in accordance with the 1993 SNA definitions, the boundary between the two must be delineated. As noted in the 1993 SNA and in Chapter 3, and as further discussed in Chapter 9, there are some difficulties with marginal cases.

Inclusion/exclusion of small-scale market production

8.9.　　A third cause of confusion arises in connection with market production activities that are on such a small scale that the enterprises responsible for them are not obliged or expected to report them to the public authorities. Even though these activities are outside the 1993 SNA definition of underground production because they do not involve any deliberate concealment, they may be included within the scope of underground production in some studies.

Total, non-observed and non-measured underground production

8.10.　　Yet another source of ambiguity in meaning is whether the underground economy is taken to cover all concealed productive activities, or just those that are not included in the official GDP estimates. According to the 1993 SNA, the underground economy includes all underground activities whether measured or not, but the interpretation of underground economy as non-measured production is also common practice. In line with the terminology presented in Chapter 1, those productive activities that are underground may be more precisely referred to as *total underground production*, those that are not recorded in the basic data as *non-observed underground production* and those that are excluded from GDP estimates as *non-measured underground production*.

Underground production, untaxed production and untaxed income

8.11.　　Underground production is sometimes used in the sense of *untaxed* production, meaning production for which the corresponding income should be but is not reported to the tax authorities.

Thus defined, untaxed production is almost but not quite coincident with underground production according to the 1993 SNA definition as the latter includes concealment from other public authorities in addition to the tax authorities.

8.12.   A more serious interpretation problem arises when underground economy is used in the context of *untaxed* income. Untaxed income cannot be directly related to untaxed production as taxable income may be generated by activities that are not productive. There is also an important distinction between untaxed production and non-measured underground production, which are sometimes confused, as noted by Tanzi (1999). The former relates to a shortfall in government revenues, the latter to a shortfall in GDP estimates.

Underground production in percentage terms

8.13.   Another source of confusion arises in quoting the extent of underground activities in percentage terms. Typically percentages are defined on the basis of the ratio of the item of interest to the whole. In the context of the underground economy this would imply expressing underground production as a percentage of total production. However, underground production is often quoted as a percentage of the official GDP estimates rather than of total (official + underground) GDP. This difference becomes increasingly significant with increase in the size of the percentages.

Other terms

8.14.   Van Eck (1987) lists nearly 30 terms that are used as synonyms for, or are closely related to, the underground economy. The list includes the following:

Alternate	Counter	Marginal	Peripheral	Twilight
Autonomous	Dual	Moonlight	Secondary	Unexposed
Black	Grey	Occult	Shadow	Unofficial
Cash	Hidden	Other	Submerged	Untaxed
Clandestine	Invisible	Parallel	Subterranean	Underwater
Concealed	Irregular			

8.15.   These terms can all have different shades of meaning. One might hypothesise that *concealed economy* meant the same as underground economy, that *grey economy* covered underground and informal sector production, and that *invisible economy* might include illegal production as well, but this would be pure speculation. There is no way of knowing what any of the terms might mean in any particular document unless the authors have included definitions.

Summary

8.16.   In conclusion, in the context of the national accounts, the appropriate definition of underground production is provided by the 1993 SNA. However, outside the immediate context of the national accounts there is no unique "correct" definition of underground and several variants are in use. Hence, as an author it is vital to specify the definition being used, and as a reader it is vital to check it. In this Handbook the 1993 SNA definition is applied.

8.3.   Measurement Tools

8.3.1. Introduction

8.17.   This section summarises the particular mechanisms that can be used to measure the underground economy. The primary tools are special surveys of underground production, labour, expenditure, and income. Another class of tools is business and household opinion surveys, and a third source of information is audit data and special studies carried out by the taxation authorities. The section builds on the material presented in Section 4.3 in connection with assessment of the national accounts, the difference being that in Chapter 4 the goal was minimising non-measured production whereas here the focus is measuring underground production separately.

8.18.   As previously noted, the results of surveys of underground activities must be interpreted very carefully, especially those focused on tax evasion. It is very likely that the non-response is selective because people who are involved in underground activities are more likely to refuse to co-operate than people who are not. Selective non-response is difficult to reduce or to adjust for. Moreover, attempts to reduce non-response may not necessarily improve the results. It may be impossible to persuade people to respond to sensitive questions, although some randomised response techniques are promising (see Landsheer et al, 1999). Too much effort to increase overall response may even reduce the reliability of the results. The challenge in surveying underground activities is to find the appropriate balance with respect to the risks of complete non-response, item non-response and incorrect response.

8.3.2. *Surveys of Expenditure on Goods and Services from Underground Production*

8.19.   In some countries it is a criminal offence to make a payment without asking for a receipt, but in most countries purchasing goods and services from underground producers is not against the law. Thus surveys of expenditure on underground production are more likely to give good results than surveys of underground income. Expenditures reported in household consumption surveys are very likely to include underground expenditures but without distinguishing them from other expenditures. Some household surveys attempt to identify expenditures on underground production by asking respondents to indicate separately those purchases that they suspect may have an underground character. Others ask respondents to describe the type of outlet or seller from among a list that includes those types most likely to be operating underground, including street-traders, independent artisans (plumbers, gardeners, electricians, etc.) and farm shops.

8.20.   For example, in a survey of the underground economy from the perspective of household consumers, the Hungarian Central Statistical Office (1998) asked the respondent:

- *How many times in the last month, and in 1997, have you or anyone in your household purchased the following personal services, what was the total amount spent and for what share was a receipt received?* – question followed by a list of personal services and boxes to enter the required data;

- *How many times in 1997 have you or anyone in your household purchased the following industrial, building and agricultural and other services, what was the total amount spent and for what share was a receipt received?* – question followed by a list of services and boxes to enter the required data;

- *For how long in the last year did you or anyone in your household purchase the following facilities, what was the total amount spent and for what share was a receipt received?* – question followed by a list of accommodation types and boxes to enter the required data;

- *How many times in the last month, and in 1997, did you or anyone in your household purchase the following products from a vendor or market seller, what was the total amount spent and for what share was a receipt received?* – question followed by a list of products and boxes to enter the required data;

- *How many times in the last month, and in 1997, did you or anyone in your household give a tip for the following services and what was the total amount spent?* – question followed by a list of personal services and boxes to enter the required data.

It should be noted that respondents find it difficult to recall information over a one year period.

8.3.3. *Surveys of Labour Input and Income Associated with Underground Production*

8.21.   Experiences in Scandinavian countries (Isachsen and Strom, 1989 and Mogensen et al, 1995), in the USA (Smith, 1985), in Romania (Ivan-Ungureanu and Pop, 1996) and in the Netherlands (Van Eck and Kazemier, 1988) suggest that the labour market is another area where surveys of underground activities can be successful. First of all, involvement is quite widespread, so there is no difficulty in locating a sample. Secondly, working has such an impact on daily activities that it is readily remembered. Thirdly, in many countries underground work is considered a minor infringement of the law and thus at least some of the workers are willing to report their activities.

8.22. As noted in Section 4.4, surveys of labour input to underground production can collect information on either demand or supply of labour.

8.23. Surveying supply of labour may provide more detail but needs careful design, involving questions that are sensitive and prone to item non-response and incorrect response. Van Eck and Kazemier (1992) describe a sequence of questions that gradually lead to underground activities. The key questions on underground activities are embedded in related but non-sensitive questions. Labour input to underground production is carefully introduced as a topic and the sensitive questions on participation in underground activities are towards the end of the question sequence. For example, the topic is foreshadowed by asking the respondent about opportunities and skills to earn some additional money. If the respondent acknowledges earning additional money further questions are asked about the kind of work, the time involved, and the hourly wage rate. Only after that is underground income introduced by asking opinions on the probability of detection if additional income is not reported to the tax authorities. Finally, it is suggested that all extra earnings are unreported, and it is assumed that this is the case unless this is explicitly denied by the respondent. In the research described, Kazemier and Van Eck noted there were seven places in their questionnaire where the respondent could deny underground activities. The result of their experiment (conducted in 1983) was that 12% of all respondents 16 years old and over admitted that they had been involved in underground activities in the previous year, earning a total underground income amounting to about 1% of GDP. This was twice as much as obtained by a survey with a conventional questionnaire in which questions about underground activities were asked directly.

8.3.4. *Surveys of Time Use*

8.24. Time use surveys can provide additional information about underground activities, as previously noted in Section 4.3. The advantage of the time use approach over labour force surveys is that it provides a framework for allocating all available time between productive and other activities. However, care must be taken to ensure that the relevant activities can be classified. It must be possible to distinguish between time spent working as an employee in an enterprise, and time spent as own account worker. It should also be possible to identify the kind of work carried out on own account in order to impute the amount of income likely to have been earned. Luttikhuizen and Oudhof (1992) provide more details.

8.3.5. *Opinion Surveys*

8.25. Opinion surveys of enterprises and households are used in several countries to monitor underground activities. As previously noted, they have several features that make them easier to manage than quantitative surveys. They can be designed to take very little time to complete. They can be addressed directly to senior managers who are likely to be well informed about underground activities in their own sector of activity. They can be made non-threatening by asking respondents to give their views about general practices in an industry or sector rather than asking respondents about their own particular underground activities. On the other hand, they do not provide quantitative information that can readily be used to make adjustments to GDP.

8.26. As an example, the Russian Federation Centre for Economic Analysis (2000) addressed questions along the following lines to retail trade enterprises. (Similar types of questions were addressed to enterprises in other branches.)

- Please estimate (in ranges < 5%, 6-15%, 16-30%, 31-50%, 51-70%, > 70%) the approximate shares of unregistered receipts by: *large and medium retailers; small retailers; individual entrepreneurs.*

- Please rate (on scale: of no importance, almost never, not often, often, almost always) the use of the following schemes and mechanisms to hide retail trade receipts: *sales without cash register;*

manipulation of cash register; manipulation of retail prices; overestimating expenses; cash settlements for goods purchases; trade without licence; fictitious agreements in settlements with suppliers; intermediate trade structures.

- Please estimate (in range < 10%, 11-20%, 21-30%, 31-50%, > 50%) the share of settlements in retail trade of the following types: *cash settlements; clearing settlements; barter; travellers cheques, letters of credit, credit cards, other financial instruments; other.*

- Please estimate (in range < 10%, 11-20%, 21-30%, 31-50%, > 50%) the share hidden from taxation by retail trade enterprises.

- Please estimate (in range at least 5%, at least 10%, at least 15%, over 20%) the minimum profitability required by retail trade enterprises to stay in regular production.

- Please rate (on scale: never, low, average, high, very high) the following purposes to which hidden share of receipts is put: *increase owners profits; increase payments to high level staff; increase payments to low level staff; to survive and function normally; to carry informal costs of doing business; other.*

- Please rate (on scale: never, low, average, high, very high) the following cases for which additional payments take place: *rent; supervising organisations; police; suppliers; local authorities; racket; criminal protection; court appeals.*

8.27.   In the household survey of the "hidden economy" (meaning in this context the underground economy) the Hungarian Central Statistical Office (1998) included some qualitative questions aimed at collecting citizens' views. On a five point scale from *totally agree with* to *totally disagree with*, and with the option of replying *don't know*, respondents were asked to give their opinion on the following statements:

- *The hidden economy is part of life.*

- *The relative size of the hidden economy is not higher in Hungary than in other countries.*

- *Too high taxes and contributions play the biggest role in the creation of the hidden economy.*

- *The high level of the hidden economy spoils our chances of joining the EU.*

- *The hidden economy benefits everybody.*

- *Products and goods needed for everyday life purchased in the hidden economy reduce household expenses.*

- *The hidden economy increases the differences in incomes.*

- *The fight against the hidden economy affects only the "small" people.*

- *The greatest incomes from the hidden economy land up in the underworld.*

- *Like it or not, in certain cases you have to give a tip or gratuity.*

8.3.6. *Tax Audit Data*

8.28.   It is generally believed that surveys on tax evasion never yield reliable results. Because of the risk of prosecution, respondents are unlikely to provide information on tax evasion even if the survey agency asserts that information supplied will never be revealed to third parties. Tax audits, on the other hand, may provide more information than surveys because the enterprises or individuals being audited cannot refuse to respond and are obliged to provide their complete accounts. As previously noted, the main limitation to their use for statistical purposes is that they are rarely conducted on a random basis and thus generalising the results to the total population is difficult if not impossible.

8.29.   Typically tax audits are carried out on enterprises in a restricted range of industry classes. The industries are chosen subjectively from amongst those for which tax evasion is believed to be largest. Within each industry samples are likely to be selected subjectively, targeting those enterprises with characteristics that are believed to correlate with higher levels of non-compliance. Even if the stated intention is to select a random sample it is prudent to check that the sample is representative across characteristics believed to relate to non-compliance.

8.30.   As described in Section 5.2.5, the *Institut national de la statistique et des études économiques*, (INSEE) in France computed estimates of adjustment coefficients for output and value added based on tax audit data. The Lithuanian Department of Statistics (1998) provides an example of the use of tax returns to estimate the size of the underground economy. The US Internal Revenue Service (1979) provides another example from the United States.

8.4. Measurements of Underground Production and Related Issues

8.4.1. Introduction

8.31.   The previous section describes the sorts of tools available for measuring various aspects of the underground economy. This section outlines the relevance and use of these tools in a number of specific circumstances commonly associated with the underground economy. It includes measurement of underground production in total and estimating the part that remains non-measured. There is also a brief discussion of tax evasion/undeclared income, shuttle trade, cross border shopping, and barter, explaining where they fit in.

8.4.2. Underground Production

8.32.   Methods for assessment and measurement of underground production were discussed in Chapters 3-4 from the viewpoint of ensuring that this production is included in GDP estimates. The focus in this section is on producing a separate estimate of total underground production. However, given that activities deliberately concealed from public authorities are equally likely to be concealed from production surveys, there is probably no difference between underground production (in total) and non-observed underground production as measured by the production approach. Thus, the systematic assessment of the scope and likely incidence of non-observed underground activities using an appropriate production based analytical framework such as described in Chapter 3 is useful. The framework helps in identifying the various kinds of activities involved and the different ways in which they might be measured.

8.33.   Following the Eurostat and Istat analytical frameworks, underground production can be considered as falling into two possible categories:

- activities that are underground because the enterprises conducting them are not registered;
- activities that are underground because the enterprises conducting them (although registered) under-report.

Activities that are underground because the enterprises conducting them are not registered

8.34.   Enterprises that are not registered and are engaged in legal productive activities are likely to be very small. Enterprises with no business address and no advertising other than by word of mouth must be operating on a small scale. However, there may be quite a large number of such enterprises. For example, persons with a regular paid job as a plumber, accountant or teacher, say, who work after hours for their own profit ("moonlighters" as they are sometimes called) count as small-scale enterprises. Because of the numbers, the total production of such enterprises may be quite substantial.

8.35.   Failure to register means that the enterprise will not be covered in any survey for which the frame is drawn from the business register. A household or mixed household-enterprise survey approach is a practical way of measuring such underground production. The first option is to obtain an estimate of the total labour input through the regular household labour force survey as described in Chapter 5, to deduct the labour input reported by enterprises in response to an enterprise-based employment survey, and thus to arrive at an estimate of the labour associated with unregistered enterprises. This presumes that the enterprise-based survey gives full coverage of all registered enterprises, and that the labour force survey gives full coverage of labour total input. The alternative is to conduct a mixed household-enterprise survey, in which the first step is to locate a sample of unregistered enterprises and the second step is to sample them. The procedures for conducting such a survey are described in detail in Section 10.3.

Activities that are underground because the enterprises conducting them under-report

8.36.   It seems fairly likely that enterprises answer survey questionnaires using the same set of accounts as they prepare for tax purposes. Thus, underreporting of production and/or receipts to the taxation authorities in order to avoid taxes is likely to be reflected in the survey data submitted to the statistical office. In some countries enterprises that sell their output to other enterprises find it difficult to underreport their sales because the purchasing enterprises usually demand receipts to support their own accounts. In such a situation, corrections are only needed for underreporting of sales to households, government and non-profit institutions serving households. In other countries, however, enterprises may collude in under-reporting their sales and purchases, and adjustments for sales to enterprises are thus also required.

8.37.   Some overall idea of the magnitude of underreporting in specific industries may be obtained through commodity balances. For example as described by Masakova (2000), crop production may be estimated from seed consumption or milk yield from estimates of forage consumed. In other industries estimates may have to be based on the results of *ad hoc* surveys that collect the incidence of "cash payments" made by households.

8.38.   Adding together estimates of all types of underground production for all components of GDP will produce an overall estimate of the total underground production, some, or hopefully even most, of which will be included in the official national accounts' estimates.

8.4.3. Non-Measured Underground Production

8.39.   The measurement that is most frequently presented in the media and of interest to many economic analysts is the *non-measured underground production, i.e.*, that part that does not get included in the official national accounts estimates. Non-measured underground production may be obtained by deducting from the estimate of total underground production described in the immediately preceding paragraphs the estimates or adjustments made for underground production during basic data collection and compilation of the accounts. This requires a systematic analysis of the collection and compilation processes to establish where estimates or adjustments for underground activities are made and what their magnitudes are. Such procedures were described in Section 4.3 in the context of computing upper bounds for non-observed and non-measured activities.

8.4.4. Tax Evasion

8.40.   Estimates of tax evasion, *i.e.*, unreported income, can be obtained through tax audits. However, as noted in the previous section, most tax audits are not based on random sampling since the auditors usually target those enterprises that they believe are more likely to be under-reporting their income. Thus the results cannot readily be weighted up to give estimates for the whole population. Furthermore the audit process does not necessarily reveal the full extent of the unreported income, uncovering only the part that can be detected in the accounts presented to the taxation authorities. In addition, tax audits cannot be directed at enterprises that are not registered.

8.41.   Given that underground production and untaxed production are essentially the same, as noted in Section 8.1, estimates of underground production can be expected to yield fairly good estimates of unreported income from productive activities. However the latter is just one component of tax evasion. A whole range of taxes can be evaded, and not just those levied on incomes.

8.4.5. Shuttle Trade

8.42.   As noted in Section 5.5.7, shuttle trade refers to the activity in which entrepreneurs buy goods abroad and import them for resale in street markets or small shops. Often the goods are imported without full declaration in order to avoid import duties. This is usually regarded as part of the underground economy whether or not it is classified as illegal. Shuttle trade is significant in many transition countries in Europe and Central Asia, and generally in countries at the borders of monetary zones.

8.43.   The primary measurement method is direct survey of shuttle traders to determine the numbers of shuttle trade journeys and the average values imported. In addition, estimates of smuggling in general and shuttle trade in particular may be obtained from comparisons of supply and demand estimates for the goods involved together with customs data on imports declared and estimates of those not declared, as described in Section 5.5.7.

8.4.6. *Cross Border Shopping*

8.44.   Cross border shopping is the name given to the activity wherein private individuals buy goods abroad because of lower taxes and import them for their own consumption, without declaring them in order to avoid paying import duties. As already noted in Chapter 5, although cross border shopping involves concealment of activities from public authorities with the intention of avoiding taxes, they are not productive activities and thus do not constitute a part of the underground economy.

8.45.   However, cross border trade may affect international trade statistics. It may be missed from exports, or imports, or both. If it is missed from exports, the GDP of the exporting country will be under-estimated when compiled by the expenditure approach. If it is missed from imports, the GDP of the importing country will be over-estimated when compiled by the expenditure approach if and only if the trade is included in the estimates of consumption.

8.4.7. *Barter Trade*

8.46.   Barter transactions are ones in which a good, a service or an asset other than cash is provided in return for a good, service or asset. According to the 1993 SNA barter transactions are to be treated like monetary transactions and the corresponding values estimated. Thus, in principle, production and subsequent exchange of home produced goods and services within the production boundary are production whether or not they are paid for in currency units or are bartered. In practice, barter on a small scale is ignored both by the taxation authorities and statistical office. However, systematically organised barter of goods and of services through large computerised *time banks* or organised *local currency systems* should not be ignored.

8.4.8. *Capital Flight*

8.47.   According to Abalkin and Walley (1999) *capital flight* may be defined as the transfer of assets denominated in a national currency into assets denominated in a foreign currency, either at home or abroad, in ways that are not part of normal transactions. In other words, transferring assets abroad into foreign banks or foreign securities that goes beyond normal portfolio diversification constitutes capital flight. Assets can be transferred in a variety of ways, in particular:

- transfer abroad of financial assets denominated in a foreign currency;
- accumulation of foreign currency abroad by the failure to repatriate profits; and
- exchanging national currency for foreign currency as a hedge against inflation.

8.48.   Laungani and Mauro (2000) note that, in the case of the Russian Federation, assets are leaving the country through under-invoicing of export earnings, fake advance import payments and bank transfers bypassing capital controls. They note that capital flight is occurring because of an unsettled economic environment, macroeconomic instability, relatively high and unevenly enforced tax rates, an insolvent banking system and weak protection of property rights. The costs to society of capital flight may be high and include reduction of domestic savings, shrinkage of the tax base and currency depreciation.

8.49.   Capital flight is sometimes approximated using the *hot money* measure, computed as the net errors and omissions in the balance of payments plus net private portfolio investment abroad. Another *broad measure* of capital flight is the net accumulation of foreign assets by the resident private sector.

8.50.   Capital flight may or may not be associated with productive activities that are underground or illegal, but it is not a productive activity in itself and it is a mistake to think it should be included in estimates of underground production.

ILLEGAL PRODUCTION

9. ILLEGAL PRODUCTION

9.1. Introduction

9.1.   As previously noted, the 1993 SNA explicitly states that productive illegal activities should be included in national accounts. There are several reasons for this. The 1993 SNA emphasises the need for overall consistency. "Clearly, the accounts as a whole are liable to be seriously distorted if monetary transactions that in fact take place are excluded." (SNA 1993: 3.54.) Not taking illegal activities fully into account gives rise to discrepancies in the accounts. The incomes earned from illegal production are largely spent on the purchase of legal goods and services, on the acquisition of legal fixed or financial assets or other legal transactions. Since all these transactions are recorded in the accounts along with those that are financed by incomes from legal activities, there is inevitably a discrepancy between supply and uses for the economy as a whole if the production and imports of illegal goods and services are omitted.

9.2.   For the same reasons the ESA 1995 includes illegal production. "All such activities are included even if they are illegal or non-registered at tax, social security, statistical and other public authorities." (ESA 1995: 3.08). Thus, both the 1993 SNA and ESA 1995 depart from a "moral" point of view in which illegal activities should not be included in GDP, because "representatives of the people have determined such products to be 'bads' rather than 'goods' with sufficient conviction to outlaw them" (Dennison, 1982).

9.3.   In addition to the consistency of the overall system, comparability of national accounts figures between countries and over time is another major reason for the inclusion of illegal activities. Some activities, for example the production and distribution of alcohol, or prostitution, may be illegal in one country and legal in another. Exclusion of illegal production may thus distort international comparisons. Likewise, it will give rise to distortions over time if some activities switch from being illegal to be legal, or conversely. Production and distribution of alcohol during to the prohibition period in the USA is an example.

9.4.   Production and distribution of illegal drugs is a relatively major economic activity in some countries of Latin America and Asia. Excluding drugs production and distribution from the accounts seriously understates value added in agriculture, manufacturing and domestic and international trade and results in GDP estimates that are grossly understated.

9.5.   Another consideration is that much of the value of illegal products – over 90% in the case of some narcotics – exists only because their illegality makes their prices high. According to Dennison (1982) "the value of the quantities of drugs now produced would be of trivial importance in the economy if they were legalised". This is sometimes used as an argument for excluding drug production and trade from the national accounts. However, following the 1993 SNA, the national accounts should describe the economic environment as it actually is. The economic behaviour of households and enterprises is based on the relative prices and costs actually existing in society. It is not based on a hypothetical situation that would exist without illegal production. Suppose that drugs were legalised and prices subsequently dropped to a third of current prices. This certainly would affect the behaviour of economic actors. The consumption patterns of drugs dealers would (have to) change dramatically due to the decrease in income. On the other hand there might be an increase of the volume of drugs consumed. Simply disregarding illegal production overlooks this reality.

9.6.   In countries where the output and value added of illegal productive activities is quantitatively insignificant, it is almost certainly a poor use of resources to try to cover them in the national accounts. Efforts are better directed to reducing the amount of underground, informal sector or own final use household production that are omitted from the GDP. In addition, the methods available to measure illegal activities are still experimental. Indeed, although there seems to be more or less agreement on the correctness, in principle, of including illegal activities, very few countries explicitly include estimates of illegal production in their national accounts figures at the present time. However, this is slowly changing. Measurement obstacles should not stop efforts to move towards the conceptually correct system, and research on finding appropriate estimation methods continues.

9.7.   In summary, the intention of this chapter is to provide a starting point for an experimental theoretical and practical investigation of illegal activities. It aims at interpreting and clarifying the SNA 1993 and ESA 1995. It builds on the previous discussion of illegal activities in Section 3.3. Section 9.2 lists and categorises the most significant types of illegal activities; Section 9.3 discusses the conceptual issues concerning the recording of illegal activities within the national accounts; Section 9.4 outlines the data sources and methods for compiling estimates for selected illegal activities; and Section 9.5 explores the issue of double counting.

9.2.   Types of Illegal Activities

9.8.   Based on Blades (1983), the following general types of illegal production are identified:

- production and distribution of illegal goods, such as banned drugs or pornographic material;
- production of illegal services, such as prostitution (in countries where this is illegal);
- production activities which are usually legal but which become illegal when carried out by unauthorised producers, such as unlicensed medical practices, unlicensed gambling activities, unlicensed production of alcohol; poaching, *e.g.* illegal fishing, hunting, tree cutting;
- production and sale of counterfeited products, such as watches and other products with false trade-marks and unauthorised copies of artistic originals, *e.g.* software, CDs and videos;
- smuggling, in particular of tobacco, weapons, alcohol, food, people, both wholesale and retail;
- fencing (resale) of stolen goods;
- bribery; and
- money laundering.

9.9.   The scale and distribution of such activities varies across countries. For example, in the Commonwealth of Independent States, the following illegal activities are of significant size:

- bribery;
- poaching, including fishing, illegal production of caviar and similar sea products, hunting, and logging;
- illegal production of alcoholic beverages which do not meet certain standards;
- provision of medical services by the persons who do not have qualification;
- production of goods whose quality does not meet established standards;
- illegal production of copies of audio and video materials, and software programmes;
- production and distribution of pornographic materials.

9.10.   In addition to the activities included in the above lists, there are many other types of illegal production, for example forgery of banknotes, contract murders, espionage, etc. For national accounts purposes, these are generally of minor importance.

9.11.   As previously noted in Chapter 3, some illegal activities do not involve mutual agreement, thus are not transactions by definition and are not productive. Examples are theft and robbery, kidnapping, and extortion. However, although not productive, they may cause underestimation of the GDP. For example, theft by employees results in less output or increased intermediate consumption and thus lower GDP estimated by the production approach.

9.3.   Issues in Recording Illegal Activities

9.12.   From a conceptual point of view, recording illegal production within the national accounts framework does not pose special problems if the production process resembles the production process for legal activities. This is the case for the production and distribution of illegal goods, services and counterfeit products, for productive activities carried out by unauthorised producers, and for smuggling. For other illegal activities such as theft and fencing, bribery, extortion, and money laundering, there are some difficult conceptual issues, as discussed in the following paragraphs. The 1993 SNA does not give much specific guidance in these cases. However the recording procedures that are proposed follow the general guidelines of the 1993 SNA as closely as possible.

Theft and fencing

9.13.   In relation to theft, a distinction can be made between i) theft of capital goods, consumer durables, money or other financial assets, and ii) theft from the inventories of producers. Both are discussed below, together with fencing, an activity related to theft.

9.14.   The 1993 SNA (Para. 3.56) states "If thefts…involve significant redistributions… of assets, it is necessary to take them into account… they are treated as *other flows* not as *transactions*". They cannot be treated as transactions because a transaction is defined as "an economic flow that is an interaction between institutional units by mutual agreement" (1993 SNA: 3.12). Theft of capital goods, consumer durables, money or other financial assets often involves significant amounts and in these cases, recording of these activities as another change in the volume of assets (*i.e.*, as a change in the value of assets (or liabilities) that does **not** take place as a result of a transaction) is appropriate.

9.15.   Theft from the inventories of producers includes theft from stocks of materials, supplies and finished goods on the one hand, and theft from stocks of goods for resale on the other. In the 1993 SNA, output and intermediate consumption are defined as sales/purchases of goods and services plus/minus the value of changes in inventories. Recurrent losses due to normal rates of wastage, theft and accidental damage are considered as (negative) changes in inventories (1993 SNA: 6.62). As a consequence, normal rates of theft from the stock of finished goods lead to a decrease of output, whereas normal rates of theft from the stock of materials and supplies lead to an increase of intermediate consumption. In both cases, value added decreases accordingly. The same holds for normal rates of theft from stocks of goods for resale. Output and value added of wholesalers and retailers are influenced negatively by theft.

9.16.   From the above, it can be concluded that normal rates of theft from inventories of producers are registered neither as a transaction nor as an other flow. Implicitly, they are completely removed from the system of national accounts. Only theft from inventories which exceeds the "normal rates" is included in the 1993 SNA as an other change in the volume of assets (1993 SNA: 12.41). Thus, leaving aside the (negative) consequences of theft from producers' inventories, value added is not affected by theft. No value added is generated; all that is happening is that assets are redistributed.

9.17.   This statement does not apply to an activity related to theft, namely trade in stolen goods, which is not explicitly addressed in the 1993 SNA. Trade in stolen goods involves action by two units in mutual agreement, namely the purchase and the subsequent sale of stolen goods by the receiver. Clearly, these actions constitute monetary transactions and should be recorded accordingly. Furthermore, if the units are involved in these activities on a regular scale, value added (trade margin) is generated, as part of distribution of the illegal goods.

9.18.   The treatment of theft recommended in the 1993 SNA requires clarification, if not elaboration, in order to take into account the special circumstances in some countries. For example, in some members of the Commonwealth of Independent States there is a widespread practice of illegal appropriation of the output of agricultural co-operatives (collective farms) by their members. This theft occurs on a large scale and is used to supplement the low compensation of the workers or members of co-operatives. The stolen goods may be sold or used for intermediate or final consumption. In many cases this supplement is an important source of income without which the collective farmers could hardly survive. In these circumstances, consideration must be given to recording the value of the theft as income in kind of employees. If the theft is of materials and supplies, its value should be moved from intermediate consumption to compensation of employees. If the theft is of final products, both output and compensation of employees have to be adjusted upwards.

9.19.   In some cases it is difficult to draw a clear distinction between theft and underreporting. For example, in the Russian Federation, the crews of the fishing ships often sell a part of the output abroad (sometimes from ship to ship) and do not show these sales in their records. The income obtained from the sale of this output may be used for a variety of purposes and the expenditure may be measured in the context of estimation of GDP by summing up expenditures on final use. It appears that this type of underreporting is actually very similar to that described in connection with collective farms. The missing production should be estimated and included in the GDP according to the 1993 SNA. Again this suggests recording such theft as income in kind.

Bribery

9.20.   Two different kinds of bribery can be distinguished, first, payments linked to the provision of services, and second, payments to persons in privileged positions. In the first case, the payments may be linked to market goods and services or to non-market services. For market goods or services, the bribe usually consists of a supplementary payment above "official" prices. For example, hotel clients are required to bribe the hotel receptionists to confirm their reservations. Examples related to non-market services are payments of (additional) amounts that are required to obtain medical services from publicly financed health care, or to get passports from civil servants. Examples of payments to persons in privileged positions are those made to officials who award contracts to the highest bribing supplier, to politicians to obtain a privileged position as a producer, or to policemen or other government officials who accept bribes in return for not prosecuting the offender.

9.21.   An important question, on which the 1993 SNA does not give guidance, is whether or not bribery should be considered as a transaction, or, to put it differently, whether bribery is an interaction between institutional units by mutual agreement. In general, it can be supposed that individuals have a freedom of choice to enter into bribery. The person paying the bribe agrees to pay the (additional) sum of money. In this case, recording as a transaction rather than as another flow is to be preferred.

9.22.   A more difficult question is whether bribery should be recorded as part of output and value added, or as an income transfer. If the bribe is linked to the provision of services, recording as part of output seems to be preferable. This is especially true for market goods/services. The official prices plus the bribes should be considered as the genuine market prices, and, from an income point of view, the bribe adds to compensation of employees or mixed income.

9.23.   In the case of non-market services, an additional criterion may be needed. If the payment to the civil servant is (implicitly) allowed by government, for example in the case of doctors or other people employed by government who receive only a small official income, or if the bribery is generally accepted as standard practice, then a bribe should be registered as additional compensation of employees. As such, it adds to total output of government. Because sales of government services are affected by the same amount, the final consumption expenditure of government remains unaffected.

9.24.   If payments linked to non-market services are not allowed or not publicly accepted or expected, then recording as an income transfer seems to be preferable. The same holds for payments to persons in privileged positions to obtain a contract.

Extortion

9.25.   Extortion consists of obligatory payments enforced by violence or blackmail. There is no mutual agreement, and, in line with the 1993 SNA, extortion should not be registered as a transaction. In this respect, it resembles theft of money (or goods or services) and it should be registered as an other change in the volume of assets.

Money laundering

9.26.   Money laundering is here defined as the transfer of money through different bank accounts so that its original source is concealed from the taxation authorities or other regulatory services. There is mutual agreement, at least implicitly, that the transactions should be registered in the system of national accounts. In so far as there is a difference between the value of the illegal cash and the value of the legalised cash, this should be looked upon as a provision of services. Often, the actors such as banks will be unaware of their involvement in money laundering, and the fees that banks charge for transferring money between different accounts should be included in the system of national accounts together with the fees from legal transactions.

Fraud and swindle

9.27.   Fraud and swindle are quite different from the other activities mentioned above. Fraud often relates to false claims for social benefits or subsidies by giving incorrect information. The relevant transactions, however, are registered in the system. Here, a breakdown into a legal and an illegal part is needed only for a complete picture of the illegal activities within a certain country. It is not a problem of exhaustiveness of GDP.

9.4.   Methods of Observation and Measurement

9.28.   By their nature, illegal activities are very difficult to measure. People involved in illegal transactions have obvious reasons to hide their involvement. The more the activities are considered unacceptable by law and by the general public, the more difficult it becomes for conventional data sources to capture them. Thus, surveys and administrative data sources are "subject to particular concerns about their suitability, coverage and reliability" (Groom and Davies, 1998).

9.29.   Notwithstanding the obvious difficulties, there are sometimes quite reasonable if unconventional data sources and methods to measure various types of illegal activity. It goes without saying that the quality of these estimates is subject to more discussion than that of estimates for activities that are well covered in regular surveys. In this section, the principal methods and data sources, and some important problems, are discussed in connection with two types of activities that have some impact on the transactions in goods and services and on GDP in nearly all countries, namely drugs and prostitution. Data sources and methods for these activities are illustrative of those available for other types.

9.30.   Parts of some illegal activities may be implicitly included in the system of national accounts. A well-known example is prostitution. Income from prostitution may be declared as income from legal "personal care" services and expenditure on prostitution may be declared, but similarly disguised, by the purchaser. However, it seems highly probable that most illegal activities are not included in the conventional data sources used in compiling the national accounts, particularly for those activities that are considered unacceptable by society. Thus, direct methods for compiling estimates of illegal production are to be preferred. In adding these estimates to the conventional estimates there is a danger of double counting, a problem that will be discussed in the next section.

9.31.   Probably the most useful approach is to use the basic national accounting identity:

- supply of goods and services (domestic output plus imports) equals use of goods and services (intermediate consumption plus final consumption plus capital formation plus exports).

In addition, estimates of value added resulting from this identity can be confronted with direct observations on income generated from illegal activities.

9.32.   For any given illegal activity, data should be collected, as far as possible independently, on each of the three angles of incidence, namely supply, use and generated income. Subsequently, the data can be confronted and integrated. In many cases, data for one of the angles may be completely absent or very weak. In that case, the identities can be used to compile the missing data.

9.33.   In general, police and survey data on criminal activities are the main data sources for the compilation of estimates. Health care institutions and charities may also provide useful information, *e.g.* on the number of addicts in the case of drugs, or the number of prostitutes. Furthermore, information may be derived from more conventional data sources for the compilation of national accounts, *e.g.* labour force surveys and other household surveys. However, serious problems in relation to underreporting, selective non-response, etc. are unavoidable.

9.34.   Illegal activities are a phenomenon frequently investigated in depth by universities and research institutes. Although these studies are often not concerned with the money flows involved in the illegal activities, they may provide useful supporting information. The last resort is to conduct a survey focusing on those aspects of illegal production for which it seems feasible to try and collect data.

Drugs

9.35.   Directly observed data are usually not available on the production, distribution and consumption of drugs. Special studies by universities and research institutes may contain useful data, *e.g.* on domestically produced drugs. Usually, however, estimates must be based on police data on seizures and estimates of the relevant seizure rates. For domestic consumption, estimates of the number of addicts and average quantities used seem to provide the most reliable data. If the country does not have substantial exports of drugs, the data on supply and use are complete, and can be confronted with each other. In such confrontation, data on seizure rates are to be considered as especially weak. Additional information on these rates, for example obtained by interviewing convicted criminals, may improve the estimates. Moreover, a sensitivity analysis using different assumptions on seizure rates may prove helpful.

9.36.   If the country also exports drugs, either domestically produced or imported, the situation becomes much more complicated. Usually, exports can be estimated only as a residual item, *i.e.*, as domestic output plus imports minus consumption minus seizures. As a consequence, the reliability of the estimates depends critically on the quality of the estimated seizure rates. Furthermore, it may be very difficult to establish the residency of the persons controlling the international trade, and therefore to establish the country to which the relevant trade and transport margins have to be allocated.

9.37.   As the identity in current prices shows, total domestic output consists of domestically produced drugs (at basic prices) plus trade and transports margins on both domestically produced drugs and imported drugs. The total of this figure can be considered to be the most important item, the distinction between output of domestically produced drugs and margin is less relevant. Total domestic output in current prices equals consumption plus exports minus imports. So, additional data on street prices, import prices and export prices are needed to arrive at an estimate.

9.38.   Reasonably good data on street prices are usually available from police sources or research studies. Data on prices of imports and exports are much more difficult to obtain. As in the case of drug purities, one needs additional information on the structure of the drug distribution network. Sometimes, such information may be available from police and/or customs. Information on prices in neighbouring countries may also be applicable. Trade in drugs is internationally organised, and it can be assumed that, leaving aside major differences in distribution channels and in law enforcement practices, import prices will not differ very much between countries.

9.39.   To arrive at an estimate of value added, assumptions have to be made on the value of intermediate consumption. Assuming that drugs dealers take care of their own transport, intermediate consumption is rather low in the case of trade in drugs. A higher share of intermediate consumption has to be assumed in the case of drugs production itself. Often, technical coefficients are available for this purpose.

9.40.   Dividing the resulting estimates of value added by estimates of the number of people involved in the drugs industry may give an insight into the plausibility of the value-added figures.

9.41. The income generated by illegal drugs transactions is used, sometimes after laundering the money, for final consumption purposes, investment in non-financial and financial assets, etc. It can be assumed that these expenditures on legitimate items will be covered implicitly in the system of national accounts.

Prostitution

9.42. The total supply of prostitution services comprises services produced domestically by residents and by non-residents and imported services, *i.e.*, prostitution services purchased by residents travelling abroad. Information on domestic output of prostitution services can be collected from health care organisations, police or prostitutes' associations. Furthermore, as prostitution is a popular theme for special studies by universities and research institutes, valuable information may be available from such sources.

9.43. Reasonable estimates of the number of prostitutes are usually available from these sources. Multiplication of the number by estimates of the average number of clients and the average price may provide a good first approximation of total domestic supply of prostitution services. Here, a breakdown into different kinds of prostitutes (call girls, prostitutes in nightclubs, "window" prostitutes, prostitutes in massage parlours, escort services, heroin prostitutes, etc.) may be needed, as the prices between these categories differ substantially. The resulting estimate of prostitution services concerns the total of these services, *i.e.*, including procurement, rents of rooms, etc. A breakdown may be possible on the basis of information on the average percentage a prostitute has to pay to the procurer, the average rent, etc. From the supply side, an estimate can also be derived of income generated by prostitutes themselves. On imports of services by residents travelling abroad, reliable data may be very scarce.

9.44. Use of prostitution services mainly consists of final use by residents (final consumption) and use by non-residents (exports). In addition, some expenditures may be paid by enterprises (intermediate consumption). Usually, data on total final use of prostitution services by residents (produced domestically plus imported) can be considered unreliable. Conventional data sources, such as household budget surveys, and also special surveys, almost inevitably contain serious underreporting. Furthermore, hardly any data will be available on expenditures by non-residents. On the other hand, from the income side, it may be possible to collect direct information on the average earnings of prostitutes, if possible broken down by categories. This can then be confronted and integrated with the relevant data from the supply side.

9.45. A problem in the measurement of the domestic output of prostitution services arises from the growing internationalisation of prostitution. One of the consequences is an increasing proportion of non-resident prostitutes staying less than one year in the host country. The services of these prostitutes are not part of domestic output and should be recorded as imports. Conversely, there may be export of services by resident prostitutes staying for short periods in other countries.

9.5. Problems of Double Counting

9.46. The previous section suggested methods to compile explicit estimates for illegal activities. Simply adding these estimates to the national accounts data on legal activities will be problematic if there are reasons to believe that part of illegal production is included implicitly. This issue of possible double counting is addressed in the following paragraphs.

9.47. As regards the output and value added of illegal activities, several possibilities for double counting can be distinguished. First of all, units providing illegal goods and services may be included in the business register. As a consequence, at least part of their output will be covered by enterprise surveys. This is a particular problem in the case of activities on the borderline of legal and illegal, *e.g.* prostitution. Often, the enterprises providing prostitution services are registered under activities such as massage salons, renting of rooms, cafés, film studios, etc.

9.48. Another reason why illegal activities may be included in the national accounts is that the units earning income from these activities want to legitimatise at least part of their earnings. For this purpose, they may provide data to the statistical office or the tax authorities but report their output and income as coming from different activities than the ones they actually undertake.

9.49.   It is also possible that illegal activities are partly included in other data sources such as household budget surveys and tax statistics. For example, payments for prostitution services and bribes that are paid by enterprises may be reported in company accounts under an "other costs" item as part of intermediate consumption. Such an overestimation of legal intermediate consumption could affect GDP in various ways depending on how supply and uses are reconciled in compiling the national accounts.

9.50.   Given an explicit estimate of illegal activities, the only one way to avoid double counting output is careful research into the contents of the basic data used for the regular compilation of the national accounts and consistent recording of adjustments for illegal activities in all three approaches to GDP, allowing for possibly different implicit coverage. The enterprises listed in the business register that are most likely to be involved in illegal production should be identified and screened. Those believed to be involved in illegal production activities for which estimates are being separately compiled should be excluded from the regular survey estimates. The same applies to other basic data. Although such research is likely to involve substantial resources, it seems to be the only approach to establishing whether or not the illegal activities have been included implicitly in GDP. Furthermore, the research results may provide valuable information in compiling the illegal production estimates.

9.51.   Another, rather different issue of double counting relates to expenditures on legal items by units involved in illegal activities. Here, the use of legal goods and services to produce illegal products may give rise to special problems. For example, the intermediate consumption needed to produce prostitution services is partly accounted for in the present national accounts, being recorded as final consumption of households. Another example is the use of raw materials and semi-manufactured products needed to produce soft drugs. Energy, lamps, fertiliser, seeds, ventilation and nutrition systems are needed to grow cannabis. Some of these outlays are probably included in final consumption or gross fixed capital formation of households or as intermediate consumption of horticulture.

9.52.   These double-counting problems result from trying to reconcile supplies and uses when the data used as input to the reconciliation process are not complete, *i.e.*, uses of legal goods and services for the purpose of illegal production are excluded. The resulting discrepancies between supply and use will be allocated to "other uses" categories. The problem is solved automatically if data for the whole economy, *i.e.*, including illegal production, are included in the supply and use framework.

Chapter 10

INFORMAL SECTOR PRODUCTION

10. INFORMAL SECTOR PRODUCTION

10.1. Introduction

10.1.   Measurements of the informal sector are of intrinsic interest in their own right as well as providing a contribution towards exhaustive measures of GDP. The informal sector represents an important part of the economy, and particularly of the labour market, in many countries, especially developing countries, and plays a major role in employment creation, production and income generation. In countries with high rates of population growth or urbanisation, the informal sector tends to absorb most of the growing labour force in the urban areas. Informal sector employment is a necessary survival strategy in countries that lack social safety nets such as unemployment insurance, or where wages and pensions are too low to cover the cost of living. In other countries, the process of industrial restructuring in the formal sector is seen as leading to a greater decentralisation of production through subcontracting to small enterprises, many of which are in the informal sector. As previously noted, the 1993 SNA makes provision for the informal sector, and a sectorial account can be compiled using the same principles and procedures as for the household sector account elaborated in United Nations (2000).

10.2.   The vast majority of informal sector activities provide goods and services whose production and distribution are perfectly legal. This is in contrast to illegal production. There is also a clear distinction between the informal sector and underground production. Informal sector activities are not necessarily performed with the deliberate intention of evading the payment of taxes or social security contributions, or infringing labour legislation or other regulations. Certainly, some informal sector enterprises prefer to remain unregistered or unlicensed in order to avoid compliance with some or all regulations and thereby reduce production costs. One should, however, make a distinction between those whose business revenue is high enough to bear the costs of regulations and those who cannot afford to comply with existing regulations because their income is too low and irregular, because certain laws and regulations are quite irrelevant to their needs and conditions, or because the State is virtually non-existent in their lives and lacks the means to enforce the regulations which it has enacted.

10.3.   In some countries at least, a sizeable proportion of informal sector enterprises are actually registered in some way, or pay taxes, even though they may not be in a position to comply with the full range of legal and administrative requirements. It should also be noted that substantial segments of underground production originate from enterprises belonging to the formal sector. Examples include the production of goods and services "off-the-books", undeclared financial transactions or property income, overstatement of tax-deductible expenses, employment of clandestine workers, and unreported wages and overtime work of declared employees. In summary, although informal sector and underground activities may overlap, the concept of the informal sector needs to be clearly separated from the concept of underground production.

10.4.   In January 1993, the Fifteenth International Conference of Labour Statisticians (15th ICLS) adopted a *Resolution concerning statistics of employment in the informal sector* (International Labour Organization, 1993b) to assist national statistical offices in developing definitions, classifications and methods of data collection for the informal sector. The Resolution covers issues relating to the definition of the informal sector and the design, content and conduct of informal sector surveys. The informal sector definition adopted by the 15th ICLS forms part of the 1993 SNA although Chapter IV of the 1993 SNA reproduces only the main parts of the definition. The 1993 SNA suggests that in countries where informal sector activities are significant the informal sector should be shown separately as a sub-sector of households (1993 SNA: 4.159). Such a distinction makes it possible for the national accounts to quantify the contribution of the informal sector to the national economy, which is an urgent statistical need for many countries. The aim of this chapter is to explain the thinking behind the 15th ICLS Resolution and the definition of informal sector and to elaborate on methods of measurement.

10.2. Definition of Informal Sector

10.2.1. *Background*

10.5.   Since its first appearance in the early 1970s, the term *informal sector* has become so popular that nowadays it is used with different meanings for different purposes. Originally, it referred to a concept for data analysis and policy-making. Now it is sometimes used in a much broader sense to refer to a concept for the collection of data on activities not covered by the existing, conventional sources of statistics. In line with the original notion behind the concept, the starting point of the 15th ICLS in defining the informal sector was an understanding of the informal sector as an *analytical/political* concept rather than a *statistical* one. Paragraph 5 (1) of the Resolution states:

> "The informal sector may be broadly characterised as consisting of units engaged in the production of goods or services with the primary objective of generating employment and incomes to the persons concerned. These units typically operate at a low level of organisation, with little or no division between labour and capital as factors of production and on a small scale. Labour relations – where they exist – are based mostly on casual employment, kinship or personal and social relations rather than contractual arrangements with formal guarantees."

10.6.   Care was taken by the 15th ICLS to make the activities included in the informal sector definition as homogeneous as possible with respect to their economic objectives and behaviour, and the requirements for data analysis. From the practical viewpoint of survey operations, a related consideration regarding the inclusion of enterprises was the need for, and usefulness of, their coverage in informal sector surveys.

10.7.   The 15th ICLS also tried to accommodate as far as possible the notion of the informal sector as a statistical concept in extending its scope to as large a universe of non-observed activities as seemed practically feasible and conceptually justifiable, but rejected its interpretation as "catch-all" concept. Thus, as noted in Chapter 3, the definition adopted does not lead to a segmentation of the economy or the employed population according to a formal/informal sector dichotomy. The 15th ICLS recognised that activities excluded from the scope of the informal sector were not necessarily formal. Examples are the household non-market production of goods, small-scale agriculture, paid domestic services, and activities presently falling outside the 1993 SNA production boundary, such as domestic or personal services provided by unpaid household members and volunteer services rendered to the community. It was recommended that such activities should be identified as belonging to a separate category outside the formal/informal sector distinction.

10.8.   The definition had to be acceptable to a wide range of countries from different parts of the world. Thus, the definition had to be broad enough to encompass the variety of ways in which the informal sector manifests itself in different countries. It had to provide flexibility for the adoption of more specific definitions at the country level, reflecting national circumstances, even though such flexibility may adversely affect the international comparability of the statistics. Finally, the 15th ICLS was requested to develop a definition of the informal sector in such a way that it could also be used for national accounting purposes. This requirement had certain implications for the nature of the definition, as explained below.

10.9.   Firstly, the informal sector had to be defined in terms of characteristics of the enterprises in which the activities take place, rather than in terms of the characteristics of the persons involved or their jobs. Accordingly, persons employed in the informal sector were defined as comprising all persons who, during a given reference period, were employed in at least one informal sector enterprise, irrespective of their status in employment and whether it was their main or a secondary job. The definition of the population employed in the informal sector stresses the distinction between *employed persons* and *jobs*. It indicates that persons are classified into the informal sector through their relationship to a job in an enterprise with specific characteristics.

10.10. Persons exclusively employed in enterprises outside the informal sector are excluded from the international definition of the informal sector, no matter how precarious their employment situation may be. Thus, the concept of employment in the informal sector is not identical with the concept of *informal employment, i.e.,* persons employed in informal jobs. The 15th ICLS was aware of the need for statistics not only on employment in the informal sector, but also on employment in informal jobs. It was believed, however, that the best way of identifying informal jobs would be through appropriate sub-categories of status-in-employment classifications.

10.11. Secondly, the informal sector was considered by the 15th ICLS to be a sub-sector of the 1993 SNA household sector. In other words, informal sector enterprises are defined as a subset of household unincorporated enterprises. As noted in Chapter 2, in contrast to corporations and quasi-corporations, a household unincorporated enterprise is a producing unit that is not constituted as a separate legal entity independently of the household members who own it. It has no complete set of accounts that would provide a means of identifying flows of income and capital between the enterprise and the owners. *Household unincorporated enterprises* include unincorporated enterprises owned and operated by individual household members or by several members of the same household, as well as unincorporated partnerships and co-operatives formed by members of different households, all provided they lack complete sets of accounts.

10.12. As previously noted, the term *enterprise* is being used in a broad sense. It covers not only producing units that employ hired labour, but also those that are owned and operated by single individuals working on own-account as self-employed persons, either alone or with the help of unpaid family members. The production activities may be undertaken inside or outside the business owner's home; they may be carried out in identifiable premises or without fixed location. Accordingly, independent street vendors, taxi drivers, home-based workers, etc., are all considered to be enterprises.

10.13. The 15th ICLS recognised that the characteristic features of household unincorporated enterprises described in the 1993 SNA corresponded well to the concept of the informal sector as commonly understood. The fixed and other capital used does not belong to the enterprises as such but to their owners. The enterprises as such cannot engage in transactions or enter into contracts with other units, nor incur liabilities on their own behalf. The owners have to raise the necessary finance at their own risk and are personally liable, without limit, for any debts or obligations incurred in the production process. Expenditure for production is often indistinguishable from household expenditure, and capital equipment such as buildings or vehicles may be used indistinguishably for business and household purposes.

10.2.2. Core Definition

10.14. The first three criteria of the informal sector definition adopted by the 15th ICLS refer to the legal organisation of the enterprises, their ownership and the type of accounts kept for them. These three criteria are all embodied in the concept of household unincorporated enterprises as described above. However, while all informal sector enterprises can be regarded as household unincorporated enterprises, not all household unincorporated enterprises belong to the informal sector. In defining the additional criteria to distinguish informal sector enterprises from other household unincorporated enterprises, the 15th ICLS adopted a modular approach, illustrated in Figure 10.1.

10.15. Within household unincorporated enterprises a distinction was made between *enterprises of employers* and *own-account enterprises*. In accordance with the definitions of employers and own-account workers of the 1993 International Classification of Status in Employment (ICSE-93), the distinction was based on whether or not an enterprise employs at least one employee on a continuous basis (in contrast to employment on an occasional basis or employment of contributing family workers). The distinction was deemed important for definitional purposes. Compared with own-account enterprises,

Figure 10.1.   **Fifteenth ICLS: Framework for informal sector definition**

Informal own-account enterprises	Other own-account enterprises	Own-account enterprises
Enterprises of informal employers	Other enterprises of employers	Enterprises of employers
Informal sector enterprises	Other household unincorporated enterprises	

enterprises of employers necessarily have a higher degree of formality in their operations, and therefore require additional criteria for being classified in the informal sector. Moreover, the distinction between these two groups of enterprises was considered useful for the purposes of data analysis and policy making and for the stratification of informal sector survey samples. Accordingly, the informal sector was defined as comprising *informal own-account enterprises* and *enterprises of informal employers* for which separate criteria were specified, as described in sections 10.2.3 and 10.2.4 below.

10.16.   There are basically two different but interrelated ways of viewing and defining the informal sector. One approach views enterprises in relation to the legal and administrative framework in force and defines the informal sector as made up of enterprises that do not conform to this framework in some way. It assumes an intrinsic relation between non-registration and the notion of informality. The second approach views the informal sector as a particular form of production, and defines it in terms of the way the enterprises are organised and carry out their activities. Supporters of the second approach maintain that the informal sector is not identical with the unregistered sector. They stress the need for a clear conceptual basis in defining the sector, and point out the problems that a criterion based on registration may pose for the comparability of informal sector statistics between countries, between different areas within a country, and over time. They also mention the practical difficulties of obtaining information on the registration of enterprises as their owners may be reluctant to provide this information, and other respondents (*e.g.* employees) may be unable to do so. They view non-registration as a characteristic of the informal sector rather than as a criterion for defining it.

10.17.   There was no agreement at the 15th ICLS as to which of the two approaches was better. Thus, the definition finally adopted by the 15th ICLS incorporated both approaches in the sense that it allows non-registration and/or employment size to be used as criteria to distinguish informal sector enterprises from other household unincorporated enterprises.

10.2.3. Informal Own-Account Enterprises

10.18.   The 15th ICLS specified that, depending on national circumstances, either all own-account enterprises should be considered informal, or only those that are not registered under specific forms of national legislation. The legislation referenced includes factories' and commercial acts, tax and social security laws, professional groups' regulatory acts, and similar acts, laws or regulations established by *national* legislative bodies. Regulations enacted by local authorities for the purpose of obtaining a trade license or a permit to operate a business are excluded from the criterion. They are not considered to be appropriate because they are governed by administrative regulations and their enforcement that may vary considerably from one country to another and, within the same country, over time or between different regions. Moreover, they are not considered to have much of an effect on the way the enterprises are organised and operate nor on their economic objectives and behaviour, and homogeneity of economic objectives and behaviour is the 1993 SNA guiding principle for distinguishing between the various institutional sectors and sub-sectors. It should be noted that in many countries the criterion of non-registration, if properly chosen, covers the criteria of lack of legal identity and lack of a complete set of accounts.

10.19.   The 15th ICLS did not include any size criterion in the definition of informal own-account enterprises. Such a criterion was considered superfluous, as by their very nature virtually all own-account enterprises are small.

10.2.4. *Enterprises of Informal Employers*

10.20. The 15th ICLS specified that enterprises of informal employers should be defined in terms of one or more of the following three criteria:

- small size of the enterprise in terms of employment;
- non-registration of the enterprise (defined as for informal own-account enterprises); or
- non-registration of its employees.

10.21. According to the 15th ICLS, the criterion of employment size can be formulated in terms of the *number of employees employed by the enterprise on a continuous basis,* or the *total number of employees* (including employees employed on an occasional basis), or the *total number of persons engaged* during a specific reference period (including the entrepreneur, business partners and contributing family workers in addition to the employees). The first of these is considered to be the ideal measure from the conceptual point of view, as it matches best the definition of informal own-account enterprises, which does not take account of the number of enterprise owners, business partners, contributing family workers and casual employees working in the enterprise. In practice, however, information on the number of all employees or on the total number of persons engaged is more easily obtained from survey respondents than information on the number of employees employed on a continuous basis, and may correspond more closely to the criterion used in practice to define the lower size cut-off point for surveys of formal sector enterprises or establishments.

10.22. In the case of enterprises composed of more than one establishment, the 15th ICLS recommended use of the *establishment* rather than the *enterprise* as the unit to which the size criterion refers. It specified that an enterprise composed of more than one establishment should be considered informal if none of its establishments exceeded the size limit. For many countries, the use of the establishment rather than the enterprise as the unit for the size criterion ensures compatibility with the criterion determining coverage of formal sector establishment surveys. Thus informal and formal sector statistics can complement each other. It also becomes possible to capture the development of informal sector enterprises that for various reasons tend to grow through the creation of additional small establishments rather than through an expansion of employment in the original establishment.

10.23. An important advantage of the size criterion in defining the informal sector is that size can be measured relatively easily by all relevant types of surveys. In addition, there is usually correlation between small size and other aspects of informality, in particular:

- small enterprises can remain unidentified by the authorities more easily than larger enterprises;
- governments with limited administrative resources tend to focus on large enterprises when trying to collect taxes or enforce labour legislation;
- unions tend to concentrate on large enterprises, which can be reached more easily, so that their efforts will achieve maximum results; and
- small enterprises tend to use more traditional technologies.

10.24. On the other hand, proponents of non-registration as the informal sector criterion note that small size, unless used in combination with other criteria, is not sufficient to define the informal sector and that the choice of the size limit is more or less arbitrary.

10.25. The size limit for enterprises of informal employers was not specified by the 15th ICLS so that it can be varied according to needs between countries and even between branches of economic activity within a country. In order to avoid an overlap with formal sector surveys, it was recommended that the choice of the size limit should take account of the coverage of enterprise/establishment surveys of the larger units in the corresponding branches of economic activity, where such surveys exist. However, some national statistical offices actually prefer to have a certain overlap in coverage, providing it can be identified, because response rates and data quality in enterprise/establishment surveys tend to be relatively poor for the smaller units.

10.26. During the 15th ICLS consideration was given to defining the informal sector residually as comprising all units that are not covered in existing enterprise/establishment surveys. It was however decided that such a definition would not be appropriate for data analysis and policy making as it would tend to be unstable over time – the informal sector would expand or contract if the coverage of the existing surveys were changed. It would also introduce substantial differences between countries depending upon the coverage of their surveys. Furthermore, it was recommended that, where the existing cut-off point used for formal sector surveys seemed too high to be the size limit for the informal sector, efforts should be made to extend formal sector survey coverage by lowering the cut-off point. Where this is not possible, it may be preferable to recognise the existence of an intermediate segment, and to cover it through a separate survey rather than to include it in the scope of informal sector surveys. This is because the survey methods used for the collection of data on informal sector enterprises may not be equally well suited to medium-sized enterprises.

10.27. The criterion of non-registration of the employees of the enterprise refers to the conditions of employment in the informal sector regarding the employees' social and legal protection. It is defined in terms of the absence of employment or apprenticeship contracts which commit the employer to pay relevant taxes and social security contributions on behalf of the employees or which make the employment relationships subject to standard labour legislation. According to this criterion, an enterprise is informal if none of its employees are registered. This criterion is especially useful in countries where the registration of workers also leads to the registration of the enterprises employing them, *e.g.* with the social security institutions. In other countries, registration of workers is likely to be more useful as an indicator of the quality of employment than as a criterion to define the informal sector.

10.2.5. *Additional Provisions*

10.28. In order to complement its definition of the informal sector, the 15th ICLS adopted a number of recommendations regarding the scope of informal sector surveys and the statistical treatment of particular situations at the borderline between the informal and other sectors.

Non-economic activities

10.29. The scope of the informal sector is restricted to economic activities, *i.e.*, activities included in the 1993 SNA production boundary. This restriction is considered necessary to ensure that employment, production and income generation in the informal sector can be measured as a share of total employment, gross domestic product and national income. Excluded are domestic and personal services provided by unpaid household members, as well as volunteer services rendered to the community. It should be noted in this connection that the 1993 SNA production boundary also includes illegal and underground production activities. In principle, such activities fall within the scope of the informal sector if they are undertaken by units meeting the criteria of the informal sector definition. In practice, however, many such activities are likely to go unreported in statistical surveys of the informal sector.

Non-market production

10.30. According to the 15th ICLS, household unincorporated enterprises that are **exclusively** engaged in the production of goods or services for own final consumption or own fixed capital formation (*e.g.* construction of own houses) are excluded from the informal sector, with the possible exception of households employing paid domestic workers (as noted below). This recommendation was based on two considerations. Firstly, units exclusively engaged in non-market production differ in their economic objectives and behaviour from informal sector enterprises, which are typically operated for the purpose of earning a living or obtaining an additional income through the production of goods and services for sale to others. Thus, they should not be merged with informal sector enterprises. Secondly, it was noted that it is difficult to determine the value of goods produced for own final use unless the same units also produce some of their goods for sale to others.

10.31. As previously noted, the boundary between enterprises exclusively engaged in production for own final use and others does not match precisely the 1993 SNA definition of a market producer as the latter includes only those enterprises (or establishments) most or all of whose output is marketed (1993 SNA: 6.52).

Agricultural activities

10.32. The 15th ICLS recognised that, from a conceptual point of view, there was nothing against the inclusion, within the scope of the informal sector, of household unincorporated enterprises engaged in agricultural and related activities, if they meet the criteria of the definition. For practical data collection reasons, however, the 15th ICLS recommended excluding agricultural and related activities from the scope of informal sector surveys and measuring them separately. The reasoning was that many developing countries have a large agricultural sector, mainly composed of small, unregistered household unincorporated enterprises and that the inclusion of such enterprises in informal sector surveys would lead to considerable expansion of survey operations and increase in costs. Moreover, most national statistical systems already have an established system of agricultural surveys whose coverage includes (or can relatively easily be extended to include) household unincorporated enterprises engaged in agricultural and related activities. In terms of concepts, definitions, classifications, survey content, questionnaire design, reference periods, sampling frames and procedures, organisation of field work, etc., agricultural surveys appear better suited than informal sector surveys to meeting the particular requirements for measuring agricultural and related activities.

10.33. However, the 15th ICLS recommended that non-agricultural activities of household unincorporated enterprises mainly engaged in the agricultural sector should be included in the informal sector if they meet the other criteria for inclusion. Experience has shown that such non-agricultural activities are frequently undertaken as secondary activities of farm households or during the agricultural slack season.

Rural areas

10.34. Recognising the large number of informal sector activities in the rural areas of many countries and their similarity with urban informal sector activities, the 15th ICLS recommended that, in principle, the informal sector should include enterprises located in rural areas as well as enterprises located in urban areas. However, countries starting to conduct informal sector surveys were given the option to confine data collection initially to urban areas until resources and appropriate sampling frames become available to cover the whole national territory.

Professional and technical services

10.35. In the past, it had been sometimes suggested that enterprises engaged in the production of professional or technical services rendered by self-employed doctors, lawyers, accountants, architects, engineers, etc., should be excluded from the informal sector because of the high level of skills involved and other particular characteristics. However, the 15th ICLS recommended that there should be no special treatment for such enterprises, *i.e.*, that they should be included or excluded on the same basis as other enterprises.

Outworkers (Homeworkers)

10.36. In accordance with the 1993 SNA, outworkers (homeworkers) were defined by the 15th ICLS as persons who agree to work for a particular enterprise, or to supply a certain quantity of goods or services to a particular enterprise, by prior arrangement or contract with that enterprise, but whose place of work is not within any of the establishments which make up that enterprise (1993 SNA: 7.26). It was recommended that outworkers should be included among informal sector enterprises if they constitute enterprises on their own as self-employed persons, and if these enterprises meet the criteria of the informal sector definition.

10.37. Criteria for distinguishing self-employed outworkers from employee outworkers include:

- the basis of remuneration (income received as a function of the value of outputs produced *versus* payment related to the amount of labour inputs provided);

- employment of paid workers by the outworker;

- non-existence of an employment contract with the enterprise receiving the goods or services produced by the outworker;

- decision-making on markets, scale of operations and finance; and

- ownership of machinery or equipment.

10.38. In respect of situations, where the number of outworkers was significant or where outworkers represented a group of particular concern for data users, it was recommended that self-employed outworkers be identified as a separate sub-category of informal sector enterprises.

Paid domestic workers

10.39. There was no agreement at the 15th ICLS regarding the treatment of paid domestic workers employed by households (*e.g.* maids, laundresses, watchmen, drivers, and gardeners) with respect to the informal sector. It was pointed out that, in many situations, it is virtually impossible to distinguish paid domestic workers who are self-employed (*i.e.*, who are owners of household unincorporated enterprises producing services for sale on the market) from those who are employees of the households employing them (*i.e.*, who are employees of household unincorporated enterprises producing services for their own final consumption). Moreover, data on paid domestic workers and their remuneration are often available from other sources, such as labour force or household income-expenditure surveys, so there may be no need to cover such workers in an informal sector survey.

10.40. For these reasons, the issue of whether or not paid domestic workers should be included in the informal sector was left by the 15th ICLS as open for determination by the countries themselves, depending upon their national circumstances and the intended uses of the statistics. However, it was recommended that, if included in the informal sector, paid domestic workers should be identified as a separate subcategory in order to enhance the international comparability of the statistics.

10.2.6. *Recommendations of the Delhi Group*

10.41. The 15th ICLS provided considerable flexibility to countries in defining and measuring the informal sector. Some elements of flexibility were desired, because the 15th ICLS resolution was the first international recommendation ever adopted on the topic, and its main purpose was to provide technical guidelines for the development of informal sector statistics rather than strive after the international comparability of data. Other elements of flexibility arose from lack of agreement. However, flexibility reduces international comparability. To address this problem, the UN Expert Group on Informal Sector Statistics (Delhi Group), which was constituted in 1997, has endeavoured to harmonise national definitions of the informal sector on the basis of the framework set by the international definition. The Delhi Group recognised that there were limits to harmonisation; nevertheless, on the basis of the largest common denominator, the Group was able to identify a subset of the informal sector that could be defined uniformly and for which countries could make internationally comparable data available. Accordingly, the Delhi Group adopted the following text.

"Since the informal sector manifests itself in different ways in different countries, national definitions of the informal sector cannot be fully harmonised at present. International agencies should disseminate informal sector data according to the national definitions used. In order to enhance the international comparability of informal sector statistics, they should also disseminate data for the subset of the informal sector, which can be defined uniformly" (Central Statistical Organisation, India 1999).

10.42. To arrive at this subset, the Delhi Group adopted the following recommendations:

1. All countries should use the criteria of legal organisation (unincorporated enterprises), of type of accounts (no complete set of accounts) and of product destination (at least some market output).

2. Specification of the employment size limit of the enterprise in the national definition of the informal sector is left to the country's discretion. For international reporting, however, countries should provide figures separately for enterprises with less than five employees. In the case of multiple-establishment enterprises, the size limit should apply to the largest establishment.

3. Countries using the employment size criterion should provide disaggregated figures for enterprises, which are not registered, as well as for enterprises, which are registered.

4. Countries using the criterion of non-registration should provide disaggregated figures for enterprises with less than five employees as well as for enterprises with five and more employees.

5. Countries, which include agricultural activities, should provide figures separately for agricultural and non-agricultural activities.

6. Countries should include persons engaged in professional or technical activities if they meet the criteria of the informal sector definition.

7. Countries should include paid domestic services unless these are provided by employees.

8. Countries should follow paragraph 18 of the Resolution adopted by the 15th ICLS regarding the treatment of outworkers/homeworkers. Countries should provide figures separately for outworkers/homeworkers included in the informal sector.

9. Countries covering urban as well as rural areas should provide figures separately for both urban and rural areas.

10. Countries using household surveys or mixed surveys should make an effort to cover not only persons whose main job is in the informal sector, but also those whose main job is in another sector and who have a secondary activity in the informal sector.

10.43. Since the subset presently covers only a relatively small part of the informal sector in any country, the Delhi Group recognised that further efforts were needed to enlarge it in future.

10.3. Measuring the Informal Sector

10.3.1. *Measurement Objectives*

10.44. The appropriate methods for measuring the informal sector depend upon the measurement objectives. If the aim is simply to monitor the evolution of informal sector employment in terms of the number and characteristics of the persons involved and the conditions of their employment and work, then the data can be obtained by adding questions to an existing labour force survey. Similarly, if the aim is to obtain information of the demand by households for goods and services produced by the informal sector, then supplementary questions can be included in a household income and expenditure survey.

10.45. On the other hand, the measurement objectives may be much more complex. For example the aim may be to collect detailed structural information on the informal sector including the number and characteristics of the enterprises involved, their production activities, employment, income generation, capital equipment, the conditions and constraints under which they operate, and their organisation and relationships with the formal sector and the public authorities. In this case, measurement requires a dedicated informal sector survey in which the informal sector enterprises themselves and their owners are the observation and reporting units. In this case, as outlined in Chapter 6, there are two basic survey design options, namely an enterprise survey or a mixed household-enterprise survey. The choice depends upon data requirements, the organisation of statistical systems, and the resources available.

The design must take into account the large number of enterprises likely to be in scope and their typical characteristics – small size, high mobility and turnover, seasonal variations in business activity, clustering in specific areas, lack of recognisable features for identification/location, lack of usable records, and eventual reluctance to participate. This may require modification of traditional survey methods or development of new ones. The following paragraphs describe the various measurement options in more detail.

10.3.2. *Labour Force Surveys*

10.46. Monitoring the number and characteristics of the persons in the informal sector and the conditions of their employment and work can be achieved by periodically including a few additional questions pertaining to the informal sector definition in an existing labour force or similar household survey. The costs of doing this are relatively low. The additional questions should be asked of all persons employed during the reference period of the survey, irrespective of their status in employment. In this way, it is possible to collect comprehensive data on the volume and characteristics of informal sector employment and to obtain information on employment and working conditions from all categories of informal sector workers, including employees and contributing family workers. These data can be related to the corresponding data on employment in the other sectors and unemployment.

10.47. Labour force or similar household surveys are often conducted at a higher frequency than specialised, in-depth informal sector surveys. Thus, the data obtained from the former concerning the evolution of labour inputs in the informal sector can be used to extrapolate data from the latter concerning other characteristics, *e.g.* value added, of the informal sector.

10.48. Employees, contributing family workers and proxy respondents may find it difficult to provide information on some of the criteria used to define the informal sector, especially the legal organisation and bookkeeping practices of the enterprise. It is, however, possible to obtain an estimate of the total number of persons employed in the informal sector using the data provided by respondents identified as employers or own-account workers regarding the characteristics of their enterprises, including legal organisation, bookkeeping practices and number of persons engaged. Another possibility is to base the estimate on all respondents irrespective of their status in employment and to obtain from respondents, who are employees or contributing family workers, approximate information on the legal organisation and type of accounts of the enterprise for which they work. For this purpose, a question on the type of enterprise (government agency, public enterprise, etc.) is required.

10.49. In many countries a large number of informal sector activities are undertaken as secondary jobs. Thus, it is essential that the questions for identification of the informal sector be asked not only in respect of the respondents' main jobs but also in respect of their secondary jobs. Furthermore, persons can be classified in the informal sector only if they have been identified as employed in the first place. To ensure that all informal sector activities are covered, it is often necessary to make special probes on activities that might otherwise go unreported as employment. For example, special probes may be required for unpaid work in small family enterprises, activities undertaken by women on their own account at or from home, undeclared activities, and informal sector businesses conducted as secondary jobs by farmers, government officials or employees of the private formal sector. In order to capture adequately the work of children in the informal sector, it may also be necessary to lower the minimum age limit that the surveys use for measurement of the economically active population. In designing the survey sample, care should be taken to include an adequate number of areas where informal sector workers live.

10.50. There are certain limitations to the use of labour force or similar household surveys for the measurement of informal sector employment.

- Informal sector employment is obtained as part of total employment, which is usually measured in relation to a short reference period such as one week. Because many informal sector activities are characterised by seasonal and other variations over time, the data on informal sector employment obtained for a short reference period are unlikely to be representative of the whole year. Improved representativeness in the time dimension may be achieved by repeating the measurement several times during the year in the case of quarterly, monthly or continuous surveys, or in using a longer reference period such as one year in the case of annual or less frequent surveys.

- Estimation of the number of informal sector enterprises is difficult, if not impossible. It is not identical to the number of informal sector entrepreneurs because of the existence of business partnerships.

- The possibilities for disaggregating the data by branch of economic activity and other characteristics depend upon the sample size and design.

10.3.3. *Household Income and Expenditure Surveys*

10.51. Household income and expenditure surveys are a potential source of information on the demand by households for goods and services produced in the informal sector. For each expenditure group, data may be collected on the distribution of expenditures by point of purchase, distinguishing, for example, supermarkets, formal shops and workshops, public sector and other formal points of purchase, ambulant vendors and street stalls, homes of vendors, small/informal shops and workshops, markets, and other informal points of purchase. However, household income and expenditure surveys cannot provide information on the total demand for informal sector products. They can only provide data on household final consumption expenditure for informal sector products, which is only a part (albeit the most important one) of the total demand.

10.3.4. *Informal Sector Enterprise Surveys*[1]

10.52. An enterprise survey presupposes the availability of a sampling frame of informal sector enterprises or establishments. List frames are usually not available. Countries with a large informal sector often do not have a business register. Even where a business register exists, it does not usually cover informal sector enterprises. In fact, it is common practice to use the presence or absence of an enterprise (establishment) in the business register to define the practical boundary between formal and informal. Thus, in most cases, enterprise surveys can be conducted only following a census of informal sector units or, better still, a general economic/establishment census covering the relevant branches of economic activity and containing the items required for the identification of informal sector units.

10.53. If an informal sector survey is conducted immediately after an economic/ establishment census, the census lists can provide the frame for selection of the informal sector sample. If the survey is conducted later, data from the most recent census can be used to construct an area sampling frame for the selection of sample areas (primary sampling units). The sampling rates should take account of the density of informal sector units of various types in the census enumeration areas. The high mobility and turnover of informal sector units usually requires a systematic updating of the lists of the enterprises/ establishments in the sample areas prior to selection of the ultimate sampling units.

10.54. Economic or establishment censuses are large-scale, costly operations that, due to resource constraints, many countries cannot undertake or can undertake only in their (major) urban areas. Furthermore, complete coverage of the informal sector without omissions or duplications is difficult.

10.55. Many informal sector enterprises are hard to identify and locate during a door to door enumeration because they lack recognisable business premises. Examples are activities conducted inside the owner's home (*e.g.* tailoring, food processing) or without fixed location (*e.g.* construction, transport, and ambulant trade). Unless substantial efforts are made, such units are likely to be omitted. An approach that has proven to be efficient and cost-effective in a number of countries is to conduct an economic census concurrently with the house-listing operation for a population census. This and similar efforts to improve the coverage of home-based and mobile activities are based on a mixed household-enterprise survey approach as discussed in section 10.3.5 below.

---

1. Throughout this section *enterprise* should be interpreted to mean *enterprise* or *establishment* according to the unit used by the statistical office as the subject of the survey.

10.56. As information is collected separately for each enterprise/establishment, it may be difficult to detect the linkages between informal sector activities undertaken by the same individuals or households and to consolidate these data at the household or enterprise level. There may be double-counting of activities in cases where, for example, some members of a household produce goods in a small workshop or at home, and other members of the same household sell these goods in a market or street stall.

10.57. Notwithstanding these limitations, enterprise censuses and surveys remain a useful and efficient method of data collection on the "upper" segment of the informal sector (*i.e.*, identifiable establishments), which are often the main target of small enterprise development programmes.

10.3.5 *Informal Sector Mixed Household-Enterprise Surveys*

10.58. There is a marked trend in recent years to survey the informal sector through *mixed-household enterprise surveys*. Such surveys are the most suitable approach when the aim is to collect comprehensive data about the informal sector as a whole and about the various segments of which it is composed. These surveys can cover all informal sector entrepreneurs (except homeless persons) and their activities, irrespective of the size of the enterprises, the kind of activity and the type of workplace used, and irrespective of whether the activities are undertaken as main or secondary jobs. In particular, they can also cover activities undertaken inside the owner's home or without fixed location.

10.59. As noted in Chapter 6, mixed household-enterprise surveys are based on area sampling and are usually conducted in two phases. In the first phase (the household survey component), a sampling frame for informal sector enterprises or, more generally, small enterprises is obtained through a household listing or survey in the selected sample areas (primary sampling units). All enterprises falling within the scope of the survey and their owners are identified. Data often have to be obtained from household members other than the enterprise owners themselves, *i.e.*, proxy respondents. Thus, it is not normally possible to obtain good quality data relating to the informal sector criteria. Instead, the focus is on ensuring good coverage of the informal sector by attempting to identify the owners of all enterprises that *may* belong to the informal sector.

10.60. In the second phase (the enterprise survey component), a sample (or all) of the enterprise owners are interviewed to obtain detailed information about them, their enterprises, and their employees (if any). The informal sector enterprises can be more precisely identified during this stage – a process known as post-sampling identification.

10.61. Mixed household-enterprise surveys make it possible to analyse jointly, at the enterprise or household level, the various kinds of informal sector activities undertaken by the same individuals or households. Moreover, data on the characteristics of the informal sector activities and enterprise owners can be related to the characteristics of the owners' households obtainable from the same survey. This is important for assessing the contribution of other household members to the household income and for analysis of the impact of the household situation on the activities of women and children working as informal sector entrepreneurs.

Independent surveys

10.62. Informal sector mixed household-enterprise surveys can be conceived either as stand-alone surveys or as modules attached to existing labour force or other household surveys. Often an independent survey is the technically better arrangement because its sample can be specifically designed to meet the informal sector measurement requirements, for example, to produce estimates of specified reliability in selected strata. Data may be required for each economic branch, or to support analysis of the differences between various informal sector segments regarding their income-generating potential, constraints and other characteristics.

10.63. Independent informal sector surveys using the mixed household-enterprise survey approach are based on a multi-stage design involving the following steps:

    1. selection of areas as primary sampling units;

    2. listing or interviewing of all households in the sample areas;

3. selection of sample households with owners of (potential) informal sector enterprises as ultimate sampling units; and

4. main interviewing of sample households and enterprise owners.

10.64. The sample design must take into consideration that some types of activities (*e.g.* transport, repair and other services) are likely to be less well represented than others (*e.g.* trade, sale of cooked food), and that some activities (*e.g.* certain types of manufacturing) tend to be concentrated in specific areas. To ensure adequate representation of all such activities in the sample and to reduce clustering effects, it is important to include a sufficient number of units in the first stage sample.

10.65. For first stage allocation and selection, an area sampling frame is used, consisting of enumeration areas of appropriate size, stratified according to the overall density of informal sector activity in these areas, or the densities of informal sector activities of different types. Information useful for construction of such a frame includes:

- data obtained from the latest population census on the density of employers and own-account workers in the enumeration areas classified by broad activity groups and, if available, by type of workplace and number of employees;

- data on the concentration of small establishments by broad activity groups as obtained from the latest establishment or economic census,

- data for stratification of enumeration areas by income level or other socio-economic criteria, data obtained during listing or data collection in previous informal sector or other surveys, or information based on local expert knowledge about the spatial distribution of informal sector activities in the regions or towns to be covered by the survey.

10.66. These data normally provide a reasonably good approximation of the density of informal sector entrepreneurs living in the enumeration areas at the time of the survey. Enumeration areas with a high density of informal sector entrepreneurs in the relevant activity groups are selected at a higher rate in order to obtain more coverage by the sample, increased sampling efficiency and reduced survey costs.

10.67. The cost aspect is particularly important for the first survey phase, which is an expensive operation unless it can be combined with a household listing for another survey. The task is to list all the households in the sample areas, to identify all the potential informal sector entrepreneurs and their enterprises, and to obtain any additional data to be used for their subsequent stratification and selection. The quality of listing is a key factor for the overall quality of the estimates obtained from the survey.

10.68. The household listing may not provide a complete coverage of informal sector activities conducted in identifiable establishments outside the homes of the enterprise owners. Thus, it is useful to undertake a dual, mutually exclusive listing of *i*) households and household-based (including mobile) entrepreneurs and *ii*) establishments in the sample areas. Some countries even use different area sampling frames for *i*) and *ii*) because they tend to be clustered in different areas. With a view to ensuring a complete coverage and accurate identification of household-based entrepreneurs, it may be useful to extend the first phase from a household listing to a household survey operation, during which detailed information is collected on the economic activities undertaken by each household member.

10.69. The listed households and establishments are then grouped in strata by industry, sex of the entrepreneur, type of workplace, etc., for second stage allocation and selection. The aim is to make the allocation of the final sample to the various strata as homogeneous as possible and to ensure that an adequate number of ultimate sampling units from each stratum is selected.

10.70. The design of an independent informal sector survey entails fairly complex survey operations and sample design and estimation procedures. It requires a team of qualified survey staff, sound training of interviewers, constant supervision and control of all survey operations, and care in keeping records of the listing operation, sample selection and sample outcome for each sample area.

Modules attached to household surveys

10.71. Attachment of an informal sector module to an existing household survey (such as a labour force survey or a household income and expenditure survey) means that the informal sector survey sample is obtained as a sub-sample of the base survey. The informal sector survey may be conducted simultaneously with the base survey or subsequently. The latter arrangement is preferred in most cases as it:

- facilitates the management and co-ordination of the two surveys;
- ensures that the survey operations for the base survey can proceed smoothly;
- is unlikely to have a negative impact on the quality of the base survey data; and
- provides a better control over the identification and selection of the sub-sample for the informal sector survey.

10.72. The modular approach is less complex and less expensive than the conduct of an independent informal sector survey because information collected during the base survey provides the basis for the identification and selection of the sub-sample of households or persons for the informal sector survey, and no special household listing or interviewing is required. From the methodological point of view, the strengths of the modular approach lie in its possibilities:

- to monitor changes of the informal sector over time, if the base survey is conducted regularly and an informal sector module is attached to it at sufficiently frequent intervals;
- to achieve a complete coverage and accurate identification of (potential) informal sector entrepreneurs in the sample households during the base survey interviews, particularly if a well-designed labour force survey is used for this purpose;
- to use the sampling weights of the base survey for the households with informal sector enterprises and thereby facilitate the estimation of the survey results; and
- to relate data on the informal sector activities to data obtained from the base survey.

10.73. However, the modular approach can only be used in situations where a suitable base survey exists, and where it is feasible in terms of survey operations and response burden to add data collection for the informal sector to data collection for the base topic. The representativeness of the data over time may be limited by the frequency and reference period of the base survey. The base survey sample is not likely to have been efficiently designed from the perspective of informal sector measurement, neither at the level of sample areas nor at the level of sample households. There is no control over the size of the informal sector sample or over its distribution by type of activity. The resulting number of informal sector entrepreneurs included in the sample may, therefore, be quite small, and insufficient to yield reliable separate estimates for each type of informal sector activity for which such estimates would be desirable (*e.g.* estimates by branch of economic activity).

10.74. There are ways to increase the size of the informal sector sample. If the information required for identification of the units eligible for the informal sector survey is obtained during the listing operation for the base survey, the informal sector survey sample can be selected on the basis of all households in the sample areas, rather than only those selected for the base survey sample. (This comes close to the design of an independent informal sector survey.) Alternatively, if resources permit, the base survey sample can be increased by adding households to it, either from the same or from additional sample areas.

Integrated surveys

10.75. *Integrated surveys* can be seen as special types of modular surveys. Integrated surveys are designed to meet several objectives at the same time, *i.e.*, the collection of data about the informal sector and other topics, *e.g.* labour force, household income and expenditure. Such surveys are especially useful for countries that do not have a household survey to which an informal sector module can be attached, and that need to collect data on a range of topics without having the resources that are necessary for separate surveys.

10.76. Integrated surveys aim at incorporating the sample design requirements for informal sector measurement into a combined survey design as an additional objective, to the extent that all the requirements can be reconciled. For this purpose, efforts are made in the sample allocation and selection to increase the number of households with informal sector enterprises included in the sample and to enhance the representation of the various types of informal sector activities in the sample. It should be noted, however, that integrated surveys are operationally complex undertakings, especially if the aim is to cover the whole country including rural areas. Moreover, the response burden for sample households tends to be high. Examples of integrated surveys are the 1-2-3 *surveys* that have been conducted in the capital cities of some French-speaking African countries. In these surveys, the first phase is a labour force survey, the second phase an informal sector survey based on a sub-sample of the labour force survey, and the third phase a household income and expenditure survey conducted on the original labour force survey sample.

10.3.6. *Design and Quality Considerations*

10.77. In addition to following the good survey design practices articulated in Chapter 6, the particular characteristics of the informal sector demand special attention. While sampling errors can be handled relatively easily by appropriate sample design and size, non-sampling errors are more difficult to control. The following measures may prove useful in reducing non-sampling errors and improving the quality of informal sector data.

10.78. A characteristic feature of many informal sector enterprises is their high mobility and turnover. In order to reduce non-contact rates and distortions of survey data resulting from sample units that have moved location or changed or stopped their activity, the time interval between the two survey phases of a mixed household-enterprise survey should be kept as short as possible.

10.79. Every possible effort should be made to trace sample units to their new location. Replacement by other units should be avoided, as it is likely to bias the survey results. In order to compensate for non-contacts, it is better to select a larger sample at the outset. Another means of increasing contact rates, as well as the quality of the data obtained, is to try to interview informal sector entrepreneurs, who conduct their business at fixed locations outside their home, at their actual place of work rather than at their residence.

10.80. Many informal sector entrepreneurs have a relatively low level of education and do not keep usable written records of their activities. They are not used to participating in surveys and are often unwilling or unable to devote much time to doing so. Some entrepreneurs are difficult to contact because they operate without fixed location, *e.g.* ambulant vendors, taxi drivers, and construction workers. There may also be respondents who are reluctant to answer the survey questions for fear of subsequent taxation or harassment by the authorities. Thus, provisions that help to improve response rates and data quality are essential, including:

- advance information for respondents regarding the survey and its purposes;
- formal assurance of confidentiality of the data provided;
- choice of the date, time and place of the interviews in consultation with the respondents themselves;
- sound motivation, training and supervision of interviewers and establishing good human relations between interviewers and respondents;
- design of survey questionnaires which are manageable in terms of content and length, and which are easy to follow and complete by interviewers;
- formulation of questions in a way that is understandable by respondents, and that refers to their specific situation and the nature of their activities; and
- use of short reference periods that enable respondents to provide the required information with sufficient accuracy.

10.81. In most circumstances, the maximum recommended length of the reference period is one month; in some cases a shorter reference period, such as one week or one day, may be essential. If respondents are allowed to choose the reference period for which they can best provide the requested data, auxiliary information has to be collected that enables data conversion to a standard reference period.

10.82. The best possible way of capturing seasonal variations and of estimating annual values in spite of using short reference periods is to spread data collection over a survey period of a whole year. The survey sample is then to be divided into independent sub-samples for different parts of the year, as repeated interviews with the same respondents are usually impossible. An alternative is to collect data for short reference periods during a short survey period, supplemented by questions on the intensity of business activity during each month of the year and on the average level of receipts/profits in the months of high/low business activity as a percentage of the average level of receipts/profits in the months of normal business activity.

Chapter 11

HOUSEHOLD PRODUCTION FOR OWN FINAL USE

11. HOUSEHOLD PRODUCTION FOR OWN FINAL USE

11.1. Introduction

11.1. Production of goods and services for own final use by household members is a significant part of total production in many countries. It comprises:

- household production of goods for own final use, including crops and livestock, production of other goods for own consumption, and own-account fixed capital formation;

- owner-occupied dwelling services; and

- paid domestic services, *i.e.*, by employment of paid domestic staff.

11.2. Household Production of Goods for Own Final Use

11.2. In defining the production boundary, the 1993 SNA (Para. 6.25) recommends that the production of a good for own final use should be measured when the amount produced is believed to be quantitatively important in relation to the total supply of the good in the country. It provides (Para. 6.24) an illustrative list of the most common types of goods that should be included, namely:

- the production of agricultural products and their subsequent storage; the gathering of berries or other uncultivated crops; forestry; wood-cutting and the collection of firewood; hunting and fishing;

- the production of other primary products such as mining salt, cutting peat, the supply of water, etc.;

- the processing of agricultural products; the production of grain by threshing; the production of flour by milling; the curing of skins and the production of leather; the production and preservation of meat and fish products; the preservation of fruit by drying, bottling, etc.; the production of dairy products such as butter or cheese; the production of beer, wine or spirits; the production of baskets and mats; etc.;

- other kinds of processing such as weaving cloth, dress making and tailoring, the production of footwear, the production of pottery, utensils or durables, making furniture or furnishings, etc.

11.3. Although not exhaustive, this list is enlightening in two respects. First, it makes clear that, in developing countries especially in Africa, production for own final use may account for an important share of the primary and secondary sectors, insofar as they are actually measured. Second, many if not most of these activities are undertaken by women, they are undertaken as secondary activities and, in most cases, the corresponding labour input is not captured in labour force statistics. Thus, their measurement in the national accounts is important, and all the more so during economic crises or periods of structural adjustment when these activities may play a major role in maintaining living standards. For example, when the CFA Franc was devalued in 1994, the purchasing power of the population was halved in francophone African countries. Dramatic falls in monetary incomes in real terms were also experienced in many transition countries in the early 1990s, leading to sharp increases in own-account production of crops and livestock in order to survive.

Agricultural production for own consumption

11.4.   Subsistence agriculture has long been the major part of non-market household production. Blades (1975) reviewed the national accounts estimates of 70 developing countries in Africa, Asia and Latin America and showed that virtually all of them included subsistence crop and livestock production in their accounts, and that over 70% also included subsistence fishing and forestry production. Subsistence agriculture is usually excluded from the scope of informal sector surveys not only because they tend to exclude agriculture, but also because they exclude enterprises solely involved in non-market activities.

11.5.   For data collection and estimation purposes, two situations must be distinguished. In developing countries, subsistence agriculture was very large a few decades ago, but now pure subsistence farmers have become more and more scarce. In the most common situation, and this is not limited to developing countries, farmers keep and store a part of their production for their own consumption and sell the rest. (Here *farmers* is used in the broad sense, including those engaged in animal husbandry, fishing, hunting, forestry, and so on.) However, more and more frequently, farmers have to sell their whole crop at the time of the harvest and to buy again as and when needed. The part kept for own consumption is usually estimated in the national accounts by use of appropriate ratios. Production as a whole is obtained from agricultural production surveys, based on the measurement of areas and yields by major crop, and the respective shares of commercialised and stored production are obtained from responses to production or income-expenditure surveys.

11.6.   In transition countries, garden plots play an important role in household consumption. In the Russian Federation, for example, more than 90% of estimated household production is for own consumption. Its measurement requires specific supplementary surveys or extra questions added to household surveys, especially where the production is a secondary activity by household members.

11.7.   Generally, the valuation of primary production for own consumption is based on market prices that are usually collected and available for primary products in rural markets as well as in urban markets. It is radically different for collection of firewood and supply of water, because even if there is a market for such goods in urban areas, there is not one in rural areas. Therefore, monetary valuation at market prices of the output, which is the preferred method according to the 1993 SNA (Para 6.84 and 6.85), is artificial, and all the more so as the time spent in these activities may be better known than the quantities involved, thanks to the recent development of time-use surveys.

Other production of goods for own consumption

11.8.   As previously noted, most of the processing activities of agricultural products are typically carried out by women. Often undertaken as secondary activities, such non-market household production is rarely measured in production or household surveys. Most labour force surveys underestimate female secondary activities, and household income-expenditure surveys usually record self-consumption for primary products only. The information available does not provide data on quantities and monetary valuation at market prices of the output is therefore difficult. Here again, time-use surveys may be particularly useful for a valuation at cost of inputs, labour being the major input.

11.9.   Although valuation at market prices is easier for household production of goods other than processed agricultural products, and although data collection on quantities of such goods is also easier, information may still be lacking. Hence, estimates may be derived indirectly from the compilation of supply-use tables. For example, the State Department of Statistics of Uzbekistan recently decided to include the household production of bread for own consumption because of a huge imbalance between production and consumption. Such a solution is consistent with the 1993 SNA because bread can be prepared a week ahead and consumed during the week, and can thus be considered as a manufactured good whose production and consumption go beyond the preparation and consumption of meals.

11.10.   Own-account construction is also a kind of household production for own final use that has long been included in the measurement of GDP. Monetary valuation of the output raises the same issues as for other non-primary goods. Where there is a local market, the value of dwellings is known. In the absence of markets, in rural areas of developing countries for instance, production costs consist mainly of individual and collective labour. The free provision of other inputs and materials – building poles, sun-dried bricks, thatch or leaves for roofing – has to be estimated in terms of the time spent in gathering and processing the materials. Thus time-use surveys can play a central role in estimation and valuation.

11.3. Household Production of Services for Own Final Use

11.11. Household production of services for own final use is outside the SNA production boundary with two exceptions: paid domestic services and owner-occupied dwelling services.

11.12. As regards paid domestic services, two cases may be distinguished. In many developed countries, domestic servants work part-time for several households and may be considered as self-employed persons (enterprises) supplying services to the households. It has been agreed by the Delhi Group that these workers are a component of the informal sector if they meet the criteria of the informal sector definition. In developing countries, on the other hand, domestic servants usually work full-time in a single household. In some developing countries of Africa and Asia, many domestic servants are unpaid workers, often children, living in the same premises as their employers. Sometimes they are indentured workers who have been either sold into service by their legal guardians or who are working to repay debts. Although such workers do not receive cash payments, they are fed and housed by their employers. They are, therefore, receiving a form of income in kind and should be treated in the same way as domestic servants who are paid cash wages.

11.13. Estimates for owner-occupied dwelling services have always been included in the national accounts, as described in Chapter 5. The methods are not further elaborated here except to note that most population censuses and household surveys collect data on the ownership of the premises where the household lives. Also, whilst monetary valuation can be easily made in urban areas where a market for renting services exist, it is more difficult in rural areas, especially in those countries that are predominantly rural.

11.4.   Data Sources

Household income-expenditure surveys

11.14. Household surveys variously described as *income-expenditure, budget-consumption, household budget, living conditions,* or *living standards* are undertaken in many developing countries on a regular basis (at least every 10 years) and fill a major gap in the national accounts.

11.15. For most types of production for own final use by rural households, reliable data can be obtained only by direct surveys of consumption. To estimate the output of subsistence agriculture, it is better to measure consumption of their own production at the time it actually occurs, rather than to ask farmers to forecast or remember the eventual disposal of their output. The same is true for other primary production, such as hunting, fishing and firewood collection. In addition, household surveys are often the best source of basic data on subsistence food processing, handicrafts, house building, and other construction and building activities.

11.16. To measure subsistence food production, all items used should be weighed and their origin established at the time meals are being prepared. Since consumption patterns usually vary from one region to another and from season to season, a nation-wide sample of households should be used, with interviews spaced evenly over a full twelve-month period. Surveys of this sort require a fairly large team of trained enumerators and supervisors, and the transport, data processing, and other administrative costs involved may also be considerable. Unfortunately, the countries where subsistence production is particularly important are those least able to undertake such large-scale household enquiries. Nevertheless, surveys of this sort provide the only sure basis for estimating the major part of subsistence output. At a very minimum they should be carried out every ten years. No major improvements in the reliability of subsistence estimates can be achieved without establishing a programme of regular surveys of rural households.

Time-use surveys

11.17. Time-use surveys are carried out on a regular basis in many developed countries and, with the support of UNDP programmes, they have recently been tested in a number of developing countries, for example, Benin and Morocco in 1998, Nigeria, India, Nepal and Philippines in 1999, and South Africa in 2000. In the context of developing countries, one of the major aims of time-use surveys is to obtain better measures of female participation in the labour force by providing estimates of the respondents' involvement in secondary activities, which are not usually recorded by regular labour force surveys.

11.18. Where available, information from time-use surveys can be of great help in the implementation of the 1993 SNA in countries where household production for own final use is widespread but where market prices for such goods exist only in urban areas and do not apply to the rural areas where the majority of the population live. In these countries, monetary valuation of the cost of production may be a more reliable method than the valuation of output at market price where labour is the main input into the production process and the time spent is known.

11.19. There are, however, some potential problems with this approach. First, the volume of labour devoted to an activity may not be the only factor determining output. Even when the link between the two is close, for example in activities like collecting firewood where labour is the only input of any kind, there may be other factors affecting output. The time spent by households collecting firewood may change without any change in output simply because firewood is getting harder or easier to find.

11.20. The second problem is to valuing the time spent on subsistence activities. The normal procedure is to use average rural wage rates on the grounds that these measure the opportunity costs, *i.e.*, the income foregone by choosing to perform a particular subsistence activity instead of working as a paid labourer. Often, however, it is quite unrealistic to assume that any such choice exists. In remote regions there may be no opportunities at all for paid employment, while elsewhere the wage levels may have been administratively fixed at levels where the supply of labour far exceeds the number of jobs available. This does not necessarily mean that no opportunity costs are involved in performing subsistence activities, but rather that income from paid employment may not be a suitable way of measuring them. It is likely that the opportunity costs of devoting labour to a particular subsistence activity can be measured realistically only in terms of other subsistence activities.

11.5. Estimation Methods

Agricultural production: crops

11.21. In most countries, peasant farmers produce an enormous range of grains, tubers, green vegetables and fruit. It is not feasible to make proper estimates for each of these items individually. Usually a relatively small number of crops – perhaps a dozen or so – account for the bulk of total subsistence output and the aim should be to get good quantity and price data for these items.

11.22. Household surveys of the size and complexity needed to make proper estimates of subsistence crop consumption cannot usually be undertaken on an annual basis. They are generally used to collect benchmark data, and current year estimates are obtained by extrapolating base year per capita consumption using an index of rural population growth. This is reasonable since subsistence consumption per head of farm population tends to remain fairly constant. However, some considerations can be given to making the estimates more realistic:

- In countries where the population is growing fairly rapidly the average age of the population is generally falling. Therefore, in the short term at least, food consumption on a per head basis, including consumption from own production, can be expected to fall.
- Subsistence food production per head or per household is related in some way to the level of total household income. In general, subsistence becomes relatively less important as total

income rises. Some estimate of this relationship can be obtained from cross-sectional analysis of household income and expenditure data, with total household income taken as the independent variable.

11.23. Crop prices normally vary both from one area to another and during the course of the year, thus the question arises as to what weights should be used to calculate average prices. Few developing countries have enough information on crop production for very elaborate weighting systems. In practice fairly simple procedures may give satisfactory results. In most countries, the major part of each crop is produced, *i.e.*, harvested, over a relatively short period in a few well-defined areas. In such cases, national annual average prices can be satisfactorily calculated as the simple average of producer prices recorded in the main growing areas during the peak harvesting season.

Crop storage

11.24. In most developing countries, storage of subsistence crops is an important activity. Peasant households often have several buildings for storing different crops from one harvest to the next. The regular inspection of these stores and their contents, fumigation and pest control, and repair and maintenance work are vital services in a subsistence economy. For the most part, however, storage activities are either excluded completely from the national accounts, or are covered only by accident through the valuation of crops at prices that implicitly include storage costs. It is generally better to use harvest time prices for valuing crop output and to make separate, explicit estimates for the gross output and value-added of crop storage.

11.25. The gross output of storage activities could be defined as the difference in the value (at producer prices) of subsistence crops on removal from the store for consumption from their value on entering the store at harvest time. This gross output consists of intermediate consumption – pesticides, repair and maintenance costs for example – and value-added – mainly labour costs and depreciation of storage buildings.

Agricultural production: livestock and livestock products

11.26. A common weakness of livestock estimates arises from the use of fixed ratios for estimating growth rates and slaughtering. The ratios used may reflect long-term trends reasonably well, but ignore short-term variations, which may be quite substantial. Disease can cause sharp annual fluctuations in the numbers of poultry and small livestock. In bad harvest years farmers may try to maintain the level of their cash receipts by selling more cattle for slaughter, while in subsequent years the take-off rate may fall as farmers replenish their herds. Few countries have accurate data on short-term variations of this sort, but it is often possible to make some rough adjustments to reproduction and take-off rates for year-to-year changes on the basis of partial information on licensed slaughtering, meat and cattle imports, or trade in hides and skins.

Food processing

11.27. For most countries the main activity in this area consists of basic processing of staple food crops – husking and polishing rice, drying and pounding cassava, or milling maize and wheat. Since virtually all crops must be processed in some way, data on quantities may be obtained directly from the estimates of crop consumption. The main problem is to find a suitable valuation procedure. Most countries make use of cost data obtained directly from commercial grain mills. When this sort of direct information is not available, a possible alternative is to compare producer or retail market prices for crops before and after processing.

House-building

11.28. For this activity, most countries calculate physical output by applying replacement and growth rates to the estimated stock of houses in a base year. In the absence of direct information on house-building activities this is a reasonable procedure, but often the rates of growth and replacement are very crudely estimated and in some cases not much is known about the housing stock either.

11.29. The growth of the stock of dwellings can be assumed to be some function of the growth of population. In countries with high population growth rates, it is reasonable to suppose that the average size of households is increasing. This implies that the housing stock is growing more slowly than total population, and half as fast seems a reasonable guess in the absence of more specific information. In practice, the growth rate assumption is usually much less important than the assumption made about the rate of replacement. Three per cent is about the highest credible rate for the growth of the housing stock whereas, depending on the durability of the construction materials, up to ten per cent of existing houses may need replacing each year, and the rate of replacement may be even higher in the event of recurrent natural disasters (earthquakes, typhoons, floods, etc.).

11.30. Even with accurate information on replacement and growth rates there is still the problem that they reflect only the underlying trend in house building. There may be substantial year-to-year changes in the level of activity. In bad harvest years, replacements of rural dwellings may be postponed. In good years, they may be brought forward. Some information about short-term changes of this sort may be obtained from imports of metal roofing sheets, sales of window frames, production of building poles, and cement consumption.

Checking consistency of basic data

11.31. The data for many subsistence activities are deficient both in terms of quantity and quality. Thus, it is vital to use all available information to check the consistency and credibility of the basic assumptions. In the case of agricultural output, for example, estimates of crop consumption must obviously be consistent with whatever information is available on crop production, and must, in addition, imply a realistic diet in terms of protein and calorie content. Data from annual livestock censuses must be credible in the light of what is known about reproduction and take-off rates; estimates of the number of animals slaughtered can be checked against data on hides and skins traded; and assumptions about reproduction rates, milk yields, egg-production and so forth must be consistent with the estimated sex and age-structure of national herds and flocks. Data on fish production can be checked against estimates of the total number of boats or nets in use. Official statistics on hunting activities can be partly verified by data on imports of hunting cartridges, licences issued, or trade in hunting trophies.

Chapter 12

MACRO-MODEL METHODS

12. MACRO-MODEL METHODS

12.1. Introduction

12.1.   *Macro-model methods* is the term used in this Handbook for methods that produce an estimate of the entire NOE, or one of its component parts such as the underground economy, by means of a single model. Such methods are discussed in this chapter not because they are considered useful in obtaining exhaustive estimates of GDP or in estimating underground production, but because they tend to produce spectacularly high measures, which attract much attention from politicians and newspapers. As Gylliane Gervais (Statistics Canada, 1994) wrote:

> "The size and growth of the "underground economy' have kindled a lot of interest in Canada in the past few years...Hardly a week goes by without the media quoting someone claiming that underground transactions amount to 10%, 15% or even 20% of GDP, or that the deficit could be eliminated if taxes were collected on these transactions. If the figures often quoted are even approximately accurate, then the level and possibly growth of Canada's GDP are considerably understated to the extent that the information given (to) policy makers about current economic conditions is misleading. Our statistical system, at least in so far as economic statistics are concerned, would be sorely inadequate if it failed to detect "hidden' transactions of such magnitude."

12.2.   Without a doubt, the media reports to which this paragraph refers were based on the use of macro-model methods. For example, Schneider and Enste (2000) quote estimates of the average level of the "shadow economy" (apparently meaning non-measured economy) in Canada over the period 1990-93 between 10.0% and 13.5%, whereas the Statistics Canada report just referenced concluded that the upper limit to the "underground economy" (defined as market production of legal goods and services that escapes measurement in the official GDP estimates) in 1992 was 2.7%.

12.3.   It is often, but entirely wrongly, conjectured that the difference between these macro-model results and the official estimates of GDP is non-measured production. However, as illustrated in this chapter, there are serious problems with macro-model methods that cast doubt on their utility for any purpose in which precision is important. In particular, they are completely unsuitable for use in compiling the national accounts. In brief the problems are:

- the activities that the models aim to measure are not precisely defined; it is often unclear whether the models are estimating non-observed or non-measured production, or whether they include informal sector or illegal activities as well as underground activities;

- the assumptions underlying the models overly simplistic;

- the results the models produce are not stable in the sense that changes in assumptions for the same model can produce quite different values;

- there are many models and they give different results;

- the methods provide only a global estimate for the economy as a whole, whereas users frequently want GDP broken down by industry or expenditure category; and

- the results can not be readily combined with other measurements, in particular those obtained by the detailed, data based methods that are used in compiling the national accounts, as described in earlier chapters of this Handbook.

12.4.   To illustrate these points, three types of macro-model methods are described in the following sections:

- *Monetary methods*, which assume that the non-measured production can be modelled in terms of stocks or flows of money.
- *Global indicator methods*, in which non-measured production is modelled in terms of a single variable (usually a physical indicator) with which it is believed to be highly correlated, electricity consumption being the most commonly used.
- *Latent variable methods*, in which modelling is in terms of two groups of variables, one group that is assumed to determine the size and growth of non-measured production and a second group that provides the "trace" (*i.e.*, evidence) of the missing activities.

12.5.   In presenting their methods, the authors refer variously to the "underground", "hidden", or "shadow" economy without always clarifying whether this includes all non-observed activities, or just those that are legal, or those that are non-measured in the official GDP estimates, or some other subset. The following descriptions should be read with this in mind.

12.2.   Monetary Methods

12.2.1. *Introduction*

12.6.   Three monetary methods are described in the following paragraphs, namely the *transaction method*, the *cash/deposit ratio* method, and the *cash demand* method. The fundamental idea behind these methods is to build relationships between monetary developments and official GDP estimates using regression techniques with a few restrictive hypotheses concerning the cash character of underground transactions, tax burdens, the relationship of holdings to deposits, etc., and to assume that all monetary developments not explained by the particular model are due to undercoverage of the official GDP.

12.2.2. *Transaction Method*

12.7.   The transaction method described by Feige (1979) is based on the following reasoning. The starting point is the equation of Fisher:

$$M * V = P * T$$

12.8.   In words, the total stock of money (M) multiplied by the velocity of circulation (V) equals the total number of transactions paid by that money (T) multiplied by the price of these transactions (P). Further it is assumed that there is a constant relationship (denoted by k) between the money flows related to these transactions and total value added, that is:

$$P * T = k * Ytotal,$$

where, by definition, total value added (Ytotal) is the sum of the official valued added (Yofficial) and underground value added (Yunder). Therefore

$$M * V = k * (Yofficial + Yunder),$$

thus $M_t * V_t = k * (Yofficial_t + Yunder_t)$, over some range of years $t = 0,1,...T$.

12.9.   The stock of money (currency plus demand deposits) is readily measurable, money velocity can be estimated and the official estimates of value added are known. Thus, if the size of the underground economy as a ratio of the official economy is assumed known for a benchmark year, then the underground component can be calculated for all subsequent years.

12.10. Feige applied the method to the United States. Following Laurant (1979), he estimated the velocity of cash as the quotient of the number of transactions a bank note survives before being worn out and the average lifetime of banknotes. The first part of this estimate was based on bank note wearing tests. He then assumed that the underground economy was zero in 1939. Based on these assumptions he calculated the size of the underground economy as 27% in 1979.

12.11. There are several problems with respect to Feige's method. The assumption of a constant ratio of transactions to official GDP seems heroic. As Cramer (1980) pointed out it is highly likely that some monetary transactions that have nothing to do with income generation are included in the calculations, for example the results of the introduction of a stricter cash management in large companies and of repurchase agreements and of euro-dollar deposits, which very frequently change ownership in the United States. Evidently part of the money notionally in circulation, in particular bills of large denomination, is not actually in circulation but kept as a store of wealth. Furthermore, the amount of money held as cash depends upon interest and inflation rates and people's perception of the likelihood of being robbed. Increased facilities for and use of cheques and credit cards can also be expected to have had an impact.

12.12. Cramer also criticised Feige's estimate of the income velocity of cash money. Cramer preferred an alternative estimate based on the number of cash withdrawals at banks and the average number of uses of a banknote between withdrawal and deposit.

12.13. Blades (1982) pointed out that the US dollar is an international currency unit and that US dollars circulate widely throughout the world, either as official legal tender (in the Virgin Islands, Liberia, Puerto Rico and Samoa for example) or as a widely accepted alternative to national currencies that lack credibility (in South East Asia and Central America for example). Because the dollar plays an international role, there is little point in relating dollars in circulation (throughout the world) to domestic activity in the United States.

12.14. Applied to the Netherlands, the transaction method yields implausible results. To address this problem, Boeschoten and Fase (1984) refined the transaction method, creating a new base method and several other variants. However, the variants all give significantly different results and there is no way to deduce which might be closest to the truth.

12.2.3. *Cash/Deposit Ratio Method*

12.15. The cash/deposit ratio method is based on information about the ratio between currency (cash) and transferable (giro) money, *i.e.*, the *cash/deposit ratio*. According to Gutmann (1977) the cash/deposit ratio is only affected by the changes in taxation and other government regulations that change the way people make payments, and the main reason that payment behaviour changes is because people want to hide certain activities to avoid taxation and restrictions. Gutmann refers to these hidden activities as the underground economy and uses the cash/deposit ratio to estimate its size.

12.16. Gutmann illustrates the method by an example from the United States. After a short rise just after the Second World War, the cash/deposit ratio for the United States remained almost constant until 1961, when it began to increase again. According to Gutmann, this conflicted with the developments that occurred before the war. Given that he expected both the pre-war and post-war developments to be the same, he concluded that the increase of the cash/deposit ratio from 1961 was the result of changed behaviour. He conjectured that an increasing proportion of transactions was being paid in cash, which pointed to the creation or increase of the underground economy. Based on the changes in the cash/deposit ratio Gutmann computed the underestimate of GNP because of the underground economy as 10% in 1976. The assumptions underlying this estimate are as follows:

- The cash/deposit ratio of the official (observed) economy has not changed since 1937-1961.

- Transferable money was only used in the official economy.

- The "surplus" of money held as cash is only used in the underground economy. This surplus is calculated as the difference between the actual amount of cash money in circulation and the amount that one would expect to be in circulation according to the cash/deposit ratio of the official economy over the period 1937-1961.

- One dollar money held in cash in the underground economy generated as much value added as one dollar of M1 (cash + transferable) money in the official economy.
- The underground economy over the period 1937-1961 was negligible.

12.17. Many people have developed variants of the cash/deposit ratio method. Feige (1980), for example, changed the assumption of an almost non-existent underground economy in the benchmark years 1937-1941. He assumed an underground economy of 5% of GNP in 1964. Based on this new assumption he arrived at an estimate of 14% of GNP in 1979. Furthermore he challenged the assumption that one dollar in the underground economy was as productive (in terms of generated GNP) as one dollar in the official economy. Because of the higher share of services in the underground economy, he conjectured that one dollar in the underground economy was at least 10% more productive. Furthermore he wondered why all underground transactions should be in cash and assumed that about one third of all underground transactions were paid through bank transfers. Based on these assumptions he estimated the size of the United States underground economy in 1979 at 28% of GNP.

12.18. Other people have criticised the underlying assumption that changes in the cash/deposit ratio are due only to the underground economy. For example, Garcia (1978) put forward different possible reasons for changes in the cash/deposit ratio. In his view, the growth of the underground economy was not the only reason, nor even the most important reason. More important were the decrease of money in the form of checking accounts and the increase of various types of savings accounts. If corrected for this shift, the cash/deposit ratio in the United States turns out to have been rather constant.

12.19. Laurent (1979) and Cramer (1980) also regarded the cash/deposit ratio as an inappropriate means of measuring the underground economy. In their view, the velocities of circulation of the different types of money develop differently, thus a better measure is the total amount of cash and bank transfer payments. This was the reason they preferred the transaction method previously outlined.

12.2.4. *Cash Demand Method*

12.20. In contrast to Gutmann, Tanzi (1980, 1982) assumed that the demand for cash money was not only affected by taxation and government regulation, but also by other factors. However, he agreed with Gutmann that changes in the total amount of cash money due to changes in taxation and government regulation go totally into the underground economy. To isolate the influence of taxation and regulation Tanzi postulated that the demand for cash as a proportion of total money, C/M2 (where M2 is cash money + transferable money + fixed period deposits), is a function of taxes, the share of wages and salaries in total personal income, the interest on fixed term deposits, and per capita real income. Based on the results of regression analyses, Tanzi arrived at two alternative estimates of the *notional demand* for cash money (defined as the demand for cash money on the assumption that there is no underground economy). They were the notional demand if taxes were unchanged since 1929 (the year when Tanzi assumed there was no underground economy), and the notional demand if there were no taxes.

12.21. In each case, the difference between the actual demand and the notional demand was considered to be the total amount of cash money in the underground economy. Assuming that the velocities of cash money in the formal and the underground economy are equal, the estimated size of the underground economy in the United States in 1976 was 3.4-5.1% of GNP according to the first variant and 8.1-11.7% according to the second variant. These values are both quite different from Gutmann's estimates previously described.

12.22. Barens (1982) demonstrated that both cash/deposit and cash-demand methods can yield counter-intuitive results. He applied both methods to the Netherlands and the results showed a decreasing underground economy since the end of the seventies, which is in contradiction to the generally accepted notion that the underground economy was increasing.

12.2.5. *Summary*

12.23. Monetary macro-models are unsuitable for estimating the underground economy primarily because they are based on modelling assumptions that cannot be justified. The crucial assumption underlying the cash/deposit ratio and the cash demand methods is that a change in the size of the underground economy is caused by changes in taxation and government regulations and that this becomes visible through changes in the demand for cash because underground transactions are mainly paid in cash. This assumption cannot be tested and may not be true. In contrast, the transaction method is not based on any assumed relation between taxation and underground activity. However, it assumes a constant relationship between monetary transactions and GDP, which again cannot be justified.

12.24. The problems with these models are evidenced by the sensitivity of the results to the benchmark year assumptions, the wide range of results that different methods give under the same circumstances, and the implausible results that are obtained in some specific cases.

12.3. Global Indicator Methods

12.25. The most prominent example of the global indicator approach is the electricity consumption method proposed by Kaufmann and Kaliberda (1996). This method uses electricity consumption as the single physical indicator of overall economic activity. It assumes a precise and stable relationship between electricity consumption and output. It is clear, however, that at least for agriculture the relationship will not be stable since output is largely determined by the weather. Moreover, in many developing and transition countries, electricity is not a major source of energy in industrial production.

12.26. The problem with the method is illustrated by an example drawn from the Russian Federation. In the years immediately following the beginning of intense economic reform in 1992, official statisticians experienced difficulties in producing sufficiently timely assessments of GDP, which was known to be in decline. Electricity consumption was one of the alternative methods tried. It produced more optimistic estimates than the official GDP and provoked considerable discussion of the NOE. Subsequent analysis indicated that these estimates could not be trusted for the following reasons.

- The relationship between electricity consumption and industrial production is not a simple ratio, even in those industries that are highly dependent upon it, because a significant part (up to a third) of consumption is a fixed cost unrelated to the volume of production. For example, factories need heating and lighting. This sort of consumption tends to change in steps rather than move smoothly with production.

- Artificial price levels further reduce the relationship between industrial production and electricity consumption. At this time in the Russian Federation, electricity prices were artificially low, thus manufacturers did not need to worry greatly about electricity consumption, nor to make efforts to reduce it when production fell. By the same token, they did not need to increase consumption much if production picked up again, either officially or through undeclared use of facilities.

- Measurements of consumption are actually derived from estimates of electricity production at the power stations. The difference between supply and consumption – transmission losses – is not large but can vary with the seasons.

12.27. Based on these arguments, the electricity consumption method was not used in the fundamental revision of the GDP undertaken by Goskomstat of Russia (1995) jointly with the World Bank. This example is typical of the problems encountered in considering such a simplistic approach to NOE measurement.

12.4. Latent Variable Method

12.28. The macro-modelling methods described in the previous paragraphs assume that the underground economy can be modelled in terms of a small number of specific variables. They ignore other background information and circumstances that can lead to the existence of underground production. This is not the case for the *latent variable method* of Frey and Weck (1983), which draws on a wide range of explanatory variables. The size of the underground economy is estimated on the basis of developments in the variables that, on the one hand, affect the size and the growth of underground production, and, on the other hand, are the traces of underground activities in the economy. The method uses a technique (known as LISREL) that enables a cross-sectional analysis of the relationship between a non-observed dependent variable and one or more observed explanatory variables. As the non-observed variable is not known it is replaced by a set of indicators. The data are drawn from a range of different countries, or time periods within a country. The results of the analysis are estimates of the relative sizes of the non-observed variable in each of the countries, or time periods. To estimate the actual sizes, benchmark estimates for two countries, or time periods are required.

12.29.   According to Frey and Weck, the size of the underground economy can be explained in terms of the actual tax burden, the perception of the tax burden, the unemployment rate, the regulation burden (for example, the number of laws), the attitude towards paying taxes (*tax morality*) and the per capita available income. Indicators of the size of underground production, in other words the traces left in the economy, are the labour force participation rate of the male population, the number of weekly working hours and the growth of the GNP. To build their model Frey and Weck used data from a large number of countries for a particular year. They calculated the relative sizes of the underground economy in these countries and then generated estimates of the actual sizes, using monetary method estimates for Norway and Sweden as benchmarks. Giles (1999) describes another application, in this case for New Zealand over a range of years.

12.30.   The method can be seriously questioned. First, one can ask about the variables chosen. For example, why is the number of weekly working hours an indicator (trace) of the underground economy? Is it a reason for the existence of the underground economy rather than a result? Second, an important variable in the model is the so-called tax morality, but this is difficult to quantify in an objective fashion. Third, the reliability of the results is never better than the reliability of the two benchmark estimates. Fourth, the results are very unstable. Helberger and Knepel (1988) show that even a small change in the countries used in the Frey and Weck example leads to quite different results. The exclusion of Finland – a country which accounts for less than 1% of the population and of the GDP of the group of countries studied by Frey and Weck – leads to insignificant estimates of almost all coefficients in the model. Helberger and Knepel conclude that the shortcomings and ambiguities in the data severely limit the utility of the model for measurement of the underground economy.

12.5.   Concluding Remarks

12.31.   The need for models in compiling national accounts is not in dispute. Models often underpin indirect methods used in compilation, providing estimates when basic data are not available. This is usually the case, for example, in making estimates of illegal production. The point is, however, that the preferred basis for statistical estimates is always empirical data. Only where data are not available should modelling be used to fill the gaps; and the models should be at the most detailed level possible so that they have the best possible chance of accurately reflecting the phenomena being modelled. The goal should be to estimate each specific, non-observed data element using closely related data for the same, or a nearby, accounting period. National accounts compilation should follow a careful, case by case approach, considering all available data sources and procedures. In this context, an electricity consumption model, for example, may have its place, not in modelling the growth of the entire economy, but at a detailed level, such as estimating the growth of a particular industry for which survey data are not available and for which electricity is a primary input and reflects the movement in output.

12.32.   In most countries, national accountants have available a rich supply of data from a variety of sources. In combination, these data are capable of producing much more accurate estimates of GDP and its components than macro-models can ever do. It is, however, incumbent on national accountants to inform users of the extent of the *non-observed economy* – i.e., how much economic activity escapes direct measurement – and the extent of the *non-measured economy* – i.e., how much of the non-observed economy may still be missing from GDP after making the various adjustments of the kind described in this Handbook. Lack of transparency in describing the procedures used to compile the national accounts is the main reason why outsiders resort to macro-models and produce estimates that undermine the credibility of the national accounts.

ANNEXES

REFERENCES

Introductory Notes

References are listed under the heading(s) of the chapter(s) in which they are cited. The idea in duplicating some references in this way is to enable readers interested in one particular chapter, for example the informal sector, to be readily able to identify all the references made in that chapter.

The 1993 SNA and two compendia are listed in the first section labelled General. The lists also include some references that are not explicitly cited in the Handbook but that provide useful background material or elaboration of the text.

The documents are in English except where otherwise noted.

General

Commission of the European Communities – Eurostat, International Monetary Fund, Organisation for Economic Co-operation and Development, United Nations, and World Bank (1993),
System of National Accounts 1993, ISBN 92-1-161352-3, Brussels/Luxemburg, New York, Paris, Washington.

United Nations (1992),
Guide-book to Statistics on the Hidden Economy, Economic Commission for Europe, Statistical Division, United Nations, New York.

United Nations (1993),
Inventory of National Practices in Estimating Hidden and Informal Economic Activities for National Accounts, Conference of European Statisticians, Economic Commission for Europe, United Nations, Geneva.

Chapter 1

Bloem, A., and M. L. Shrestha (2000),
Comprehensive Measures of GDP and the Unrecorded Economy, IMF Working Paper WP/00/204, International Monetary Fund, Washington.

Calzaroni, M. (2000),
The Exhaustiveness of Production Estimates: New Concepts and Methodologies, Proceedings of the International Conference on Establishment Surveys, Buffalo, 2000, Statistics Canada, Ottawa.

Calzaroni M., and S. Ronconi (1999),
Issues and activities to ensure the coverage of the non-observed economy in national accounts: implications for national statistical offices, Conference of European Statisticians, 47th plenary session, Neuchatel, June 1999, Economic Commission for Europe, Geneva: available at *www.unece.org/stats/documents/1999.06.ces.htm*.

Calzaroni M., and A. Puggioni (2001),
Evaluation and Analysis of the Quality of the National Accounts Aggregates, Essays No. 10, Istat, Rome.

Commission of the European Communities – Eurostat, International Monetary Fund, Organisation for Economic Coloperation and Development, United Nations, and World Bank (1993),
System of National Accounts 1993, ISBN 92-1-161352-3, Brussels/Luxemburg, New York, Paris, Washington.

Dallago B. (1990),
The irregular economy: the "underground" economy and the "black" labour market, Dartmouth, England.

Goskomstat of Russia (1998),
Guidelines for Statistical Methods: Volume 2, ISBN 5-89476-017-8, Goskomstat of Russia, Moscow (in Russian).

Luttikhuizen, R., and B. Kazemier (2000),
A *Systematic Approach to the Hidden and Informal Activities*, Proceedings of the International Conference on Establishment Surveys, Buffalo, 2000, Statistics Canada, Ottawa.

Masakova, I. (2000),
   Estimation of the Non-Observed Economy: the Statistical Practices in Russia, Proceedings of the International Conference on Establishment Surveys, Buffalo, 2000, Statistics Canada, Ottawa.

Organisation for Economic Co-operation and Development (1997),
   Framework for the Measurement of Unrecorded Economic Activities in Transition Economies, OECD/GD(97)177, Organisation for Economic Co-operation and Development, Paris.

Goskomstat of Russia (1998),
   Guidelines for Statistical Methods: Volume 2, ISBN 5-89476-017-8, Goskomstat of Russia, Moscow (in Russian).

Stapel, S. (2001),
   The Eurostat Pilot Project on Exhaustiveness with the Candidate Countries – Concepts and General Results, Proceedings, Conference on National Accounts of the Candidate Countries, January, 2001, Eurostat, Brussels.

Wroe D., P. Kenny, U. Rizki, and I. Weerakkody (1999),
   Reliability and Quality Indicators for National Accounts Aggregates, Report Project SUP.COM, Eurostat, Luxembourg.

Chapter 2

Bloem, A., R. Dippelsman, and N. Maehle (2001),
   Quarterly National Accounts Manual: Concepts, Data Sources, and Compilation, International Monetary Fund, Washington.

Eurostat (1995),
   European system of accounts, ISBN 92-827-7954-8, Eurostat, Luxembourg.

International Labour Organization (1993),
   Resolution concerning economically active population, employment, unemployment and underemployment, 13th International Conference of Labour Statisticians, International Labour Organisation, Geneva.

Vanoli, A. (1995),
   Foundations of a system of national accounts. A short discussion of some basic concepts, Verso il nuovo sistema di contabilità nazionale, Istat, Annali di Statistica Serie X, 1996 Roma.

Chapter 3

Calzaroni, M. (2000),
   The Exhaustiveness of Production Estimates: New Concepts and Methodologies, Proceedings of the International Conference on Establishment Surveys, Buffalo, 2000, Statistics Canada, Ottawa.

Calzaroni, M., and S. Ronconi (1999),
   Issues and activities to ensure the coverage of the non-observed economy in national accounts: implications for national statistical offices, Conference of European Statisticians, 47th plenary session, Neuchatel, June 1999, Economic Commission for Europe, Geneva: available at *www.unece.org/stats/documents/1999.06.ces.htm*.

Calzaroni, M., Pascarella C., and Pisani S. (2000),
   Il sommerso. Aspetti metodologici e quantificazioni per una stima esaustiva dell'input di lavoro e del PIL, Seminar La Nuova Contabilita' Nazionale, 12-13 January, Istat, Rome (in Italian).

Dallago, B. (1990),
   The irregular economy: the "underground" economy and the "black" labour market, Dartmouth, England.

European Commission (1994),
   Decision 94/168/EC, Euratom of 22 February 1994, Official Journal L77, Volume 37 of 19 March 1994, Office for Official Publications of the European Communities, Luxembourg.

Hein, R. (1998),
   Guidelines for the Pilot Study on Exhaustiveness, First Workshop of the Pilot Project on Exhaustiveness, Luxembourg, December 1998, Eurostat, Luxembourg.

International Labour Organization (1993),
   Highlights of the Conference and text of the three resolutions adopted, 15th International Conference of Labour Statisticians, in Bulletin of Labour Statistics 1993-2, International Labour Organisation, Geneva: pp. IX-XXI.

Luttikhuizen, R., and B. Kazemier (2000),
   A Systematic Approach to the Hidden and Informal Activities, Proceedings of the International Conference on Establishment Surveys, Buffalo, 2000, Statistics Canada, Ottawa.

Pedullà M.G. (1987),
   Concetti e metodi utilizzati in contabilità nazionale per la stima delle unità di lavoro, Economia e Lavoro, No. 3, July-September (in Italian).

Rey G. (1992),
   Analisi economica ed evidenza empirica dell'attivita' illegale in Italia, Quaderni di ricerca, Istat, Rome (in Italian).

Stapel, S. (2001),
   The Eurostat Pilot Project on Exhaustiveness with the Candidate Countries – Concepts and General Results, Conference on National Accounts of the Candidate Countries, Brussels, January 2001, Eurostat, Luxembourg.

Chapter 4

Broesterhuizen, G.A.A.M. (1985),
   The Unobserved Sector and the National Accounts in the Netherlands, in Gaertner W. and A. Wenig (eds) (1985), The Economics of the Shadow Economy, Proceedings of Conference, Bielefeld, 1983, Springer-Verlag, Berlin: pp. 277-287.

Calzaroni M., and S. Ronconi (1999),
   Issues and activities to ensure the coverage of the non-observed economy in national accounts: implications for national statistical offices, Conference of European Statisticians, 47th plenary session, Neuchatel, June 1999, Economic Commission for Europe, Geneva: available at *www.unece.org/stats/documents/1999.06.ces.htm*.

Carson, C.S. (2001),
   Toward a Framework for Assessing Data Quality, Working Paper WP/01/25, International Monetary Fund, Washington.

Dallago B. (1990),
   The irregular economy: the "underground" economy and the "black" labour market, Dartmouth, England.

Dennison, E. F. (1982),
   Is US growth understated because of underground economy? Employment ratios suggest not, The Review of Income and Wealth, March 1982.

Dilnot, A., and C.N. Morris (1981),
   What Do We Know About the Black Economy? Fiscal Studies 2(1): pp. 58-73.

European Commission (1994),
   Decision 94/168/EC, Euratom of 22 February 1994, Official Journal L77, Volume 37 of 19 March 1994, Office for Official Publications of the European Communities, Luxembourg.

Eurostat (2000),
   Energy in Europe: 1999 Annual Energy Review, Eurostat, Luxembourg.

Eurostat (2001),
   Report from the Task Force on Accuracy Assessment in National Accounts, document CPNB-296, Eurostat.

Goldschmidt-Clermont, L. (1987),
   Economic Evaluations of Unpaid Household Work: Africa, Asia, Latin America and Oceania, in Women, Work and Development No. 14, International Labour Organisation, Geneva.

Goldschmidt-Clermont, L., and E. Pagnossin-Aligisakis (1995),
   Measures of Unrecorded Economic Activities in Fourteen Countries, in Human Development Report, Occasional Papers No. 20, UNDP, New York.

Hayes, K. (1996),
   The Exhaustiveness of the GNP Estimates in the EU Member States, presented at joint UNECE/Eurostat/OECD meeting on National Accounts, Geneva, April/May 1996, Economic Commission for Europe, United Nations, Geneva.

Hayes, K., and E. Lozano (1998),
   Validating the Exhaustiveness of the GNP Estimates of the European Union Member States, Proceedings of the Joint IASS/IAOS Conference, Statistics for Economic and Social Development, September 1998, International Statistical Institute, Voorburg.

Hungarian Central Statistical Office (1998),
   Hidden Economy in Hungary 1998, Hungarian Central Statistical Office, Budapest.

Kazemier, B. (1991),
   Concealed Interest Income of Households in the Netherlands: 1977, 1979 and 1981, Public Finance 46(3): pp. 443-453.

Kazemier, B., and R. Van Eck (1992),
   Survey Investigations of the Hidden Economy, Some Methodological Results, Journal of Economic Psychology 13: pp. 569-587.

Leunis, W., and K. Verhagen (1999),
   Labour Accounts in Theory and Practice; The Dutch Experience, Statistics Netherlands, Voorburg.

MacAfee, K. (1980),
   A *Glimpse of the Hidden Economy in the National Accounts*, Economic Trends, 1980(8),
   Central Statistical Office: pp. 81-87.

Organisation for Economic Co-operation and Development (1985),
   Household Production in OECD Countries: Data Sources and Measurement Methods, (ed. A. Chadeau) Organisation for Economic Co-operation and Development, Paris.

O'Higgins, M. (1989),
Measuring the Hidden Economy: A Review of Evidence and Methodologies, Outer Circle Policy Unit, London.

Parker, R.P. (1984),
Improved Adjustment for Mis-reporting of Tax Return Information Used to Estimate the National Income and Product Accounts, 1977, Survey of Current Business 64(6): pp. 17-25.

Russian Federation Centre for Economic Analysis (2000),
Business Tendency Survey Questionnaires, survey questionnaires, Russian Federation Centre for Economic Analysis, Moscow.

Statistics Canada (1994),
The Size of the Underground Economy in Canada, (by Gylliane Gervais) Studies in National Accounting, ISSN 1192-0106, Statistics Canada, Ottawa.

United States Internal Revenue Service (1979),
Estimates of Income Unreported on Individual Income Tax Returns, Publication 1104, Government Printing Office, Washington.

Van de Laan, P., and J.W.B. De Waard (1985),
Vergellijking tussen de inkomensstatistiek en de Nationale rekeningen, Central Bureau of Statistics, Voorburg (in Dutch).

Willard, J.C. (1989),
The Underground Economy in National Accounts, in Guide-book to Statistics on the Hidden Economy, United Nations, 1992: pp. 79-103; also in Économie et Statistique, 226, 1989: pp. 35-51 (in French).

Zienkowski, L. (1996),
Polish Experience in Estimating Hidden Economy, joint UNECE/Eurostat/OECD meeting on National Accounts, Geneva, April/May 1996.

Chapter 5

AFRIstat (1997),
Proceedings of the Seminar on the Informal Sector and Economic Policy in SubSaharan Africa, March 10-14, 1997, Bamako, BPE1600, Vol. 2 AFRIstat, Bamako: pp. 167-168.

Bloem, A., P., Cotterel, and T. Gigantes (1996),
National Accounts in Transition Countries: Distortions and Biases, working paper WP/96/130, International Monetary Fund, Washington.

Bloem, A., R. Dippelsman, and N. Maehle (2001),
Quarterly National Accounts Manual: Concepts, Data Sources, and Compilation, International Monetary Fund, Washington.

Calzaroni, M. (2000),
The Exhaustiveness of Production Estimates: New Concepts and Methodologies, Proceedings of the International Conference on Establishment Surveys, Buffalo, 2000, Statistics Canada, Ottawa.

Calzaroni M., and S. Ronconi (1999),
Issues and activities to ensure the coverage of the non-observed economy in national accounts: implications for national statistical offices, Conference of European Statisticians, 47th plenary session, Neuchatel, June 1999, Economic Commission for Europe, Geneva: available at www.unece.org/stats/documents/1999.06.ces.htm.

Calzaroni M., Pascarella C., and Pisani S. (2000),
Il sommerso. Aspetti metodologici e quantificazioni per una stima esaustiva dell'input di lavoro e del PIL, Seminar La Nuova Contabilita' Nazionale, 12-13 January, Istat, Rome (in Italian).

Calzaroni, M., and V. Madelin (2000),
Exhaustiveness of GDP Measurement: French and Italian Approaches, presented at Twenty-Fourth General Conference of the International Association for Research in Income and Wealth, Lillehammer, Norway.

Central Bureau of Statistics, Nepal (1994),
The Revised GDP Series of Nepal: 1984/85 – 1993/94, Central Bureau of Statistics, Kathmandu.

Central Statistical Organization, Government of India (1989),
National Accounts Statistics: Sources and Methods, Central Statistical Organization, Delhi.

Dallago B. (1990),
The irregular economy: the "underground" economy and the "black" labour market, Dartmouth, England.

Goskomstat of Russia (1998),
Guidelines for Statistical Methods: Volume 2, ISBN 5-89476-017-8, Goskomstat of Russia, Moscow (in Russian).

Hayes, K., and E. Lozano (1998),
Validating the Exhaustiveness of the GNP Estimates of the European Union Member States, in Proceedings of the Joint IASS/IAOS Conference, Statistics for Economic and Social Development, September 1998, International Statistical Institute, Voorburg.

Istat (1993),
> The underground economy in Italian economic accounts, Annali di Statistica, Series X, Vol. 2, Rome.

Pedullà M.G. (1987),
> Concetti e metodi utilizzati in contabilità nazionale per la stima delle unità di lavoro, Economia e Lavoro, No. 3, July-September (in Italian).

United Nations (1998),
> International Merchandise Trade Statistics: Concepts and Definitions, Studies in Methods, Series M, No. 52, Rev. 2, United Nations, New York.

United Nations (1999),
> Handbook of Input-Output Tables: Compilation and Analysis, Studies in Methods, Series F, No. 74, United Nations, New York.

Chapter 6

Booleman, M. (1998),
> Improving Basic Statistics in Relation to the Non Observed Economy, presented at the Workshop on Non-Observed Economy, Chisnau, 1999, Eurostat, Luxembourg.

Brackstone, G. (1999),
> Managing Data Quality in a Statistical Agency, Survey Methodology Journal, Volume 24, No. 2: pp. 139-149.

Carson, C.S. (2001),
> Toward a Framework for Assessing Data Quality, Working Paper WP/01/25, International Monetary Fund, Washington.

Castonguay E., and A. Monty (2000),
> Recent Developments in the Statistics Canada Business Register, Proceedings of the Second International Conference on Establishment Surveys, American Statistical Association, Virginia: pp. 61-66.

Cochran, W. G. (1977),
> Sampling Techniques, Third Edition, Wiley, New York.

Colledge, M. J. (1995),
> Frames and Business Registers; An Overview, Chapter 2 in Business Survey Methods, Cox, B.G., et al. (editors), ISBN 0-471-5985-6, Wiley, New York.

Colledge, M. J., and M. March (1993),
> Quality Management, Journal of Business and Economic Statistics, April 1993.

Colledge, M. J. (1999),
> Statistical Integration through Metadata Management, International Statistical Review 67, 1, International Statistical Institute, Voorburg: pp. 79-98.

European Commission (1993),
> Council Regulation (EEC) concerning the statistical units for the observation and analysis of the production system in the community, 15 March, 1993, Official Journal of the European Communities No. L76.2, 1993 European Commission, Brussels.

European Commission (1996),
> Council Regulation (EC, EURATOM) concerning structural business statistics, 20 December 1996, Official Journal of the European Communities No. L14/1, 1997, European Commission, Brussels.

Eurostat (1996),
> Business Registers for Statistical Purposes: Methodological Recommendations, Volume 1, ISBN 92-827-9034-7, Eurostat, Luxembourg.

Eurostat (1998),
> Handbook on the Design and Implementation of Business Surveys, ISBN 92-828-3234-1, Eurostat, Luxembourg.

Eurostat (1998),
> Statistical Requirements Compendium, Wurm, N., et al. (editors), July 1998, Eurostat, Luxembourg.

Eurostat, (1999a),
> Statistical Law, Meeting of Steering Group on EU statistical co-operation with the New Independent Staes and Mongolia, Luxembourg, May 1999, Eurostat, Luxembourg.

Eurostat (1999b),
> Multi-annual Integrated Statistical Programme, Meeting of Steering Group on EU statistical co-operation with the New Independent Staes and Mongolia, Luxembourg, May 1999, Eurostat, Luxembourg.

Eurostat (1999c),
> Handbook on Information Technologies for a National Statistical Office, Tacis Task Force Report, Eurostat, Luxembourg.

Eurostat (1999*d*),
Standard Quality Report, Data Quality Working Group Meeting on Assessment of Quality in Statistics, Luxembourg, November 1999, Eurostat, Luxembourg.

Fellegi, I.P. (1996),
Characteristics of an Effective Statistical System, 1995 Morris Hansen Lecture, Washington Statistical Society, Washington.

Fellegi, I., and J. Ryten (2001),
A Peer Review of the Hungarian Statistical System. Hungarian Central Statistical Office, Budapest and Statistics Canada, Ottawa: available at: *www.ksh.hu/pls/ksh/docs/news/eszakvizs.doc*.

International Monetary Fund (2002*a*),
Special Data Dissemination Standard, International Monetary Fund: document available at: *http://dsbb.imf.org/ sddsindex.htm*.

International Monetary Fund (2002*b*),
General Data Dissemination Standard, International Monetary Fund: document available at *http://dsbb.imf.org/ sddsindex.htm*.

Masakova, I. (2000),
Estimation of the Non-Observed Economy: the Statistical Practices in Russia, Proceedings of the International Conference on Establishment Surveys, Buffalo, 2000, Statistics Canada, Ottawa.

Monsour, N. (1976),
US Retail Trade Survey, US Bureau of the Census, Washington.

Office of National Statistics (1998),
Statistical Quality Checklist. Office of National Statistics, London.

Statistics Canada (1998),
Statistics Canada Quality Guidelines, Catalogue No. 12-539-XIE, Statistics Canada, Ottawa.

Statistics Canada (2001),
Seminar on Statistical Output Databases and Marketing, May 2001, Statistics Canada, Ottawa: documents available at *www.statcan.ca*

Sundgren, B. (1997),
Sweden's Statistical Databases; an Infrastructure for Flexible Dissemination of Statistics, Report to UN/ECE Conference of European Statisticians, June 1997, Economic Commission for Europe, United Nations.

UN/ECE (2002),
Work Session on Statistical Metadata, March 2002, Luxembourg, United Nations Economic Commission for Europe, Statistical Division, Geneva: documents available at *www.unece.org/stats/documents/2002.03.metis.htm*.

United Nations Statistical Commission (1997),
Fundamental Principles of Official Statistics, in Official Records of the Economic and Social Council, 1994 Supplement No. 29 (E/1994/29), United Nations, New York: available at *www.unece.org/stats/documents/1997.06.ces.htm*

World Bank (2001),
Establishment of a Statistical Business Register, Strengthening the Statistical Infrastructure, working paper, Subcomponent of the Project for Reform of the State Statistics System of Ukraine, World Bank, Washington.

Chapter 7

Charmes J. (1989),
35 years of national accounts of the informal sector in Burkina Faso (1954-89). Lessons from an experience and perspectives for improvement, Ministère du Plan et de la Coopération, PNUD-DTCD, Ouagadougou, Burkina Faso, (108 pages, in French).

Charmes J. (1996),
Informal sector in Burkina Faso. Long term trends and short term follow up, Ministère de l'Economie, des Finances et du Plan, GTZ, Ouagadougou, (30 pages, in French).

Charmes J. (1998),
Progress in Measurement of the Informal Sector: Employment and Share of GDP, in Handbook of National Accounting. Household Accounting: Experiences in the Use of Concepts and Their Compilation, Volume 1: Household Sector Accounts. Statistics Division, United Nations, New York: pp. 171-188.

Charmes J. (1999),
Results and Lessons of a National Time-Use Survey in Benin, and Consequences on Re-estimation of Women's Participation to the Labour Force and Contribution to GDP, presented at a Conference of the International Association of Time-Use Researchers (IATUR), Colchester, October 1999, University of Essex, Colchester.

Charmes J. (2000*a*),

> The Contribution of Informal Sector to GDP in Developing Countries: Assessment, Estimates, Methods, Orientations for the Future, presented at joint Goskomstat of Russia/ Eurostat/ OECD Workshop on Measurement of the Non-Observed Economy, Sochi, October 2000, Organisation for Economic Co-operation and Development, Paris.

Charmes J. (2000*b*),

> African women in food processing: a major, but still underestimated sector of their contribution to the national economy, IDRC, Ottawa.

Hussmanns, R. (2000),

> Informal sector surveys: Advantages and limitations of different survey methods and survey designs for the data collection, Fourth Meeting of the Expert (Delhi) Group on Informal Sector Statistics, Geneva, August 2000, International Labour Office, Geneva.

Organisation for Economic Co-operation and Development (1997),

> Framework for the Measurement of Unrecorded Economic Activities in Transition Economies, OECD/GD(97)177, Organisation for Economic Co-operation and Development, Paris.

Chapter 8

Albakin A., and J. Walley (1999),

> The Problem of Capital Flight from Russia, report from joint project of Institute of Economics, Moscow and Centre for the Study of International Economic Relations, University of Western Ontario, in The World Economy, Blackwell Publishers, Oxford.

Gaertner W., and A. Wenig (eds) (1985),

> The Economics of the Shadow Economy, Proceedings of Conference, Bielefeld, 1983, Springer-Verlag, Berlin.

Giles, D.E.A.. (1999),

> Modelling the Hidden Economy and the Tax Gap in New Zealand, Empirical Economics 24 Springer-Verlag: pp. 621-640.

Gismondi R., and Ronconi S. (2001),

> Estimating the Non-Observed Economy in Relation to Tourist Flows, Proceedings, ETK/NTTS 2001 Conference, Crete, June, 2001, European Commission, Brussels.

Hungarian Central Statistical Office (1998),

> Hidden Economy in Hungary 1998, Hungarian Central Statistical Office, Budapest.

Isachsen, A.J., and S. Strom (1989),

> The Hidden Economy in Norway with Special Emphasis on the Hidden Labor Market in Feige (1989): pp. 251-266.

Ivan-Ungureanu, C., and C. Pop (1996). Hidden Economy in Romania and Its Integration in the National Accounts, presented at the joint UNECE/ Eurostat/ OECD meeting on National Accounts, Geneva, April/May 1996.

Landsheer, J. A., P., Van der Heijden, and G. Van Gils (1999),

> Trust and Understanding, Two Psychological Aspects of Randomized Response in Quality and Quantity, 33: pp. 1-12.

Laungani, P., and P. Mauro (2000),

> Capital Flight from Russia, policy discussion paper, International Monetary Fund, Washington.

Lithuanian Department of Statistics (1998),

> Non-Observed Economy: Concepts, Surveys, Problems, Lithuanian Department of Statistics, Vilnius.

Luttikhuizen, R., and J. Oudhof (1992),

> Informal Economy, A Time Use Approach, in Guide-book to Statistics on the Hidden Economy, Economic Commission for Europe, Statistical Division, United Nations, New York: pp. 283-304.

Masakova, I. (2000),

> Estimation of the Non-Observed Economy: the Statistical Practices in Russia, Proceedings of the International Conference on Establishment Surveys, Buffalo, 2000, Statistics Canada, Ottawa.

Mogensen, G. V., H. K. Kvist, E. Körmendi, and S. Pedersen (1995),

> The Shadow Economy in Denmark 1994 Measurement and Results, Rockwool Foundation Research Unit, Copenhagen.

Russian Federation Centre for Economic Analysis (2000),

> Business Tendency Survey Questionnaires, working questionnaires, Russian Federation Centre for Economic Analysis, Moscow.

US Internal Revenue Service (1979),

> Estimates of Income Unreported on Individual Income Tax Returns, Publication 1104, Government Printing Office, Washington.

Van Eck, R. (1987),

> Secondary Activities and the National Accounts, working paper, Central Bureau of Statistics, Voorburg.

Van Eck, R., and B. Kazemier (1988),

> Features of the Hidden Economy in the Netherlands, Review of Income and Wealth 34(3): pp. 251-273.

Van Eck, R., and B. Kazemier (1992), *Hidden Labour in the Netherlands*, in Guide-book to Statistics on the Hidden Economy, Economic Commission for Europe, Statistical Division, United Nations, New York: pp. 242-282.

Chapter 9

Blades, D. W. (1983),
Crime: what should be included in the National Accounts and what difference would it make, Organisation for Economic Co-operation and Development, Paris.

Commission of the European Communities – Eurostat, International Monetary Fund, Organisation for Economic Co-operation and Development, United Nations, and World Bank (1993),
System of National Accounts 1993, ISBN 92-1-161352-3, Brussels/Luxemburg, New York, Paris, Washington.

Groom, C., and T. Davies (1998),
Developing a methodology for measuring illegal activity for the UK *national accounts*, Economic Trends No. 536, July 1998.

Rey G. (1992),
Analisi economica ed evidenza empirica dell'attivita' illegale in Italia, Quaderni di ricerca, Istat, Rome (in Italian).

Chapter 10

Central Statistical Organisation, India (1999),
*Expert Group on Informal Sector Statistics (Delhi Group) Report of the Third Meeting,*New Delhi, May 1999, Central Statistical Organisation, New Delhi.

Charmes J. (1998),
Progress in Measurement of the Informal Sector: Employment and Share of GDP, in *Handbook of National Accounting. Household Accounting: Experiences in the Use of Concepts and Their Compilation, Volume* 1: *Household Sector Accounts*. Statistics Division, United Nations, New York: pp. 171-188.

Hussmanns, R. (1996),
ILO *recommendations on methodologies concerning informal sector data collection*, in Herman, B. and W. Stoffers (eds.) (1996) Unveiling the informal sector – More than counting heads, Aldershot/Brookfield/ Hong Kong/Singapore/Sydney/ Avebury: pp. 15-29.

Hussmanns, R. (1998*a*),
Developments in the design and implementation of informal sector and similar surveys – a review of national practices and experiences, Sixteenth International Conference of Labour Statisticians, Geneva, October 1998, doc. ICLS/16/RD2, International Labour Organization, Geneva.

Hussmanns, R. (1998*b*),
The impact of questionnaire design and field operations on the quality of informal sector survey data – a note on lessons learnt from past survey experiences, Second Meeting of the Expert Group on Informal Sector Statistics (Delhi Group), Ankara, April 1998, International Labour Organization, Geneva.

Hussmanns, R. (2000*a*),
Informal sector surveys: Advantages and limitations of different survey methods and survey designs for the data collection, presented at Fourth Meeting of the Expert Group on Informal Sector Statistics (Delhi Group), Geneva, August 2000, International Labour Organization, Geneva.

Hussmanns, R. (2000*b*),
The informal sector – statistical definition and survey methods in Handbook of National Accounting, Household Accounting: Experience in Concepts and Compilation, Volume 1: Household Sector Accounts, doc. ST/ESA/ STAT/SERF/75 (Vol. 1), United Nations, New York: pp. 59-92.

Hussmanns, R. (2001),
Informal Sector and Informal Employment: Elements of a Conceptual Framework, presented at ILO/WIEGO Workshop on Informal Employment Statistics in Latin America, Santiago, October 2001, International Labour Organization, Geneva.

Hussmanns, R., and F. Mehran (1999),
Statistical definition of the informal sector – international standards and national practices, 52nd Session of the International Statistical Institute, Helsinki, August 1999, International Labour Organization, Geneva.

International Labour Organisation (1992),
Report III: *Statistics of employment in the informal sector*, Fifteenth International Conference of Labour Statisticians, Geneva, January 1993, doc. ICLS/15/III, International Labour Organisation,Geneva.

International Labour Organisation (1993),
Highlights of the conference and text of the three resolutions adopted, Fifteenth International Conference of Labour Statisticians, Geneva, January 1993, in Bulletin of Labour Statistics 1993-2, International Labour Organisation, Geneva: pp. IX-XXI.

International Labour Organisation (1993a),
    Report of the conference, Fifteenth International Conference of Labour Statisticians, Geneva, January 1993, doc. ICLS/15/D.6 (rev.1), International Labour Organisation, Geneva.

United Nations (2000),
    Household Accounting: Experience in Concepts and Compilation, Volume 1: Household Sector Accounts; *Handbook of National Accounting*, Studies in Methods, Series F, No. 75 (Vol. 1), document # ST/ESA/STAT/SER.F/75 (Vol. 1), Department of Economic and Social Affairs, Statistics Division, United Nations, New York.

Chapter 11

Blades, D. W. (1975),
    Non-Monetary (Subsistence) Activities in the National Accounts of Developing Countries, Organisation for Economic Co-operation and Development, Paris.

Charmes J. (1998a),
    Progress in Measurement of the Informal Sector:Employment and Share of GDP, in Handbook of National Accounting, Household Accounting: Experiences in the Use of Concepts and their Compilation, Volume 1: Household Sector Accounts, Statistics Division, United Nations, New York: pp. 171-188.

Charmes J. (1989),
    35 years of national accounts of the informal sector in Burkina Faso (1954-89). Lessons from an experience and perspectives for improvement, Ministère du Plan et de la Coopération, PNUD-DTCD, Ouagadougou, Burkina Faso, (108 pages, in French).

Charmes J. (2000a),
    The Contribution of Informal Sector to GDP in Developing Countries: Assessment, Estimates, Methods, Orientations for the Future, presented at joint Goskomstat of Russia/ Eurostat/ OECD Workshop on Measurement of the Non-Observed Economy, Sochi, October 2000, Organisation for Economic Co-operation and Development, Paris.

Goldschmidt-Clermont L., E. Pagnossin-Aligisakis, and C. Samii-Etemad (1998),
    Direct Measurement of Household Non-Market Production, A Methodological Contribution, joint ECE/INSTRAW/UNSD Work Session on Gender Statistics, Geneva, 1998, Working Paper 12.

Goldschmidt-Clermont, L. (1987),
    Economic Evaluations of Unpaid Household Work: Africa, Asia, Latin America and Oceania, Women, Work and Development, No. 14, International Labour Organisation, Geneva.

Chapter 12

Barens, J. J. (1982),
    Macro-economic methods for the estimation of the size of the underground economy, thesis, Erasmus University (in Dutch).

Blades, D. (1982),
    The Hidden Economy, Occasional Studies, Organisation for Economic Co-operation and Development, Paris.

Boeschoten, W.C., and M.M.G. Fase (1984),
    Money transfer and the underground economy in the Netherlands 1965-1982, De Nederlandsche Bank, Amsterdam (in Dutch).

Cramer, J.S. (1980),
    The Regular and Irregular Circulation of Money in the United States, A&E report 11/80, University of Amsterdam, Amsterdam.

Feige, E.L. (1979),
    How Big is the Irregular Economy? Challenge 22(5): pp. 5-13.

Feige, E.L. (1980),
    A New Perspective on Macroeconomic Phenomena, Netherlands Institute for Advanced Studies, Wassenaar.

Frey, B.S., and H. Weck (1983),
    Estimating the shadow economy: A 'Naive' Approach, Oxford Economic Papers 35: pp. 23-44.

Garcia, G. (1978),
    The Currency Ratio and the Subterranean Economy, Financial Analysts Journal, Nov/Dec 1978.

Goskomstat of Russia (1995),
    Russian Federation: Report on the National Accounts, October 1995, The World Bank, ECA Country Department III, Government of Russia, State Statistical Committee, Moscow.

Gutmann, P.M. (1977),
    The Subterranean Economy, Financial Analysts Journal 34: pp. 26-28.

Helberger, C., and H. Knepel (1988),
How Big is the Shadow Economy? A Re-Analysis of the Unobserved-Variable Approach of B.S. Frey and H.Weck-Hannemann, European Economic Review 32: pp. 965-976.

Kaufmann D., and A. Kaliberda (1996),
Integrating the Unofficial Economy into the Dynamics of Post-Socialist Economies: A Framework of Analysis and Evidence, in Kaminski and Barlomiej (ed.) Economic Transition in Russia and the new states of Eurasia, International Politics of Eurasia Series, Vol. 8., Armonk and London: Sharpe, 1996: pp. 81-120

Laurent, R.D. (1979),
Currency and Subterrenean Economy, in Economic Perspectives, Federal Reserve Bank of Chicago, March/April 1979.

Schneider, F., and D. Enste (2000),
Shadow Economies Around the World: Size, Causes, and Consequences, Working Paper WP/00/26, International Monetary Fund, Washington.

Statistics Canada (1994),
The Size of the Underground Economy in Canada, (by Gylliane Gervais) Studies in National Accounting, ISSN 1192-0106, Statistics Canada, Ottawa.

Tanzi, V. (1980),
Underground Economy Built on Illicit Pursuits is Growing Concern of Economic Policymakers, Survey 4-2-1980, International Monetary Fund: pp. 34-37.

Tanzi, V. (ed.) (1982),
The Underground Economy in the United States and Abroad, Lexington Books, Toronto.

Annex 2

GLOSSARY

Notes: 1) The sources of the definitions are indicated in parentheses. 2) The definitions labelled NOE H*andbook* were developed specifically for this Handbook. 3) All terms other than those labelled NOE Handbook are in the OECD Glossary, accessible through the Internet via *www.oecd.org*. 4) All definitions should be interpreted in the context of collection, processing, compilation or dissemination of statistical data.

Account	An *account* is a tool which records, for a given aspect of economic life, *a*) the uses and resources or *b*) the changes in assets and the changes in liabilities and/or *c*) the stock of assets and liabilities existing at a certain time; the transactions accounts include a balancing item which is used to equate the two sides of the accounts (*e.g.* resources and uses) and which is a meaningful measure of economic performance in itself. (SNA 2.85 and 2.87)
Activity classification	The main purpose of an *activity classification* is to classify productive economic activities. The main aim is to provide a set of activity categories that can be utilised when dissecting statistics according to such activities. ISIC is the United Nations International Standard Industrial Classification of All Economic Activities. The third revision of ISIC is used in the 1993 SNA. (ISIC Rev. 3, para. 16)
Administrative data collection	The set of activities involved in the collection, processing storage and dissemination of statistical data from one or more *administrative sources*. The equivalent of a *survey* but with the source of data being administrative records rather direct contact with respondents. (NOE Handbook)
Administrative data	The set of units and data derived from an *administrative source*. (NOE Handbook)
Administrative source	The organisational unit responsible for implementing an administrative regulation (or group of regulations), for which the corresponding register of units and the transactions are viewed as a source of statistical data. (NOE Handbook)
Aggregate (data)	Data obtained by *aggregation*, as distinct from *unit record data*. (NOE Handbook)
Aggregation	*Aggregation* is the combination of related categories, usually within a common branch of a hierachy, to provide information at a broader level to that at which detailed observations are taken. (*United Nations Glossary of Classification Terms*. Prepared by the Expert Group on International Economic and Social Classifications. Available at: *www.un.org/Depts/unsd/class/glossary_short.htm*)
Analytical unit	For more refined analysis of the production process, use is made of an *analytical unit* of production: this unit, which is not always observable, is the unit of homogeneous production, defined as covering no secondary activities. (SNA 2.48) See also *Statistical units and Observation units*.
Assets	*Assets* are entities functioning as stores of value and over which ownership rights are enforced by institutional units, individually or collectively, and from which economic benefits may be derived by their owners by holding them, or using them, over a period of time (the economic benefits consist of primary incomes derived from the use of the asset and the value, including possible holding gains/losses, that could be realised by disposing of the asset or terminating it). (SNA 10.2 and 13.12 [1.26])

205

Balance of payments	The *balance of payments* is a statistical statement that systematically summarises, for a specific time period, the economic transactions of an economy with the rest of the world. Transactions for the most part between residents and non-residents, consist of those involving: goods, services and income; those involving financial claims on, and liabilities to, the rest of the world; and those (such as gifts) classified as transfers which involve offsetting entries to balance, in an accounting sense, one-sided transactions.
	The standard components of the balance of payments comprise two main groups of accounts:
	• the current account, which pertains to goods and services, income, and current transfers; and
	• the capital and financial account, which pertains to *i)* capital transfers and acquisition or disposal of non-produced, non-financial assets and *ii)* financial assets and liabilities. (BPM, paras. 13, 149)
Balance sheet	A *balance sheet* is a statement, drawn up at a particular point in time, of the values of assets owned by an institutional unit or sector and of the financial claims (*i.e.*, liabilities) incurred by this unit or sector; for the economy as a whole, the balance sheet shows what is often referred to as "national wealth" – the sum of non-financial assets and net claims on the rest of the world. (SNA 13.1 and 13.2 [1.11, 2.93, 10.1])
Balancing item	An account is closed by introducing a *balancing item* defined residually as the difference between the two sides of the account; a balancing item typically encapsulates the net result of the activities covered by the account in question and is therefore an economic construct of considerable interest and analytical significance – for example, value added, disposable income, saving, net lending and net worth. (SNA 1.3 [3.64])
Barter transaction	A b*arter transaction* involves two parties, with one party providing a good, service or asset other than cash to the other in return for a good, service or asset other than cash. (SNA 3.37)
Base period	The *base period* is the period that provides the weights for an index. (SNA 16.16)
Basic data	Same as *basic statistical data.* (NOE Handbook)
Basic data collection programme	The *basic data collection programme* is the data collection infrastructure and survey procedures that are in place within a *national statistical system* to collect, process and disseminate basic statistical data. (NOE Handbook)
Basic price	The *basic price* is the amount receivable by the producer from the purchaser for a unit of a good or service produced as output minus any tax payable, and plus any subsidy receivable, on that unit as a consequence of its production or sale; it excludes any transport charges invoiced separately by the producer. (SNA 6.205, 15.28 [3.82])
Basic statistical data	Data collected on a regular basis by *survey* from respondents, or from *administrative sources,* by *survey statisticians* in the *national statistical system* are edited, imputed and aggregated to become the *basic statistical data* that are published as *official statistics* and/or used in compilation of the national accounts. (NOE Handbook)
Capital account	The *capital account* records all transactions in non-financial assets. (SNA 10.20 and 1.9)
Capital flight	Capital flight may be defined as transfer of assets denominated in a national currency into assets denominated in a foreign currency, either at home or abroad, in ways that are not part of normal transactions. (Abalkin and Walley (1999) – for full reference see NOE Handbook Chapter 10)
Capital stock	*Gross capital stock* is the value of all fixed assets still in use at the actual or estimated current purchasers' prices for new assets of the same type, irrespective of the age of the assets. (SNA 6.199).
	Net capital stock can be described as the difference between gross capital stock and consumption of fixed capital. (SNA 6.199)
Census	A *census* is a survey conducted on the full set of observation objects belonging to a given population or universe. (*Terminology on Statistical Metadata*, Conference of European Statisticians Statistical Standards and Studies, No. 53, UNECE, Geneva 2000)

Central government	The political authority of *central government* extends over the entire territory of the country; central government has the authority to impose taxes on all resident and non-resident units engaged in economic activities within the country. (SNA 4.118)
Central product classification	The *central product classification* (CPC) is a classification based on the physical characteristics of goods or on the nature of the services rendered; each type of good or service distinguished in the CPC is defined in such a way that it is normally produced by only one activity as defined in ISIC. (SNA 5.44) The classification structure comprises: Sections – one digit code; Divisions – two-digit code; Groups – three-digit code; Classes – four-digit code; Subclasses – five-digit code. The current version (Version 1.0) was last revised in 1997 and is expected to be updated by 2002. (*Central Product Classification* (CPC). Version 1.0. United Nations, New York, 1998, Series M, No. 77, Ver. 1.0)
Centre of economic interest	An institutional unit is said to have a *centre of economic interest* within a country when there exists some location within the economic territory of the country on or from which it engages, and intends to continue to engage, in economic activities and transactions on a significant scale, either indefinitely or over a finite but long period of time. (SNA 14.12 [4.15])
Chain index	A *chain index* is obtained by linking price (or volume) indices for consecutive periods; the short-term movements that are linked are calculated using weighting patterns appropriate to the periods concerned. (SNA 16.41). The key difference to the fixed-weight aggregation is that the prices are continuously updated so that "substitution bias" is avoided and that measures are independent of the choice of base year. (OECD – *Economic Outlook: Sources and Methods*)
C.i.f. price	The *c.i.f. price* (i.e., *cost, insurance and freight price*) is the price of a good delivered at the frontier of the importing country, including any insurance and freight charges incurred to that point, or the price of a service delivered to a resident, before the payment of any import duties or other taxes on imports or trade and transport margins within the country. (*International Merchandise Trade Statistics, Concepts and Definitions*, United Nations, New York, 1998, Studies in Methods, Series M, No. 52, Rev. 2, page 35, para. 7) In 1993 SNA this concept is applied only to detailed imports. (SNA 15.35 [14.40])
Classification	A *classification* is a set of discrete, exhaustive and mutually exclusive observations which can be assigned to one or more variables to be measured in the collation and/or presentation of data. The terms "classification" and "nomenclature" are often used interchangeably, despite the definition of a "nomenclature" being narrower than that of a "classification". The structure of classification can be either hierarchical or flat. (*United Nations Glossary of Classification Terms*. Prepared by the Expert Group on International Economic and Social Classifications. Available at: *www.un.org/Depts/unsd/class/glossary_short.htm*)
Classification of individual consumption by purpose (COICOP)	The *classification of individual consumption by purpose* (COICOP) is a classification used to identify the objectives of both individual consumption expenditure and actual individual consumption. (SNA 18.7)
Classification of the functions of government (COFOG)	The *classification of the functions of government* (COFOG) is a classification used to identify the socio-economic objectives of current transactions, capital outlays and acquisition of financial assets by general government and its sub-sectors. (SNA 18.9)
Concealed production	Same as *underground production*. (SNA 6.34)
Compensation of employees	*Compensation of employees* is the total remuneration, in cash or in kind, payable by an enterprise to an employee in return for work done by the latter during the accounting period. No compensation of employees is payable in respect of unpaid work undertaken voluntarily, including the work done by members of a household within an unincorporated enterprise owned by the same household. Compensation of employees does not include any taxes payable by the employer on the wage and salary bill – for example, a payroll tax. Such taxes are treated as taxes on production. (SNA 7.21 [7.31])

207|

Concept	*Concepts* are abstract summaries, general notions, knowledge, etc., of a whole set of behaviours, attitudes or characteristics which are seen as having something in common. Concepts are used to assist in presenting/conveying precise meaning, categorising, interpreting, structuring and making sense of phenomena (such as classifications).
	(*United Nations Glossary of Classification Terms*. Prepared by the Expert Group on International Economic and Social Classifications. Available at: *www.un.org/Depts/unsd/class/glossary_short.htm*)
Constant price	*Constant prices* are obtained by directly factoring changes over time in the values of flows or stocks of goods and services into two components reflecting changes in the prices of the goods and services concerned and changes in their volumes (*i.e.*, changes in "constant price terms"); the term "at constant prices" commonly refers to series which use a fixed-base Laspeyres formula. (SNA 16.2)
Consumer goods	Good or service that is used without further transformation in production by households, non-profit institutions serving households or government units for the direct satisfaction of individual needs or wants or the collective needs of members of the community. (SNA, para. 9.41)
Consumer price index	The *consumer price index* measures changes over time in the general level of prices of goods and services that a reference population acquires, uses or pays for consumption. A consumer price index is estimated as a series of summary measures of the period-to-period proportional change in the prices of a fixed set of consumer goods and services of constant quantity and characteristics, acquired, used or paid for by the reference population. Each summary measure is constructed as a weighted average of a large number of elementary aggregate indices. Each of the elementary aggregate indices is estimated using a sample of prices for a defined set of goods and services obtained in, or by residents of, a specific region from a given set of outlets or other sources of consumption goods and services. (International Labour Organisation Resolution Concerning Consumer Price Indices Adopted by the 14th International Conference of Labour Statisticians, October-November 1988, para. 2)
Consumption of fixed capital	*Consumption of fixed capital* represents the reduction in the value of the fixed assets used in production during the accounting period resulting from physical deterioration, normal obsolescence or normal accidental damage. (SNA 10.27 [6.179, 10.118])
Corporation	A *corporation* is a legal entity, created for the purpose of producing goods or services for the market, that may be a source of profit or other financial gain to its owner(s); it is collectively owned by shareholders who have the authority to appoint directors responsible for its general management. (SNA 4.23 [4.18])
Coverage	*Coverage* refers to the population from which observations for a particular topic can be drawn. An understanding of coverage is required to facilate the comparison of data. The rules and conventions of coverage are largely determined by concept definitions, scope rules, information requirements and, in the case of statistical collections and classifications, collection and counting units and the collection methodology. (*United Nations Glossary of Classification Terms*. Prepared by the Expert Group on International Economic and Social Classifications. Available at: *www.un.org/Depts/unsd/class/glossary_short.htm*)
	In the context of the 1993 SNA, coverage relates to production activities within the production boundary. (NOE Handbook)
Cross border shopping	*Cross border shopping* is the name given to the activity wherein private individuals buy goods abroad because of lower taxes and import them for their own consumption, without declaring them in full in order to avoid paying import duties. (NOE Handbook)
Cumulative data	Same as *year to date data*. (OECD – *Main Economic Indicators*)
Currency	*Currency* comprises those notes and coins in circulation that are commonly used to make payments. (SNA 11.70, (AF.21) – Annex to Chapter XIII)
Current accounts	*Current accounts* record the production of goods and services, the generation of incomes by production, the subsequent distribution and redistribution of incomes among institutional units, and the use of incomes for purposes of consumption or saving. (SNA 1.5 [2.102])
Currently active population	Same as *labour force*. (International Labour Organization Resolution Concerning Statistics of the Economically Active Population, Employment, Unemployment and Underemployment Adopted by the 13th International Conference of Labour Statisticians, October 1982, para. 8)

Cut-off survey	*Survey* in which the sample excludes all units that are less than a specified size. (NOE Handbook)
Data	*Data* is the physical representation of information in a manner suitable for communication, interpretation, or processing by human beings or by automatic means. (*Terminology on Statistical Metadata*, Conference of European Statisticians Statistical Standards and Studies, No. 53, UNECE, Geneva 2000)
Data collection	*Data collection* is an activity of the survey life cycle for gathering data from respondents and recording it for further processing. (*Terminology on Statistical Metadata*, Conference of European Statisticians Statistical Standards and Studies, No. 53, UNECE, Geneva 2000) *Data collection* is also used in a broader sense to mean the whole survey or administrative data collection process, including design, collection, editing, imputation, aggregation and dissemination. (NOE Handbook)
Data collection programme	Same as *basic data collection programme*. (NOE Handbook)
Data element	A *data element* is the smallest identifiable unit of data within a certain context for which the definition, identification, permissible values and other information is specified by means of a set of attributes. (*Terminology on Statistical Metadata*, Conference of European Statisticians Statistical Standards and Studies, No. 53, UNECE, Geneva 2000) Synonymous with *data item* and *variable* (NOE Handbook)
Data item	Same as *data element* (NOE Handbook)
Demand deposit	*Demand deposits* are funds deposited at a depository institution that are payable on demand (immediately or within a very short period). The most common forms of demand deposits are checking accounts. (OECD *Economic Outlook: Sources and Methods*. Available at *www.oecd.org/eco/sources-and-methods*)
Depreciation	*Depreciation* as usually calculated in business accounts is a method of allocating the costs of past expenditures on fixed assets over subsequent accounting periods; note that the depreciation methods favoured in business accounting and those prescribed by tax authorities almost invariably deviate from the concept of consumption of fixed capital employed in the SNA and so the term "consumption of fixed capital" is used in the SNA to distinguish it from "depreciation" as typically measured in business accounts. (SNA 1.62, 3.77 and 6.183)
Derived data element	A *data element derived* from other data elements using a mathematical, logical, or other type of transformation, *e.g.* arithmetic formula, composition, aggregation. (*Terminology on Statistical Metadata*, Conference of European Statisticians Statistical Standards and Studies, No. 53, UNECE, Geneva 2000)
Disaggregation	*Disaggregation* is the breakdown of observations, usually within a common branch of a hierachy, to a more detailed level to that at which detailed observationsare taken. (*United Nations Glossary of Classification Terms*. Prepared by the Expert Group on International Economic and Social Classifications. Available at: *www.un.org/Depts/unsd/class/glossary_short.htm*)
Distribution and use of income accounts	The *distribution and use of income accounts* consist of a set of articulated accounts showing how incomes are: *a)* generated by production; *b)* along with property income, distributed to institutional units with claims on the value added created by production; *c)* redistributed among institutional units, mainly by government units through social security contributions and benefits and taxes; and *d)* eventually used by households, government units or non-profit institutions serving households (NPISHs) for purposes of final consumption or saving. (SNA 1.7 and Table 2.8)
Distributive trades	*Distributive trades* corresponds to the wholesale and retail trade; repair of motor vehicles, motorcycles and personal and household goods Tabulation Category (G) of ISIC Rev. 3. It includes the following Divisions: • Sale, maintenance and repair of motor vehicles and motorcycles; retail sale of automotive fuel • Wholesale trade and commission trade, except of motor vehicles and motorcycles • Retail trade, except of motor vehicles and motorcycles; repair of personal and household goods (ISIC Rev. 3 and NACE Rev. 1)

Documentation	Descriptive text used to define or describe an object, design, specification, instructions or procedure. (*Terminology on Statistical Metadata*, Conference of European Statisticians Statistical Standards and Studies, No. 53, UNECE, Geneva 2000)
Double deflation	*Double deflation* is a method whereby gross value added is measured at constant prices by subtracting intermediate consumption at constant prices from output at constant prices; this method is feasible only for constant price estimates which are additive, such as those calculated using a Laspeyres' formula (either fixed-base or for estimates expressed in the previous year's prices). (SNA 16.5)
Double entry	For a unit or sector, national accounting is based on the principle of *double entry*, as in business accounting, whereby each transaction must be recorded twice, once as a resource (or a change in liabilities) and once as a use (or a change in assets). (SNA 2.57)
Earnings	The concept of earnings, as applied in wage statistics, relates to remuneration in cash and in kind paid to employees for time worked or work done together with remuneration for time not worked, such as annual vacation and other paid leave or holidays.
	Earnings exclude employers' contributions in respect of their employees paid to social security and pension schemes and also the benefits received by employees under these schemes. Earnings also exclude severance and termination pay. (International Labour Organisation Resolution Concerning an Integrated System of Wages Statistics Adopted by the 12th International Conference of Labour Statisticians, October 1973, para. 8)
Economic activity	An economic *activity* is a process, *i.e.*, the combination of actions, that result in economic production (ISIC Rev. 3, para. 29)
Economic activity classification	Same as *activity classification* (NOE Handbook)
Economic asset	*Economic assets* are entities functioning as stores of value and over which ownership rights are enforced by institutional units, individually or collectively, and from which economic benefits may be derived by their owners by holding them, or using them, over a period of time (the economic benefits consist of primary incomes derived from the use of the asset and the value, including possible holding gains/losses, that could be realised by disposing of the asset or terminating it). (SNA 10.2 and 13.12 [11.16])
Economic flow	*Economic flows* reflect the creation, transformation, exchange, transfer or extinction of economic value; they involve changes in the volume, composition, or value of an institutional unit's assets and liabilities. (SNA 3.9)
Economic production	*Economic production* is consists of processes or activities carried out under the control and responsibility of an institutional unit that uses inputs of labour, capital, and goods and services to produce outputs of goods or services. (SNA 5.4, 6.15)
Economic territory (of a country)	The *economic territory of a country* consists of the geographic territory administered by a government within which persons, goods, and capital circulate freely; it includes: *a*) the airspace, territorial waters, and continental shelf lying in international waters over which the country enjoys exclusive rights or over which it has, or claims to have, jurisdiction in respect of the right to fish or to exploit fuels or minerals below the sea bed; *b*) territorial enclaves in the rest of the world; and *c*) any free zones, or bonded warehouses or factories operated by offshore enterprises under customs control (these form part of the economic territory of the country in which they are physically located). (SNA 14.9 and *International Merchandise Trade Statistics, Concepts and Definitions*, United Nations, New York, 1998, Studies in Methods, Series M, No. 52, Rev. 2, page 27, para. 3)
Economically active population	*Economically active population* comprises all persons of either sex who furnish the supply of labour for the production of economic goods and services as defined by the United Nations System of National Accounts during a specified time-reference period. (International Labour Organisation Resolution Concerning Statistics of the Economically Active Population, Employment, Unemployment and Underemployment Adopted by the 13th International Conference of Labour Statisticians, October 1982, para. 5)
	Economically active persons are persons engaged in production included within the boundary of production of the SNA. (SNA 6.22)

Economically significant prices	*Prices* are said to be *economically significant* when they have a significant influence on the amounts the producers are willing to supply and on the amounts purchasers wish to buy. (SNA 6.45 [4.58])
Employed persons	The *employed* comprise all persons above a specified age who during a specified brief period, either one week or one day, were in the following categories:

a) paid employment:

- at work: persons who during the reference period performed some work for a wage or salary, in cash or in kind;

- with a job but not at work: persons who, having already worked in their present job, were temporarily not at work during the reference period and had a formal attachment to their job. This formal attachment should be determined in the light of national circumstances, according to one or more of the following criteria: the continued receipt of wage or salary; an assurance of return to work following the end of the contingency, or an agreement as to the date of return; the elapsed duration of absence from the job which, wherever relevant, may be that duration for which workers can receive compensation benefits without obligations to accept other jobs;

b) self-employment

- at work; persons who during the reference period performed some work for profit or family gain, in cash or in kind;

- with an enterprise but not at work: persons with an enterprise, which may be a business enterprise, a farm or a service undertaking, who were temporarily not at work during the reference period for any specific reason.

For operational purposes the notion of "some work" may be interpreted as work for at least one hour. (International Labour Organisation Resolution Concerning Statistics of the Economically Active Population, Employment, Unemployment and Underemployment Adopted by the 13th International Conference of Labour Statisticians, October 1982, para. 9)

Employee	An *employee* is a person who enters an agreement, which may be formal or informal, with an enterprise to work for the enterprise in return for remuneration in cash or in kind. (SNA 7.23)

Employees are all those workers who hold the type of job defined as paid employment jobs. Employees with stable contracts are those employees who have had, and continue to have, an explicit (written or oral) or implicit contract of employment, or a succession of such contracts, with the same employer on a continuous basis. On a continuous basis implies a period of employment which is longer than a specified minimum determined according to national circumstances. *Regular employees* are those employees with stable contracts for whom the employing organisation is responsible for payment of taxes and social security contributions and/or where the contractual relationship is subject to national labour legislation. International Labour Organisation Resolution Concerning the International Classification of Status in Employment Adopted by the 15th International Conference of Labour Statisticians, January 1993, para. 8)

Employer	*Employers* are self-employed persons with paid employees. (SNA 7.25)

Employers are those workers who, working on their own account or with one or a few partners, hold the type of job defined as a *self-employed job*, and in this capacity, on a continuous basis (including the reference period) have engaged one or more persons to work for them in their business as *employees*. (International Labour Organisation Resolution Concerning the International Classification of Status in Employment Adopted by the 15th International Conference of Labour Statisticians, January 1993, para. 9)

Employment	Persons in *employment* comprise all persons above a specified age who during a specified brief period, either one week or one day, were in paid employment or self employment.

(International Labour Organisation Resolution Concerning Statistics of the Economically Active Population, Employment, Unemployment and Underemployment Adopted by the 13th International Conference of Labour Statisticians, October 1982, para. 9)

211

Employment (establishment surveys)	*Employment* in establishment surveys is the total number of persons who work in or for the etablishment including working proprietors, active business partners and unpaid family workers, as well as persons working outside the establishment when paid by and under the control of the establishment, for example, sales representatives, outside service engineers and repair and maintenance personnel. Also included are salaried managers and salaried directors of incorporated enterprises. The total should include part-time workers and seasonal workers on the payroll, persons on short-term leave (sick leave, maternity leave, annual leave or vacation) and on strike, but not persons on indefinite leave, military leave or pension.
	Excluded are directors of incorporated enterprises and members of shareholders committees who are paid solely for their attendance at meetings, labour made available to the establishment by other units and charged for, such as contract workers paid through contractors, persons carrying out repair and maintenance work in the establishment on behalf of other units and all homeworkers.
	The enumeration may refer to a specified day, pay period or calendar week in the inquiry period. (*International Recommendations for Industrial Statistics*, United Nations, New York, 1983, Statistical Papers, Series M, No. 48, Rev. 1, paras. 92-94)
Employment rate	The *employment rate* is the number of persons in employment as a percentage of the population of working age.
Employment status	*Status in employment* refers to the status of an economically active person with respect to his or her employment, that is to say, the type of explicit or implicit contract of employment with other persons or organisations that the person has in his/her job. The basic criteria used to define the groups of the classification are the economic risk, an element of which is the strength of the attachment between the person and the job, and the type of authority over establishments and other workers that the person has or will have in the job. Care should be taken to ensure that an economically active person is classified by status in employment on the basis of the same job(s) as used for classifying the person by "occupation", "industry" and "sector".
	It is recommended that the economically active population should be classified by status in employment as follows: employees, employers; own-account workers; contributing family workers; members of producers' co-operatives; persons not classifiable by status.
	(*Principles and Recommendations for Population and Housing Censuses*, Revision 1. United Nations, New York, 1998, Series M, No. 67, Rev. 1, paras. 2.226-2.227)
Enterprise	An *enterprise* is an institutional unit in its capacity as a producer of goods and services; an enterprise may be a corporation, a quasi-corporation, a non-profit institution, or an unincorporated enterprise. (SNA 5.17 [5.1])
	An *enterprise* is an institutional unit or the smallest combination of institutional units that encloses and directly or indirectly controls all necessary functions to carry out its production activities (ISIC Rev. 3, para. 79)
Establishment	An *establishment* is an enterprise, or part of an enterprise, that is situated in a single location and in which only a single (non-ancillary) productive activity is carried out or in which the principal productive activity accounts for most of the value added. (SNA 5.21, 6.80)
	An *establishment* is an enterprise, or part of an enterprise, which engages in one, or predominantly one, kind of economic activity at or from one location or within one geographic area, for which data are available, or can meaningfully be compiled, that allow the calculation of the operating surplus. (ISIC Rev. 3, para. 106)
Exhaustive(ness)	GDP estimates are said to be *exhaustive* when they include all productive activities within the 1993 SNA production boundary, *i.e.*, there are no *non-measured* productive activities. *Exhaustiveness* is the state of being exhaustive. (NOE Handbook)
Expenditure	*Expenditures* are the values of the amounts that buyers pay, or agree to pay, to sellers in exchange for goods or services that sellers provide to them or to other institutional units designated by the buyers. (SNA 9.22)

Exports of goods and services	*Exports of goods and services* consist of sales, barter, or gifts or grants, of goods and services from residents to non-residents. The treatment of exports and imports in the SNA is generally identical with that in the balance of payments accounts as described in the Balance of Payments Manual. (SNA 14.88 [14.91, 14.94])
	The international standard for the concepts and definitions for merchandise trade are outlined in the UN publication, *International Merchandise Trade Statistics, Concepts and Definitions,* United Nations, New York, 1998, Studies in Methods, Series M, No. 52, Rev. 2.
Externalities	*Externalities* are changes in the condition or circumstances of institutional units caused by the economic actions of other units without the consent of the former. (SNA [3.51])
Final consumption	*Final consumption* consists of goods and services used up by individual households or the community to satisfy their individual or collective needs or wants. (SNA 1.49)
Final expenditure	*Final expenditure* consists of *final consumption expenditure* and *gross fixed capital formation.* (SNA [1.57])
Financial account	The *financial account* records all transactions in financial assets and liabilities. (SNA 11.1 [1.9, 11.103])
Financial asset	*Financial assets* are entities over which ownership rights are enforced by institutional units, individually or collectively, and from which economic benefits may be derived by their owners by holding them, or using them over a period of time; they differ from other assets in the SNA in that there is a counterpart liability on the part of another institutional unit (except for monetary gold and Special Drawing Rights (SDRs). (SNA 13.20 [10.5, 11.16, 11.17, (AF) – Annex to Chapter XIII])
Financial corporation	*Financial corporations* consist of all resident corporations or quasi-corporations principally engaged in financial intermediation or in auxiliary financial activities which are closely related to financial intermediation. (SNA 4.77 [2.20])
Financial intermediary	*Financial intermediaries* are units which incur liabilities on their own account on financial markets by borrowing funds which they lend on different terms and conditions to other institutional units. (SNA 6.121)
Financial intermediation	*Financial intermediation* is a productive activity in which an institutional unit incurs liabilities on its own account for the purpose of acquiring financial assets by engaging in financial transactions on the market; the role of financial intermediaries is to channel funds from lenders to borrowers by intermediating between them. (SNA 4.78)
Financial intermediation services indirectly measured	*Financial intermediation services indirectly measured* (FISIM) is an indirect measure of the value of financial intermediation services provided but for which financial institutions do not charge explicitly. (SNA 6.124)
Financial transaction	*Financial transactions* between institutional units and between institutional units and the rest of the world cover all transactions involving change of ownership of financial assets, including the creation and liquidation of financial claims. (SNA 11.13)
First in first out	*First-in-first-out* (FIFO) is an inventory valuation method based on the assumption that goods are withdrawn from inventories in the same order as they entered. (SNA 6.70)
Fixed asset	*Fixed assets* are tangible or intangible assets produced as outputs from processes of production that are themselves used repeatedly or continuously in other processes of production for more than one year. (SNA 10.33 [1.49, 10.7, 10.26, 13.15, (AN.11) – Annex to Chapter XIII])
Flow data	*Flow data* are cumulated over a reference period, for example, passenger car registrations, where the figure for the reference period is the sum of daily registrations. In contrast to *stock data.* (OECD – Main Economic Indicators)
F.o.b. price	The *f.o.b. price* (free on board price) of exports and imports of goods is the market value of the goods at the point of uniform valuation, (the customs frontier of the economy from which they are exported). It is equal to the c.i.f. price less the costs of transportation and insurance charges, between the customs frontier of the exporting (importing) country and that of the importing (exporting) country. (SNA 14.36 and 14.40 [15.36] and *International Merchandise Trade Statistics, Concepts and Definitions,* United Nations, New York, 1998, Studies in Methods, Series M, No. 52, Rev. 2, page 35, para. 5)

213|

Foreign direct investment	*Foreign direct investment* is the category of international investment that reflects the objective of a resident entity in one economy to obtain a lasting interest in an enterprise resident in another economy. (SNA 14.151 and 14.152 [Table 11.2, BPM 359 and 362])
Full coverage survey	Same as *census*
Full-time equivalent employment	*Full-time equivalent employment* is the number of full-time equivalent jobs, defined as total hours worked divided by average annual hours worked in full-time jobs. (SNA 17.14 [15.102, 17.28])
General government	The *general government* sector consists of the totality of institutional units which, in addition to fulfilling their political responsibilities and their role of economic regulation, produce principally non-market services (possibly goods) for individual or collective consumption and redistribute income and wealth. (SNA 2.20)
General sales taxes	*General sales taxes* consist of all general taxes levied at one stage only (*e.g.* manufacturing or wholesale or retail) plus multi-stage cumulative taxes (also known as cascade taxes) where tax is levied each time a transaction takes place without any deduction for tax paid on inputs. (OECD 5112 and 5113 [7.69])
Generation of income account	The *generation of income account* shows the types of primary incomes and the sectors, sub-sectors or industries in which the primary incomes originate, as distinct from the sectors or sub-sectors destined to receive such incomes. (SNA 7.3)
Goods	*Goods* are physical objects for which a demand exists, over which ownership rights can be established and whose ownership can be transferred from one institutional unit to another by engaging in transactions on markets; they are in demand because they may be used to satisfy the needs or wants of households or the community or used to produce other goods or services. (SNA 6.7)
Goods and services account	The *goods and services account* shows for the economy as a whole and for groups of products, the total resources in terms of output and imports, and the uses of goods and services in terms of intermediate consumption, final consumption, gross capital formation and exports. (SNA 15.5)
Government units	*Government units* are unique kinds of legal entities established by political processes which have legislative, judicial or executive authority over other institutional units within a given area. (SNA 4.104 [4.19])
Gross	The term *gross* is a common means of referring to values before deducting consumption of fixed capital (generally used as in "gross capital stock" or "gross domestic product"); all the major balancing items in the accounts from value added through to saving may be recorded gross or net. (SNA 6.201)
Gross domestic product	*Gross domestic product* is an aggregate measure of production equal to the sum of the gross values added of all resident institutional units engaged in production (plus any taxes, and minus any subsidies, on products not included in the value of their outputs). The sum of the final uses of goods and services (all uses except intermediate consumption) measured in purchasers' prices, less the value of imports of goods and services, or the sum of primary incomes distributed by resident producer units. (SNA 1.28 and 2.173-2.174) UNSD
Gross domestic product deflator	Volume of GDP calculated by recalculating the values of the various components of GDP at the constant prices of the previous year or of some fixed base year, frequently referred to as "GDP at constant prices", divided by GDP at current prices. (SNA para. 16.71)

Gross domestic product – expenditure based	*Expenditure based gross domestic product* is total final expenditures at purchasers' prices (including the f.o.b. value of exports of goods and services), less the f.o.b. value of imports of goods and services. (SNA 6.235)
Gross domestic product – income based	*Income based gross domestic product* is compensation of employees, plus taxes less subsidies on production and imports, plus gross mixed income, plus gross operating surplus. (SNA 2.222)
Gross domestic product – output based	*Output-based gross domestic product* is the sum of the gross values added of all resident producers at basic prices, plus all taxes less subsidies on products. (SNA 6.235-6.237)
Gross domestic product at market prices	*Gross domestic product at market prices* is the sum of the gross values added of all resident producers at market prices, plus taxes less subsidies on imports. (SNA 6.235). Non-deductable VAT should be added (SNA 6.236-7)
Gross fixed capital formation	*Gross fixed capital formation* is measured by the total value of a producer's acquisitions, less disposals, of fixed assets during the accounting period plus certain additions to the value of non-produced assets (such as subsoil assets or major improvements in the quantity, quality or productivity of land) realised by the productive activity of institutional units. (SNA 10.33 and 10.51 [10.26])
Gross national income	*Gross national income* (GNI) is GDP less net taxes on production and imports, less compensation of employees and property income payable to the rest of the world plus the corresponding items receivable from the rest of the world (in other words, GDP less primary incomes payable to non-resident units plus primary incomes receivable from non-resident units); an alternative approach to measuring GNI at market prices is as the aggregate value of the balances of gross primary incomes for all sectors; (note that gross national income is identical to gross national product (GNP) as previously used in national accounts generally). (SNA 2.81 and 7.16 and Table 7.2 [2.181])
Gross value added	*Gross value added* is the value of output less the value of intermediate consumption; it is a measure of the contribution to GDP made by an individual producer, industry or sector; gross value added is the source from which the primary incomes of the SNA are generated and is therefore carried forward into the primary distribution of income account. (SNA 1.6 [2.172, 6.4, 6.222])
	Gross value added at basic prices is output valued at basic prices less intermediate consumption valued at purchasers' prices. (SNA 6.226, 15.37 [6.231])
	Gross value added at producers' prices is output valued at producers' prices less intermediate consumption valued at purchasers' prices. (SNA 6.227, 15.37)
Harmonised system	The complex nature of the basic customs and statistical needs makes it necessary to have a rather detailed commodity classification. The Harmonised Commodity Description and Coding System (*Harmonised System*, or HS provides such details. Classification using these nomenclatures is based on the nature of the commodity. The HS is in principle, revised every few years. The next revision is planned to come into force on 1 January 2002. It is managed by the World Customs Organisation. (*International Merchandise Trade Statistics, Concepts and Definitions*, United Nations, New York, 1998, Studies in Methods, Series M, No. 52, Rev. 2, page 35, para. 92)
Hidden economy	Frequently but not invariably used by other authors as a synonym for *underground economy*. (NOE Handbook)
Hidden production	Frequently but not invariably used by other authors as a synonym for *underground production*. (NOE Handbook)
Holding gain	Positive or negative *holding gains* may accrue during the accounting period to the owners of financial and non-financial assets and liabilities as a result of a change in their prices (holding gains are sometimes referred to as "capital gains"). (SNA 3.62)
Homogeneous production unit	A *unit* of *homogeneous production* is a producer unit in which only a single (non-ancillary) productive activity is carried out; this unit is not normally observable and is more an abstract or conceptual unit underlying the symmetric (product-by-product) input-output tables. (SNA 15.14)

215|

Hours worked	*Total hours worked* are the aggregate number of hours actually worked during the reference period in employee and self-employment jobs. (SNA 15.102) Statistics on *hours worked* should include: • hours actually worked during normal hours of work; • time worked in addition to hours worked during normal periods of work, and generally paid at higher than normal rates (overtime); • time spent at the place of work on work such as preparation of the workplace, repairs and maintenance, preparation and cleaning of tools, and the preparation of receipts, time sheets and reports; • time spent at the place of work waiting or standing by for such reasons as lack of supply of work, breakdown of machinery, or accidents, or time spent at the place of work during which no work is done but for which payment is made under a guaranteed employment contract; • time corresponding to short rest periods at the workplace, including tea and coffee breaks. Statistics of hours worked should exclude: • hours paid for but not worked, such as paid annual leave, paid public holidays, paid sick leave; • meal breaks; • time spent on travel from home to work and *vice versa* . (International Labour Organization Resolution Concerning Statistics of Hours Worked Adopted by the 10th International Conference of Labour Statisticians, October 1962, para. 5)
Household	A *household* is a small group of persons who share the same living accommodation, who pool some, or all, of their income and wealth and who consume certain types of goods and services collectively, mainly housing and food. (SNA 4.132 [4.20])
Household production for own use	*Household production for own use* comprises those activities that are carried out by household unincorporated enterprises that are not involved in market production. By definition, such enterprises are excluded from the informal sector. (NOE Handbook)
Household unincorporated market enterprise	*Household unincorporated market enterprises* are created for the purpose of producing goods or services for sale or barter on the market; they can be engaged in virtually any kind of productive activity and they include unincorporated partnerships but the liability of the partners for the debts of the businesses must be unlimited for the partnerships to be treated as unincorporated enterprises. (SNA 4.144 and 4.145)
Illegal production	*Illegal production* comprises: • the production of goods or services whose sale, distribution or possession is forbidden by law; and • production activities which are usually legal but which become illegal when carried out by unauthorised producers, *e.g.* unlicensed medical practicioners (SNA 6.30); There may be no clear borderline between the underground economy and illegal production. For example production which does not comply with certain safety, health or other standards could be defined as illegal. (SNA 6.35) The scope of illegal production in individual countries depends upon the laws in place. For example, prostitution is legal in some countries but illegal in others. (NOE Handbook)
Implicit price deflator	An *implicit price deflator* (IPD) is obtained by dividing a current price value by its real counterpart (the chain volume measure). When calculated from the major national accounting aggregates such as GDP, IPDs relate to a broader range of goods and services in the economy than that represented by any of the individual price indexes (such as CPIs, PPIs). Movements in an implicit price deflator reflect both changes in price and changes in the composition of the aggregate for which the deflator is calculated. (*Australian National Accounts: Concepts, Sources and Methods: Glossary*, Australian Bureau of Statistics, Canberra, 2000)
Import of goods and services	*Imports of goods and services* consist of purchases, barter, or receipts of gifts or grants, of goods and services by residents from non-residents. The treatment of exports and imports in the SNA is generally identical with that in the balance of payments accounts as described in the Balance of Payments Manual. (SNA 14.88 [14.91, 14.94]) The international standard for the concepts and definitions for merchandise trade are outlined in the UN publication, *International Merchandise Trade Statistics, Concepts and Definitions*, United Nations, New York, 1998, Studies in Methods, Series M, No. 52, Rev. 2.

Income	*Income* is the maximum amount that a household, or other unit, can consume without reducing its real net worth provided the net worth at the beginning of the period is not changed by capital transfers, other changes in the volume of assets or real holding gains or losses. (SNA 8.15)
Index	*Indexes* show on average how a variable changes over time, by comparing data expressed relative to a given base value (100). Changes are shown as an increase or decrease from the base value. (OECD)
Indirect compilation method	An *indirect compilation method* is one in which a national accounts' *data item* is obtained indirectly, often through the use of indicators, rather than from direct observation through *survey* or *administrative source*. (NOE Handbook)
Industrial production	*Industrial production* comprises the output of industrial establishments, covering: mining and quarrying; manufacturing; and electricity, gas and water supply. (United Nations (1983). *International Recommendations for Industrial Statistics*. Statistical Office, Series M, No. 48, Rev. 1, para. 25)
Industry	An *industry* consists of a group of establishments engaged on the same, or similar, kinds of production activity. The classification of productive activities used in the SNA is ISIC (Rev.3). (SNA 5.5 and 5.40)
	Industry comprises Divisions 10-45 of ISIC Rev. 3. These comprise ISIC Rev. 3 Tabulation Categories C, D and E: – mining and quarrying; manufacturing; electricity, gas and water (ISIC Rev. 3)
Industry-by-industry table	An *industry-by-industry table* is a symmetric input-output table with industries as the dimension of both rows and columns; as a result it shows which industry uses the output of which other industry. (SNA 15.150)
Informal sector	The *informal sector* is broadly characterised as consisting of units engaged in the production of goods or services with the primary objective of generating employment and incometo the persons concerned. These units typically operate at a low level of organisation, with little or no division between labour and capital as factors of production and on a small scale. Labour relations – where they exist – are based mostly on casual employment, kinship or personal and social relations rather than contractual arrangements with formal guarantees. This broad definition is operationalised for statistical purposes and the informal sector defined as comprising those household unincorporated enterprises with market production that are:
	• informal own account enterprises (optionally, all, or those that are not registered under specific forms of national legislation);
	• enterprises of informal employers (optionally all those with less than a specified level of employment and/or not registered and/or employees not registered.
	(International Labour Organisation Resolution Concerning Statistics of Employment in the Informal Sector Adopted by the 15th International Conference of Labour Statisticians, January 1993, paras. 5, 8 and 9.)
Input-output table	An *input-output table* is a means of presenting a detailed analysis of the process of production and the use of goods and services (products) and the income generated in that production.; they can be either in the form of:
	a) supply and use tables or
	b) symmetric input-output tables
	(SNA 2.211, 15.1 15.2 and 15.8)
Institution	An *Institution* comprises a set of premises in a permanent structure or structures designed to house (usually large) groups of persons who are bound by either a common public objective or a common personal interest. Such sets of living quarters usually have certain common facilities shared by the occupants (baths, lounges, dormitories and so forth). Hospitals, military barracks, boarding schools, convents, prisons and so forth fall within this category. (*Principles and Recommendations for Population and Housing Censuses*, Revision 1. United Nations, New York, 1998, Series M, No. 67, Rev. 1, para. 2.359)
Institutional sectors	Institutional units are grouped together to form *institutional sectors*, on the basis of their principal functions, behaviour, and objectives. (SNA 2.20) The resident institutional units that make up the total economy are grouped into five mutually exclusive institutional sectors: *non-financial corporations*; *financial corporations*; *general government*; *non-profit institutions serving households*; and *households*. (SNA 4.6)

Institutional unit	An *institutional unit* is an economic entity that is capable, in its own right, of owning assets, incurring liabilities and engaging in economic activities and in transactions with other entities. (SNA 4.2 [1.13, 2.19, 3.13])
Integrated economic accounts	The *integrated economic accounts* comprise the full set of accounts of institutional sectors and the rest of the world, together with the accounts for transactions (and other flows) and the accounts for assets and liabilities. (SNA 2.88)
Interest	*Interest* is the amount that the debtor becomes liable to pay to the creditor over a given period of time without reducing the amount of principal outstanding, under the terms of the financial instrument agreed between them. (SNA 7.93 and ESA 4.42)
Intermediate product	*Intermediate products* are goods and services consumed as inputs by a process of production, excluding fixed assets. (SNA 6.147)
Internal transaction	The SNA treats as transactions certain kinds of actions within a unit to give a more analytically useful picture of final uses of output and of production; these transactions that involve only one unit are called *internal*, or intra-unit, *transactions*. (SNA 3.44)
Inventory	*Inventories* consist of stocks of outputs that are still held by the units that produced them prior to their being further processed, sold, delivered to other units or used in other ways, and stocks of products acquired from other units that are intended to be used for intermediate consumption or for resale without further processing. (SNA 10.7 [13.15, 13.46, (AN.12) – Annex to Chapter XIII])
International standard industrial classification	ISIC is the United Nations International Standard Industrial Classification of All Economic Activities. This classification is the international standard for the classification of productive economic activities. The main purpose is to provide a standard set of economic activities so that entities can be classified according to the activity they carry out. The hierarchical structure of the classification comprises: • Tabulation Categories – one letter alpha code A to Q; • Divisions – two-digit codes; • Groups – three-digit codes; • Classes – four-digit codes The third revision of ISIC is used in the 1993 SNA. (*International Standard Industrial Classification of all Economic Activities*, Rev. 3, United Nations, New York, 1990, Statistical Papers Series M, No. 4 Rev. 3)
Job	A *job* is a contract (explicit or implicit) between a person and an institutional unit to perform work in return for compensation (or mixed income) for a defined period or until further notice. (SNA 15.102 [17.8])
Kind-of-activity unit	A *kind-of-activity unit* is an enterprise, or a part of an enterprise, which engages in only one kind of (non-ancillary) productive activity or in which the principal productive activity accounts for most of the value added. (SNA 5.19)
Labour cost	For the purpose of *labour cost* statistics, labour cost is the cost incurred by the employer in the employment of labour. The statistics concept of labour cost comprises remuneration for work performed, payments in respect of time paid for but not worked, bonuses and gratuities, the cost of food, drink and other payments in kind, cost of workers' housing borne by employers, employers' social security expenditures, cost to the employer for vocational training, welfare services and miscellaneous items, such as transport of workers, work clothes and recruitment, together with taxes regarded as labour cost. (International Labour Organization Resolution Concerning Statistics of Labour Cost Adopted by the 11th International Conference of Labour Statisticians, October 1966, para. 3)
Labour force	The *labour force* comprises all persons who fulfil the requirements for inclusion among the *employed* or the *unemployed* during a short reference period. (International Labour Organization Resolution Concerning Statistics of the Economically Active Population, Employment, Unemployment and Underemployment adopted by the 13th International Conference of Labour Statisticians, October 1982, para. 8)

Labour force participation rate	The *labour force participation rate* is the ratio between the *total labour force* divided by the total population (of working age). (International Labour Organization Resolution Concerning Statistics of the Economically active Population, Employment, Unemployment and Underemployment, adopted by the 13th International Conference of Labour Statisticians, October 1982)
Last-in-first-out	*Last-in-first-out* (LIFO) is an inventory valuation method based on the assumption that the first good withdrawn from inventory is the last one which entered. (SNA 6.70)
Legal entity	*Legal entities* are types of institutional units which are created for purposes of production, mainly corporations and non-profit institutions (NPIs), or government units, including social security funds; they are capable of owning goods and assets, incurring liabilities and engaging in economic activities and transactions with other units in their own right. (SNA 1.13 [4.5])
Local government	*Local government* units are institutional units whose fiscal, legislative and executive authority extends over the smallest geographical areas distinguished for administrative and political purposes. (SNA 4.128)
Local kind of activity unit	A *local unit* is an enterprise, or a part of an enterprise, which engages in productive activity at or from one location. (SNA 5.20)
	The *local kind-of activity unit* (local KAU) is the part of a KAU which corresponds to a local unit. Accoding to the European System of Accounts (ESA) the local KAU is called the establishment in the SNA and ISIC Rev. 3. (Council Regulation (EEC), No. 696/93, Section III G of 15.03.1993 on the statistical units for the observation and analysis of the production system in the Community and ESA 2.106, footnote 15)
Local unit	The concept of the *local unit* covers all economic activities carried out by an enterprise at or from one location. (ISIC Rev. 3, para. 99)
	The definition has only one dimension in that it does not refer to the kind of activity that is carried out. Location may be interpreted according to the purpose, narrowly, such as specific address, or more broadly, such as within province, state, country, etc. (*United Nations Glossary of Classification Terms*. Prepared by the Expert Group on International Economic and Social Classifications. Available at: *www.un.org/Depts/unsd/class/glossary_short.htm*)
Manufacturing	*Manufacturing* comprises Tabulation Category D and Divisions 15-37 in ISIC Rev. 3.
	Manufacturing is defined as the physical or chemical transformation of materials of components into new products, including assembly of component parts of manufactured products and recycling of waste materials. (ISIC Rev. 3)
Market output	*Market output* is output that is sold at prices that are economically significant or otherwise disposed of on the market, or intended for sale or disposal on the market. (SNA 6.45)
Market price	*Market prices* for transactions are the amounts of money willing buyers pay to acquire something from willing sellers. (BPM 92 [2.68])
Market producer	*Market producers* are producers that sell most or all of their output at prices that are economically significant. (SNA 4.58 [6.52])
Metadata	*Metadata* comprises data and other documentation that describes objects in a formalised way. (*Terminology on Statistical Metadata*, Conference of European Statisticians Statistical Standards and Studies, No. 53, UNECE, Geneva 2000)
Methodology	A *methodology* is a structured approach to solve a problem. (*Terminology on Statistical Metadata*, Conference of European Statisticians Statistical Standards and Studies, No. 53, UNECE, Geneva 2000)
Mixed income	*Mixed income* is the surplus or deficit accruing from production by unincorporated enterprises owned by households; it implicitly contains an element of remuneration for work done by the owner, or other members of the household, that cannot be separately identified from the return to the owner as entrepreneur but it excludes the operating surplus coming from owner-occupied dwellings. (SNA 7.8 [4.143, 7.81])
Monetary transaction	A *monetary transaction* is one in which one institutional unit makes a payment (receives a payment) or incurs a liability (receives an asset) stated in units of currency. (SNA 3.16)

Money supply	The *money supply* is the total amount of money in circulation in a country or group of countries in a monetary union. There are several ways in which this can be calculated:
	M1 is a measure of money supply including all coins and notes plus personal money in current accounts;
	M2 is M1 plus personal money in deposit accounts;
	M3 is M2 plus government and other deposits.
	(*Dictionary of Banking and Finance*, Second Edition, P.H. Collins, 1991, Peter Collins Publishing)
National accountant	A *national accountant* is a person involved in the preparation of the national accounts. See also System of National Accounts. (NOE Handbook)
National expenditure	Capital formation and final consumption grouped together constitute *national expenditure*. (SNA 2.187)
National statistical office	The *national statistical office* is the leading statistical agency within a *national statistical system*. (NOE Handbook)
National statistical system	The *national statistical system* (NSS) is the ensemble of statistical organisations and units within a country that jointly collect, process and disseminate statistics on behalf of the national government. (NOE Handbook)
	See also: *national statistical office* and *official statistics*. (NOE Handbook)
Net	The term *"net"* is a common means of referring to values after deducting consumption of fixed capital (generally used as in "net capital stock" or "net domestic product"); all the major balancing items in the accounts from value added through to saving may be recorded gross or net; it should be noted, however, that the term "net" can be used in different contexts in the national accounts, such as "net income from abroad" which is the difference between two income flows. (SNA 6.201)
Non-financial corporation	*Non-financial corporations* are corporations whose principal activity is the production of market goods or non-financial services. (SNA 4.68 [2.20])
Non-monetary transaction	*Non-monetary transactions* are transactions that are not initially stated in units of currency; barter is an obvious example. (SNA 3.34)
Non-observed activity	An activity within the 1993 SNA production boundary that is not observed, *i.e.*, not directly measured in the basic data from which the national accounts are compiled. (NOE Handbook)
Non-observed economy	The groups of activities most likely to be non-observed are those that are *underground, illegal, informal sector,* or *undertaken by households for their own final use*. Activities may also be missed because of *deficiencies in the basic statistical data collection programme*. These groups of activities are referred to (in the NOE Handbook) as the *problem areas*. Activities not included in the basic data because they are in one or more of these problem areas are collectively said to comprise the *non-observed economy* (NOE). (NOE Handbook)
Non-measured activity	A *non-measured activity* is an activity within the 1993 SNA production boundary that is not included in GDP estimates. (NOE Handbook)
Non-measured economy	The *non-measured economy* is the group of activities within the 1993 SNA production boundary that are non-measured. (NOE Handbook)
Non-profit institution	*Non-profit institutions* (NPIs) are legal or social entities created for the purpose of producing goods and services whose status does not permit them to be a source of income, profit or other financial gain for the units that establish, control or finance them. (SNA 4.54 [4.18, 4.161])
Non-profit institutions serving households	*Non-profit institutions serving households* (NPISHs) consist of NPIs which are not predominantly financed and controlled by government and which provide goods or services to households free or at prices that are not economically significant. (SNA 4.64 and 4.65 [2.20])

Non-resident	A unit is *non-resident* if its centre of economic interest is not in the economic territory of a country. (BPM para. 58 [1.14])
Not currently active population	The *not currently active population* or, equivalently, *persons not in the labour force*, comprises all persons who were neither employed or unemployed during the short reference period used to measure current activity. (*Principles and Recommendations for Population and Housing Censuses*, Revision 1. United Nations, New York, 1998, Series M, No. 67, Rev. 1, para. 2.205)
Observation unit	*Observation units* are those entities on which information is received and statistics are compiled. (ISIC Rev. 3, para. 63) During the collection of data, this is the unit for which data is recorded. It should be noted that this may, or may not be, the same as the reporting unit. (Eurostat) See also *Statistical unit* and *Analytical unit*.
Occupation	*Occupation* refers to the type of work done during the time-reference period by the person employed (or the type of work done previously, if the person is unemployed), irrespective of the industry or the status in employment in which the person should be classified. (*Principles and Recommendations for Population and Housing Censuses*, Revision 1. United Nations, New York, 1998, Series M, No. 67, Rev. 1, paras. 2.214-2.215) The international standard for classification of occupations is the *International Standard Classification of Occupations* (ISCO-88), International Labour Office, Geneva, 1990
Official statistics	*Official statistics* are the statistics disseminated by the *national statistical system*, excepting those that are explicitly stated not to be official. (NOE Handbook)
Operating surplus	The *operating surplus* measures the surplus or deficit accruing from production before taking account of any interest, rent or similar charges payable on financial or tangible non-produced assets borrowed or rented by the enterprise, or any interest, rent or similar receipts receivable on financial or tangible non-produced assets owned by the enterprise; (note: for unincorporated enterprises owned by households, this component is called "mixed income"). (SNA 7.8)
Other flow	*Other flows* are changes in the value of assets and liabilities that do not take place in transactions; these entries are of two broad kinds – the first kind consists of changes due to factors such as discoveries or depletion of subsoil resources, or destruction by war or other political events or by natural catastrophes while the second kind consists of changes in the value of assets, liabilities, and net worth due to changes in the level and structure of prices, which are reflected in holding gains and losses. (SNA 3.57)
Output	*Output* consists of those goods or services that are produced within an establishment that become available for use outside that establishment, plus any goods and services produced for own final use. (SNA 6.38)
Output produced for own final use	*Output produced for own final use* consists of goods or services that are retained for their own final use by the owners of the enterprises in which they are produced. (SNA 6.46)
Outworker	An *outworker* is a person who agrees to work for a particular enterprise or to supply a certain quantity of goods or services to a particular enterprise, by prior arrangement or contract with that enterprise, but whose place of work is not within any of the establishments which make up that enterprise; the enterprise does not control the time spent at work by an outworker and does not assume responsibility for the conditions in which that work is carried out. (SNA 7.26)
Overtime	*Overtime* is time worked in addition to hours worked during normal periods of work, and which is generally paid at higher than normal rates. (International Labour Organisation Resolution Concerning Statistics of Hours Worked Adopted by the 10th International Conference of Labour Statisticians, October 1962, para. 5)
Own-account producer	*Own-account producers* consist of establishments engaged in gross fixed capital formation for the enterprises of which they form part, or unincorporated enterprises owned by households all or most of whose output is intended for final consumption or gross fixed capital formation by those households. (SNA 6.52)

221

Own-account worker	*Own-account workers* are self-employed persons without paid employees. (SNA 7.25) *Own-account workers* are those workers who, working on their own account or with one or more partners, hold the type of job defined as a *self-employed job*, and have not engaged on a continuous basis any *employees* to work for them during the reference period. It should be noted that during the reference period the members of this group may have engaged *employees*, provided that this is on a non-continuous basis. The partners may or may not be members of the same family or household. (International Labour Organisation Resolution Concerning the International Classification of Status in Employment Adopted by the 15th International Conference of Labour Statisticians, January 1993, para. 10)
Paid employment job	*Paid employment jobs* are those jobs where the incumbents hold explicit (written or oral) or implicit employment contracts which give them a basic remuneration which is not directly dependent upon the revenue of the unit for which they work. This unit can be a corporation, a non-profit institution, a government unit or a household. Persons in paid employment jobs are typically remunerated by wages and salaries, but may be paid by commission from sales, piece-rates, bonuses or in-kind payments such as food. (International Labour Organisation Resolution Concerning the International Classification of Status in Employment Adopted by the 15th International Conference of Labour Statisticians, January 1993, para. 6)
Partnership	*Partnerships* are separate legal entities which behave like corporations but whose members enjoy limited liability; in effect, the partners are at the same time both shareholders and managers. (SNA 4.46)
Part-time employee	*Part-time employees* are persons whose usual hours of work are less than the normal working hours established for full-time jobs. This definition encompasses all forms of part-time work (half-day work, work for one, two or three days a week, etc.). This number may be established at the national, regional, industrial or unit level. The number of part-time employees is calculated by reference to the number of hours worked per week for which they are paid. The number of hours is considered in relation to the length of what is considered to be a full-time working week in the Member State or the sector of the unit or the unit itself. (Definitions of Structural Business Statistics Regulation , Commission Regulation (EC) No. 2700/98 of 17 December 1998)
Population	*Population* is the total membership or population or "universe" of a defined class of people, objects or events. There are two types of population, viz, target population and survey population. A target population is the population outlined in the survey objects about which information is to be sought and a survey population is the population from which information can be obtained in the survey. The target population is also known as the scope of the survey and the survey population is also known as the coverage of the survey. For administrative records the corresponding populations are: the "target" population as defined by the relevant legislation and regulations, and the actual "client population". (*United Nations Glossary of Classification Terms*. Prepared by the Expert Group on International Economic and Social Classifications. Available at: *www.un.org/Depts/unsd/class/glossary_short.htm*)
Price	The *price* of a good or service is the value of one unit of that good or service. (SNA 16.9)
Price index	A *price index* reflects an average of the proportionate changes in the prices of a specified set of goods and services between two periods of time. (SNA 16.14)
Primary income	*Primary incomes* are incomes that accrue to institutional units as a consequence of their involvement in processes of production or ownership of assets that may be needed for purposes of production. (SNA 7.2)
Principal activity	The principal activity of a producer unit is the activity whose value added exceeds that of any other activity carried out within the same unit (the output of the principal activity must consist of goods or services that are capable of being delivered to other units even though they may be used for own consumption or own capital formation). (SNA 15.16) The *principal activity* of a producer unit is the activity that contributes most to the value added of the entity, or the activity the value added of which exceeds that of an other activity of the entity. (ISIC Rev. 3, para 34)

Produced asset	*Produced assets* are non-financial assets that have come into existence as outputs from processes that fall within the production boundary of the SNA; produced assets consist of fixed assets, inventories and valuables. (SNA 10.6 and 10.7 [13.14, (AN.1) – Annex to Chapter XIII])
Producer's price	The *producer's price* is the amount receivable by the producer from the purchaser for a unit of a good or service produced as output minus any VAT, or similar deductible tax, invoiced to the purchaser; it excludes any transport charges invoiced separately by the producer. (SNA 6.205, 15.28 [3.82])
Producer price index	*Producer price indices* (PPIs) provide a measure of average movements of prices received by producers of commodities. In principle, transport costs and consumption taxes are excluded. Producer price indices are not a measure of average price levels nor a measure of costs of production. In principle, PPIs should include service industries, but in practice in may countries they are limited to the domestic agricultural and industrial sectors. (*Producer Price Indices: Sources and Methods*, OECD, Paris, 1994, page 7)
Product (commodity) technology assumption	*Product (commodity) technology assumption* is one of two types of technology assumptions used in converting supply and use tables into symmetric input-output tables; it assumes that a product has the same input structure in whichever industry it is produced. (SNA 15.144)
Product-by-product table	A *product-by-product table* is a symmetric input-output table with products as the dimension of both rows and columns; as a result it shows which products are used in the production of which other products. (SNA 15.150)
Production	*Production* is an activity, carried out under the responsibility, control and management of an institutional unit, that uses inputs of labour, capital and goods and services to produce outputs of goods and services. (SNA 6.15 [1.20 5.4, 6.6])
Production boundary	The *production boundary* includes *a*) the production of all individual or collective goods or services that are supplied to units other than their producers, or intended to be so supplied, including the production of goods or services used up in the process of producing such goods or services; *b*) the own-account production of all goods that are retained by their producers for their own final consumption or gross capital formation; *c*) the own-account production of housing services by owner-occupiers and of domestic and personal services produced by employing paid domestic staff. (SNA 6.18 [1.20 and 1.22])
Product	*Products*, also called "goods and services", are the result of production; they are exchanged and used for various purposes: as inputs in the production of other goods and services, as final consumption or for investment. (SNA 2.49)
Provincial government	Same as *state government*. (OECD Glossary)
Public corporation	*Public corporations* are resident corporations and quasi-corporations that are subject to control by government units, with control over a corporation being defined as the ability to determine general corporate policy by choosing appropriate directors, if necessary. (SNA 4.72 and 4.84)
Purchaser's price	The *purchaser's price* is the amount paid by the purchaser, excluding any deductible VAT or similar deductible tax, in order to take delivery of a unit of a good or service at the time and place required by the purchaser; the purchaser's price of a good includes any transport charges paid separately by the purchaser to take delivery at the required time and place. (SNA 6.215, 15.28 [2.73, 3.83])
Purchasing power parity	A *purchasing power parity* (PPP) is a price relative which measures the number of units of country B's currency that are needed in country B to purchase the same quantity of an individual good or service as 1 unit of country A's currency will purchase in country A. (SNA 16.82)
Qualitative data	*Qualitative data* are data describing the attributes or properties that an object possesses. (*Terminology on Statistical Metadata*, Conference of European Statisticians Statistical Standards and Studies, No. 53, UNECE, Geneva 2000)

Quality	Quality is defined in the ISO 8402 - 1986 as: "the totality of features and characteristics of a product or service that bear on its ability to satisfy stated or implied needs." For statistical data the components of quality include: relevance, accuracy, timeliness, comparability, coherence (Assessment of Quality in Statistics, Eurostat, April 2000)
Quantitative data	Quantitative data is data expressing a certain quantity, amount or range of values related to an object. The quantitative data is usually associated with measurement units. (Terminology on Statistical Metadata, Conference of European Statisticians Statistical Standards and Studies, No. 53, UNECE, Geneva 2000)
Quasi-corporation	Quasi-corporations are unincorporated enterprises that function as if they were corporations, and which have complete sets of accounts, including balance sheets. (SNA 4.49)
Questionnaire	A questionnaire is an identifiable instrument containing questions for gathering data from respondents. (Terminology on Statistical Metadata, Conference of European Statisticians Statistical Standards and Studies, No. 53, UNECE, Geneva 2000)
Reference period	In connection with price or volume indices, the reference period means the period to which the indices relate; it is typically set equal to 100 and it does not necessarily coincide with the "base" period that provides the weights for the indices. (SNA 16.16)
Reporting unit	A reporting unit is a unit that supplies the data for a given survey instance. (Terminology on Statistical Metadata, Conference of European Statisticians Statistical Standards and Studies, No. 53, UNECE, Geneva 2000)
Resident	An institutional unit is resident in a country when it has a centre of economic interest in the economic territory of that country. (SNA 4.15 [1.28, 14.8])
Resources	Resources refers to the side of the current accounts where transactions which add to the amount of economic value of a unit or a sector appear (for example, wages and salaries are a resource for the unit or sector receiving them); by convention, resources are put on the right side of the account. (SNA 2.54)
Respondent	Respondents are businesses, authorities, individual persons, etc, from whom data and associated information are collected for use in compiling statistics. (NOE Handbook)
Rest of the world	The rest of the world consists of all non-resident institutional units that enter into transactions with resident units, or have other economic links with resident units. (SNA 4.163 [1.14, 14.3])
Rest of the world account	The rest of the world account comprises those categories of accounts necessary to capture the full range of transactions that take place between the total economy and the rest of the world (i.e., between residents and non-residents). (SNA 14.3 [1.14])
Retail trade	Retail trade is defined in ISIC as the re-sale (sale without transformation) of new and used goods to the general public, for personal or household consumption or utilisation.Retail trade includes the following ISIC Rev. 3 Groups in Division 52 (except repair of personal and household goods). non-specialised retail trade in stores; retail sale of food, beverages and tobacco in specialised stores; other retail trade of new goods in specialised stores; retail sale of second-hand goods in stores; retail trade not in stores. (ISIC Rev. 3)
Sales	See Turnover (OECD Glossary)
Sample	A sample is a subset of a frame where elements are selected based on a randomised process with a known probability of selection. (Terminology on Statistical Metadata, Conference of European Statisticians Statistical Standards and Studies, No. 53, UNECE, Geneva 2000)
Sample survey	A sample survey is a survey which is carried out using a sampling method, i.e., in which a portion only, and not the whole population is surveyed. (A Dictionary of Statistical Terms, 5th Edition, F.H.C. Marriott, prepared for the International Statistical Institute, Longman Scientific and Technical, 1990)
Satellite account	A satellite account provides a framework linked to the central accounts that enables attention to be focussed on a certain field or aspect of economic and social life in the context of national accounts; common examples are satellite accounts for the environment, or tourism, or unpaid household work. (SNA 2.246 [21.4])

Saving	*Saving* is disposable income less final consumption expenditure (or adjusted disposable income less actual final consumption), in both cases after taking account of an adjustment for pension funds; saving is an important aggregate which can be calculated for each institutional sector or for the whole economy. (SNA 9.17 [1.10, 9.2, 9.19])
Seasonal adjustment	*Seasonal adjustment* is a statistical technique to remove the effects of seasonal calendar influences operating on a series. Seasonal effects usually reflect the influence of the seasons themselves either directly or through production series related to them, or social conventions. Other types of calendar variation occur as a result of influences such as number of days in the calendar period, the accounting or recording practices adopted or the incidence of moving holidays (such as Easter). (*An Analytical Framework for Price Indexes in Australia: Glossary and References*, Australian Bureau of Statistics, Canberra, 1997)
Secondary activity	A *secondary activity* is an activity carried out within a single producer unit in addition to the principal activity and whose output, like that of the principal activity, must be suitable for delivery outside the producer unit. (SNA 5.8 [15.16])
Sector	Institutional units are grouped together to form *institutional sectors*, on the basis of their principal functions, behaviour, and objectives. (SNA 2.20)
Self-employed worker	*Self-employed workers* are persons who are the sole owners, or joint owners, of the unincorporated enterprises in which they work, excluding those unincorporated enterprises that are classified as quasi-corporations. Contributing family workers, too, are considered self-employed workers. (SNA 7.24)
Self-employment job	*Self-employment jobs* are those jobs where the remuneration is directly dependent upon the profits (or the potential for profits) derived from the goods or services produced (where own consumption is considered to be part of profits). The imcumbants make the operational decisions affecting the enterprise, or delegate such decisions while retaining responsibility for the welfare of the enterprise. In this context "enterprise" includes one-person operations. (International Labour Organisation Resolution Concerning the International Classification of Status in Employment Adopted by the 15th International Conference of Labour Statisticians, January 1993, para. 7)
Services	*Services* are outputs produced to order and which cannot be traded separately from their production; ownership rights cannot be established over services and by the time their production is completed they must have been provided to the consumers; however as an exception to this rule there is a group of industries, generally classified as service industries, some of whose outputs have characteristics of goods, *i.e.*, those concerned with the provision, storage, communication and dissemination of information, advice and entertainment in the broadest sense of those terms; the products of these industries, where ownership rights can be established, may be classified either as goods or services depending on the medium by which these outputs are supplied.
	The service sector covers both market and non-market services. (SNA 6.8 [6.13])
Shuttle trade	*Shuttle trade* refers to the activity in which individual entrepreneurs buy goods abroad and import them for resale in street markets or small shops. Often the goods are imported without full declaration in order to avoid import duties. (NOE Handbook)
Social accounting matrix	A *social accounting matrix* (SAM) is a means of presenting the SNA accounts in a matrix which elaborates the linkages between a supply and use table and institutional sector accounts; a typical focus of a SAM on the role of people in the economy may be reflected by, among other things, extra breakdowns of the household sector and a disaggregated representation of labour markets (*i.e.*, distinguishing various categories of employed persons). (SNA 20.4)

225|

Standard industrial trade classification	The *Standard International Trade Classification* (SITC) is a statistical classification of the commodities entering external trade. It is designed to provide the commodity aggregates requited for purposes of economic analysis and to facilitate the international comparison of trade-by-commodity data.
	The hierarchical structure of the classification comprises:
	• Sections – one-digit code; - Divisions – two-digit codes; - Groups – three-digit codes;
	• Subgroups – four digit codes; - Items – five-digit codes
	The current international standard is the SITC, Revision 3.
	(*Commodity Indexes for the Standard International Trade Classification*, Revision 3, United Nations, New York, Statistical Papers, Series M, No. 38/Rev. 2, Vol. 1 page v.)
Standard statistical unit	The *standard statistical units* defined in ISIC Rev. 3 comprise: enterprise; enterprise group; kind-of-activity unit (KAU); local unit; establishment; homogeneous unit of production (ISIC Rev. 3, paragraph 76)
State government	*State governments* are institutional units exercising some of the functions of government at a level below that of central government and above that of the governmental institutional units existing at a local level; they are institutional units whose fiscal, legislative and executive authority extends only over the individual "states" (often referred to as "provinces") into which the country as a whole may be divided. (SNA 4.124)
Statistical data	*Statistical data* are data from a *survey* or *administrative source* used to produce statistics and/or the data comprising such statistics. (NOE Handbook)
Statistical data collection	*Statistical data collection* is the operation of statistical data processing aimed at gathering of statistical data and producing the input object data of a statistical survey. (*Terminology on Statistical Metadata*, Conference of European Statisticians Statistical Standards and Studies, No. 53, UNECE, Geneva 2000)
Statistical data editing	*Statistical data editing* is the operation of detecting and correcting errors in statistical data. (*Terminology on Statistical Metadata*, Conference of European Statisticians Statistical Standards and Studies, No. 53, UNECE, Geneva 2000)
Statistical metadata	*Statistical metadata* are metadata describing statistical data. (*Terminology on Statistical Metadata*, Conference of European Statisticians Statistical Standards and Studies, No. 53, UNECE, Geneva 2000)
Statistical territory (of a country)	In international merchandise trade statistics, the objective is to record goods entering and leaving the economic territory of a country. In practice, what is recorded is goods that enter or leave the *statistical territory*, which is the territory with respect to which data are being collected. The statistical territory may coincide with the economic territory of a country or with some part of it. It follows that when the statistical territory of a country and its economic territory differ, international merchandise trade statistics do not provide a complete record of inward and outward flows of goods. (*International Merchandise Trade Statistics, Concepts and Definitions*, United Nations, New York, 1998, Studies in Methods, Series M, No. 52, Rev. 2, page 9, para. 64)
Statistical unit	*Statistical units* are the entities for which information is sought and for which statistics are ultimately compiled. These units can, in turn, be divided into observation units and analytical units. (ISIC Rev. 3, para. 63)
Statistical units model	The *statistical units model* for a *national statistical system* comprises the set of *standard statistical units* defined and used in that system. This may or may not include the full set of standard statistical units defined in the 1993 SNA. (NOE Handbook)
Stock data	*Stock data* are data measured at some particular point of time within the reference period, for example, money supply data which can refer to an observation on the last working day of the reference period. In contrast to *flow data*. (OECD – Main Economic Indicators)
Stocks	*Stocks* are a position in, or holdings of, assets and liabilities at a point in time and the SNA records stocks in accounts, usually referred to as balance sheets, and tables at the beginning and end of the accounting period; stocks result from the accumulation of prior transactions and other flows, and they are changed by transactions and other flows in the period (note that stocks of goods are referred to as "inventories" in the SNA. (SNA 3.66)
Subject matter statistician	Statistician concerned with processing, analysis or dissemination of data within a particular subject area, for example, labour, manufacturing, or health. (NOE Handbook)

Subsidy	*Subsidies* are current unrequited payments that government units, including non-resident government units, make to enterprises on the basis of the levels of their production activities or the quantities or values of the goods or services which they produce, sell or import. (SNA 7.71 [15.52])
Subsistence worker	*Subsistence workers* are workers who hold a *self-employment job* and in this capacity produce goods or services which are predominantly consumed by their own household and constitute an important basis for its livelihood. (International Labour Organisation Resolution Concerning the International Classification of Status in Employment Adopted by the 15th International Conference of Labour Statisticians, January 1993, para. 14(s))
Supply and use table	*Supply and use tables* are in the form of matrices that record how supplies of different kinds of goods and services originate from domestic industries and imports and how those supplies are allocated between various intermediate or final uses, including exports. (SNA 1.16 [15.1])
Survey	A *survey* is an investigation about the characteristics of a given population by means of collecting data from a sample of that population and estimating their characteristics through the systematic use of statistical methodology. (*Terminology on Statistical Metadata*, Conference of European Statisticians Statistical Standards and Studies, No. 53, UNECE, Geneva 2000)
	If every unit of the population is included in the sample, the survey may be referred to as a *full coverage survey* or *census*. Thus the term "survey" includes census as a special case. (NOE Handbook)
Survey statistician	Person involved in design, collection, processing, analysis and dissemination of basic statistical data; includes survey statistician and methodologist; excludes national accountant. (NOE Handbook)
Symmetric input-output table	*Symmetric (input-output) tables* are tables in which the same classifications or units (*i.e.*, the same groups of products or industries) are used in both rows and columns. (SNA 15.2)
System of National Accounts	The *System of National Accounts* (SNA) consists of a coherent, consistent and integrated set of macroeconomic accounts, balance sheets and tables based on a set of internationally agreed concepts, definitions, classifications and accounting rules. (SNA 1.1)
Taxes	*Taxes* are compulsory, unrequited payments, in cash or in kind, made by institutional units to government units; they are described as unrequited because the government provides nothing in return to the individual unit making the payment, although governments may use the funds raised in taxes to provide goods or services to other units, either individually or collectively, or to the community as a whole. (SNA 7.48 [8.43])
Taxes on income	*Taxes on income* consist of taxes on incomes, profits and capital gains; they are assessed on the actual or presumed incomes of individuals, households, NPIs or corporations. (SNA 8.52 [OECD 1110, 1120, 1130, 1210])
Taxes on production and imports	*Taxes on production and imports* consist of taxes payable on goods and services when they are produced, delivered, sold, transferred or otherwise disposed of by their producers plus taxes and duties on imports that become payable when goods enter the economic territory by crossing the frontier or when services are delivered to resident units by non-resident units; they also include other taxes on production, which consist mainly of taxes on the ownership or use of land, buildings or other assets used in production or on the labour employed, or compensation of employees paid. (SNA 7.49)
Taxes on products	*Taxes on products*, excluding VAT, import and export taxes, consist of taxes on goods and services that become payable as a result of the production, sale, transfer, leasing or delivery of those goods or services, or as a result of their use for own consumption or own capital formation. (SNA 7.69, 15.47 [OECD 5110-5113, 5121, 5122, 5126, 4400])
Total economy	The *total economy* consists of all the institutional units which are resident in the economic territory of a country. (SNA 2.22)
Total labour force	Same as *labour force*. (OECD Glossary)
Trade balance	The *trade balance* is the difference between exports and imports of goods. (SNA 2.166)

Trade margin	A *trade margin* is the difference between the actual or imputed price realised on a good purchased for resale (either wholesale or retail) and the price that would have to be paid by the distributor to replace the good at the time it is sold or otherwise disposed of. (SNA 6.110)
Transaction	A *transaction* is an economic flow that is an interaction between institutional units by mutual agreement or an action within an institutional unit that it is analytically useful to treat like a transaction, often because the unit is operating in two different capacities. (SNA 3.12)
Transfer	A *transfer* is a transaction in which one institutional unit provides a good, service or asset to another unit without receiving from the latter any good, service or asset in return as counterpart. (SNA 8.3, 8.27)
Transfer price	A *transfer price* is a price, adopted for book-keeping purposes, which is used to value transactions between affiliated enterprises integrated under the same management at artificially high or low levels in order to effect an unspecified income payment or capital transfer between those enterprises. (SNA 3.79, BPM 97)
Transport margin	A *transport margin* consists of those transport charges paid separately by the purchaser in taking delivery of the goods at the required time and place. (SNA 15.40 [15.42])
Turnover	Turnover comprises the totals invoiced by the observation unit during the reference period, and this corresponds to market sales of goods or services supplied to third parties.Turnover includes all duties and taxes on the goods or services invoiced by the unit with the exception of the VAT invoiced by the unit *vis-à-vis* its customer and other similar deductible taxes directly linked to turnover.It also includes all other charges (transport, packaging, etc.) passed on to the customer, even if these charges are listed separately in the invoice. Reduction in prices, rebates and discounts as well as the value of returned packing must be deducted.Income classified as other operating income, financial income and extra-ordinary income in company accounts is excluded from turnover. Operating subsidies received from public authorities or the institutions of the European Union are also excluded.
Underground economy	Producers engaged in *underground production* are described as belonging to the *underground economy*. (SNA 6.34)
Underground production	*Underground production* consists of activities that are productive in an economic sense and quite legal (provided certain standards or regulations are complied with), but that are deliberately concealed from public authorities for the following kinds of reasons:
	a) to avoid the payment of income, value added or other taxes;
	b) to avoid payment of social security contributions;
	c) to avoid having to meet certain legal standards such as minimum wags, maximum hours, safety or health standards, etc.;
	d) to avoid complying with certain administrative procedures, such as completing statistical quetionnaires or other administrative forms (SNA 6.34)
Unemployed	The *unemployed* comprise all persons above a specified age who during the reference period were:
	• without work, that is, were not in *paid employment* or *self employment* during the reference period;
	• currently available for work, that is, were available for *paid employment* or *self-employment* during the reference period; and
	• seeking work, that is, had taken specific steps in a specified recent period to seek *paid employment* or *self-employment*. The specific steps may include registration at a public or private employment exchange; application to employers; checking at worksites, farms, factory gates, market or other assembly places; placing or answering newspaper advertisements; seeking assistance of friends or relatives; looking for land, building, machinery or equipment to establish own enterprise; arranging for financial resources; applying for permits and licences, etc. (International Labour Organisation Resolution Concerning Statistics of the Economically Active Population, Employment, Unemployment and Underemployment Adopted by the 13th International Conference of Labour Statisticians, October 1982, para. 10)

Unemployment	Unemployment is the fact of being *unemployed* (OECD Glossary)
Unemployment rate	The *unemployment rate* is the number of *unemployed* divided by the *total labour force*.
Unincorporated enterprise	An *unincorporated enterprise* is a producer unit which is not incorporated as a legal entity separate from the owner (household, government or foreign resident); the fixed and other assets used in unincorporated enterprises do not belong to the enterprises but to their owners, the enterprises as such cannot engage in transactions with other economic units nor can they enter into contractual relationships with other units nor incur liabilities on their own behalf; in addition, their owners are personally liable, without limit, for any debts or obligations incurred in the course of production. (SNA 4.140 and 4.141)
Unit	U*nits* refer to entities, respondents to a survey or things used for the purpose of calculation or measurement. Their statistics are collected, tabulated and published. They include, among others, businesses, government institutions, individual organisations, institutions, persons, groups, geographical areas and events. They form the population from which data can be collected or upon which observations can be made. (U*nited Nations Glossary of Classification Terms*. Prepared by the Expert Group on International Economic and Social Classifications. Available at: *www.un.org/Depts/unsd/class/glossary_short.htm*)
Uses	The term *uses* refers to transactions in the current accounts that reduce the amount of economic value of a unit or sector (for example, wages and salaries are a use for the unit or sector that must pay them); by convention, uses are put on the left side of the account. (SNA 2.54)
Value	*Value* at the level of a single, homogeneous good or service is equal to the price per unit of quantity multiplied by the number of quantity units of that good or service; in contrast to price, value is independent of the choice of quantity unit. (SNA 16.9)
Value added	*Gross value added* is the value of output less the value of intermediate consumption; it is a measure of the contribution to GDP made by an individual producer, industry or sector. (SNA 1.6 [2.172, 6.4, 6.222]) *Net value added* is gross value added less consumption of fixed capital. (SNA 6.4, 6.222 [1.6])
Value added tax	A *value added tax* (VAT) is a tax on products collected in stages by enterprises; it is a wide-ranging tax usually designed to cover most or all goods and services but producers are obliged to pay to government only the difference between the VAT on their sales and the VAT on their purchases for intermediate consumption or capital formation, while VAT is not usually charged on sales to non-residents (*i.e.*, exports). (SNA 6.207 and 6.208 [15.47])
Variable	A variable is a characteristic of a unit being observed that may assume more than one of a set of values to which a numerical measure or a category from a classification can be assigned (*e.g.* income, age, weight, etc., and "occupation", "industry", "disease", etc. (U*nited Nations Glossary of Classification Terms*. Prepared by the Expert Group on International Economic and Social Classifications. Available at: *www.un.org/Depts/unsd/class/glossary_short.htm*) Same as *data element*. (NOE Handbook)
Volume index	A *volume index* is most commonly presented as a weighted average of the proportionate changes in the quantities of a specified set of goods or services between two periods of time; volume indices may also compare the relative levels of activity in different countries (*e.g.* those calculated using purchasing power parities). (SNA 16.11)

Wages and salaries	*Wages and salaries* consist of the sum of wages and salaries in cash and wages and salaries in kind. (SNA 7.33 and 7.37)
	Wages and salaries are defined as "the total remuneration, in cash or in kind, payable to all persons counted on the payroll (including homeworkers), in return for work done during the accounting period" regardless of whether it is paid on the basis of working time, output or piecework and whether it is paid regularly or not. Wages and salaries include the values of any social contributions, income taxes, etc. payable by the employee even if they are actually withheld by the employer and paid directly to social insurance schemes, tax authorities, etc. on behalf of the employee. Wages and salaries do not include social contributions payable by the employer. Wages and salaries include: all gratuities, bonuses, ex gratia payments, "thirteenth month payments", severance payments, lodging, transport, cost-of-living, and family allowances, tips, commission, attendance fees, etc. received by employees, as well as taxes, social security contributions and other amounts payable by employees and withheld at source by the employer. Wages and salaries which the employer continues to pay in the event of illness, occupational accident, maternity leave or short-time working may be recorded here or under social security costs, dependent upon the unit's accounting practices.
Wholesale prices index	*Wholesale price indices* refer to prices received by the wholesalers while producer price indices refer to prices do not take into account the organisation of the distribution chain. Many commodities are now sold through many different channels of which wholesale is a part. Moreover, wholesale prices include commercial mark-ups which are not included in producer prices.
	For some countries the name *Producer price index* replaced the name Wholesale price index in the 1970s or 1980s after a change in methodology. For some countries, the name Wholesale price index is used for historical reasons and in fact refers to a price index following the same methodology as for a Producer price index. (*Producer Price Indices: Sources and Methods*, OECD, Paris, 1994, page 7)
Wholesale trade	*Wholesale trade* is defined in ISIC as the resale (sale without transformation) of new and used goods to retailers; to industrial, commercial, institutional or professional users; to other wholesalers; or acting as agents in buying merchandise for, or selling merchandise to, such persons or companies. Wholesale trade is defined in ISIC Rev. 3 as comprising the following Groups in Division 51): wholesale on a fee or contract basis; wholesale of agricultural raw materials, live animals, food, beverages and tobacco; wholesale of household goods; wholesale of non-agricultural intermediate products, waste and scrap; wholesale of machinery, equipment and supplies; other wholesale. (ISIC Rev. 3)
Year to date data	*Year to date data* are data expressed in period to date terms; they are sometimes (especially in transition economies) referred to as cumulative data. (OECD – Main Economic Indicators)

Annex 3

DATA REQUIREMENTS AND SOURCES

Annex 3.1. Outputs of Basic Data Collection Programme by Use

Note: The list of outputs is for illustration. It was developed for the Australian Bureau of Statistics. In other countries, other use categories may be more appropriate.

Note: M. = Ministry of

	Macro-Economic Structural	Macro-Economic Short Term	Micro-Economic Industry	Micro-Economic Activity	Micro-Economic Short Term	Micro-Economic Dynamics	Regional
Principal users/Uses	National Bank, Treasury, M. Finance, National Accounts	National Bank, Treasury, M. Finance, National Accounts	National Bank, Treasury, M. Finance, M. Industry, Industry Associations	M. Industry, M. Environ, M. Technology, Industry Associations	Industry Associations, Marketing Agencies	M. Small Business, Monopolies Commission, Enterprises	M. Regional Develop, Regional Government, Development Enterprises
Reference period	Year	Month/Quarter	Year	Year	Month/Quarter	Year Longitudinal	Year
Data items	Turnover, expenses, purchases, stocks, earnings, hours, employment, capital expenditure, labour costs, operating surplus, assets, liabilities	Retail sales, stocks, earnings, hours, employment, capital expenditure, business opinions	Retail sales, stocks, earnings, hours, employment, capital expenditure	Commodities produced, services rendered, research and development expenditure, environmental impacts and expenditure	Retail sales, commodities produced, services rendered, motor vehicle registrations	As for second col + counts by enterprise/establishment of births, deaths & organisation changes (by type)	Turnover, employment, earnings
Industrial breakdown	Division/	Division	Class	Varies	None	Branch	Branch
Geographic breakdown	None	None	Region	Region	Region	region	Locality
Size breakdown	None	None	2-6 classes	2-6 classes	None	2-6 classes	2-6 classes
Output frequency	Aannual	Monthly/quarterly	Annual/occasional	Annual/Occasional	Monthly/quarterly	Annual/occasional	Annual/occasional

Annex 3.2. Minimal Data Requirements and Sources for Annual National Accounts

Note: The list is for illustration. It was developed in the context of the Commonwealth of Independent States. In other countries, this list of data requirements may be considered less than, or in excess of minimal; also the sources of data may not all be available and there may be others.

Types of data	Sources of data
Production (by industries)	
1. Output	
1.1. Market output	
1.1.1. Sales	Reports and surveys of enterprises on their performance
	Bank reports on profits and losses
	Reports of insurance companies on profits and losses
	Households budget surveys
	Special sample households surveys
	Business registers
	Tax authorities statistics
1.1.2. Change in stocks of finished but not sold goods and work in progress	Balance sheets of enterprises (business accounts)
1.2. Non-market and other output	Reports on execution of the state budget
	Sample surveys of NPISH
	Households budget surveys
	Special sample households surveys
2. Intermediate consumption	Reports and surveys of enterprises on production costs
	Reports on execution of the state budget
	Sample surveys of NPISH
	Households budget surveys
3. Gross value added	Balancing item
Generation of income	
4. Compensation of employees	
4.1. Gross wage (paid out by resident producers)	Reports and surveys of enterprises on wages and labour force
	Bank reports on profits and losses
	Report on execution of the state budget
	Sample surveys of NPISH
4.2. Social contributions	Reports of social insurance and pension funds on execution of their budget
5. Taxes on production and imports	
5.1. Taxes on products	Report on execution of the state budget
5.2. Other taxes on production	Report on execution of the state budget
6. Subsidies on production and imports	
6.1. Subsidies on products	Report on execution of the state budget
6.2. Other subsidies on production	Report on execution of the state budget
7. Gross operating surplus/gross mixed income	Balancing item
Final disposition of goods and services	
8. Final consumption expenditure	
8.1. Households	Reports and surveys of enterprises on trade turnover and sales of services
	Households budget surveys
	Special sample households surveys
8.2. General government	Reports on execution of the state budget
8.3. NPISH	Sample surveys of HPISH

233

Types of data	Sources of data
9. Gross capital formation	
9.1. Gross fixed capital formation	Reports of enterprises on investments in fixed assets
	Reports of local authorities on households dwelling construction
	Sample surveys of households construction
	Reports on execution of the state budget
	Censuses of livestock and plantations
9.2. Change in inventories	Balance sheets of enterprises (business accounts)
9.3. Net acquisition of valuables	Reports and surveys of enterprises on trade turnover
10. Net exports of goods and services	External trade statistics
	Customs statistics
	Reports of enterprises on exports and imports of items not covered by customs statistics
	Surveys of unorganized external trade (shuttle traders)

Annex 3.3. Minimal data requirements and sources for sector accounts

Note: The list is for illustration. It was developed in the context of the Commonwealth of Independent States. In other countries, this list of data requirements may be considered less than, or in excess of minimal; also the sources of data may not all be available and there may be others.

Types of data	Sources of data
Production (by sectors)	
1. Output	
1.1. Market output	
1.1.1. Sales	Reports and surveys of enterprises on their performance
	Bank reports on profits and losses
	Reports of insurance companies on profits and losses
	Households budget surveys
	Special sample households surveys
	Business registers
	Tax authorities statistics
1.1.2. Change in stocks of finished but not sold goods and work in progress	Balance sheets of enterprises (business accounts)
1.2. Non-market and other output	Reports on execution of the state budget
	Sample surveys of NPISH
	Households budget surveys
	Special sample households surveys
2. Intermediate consumption	Reports and surveys of enterprises on production costs
	Reports on execution of the state budget
	Sample surveys of NPISH
	Households budget surveys
3. Gross value added	Balancing item
Generation of income	
4. Compensation of employees	
4.1. Gross wage (paid out by resident producers)	Reports and surveys of enterprises on wages and labour force
	Bank reports on profits and losses
	Report on execution of the state budget
	Sample surveys of NPISH

Types of data	Sources of data
4.2. Social contributions	Reports of social insurance and pension funds on execution of their budget
5. Taxes on production and imports	
5.1. Taxes on products	Report on execution of the state budget
5.2. Other taxes on production	Report on execution of the state budget
6. Subsidies on production and imports	
6.1. Subsidies on products	Report on execution of the state budget
6.2. Other subsidies on production	Report on execution of the state budget
7. Gross operating surplus/gross mixed income	Balancing item

Allocation of primary incomes

4. Compensation of employees	
4.1. Gross wage (received by residents)	Reports and surveys of enterprises on wages and labour force
	Bank reports on profits and losses
	Report on execution of the state budget
	Sample surveys of NPISH
	Balance of payments
4.2. Social contributions	Reports of social insurance and pension funds on execution of their budget
5. Taxes on production and imports	
5.1. Taxes on products	Report on execution of the state budget
5.2. Other taxes on production	Report on execution of the state budget
6. Subsidies on production and imports	
6.1. Subsidies on products	Report on execution of the state budget
6.2. Other subsidies on production	Report on execution of the state budget
7. Gross operating surplus/gross mixed income	Balancing item from the generation of income account
8. Property income	Bank reports on profits and losses
	Report on execution of the state budget
	Reports of insurance companies on profits and losses
	Reports and surveys of enterprises on production costs and use of profit
	Balance of payments
9. Balance of primary incomes	Balancing item

Secondary distribution of income

10. Current transfers	
10.1. Taxes on income and wealth, etc.	Reports on execution of the state budget
10.2. Social contributions	Reports of social insurance and pension funds on execution of their budget
10.3. Other current transfers	Reports of insurance companies on profits and losses
	Reports on execution of the state budget
	Reports and surveys of enterprises on production costs and use of profit
	Balance of payments
11. Disposable income	Balancing item

Use of income

12. Final consumption expenditure	
12.1. Households	Reports and surveys of enterprises on trade turnover and sales of services
	Households budget surveys
	Special sample households surveys
12.2. General government	Reports on execution of the state budget
12.3. NPISH	Sample surveys of HPISH
13. Saving	Balancing item

Types of data	Sources of data
Capital transactions	
14. Capital transfers	Reports on execution of the state budget
	Reports and surveys of enterprises on use of profit
	Balance of payments
15. Gross fixed capital formation	Reports of enterprises on investments in fixed assets
	Reports of local authorities on households dwelling construction
	Sample surveys of households construction
	Reports on execution of the state budget
	Censuses of livestock and plantations
16. Change in inventories	Balance sheets of enterprises (business accounts)
17. Net acquisition of valuables	Reports and surveys of enterprises on trade turnover
18. Net acquisition of non-financial non-produced assets	Reports on execution of the state budget
	Reports and surveys of enterprises on use of profit
	Balance of payments
19. Net lending/Net borrowing	Balancing item
Rest of the world transactions	
20. Exports of goods and services	External trade statistics
	Customs statistics
	Reports of enterprises on exports and imports of items not covered by customs statistics
	Surveys of unorganized external trade (shuttle traders)
21. Imports of goods and services	External trade statistics
	Customs statistics
	Reports of enterprises on exports and imports of items not covered by customs statistics
	Surveys of unorganized external trade (shuttle traders)
22. Primary incomes to and from abroad	Balance of payments
23. Current transfers to and from abroad	Balance of payments
24. Capital transfers to and from abroad	Balance of payments

Annex 3.4. Statistical surveys typically included in a national statistical system

Note: The list is for illustration. It is based on the Australian Bureau of Statistics. In other countries, some of these surveys may not be conducted, or may be combined with one another or divided into parts.

Survey	Reference period	Data items
Manufacturers stocks and sales	Monthly/Quarterly	Stocks, sales: by industry branch
Retail sales	Monthly/Quarterly	Retail sales: by retail trade branch
Capital expenditures	Monthly/Quarterly	
Building and engineering construction	Monthly/Quarterly	
Producer price indices	Monthly/Quarterly	
Employment, earnings and hours	Monthly/Quarterly	Employment, earnings, hours: by industry branch
Labour force	Monthly/Quarterly	Employment, hours: by self-employed/ employee; by industry branch
Household expenditure	Monthly/Quarterly	

Survey	Reference period	Data items
Consumer price index	Monthly/Quarterly	
Industrial production	Annual	Income items: receipts from sales; rental leasing and hiring income; contract and commission: changes in inventories; own account fixed capital formation; interest and dividends; subsidies; insurance claims; other.
		Expenditure items: wages and salaries; employers social security payments; provision for employee entitlements; contact and commission; transport; equipment rental leasing and hiring; purchases; other operating expenses; interest; taxes on products; insurance premiums.
Agricultural production	Annual	(similar to industrial production)
Transportation	Annual	(similar to industrial production)
Other services	Annual	(similar to industrial production)
Financial institutions	Annual	
Government	Annual	
Labour costs	Annual/Occasional	
Population and housing census	Occasional	Population: by region

Annex 3.5. Administrative sources typically used in a national statistical system

Note: The list is for illustration. It is based on the Australian Bureau of Statistics. In other countries, these sources of administrative data may not all be available and there may be others.

Administrative Programme	Reference period	Data items
Corporate income tax	Annual	Income, expenses
Personal income tax	Annual	Income, expenses
National government budget	Annual	(Intended) expenditures
National government accounts	Annual	Expenditures, employment, wages and salaries
Regional government budget	Annual	(Intended) expenditures
Regional government accounts	Annual	Expenditures, employment, wages and salaries
Building permits	Daily/monthly	Building approvals: numbers and values
New motor vehicle registrations	Daily/monthly	New motor vehicle registrations: numbers and values
Merchandise exports	Daily/monthly	Export transaction: by commodity, quantity and value
Merchandise imports	Daily/monthly	Import transaction: by commodity, quantity and value
Social security	Weekly/monthly	Social security payments made by employers for/ on behalf of employees: by industry, type
Payroll deductions	Weekly/monthly	Payroll deductions made by employers on behalf of employees: by industry, type
Sales tax	Weekly/monthly	Taxes collected: by industry, taxable item
Value added/ goods and services/ manufacturers tax	Weekly/monthly	Taxes collected: by industry, taxable item
Multi-purpose business registration	Daily/monthly	Registration details: name, address, location, industrial classification, size group

Annex 4

ANALYTICAL FRAMEWORKS FOR THE NON-OBSERVED ECONOMY

Annex 4.1. Eurostat Candidate Country Exhaustiveness Project: Tabular Framework

Non-Observed Economy: Classification by Type

T1: *Statistically non-observed: non-response*

Undercoverage occurs as a result of non-response to statistical questionnaires or non-coverage of active units in administrative files. Possible methods to ensure exhaustiveness include:

- use of data from similar units (industries, size groups), former year's data or similar appropriate data;
- adjustment of sample weighting;
- use of global verification procedures such as labour input method.

T2: *Statistically non-observed: out of date registers*

Undercoverage occurs due to units being missing from statistical register when defining the survey population and selecting the survey sample, or due to problems resulting from out-of-date information about the units. Possible methods to ensure exhaustiveness include:

- detailed investigation of the register quality and expert estimates of its deficiencies;
- comparison of various statistical and administrative sources (preferably at the unit level);
- use of global verification procedures such as labour input method;
- use of information from other surveys.

T3: *Statistically non-observed: units not registered or not surveyed*

Undercoverage occurs due to:

- non-coverage of units in the statistical registers because of thresholds for registration or non-coverage of certain activities in the register;
- non-coverage of units in the survey because they were newly created or disappeared during the year.

Possible methods to ensure exhaustiveness include:

- adjustments for thresholds based on other sources or expert estimates;
- comparison of different statistical and administrative sources (preferably at the unit level);
- estimates based on the number of newly created and closed (non-active) units;
- use of global verification procedures such as labour input method.

T4: *Non-observed for economic reasons: underreporting of turnover/ income*

Undercoverage occurs due to intentional under-reporting of gross output, over-reporting of intermediate consumption in order to evade income tax, value added tax or other taxes, or social security contributions, for example. in the form of double bookkeeping, envelope salaries, without-bill-settlements. Possible methods to ensure exhaustiveness include:

- use of fiscal audit information;
- comparison of turnover in the national accounts with turnover in VAT or other tax files, taking into account differences in types of units, tax thresholds, and branch classification;
- comparison of wages and salaries and mixed income per capita by industries, preferably by size groups;

- comparison of the intermediate consumption ratios for different sub-groups of units operating in the same industry, *e.g.* different size groups, public and private enterprises, legal and unincorporated units.

T5: *Non-observed for economic reasons: units intentionally not registered*

Undercoverage occurs because of intentional non-registration of units or production (or parts of these). Possible methods to ensure exhaustiveness include use of global verification procedures such as labour input method.

T6: *Informal sector (not registered, underreporting)*

Undercoverage occurs because of:

- missing productive units or production activities because units are not required to register their activities under any kind of administrative act, including agricultural production in non-agricultural households for own use, production of goods (other than agricultural) in households for own use, own construction of residential buildings by households, occasional and temporary activities, and work on service contracts;
- missing gross output for persons with secondary self-employed jobs;
- missing units or production even if reported to fiscal authorities.

Possible methods to ensure exhaustiveness include estimates for the important types of informal activities of households using household budget survey data, data on construction permits or other administrative information, also use of global verification procedures.

T7: *Illegal activities*

Undercoverage occurs because the producing units do not register or report their illegal activities. Possible methods to ensure exhaustiveness include special studies, use of administrative data from customs, police medical authorities, etc.

T8: *Other types of* GDP *under-coverage*

Other types of undercoverage include:

- production for own final use;
- tips;
- wages and salaries in kind;
- valuation of NOE adjustments;
- taxes and subsidies on products;
- reliability of quantity-price methods and product balances.

Production for own final use includes:

- production of agricultural or other products in the household sector for own final consumption – this concerns unincorporated units, *e.g.* farmers or self-employed, as well as informal activities of households;
- dwellings, extensions to dwellings, capital repairs of dwellings produced by households;
- own account construction including capital repairs in agriculture (all sectors);
- own account construction including capital repairs in other industries (all sectors);
- machinery and equipment produced for own capital formation or own account capital repairs (all sectors).

Tips may occur in hotels and restaurants, repair services, personal services, hospitals and other health services, banks, and insurance companies. Possible data sources and estimation methods for tips include use of household budget survey data, special surveys and expert estimates, comparison of wages and salaries/ mixed income with other branches, and regulations for the taxation of tips.

Wages and salaries in kind include:

- goods and services produced by the employer either as main production, *e.g.* coal or free train or railway tickets, or secondary production, including the provision of sports, recreation or holiday facilities for employees and their families, and free or cheap crèches for employees' children;
- goods and services purchased or financed by the employer, including: meals and drinks, including those when travelling on business; housing or accommodation services; uniforms or other forms of special clothing; private use of business cars; sports, recreation or holiday facilities for employees and their families, and free or cheap crèches for employees' children.

Further information on these other types of GDP under-coverage is available from relevant tax and social legislation and bookkeeping practices, and another possible source of data is a labour cost survey.

Eurostat Tabular Framework (Pilot Project on Exhaustiveness)

Table 1. **Non-observed activities by type and adjustment method**

National accounts component	NOE types	Adjustment method in national accounts		
		Explicit method(s) "–" if not covered "I" if implicitly covered	Correspondence to Tables 2A – 2C (give cross reference to adjustment number in Tables 2A, 2B, 2C)	
Detailed breakdown that allows allocation of possible types of under-coverage	For each line, indicate relevant types of under-coverage		Table 2A Table 2B	Table 2C

Table 1A : Output approach

Public non-financial corporations

NACE A
 large units
 medium-size units
 small units

NACE B
 large units
 medium-size units
 small units

(by NACE A – P, or groups with similar data sources)

Private non-financial corporations

NACE A
 large units
 medium-size units
 small units

NACE B
 large units
 medium-size units
 small units

…by NACE A – P, or groups with similar data sources

Financial corporations

General Government
 Central and local government units
 Extra-budgetary funds

NPISH

Households

NACE A
 Unincorporated units
 Informal/Other activities/
 Market production
 Production for own use
  farmers
  non-agricultural households

Eurostat Tabular Framework (Pilot Project on Exhaustiveness)
Table 1. **Non-observed activities by type and adjustment method** (*cont.*)

National accounts component	NOE types	Adjustment method in national accounts			
		Explicit method(s) "–" if not covered "I" if implicitly covered	Correspondence to Tables 2A – 2C (give cross reference to adjustment number in Tables 2A, 2B, 2C)		
Detailed breakdown that allows allocation of possible types of under-coverage	For each line, indicate relevant types of under-coverage		Table 2A	Table 2B	Table 2C
NACE B Unincorporated units Informa/Other activities Market production Production for own use (... by NACE A – P, or groups with similar data sources) Taxes and subsidies on products					

Table 1B : Expenditure approach
Household final consumption expenditure
Purchases of goods and services
(COICOP, 1and/or 2-digit level)
Production for own final use
   Agricultural goods
   Other household productof goods
   Unincorporated units
   Other HFC-components

Final consumption general government
Final consumption of NPISH

Gross Fixed Capital Formation with breakdown by
   Institutional sectors
   NACE Positions
   Size of units, special units/activities

Changes in Inventories
(with a breakdown similar to GFCF)

Export and Import
   Export and Import of goods
   Export and Import of services
   Purchases of non-residents
   Purchases of residents abroad
   Shuttle trade

Table 1C : Income approach
(with breakdown similar to the output approach)

Eurostat Tabular Framework (Pilot Project on Exhaustiveness)

Table 1. **Non-observed activities by type and adjustment method** (*cont.*)

National accounts component	NOE types	Adjustment method in national accounts			
			Correspondence to Tables 2A – 2C (give cross reference to adjustment number in Tables 2A, 2B, 2C)		
Detailed breakdown that allows allocation of possible types of under-coverage	For each line, indicate relevant types of under-coverage	Explicit method(s) "–" if not covered "!" if implicitly covered	Table 2A	Table 2B	Table 2C
Table 1D : Illegal activities					
Smuggling					
Tobacco					
Weapons					
Alcohol					
Food					
Stolen cars					
Other					
Trade and production of narcotics					
Prostitution					
Clandestine gambling					
Corruption					
Usury					
Fake brands					
Fake money					
Dealing with stolen goods					
Other					

Eurostat Tabular Framework (Pilot Project on Exhaustiveness)
Table 2. – **Exhaustiveness adjustments**
Table 2A. Output Approach

Adjust. No.	Type of adjustment	National accounts component	NACE Code, Type of units	Data sources	Absolute size Currency unit	Relative size as % of component	of GDP

Table 2B. Expenditure Approach

Adjust. No.	Type of adjustment	National accounts component / Type of Expenditure	NACE, COICOP, etc. Code, Type of units	Data sources	Absolute Size Currency unit	Relative size as % of component	of GDP

Table 2C. Income Approach

Adjust. No.	Type of adjustment	National accounts component / Type of Income	NACE Code, Type of units	Data sources	Absolute size Currency unit	Relative size as % of component	of GDP

Eurostat Tabular Framework (Pilot Project on Exhaustiveness)
Table 3. – **Summary of exhaustiveness adjustments**
Table 3A. Output Approach

NA component Type of unit	Type of NOE/other GDP under-coverage								Total	
Similar breakdown to Table 1A incl. illegal	T1	T2	T3	T4	T5	T6	T7	T8	Absolute	Percentage of GDP
For each: Gross output, Intermediate Cons, Gross Value added										
Total										

Table 3B. Expenditure approach

Expenditure component	Type of NOE/other GDP under-coverage								Total	
Similar breakdown to Table 1B incl illegal	T1	T2	T3	T4	T5	T6	T7	T8	Absolute	Percentage of GDP
Expenditure components										
Total										

Table 3C. Income approach

Type of income Type of unit	Type of NOE/other GDP under-coverage								Total	
Similar breakdown to Table 1C incl. illegal	T1	T2	T3	T4	T5	T6	T7	T8	Absolute	Percentage of GDP
Sector, industry, type of unit, For each : Compens of Employees, Gross OS, Cons Fixed Cap, NOS										
Total										

243

Annex 4.2. Unit and Labour Input Framework (developed by Statistics Netherlands)

Classification of NOE by registration of units and labour input

Labour input	Production units			
	Enterprises registered in business register	Enterprises not registered in business register		
		Other	Own account	Production for own use
Registered	C1	C3		
Not registered	C2	C4	C5	C6

Non-Observed Economy: Classification by Type

NOE types C1 and C3: activities not related to unregistered labour inputs

NOE Type C1 represents the output of registered enterprises using registered labour. The most important reason for errors of this type is a statistical one. Here non-observed activities can occur because of an explicit constraint in selecting the sample (for example when surveying is restricted to enterprises with more than a given number of employees), errors in the sample frame, and misreporting or non-response for other reasons than tax evasion or illegal activities.

Adjustment for restrictions of the sample to larger enterprises can be made by assuming that the production, turnover, value added etc. per worker of the smaller enterprises equal those of the smallest enterprises included in the sample. This can only be done if the number of employees is the available in the sample frame. If it is not, and, the size measure is based, for example, on the reported turnover in last year's tax return, then this latter variable can be used for adjustment.

Sample frame deficiencies can be adjusted for by means of the labour force survey. Provided that the employment data from the survey is of sufficient quality, it can be used to reweight other data from business surveys, like production, intermediate consumption, operating surplus, value added, etc., and hence to correct for errors.

Underreporting of turnover and over-reporting of costs both cause a decrease in value added. Enterprises that over-report costs are not necessarily committing fraud. Over-reporting may also be caused by the differences between business accounting and national accounting standards. For example, income in kind is often correctly booked as intermediate consumption in terms of business accounting and tax laws, while in terms of national accounting it should be booked as part of the wages and salaries, and thus as part of the value added. Other reasons for misreporting are inadequate bookkeeping practices.

A special case is simultaneous over-reporting (or underreporting) of both turnover and cost. Such misreporting may not affect value added, but it does affect the confrontation of supply and use of goods and services and the estimates of the final consumption, especially if these are calculated as a residual. As this may lead to difficulties in the compilation of the sector accounts, it should be corrected if possible.

To correct for partial non-response, values can be imputed using other data in the response. For example, if an enterprise does not provide a breakdown of intermediate consumption by product, the structure can be borrowed from enterprises of similar size in the same branch of industry. A similar technique can be used to impute values for enterprises, which were not surveyed because of a size cut off in sample selection.

NOE type C3 reflects problems in the registration process. One possible reason is that enterprises are wrongly classified and hence are missed when the sample is selected. The most common errors occur in the industry code and in the size code. A wrong industry code may lead to inappropriate exclusion from the sample. A wrong code may equally lead to inappropriate inclusion in the sample frame of a survey of another branch of industry. (This is not addressed in the description of NOE type C1 as it is assumed that such errors are corrected during the normal data editing.) Keeping track of the number of enterprises inappropriately included in the sample gives some insight in the size of this problem. If this number is very small, then the problem can probably be ignored.

A second reason is that the register is not up to date. It is missing new enterprises and contains dead ones. However, the number of employees in new enterprises is not usually high, so the impact on employment, wages and salaries, operating surplus and value added is likely to be modest. The long-term solution to this problem is to put extra effort in the maintenance of the business register, while a short time solution is to use labour force survey data to re-weight the data as described in Section 5.2.3.

The third and probably most common reason in terms of the number of enterprises, is that enterprises are missing because there is no need or obligation for them to register. A labour force survey may give a first impression of the relative importance of the problem, measured in terms of number of employees of these enterprises. If the number of unregistered enterprises is low, estimation using per employee characteristics based on surveyed enterprises may be acceptable. However, if there are reasons to assume that such enterprises differ significantly from those that register, then special investigations into their size and structure is needed, for example using city market surveys.

NOE type C2: activities of registered enterprises with unregistered labour inputs

NOE type C2 reflects the output of registered enterprises by the use of unregistered labour. If labour is concealed it is most likely that this is done to evade taxes and social contributions. Actually, it is underreporting of labour costs. If the only purpose is to evade income taxes and social contributions, it is possible that other variables are not biased. However, to decrease the risk of being caught (and to evade taxes on operating surplus), enterprises may also underreport other variables to such an extent that the reported figures suggest a normal production structure. Although, in principle, all enterprises (perhaps except governmental organisations) might commit such a fraud, the opportunities to do so are the greatest for small enterprises with a rather simple production structure and relatively high labour input, for example in the areas of trade, construction, repair, and services.

This kind of misreporting can be corrected by using data from a labour force survey to re-weight the outcomes of the business surveys in a similar way to adjusting for sample frame deficiencies and sampling restrictions, but with the additional requirement that the labour force survey results must implicitly or explicitly include the supply of unregistered labour.

Misreporting in this group of enterprises may also be due to the lack of a proper administration. This is especially the case for smaller units in the register, for example the own account enterprises.

NOE types C4 and C5: activities by unregistered market enterprises related to unregistered labour

The main part of NOE type C4 is production by unregistered labour in enterprises that are not included in the business register for statistical reasons, such as wrong classification, wrong size code, incorrect register update, etc., not because they have deliberately evaded registration. If the register were to improve, such enterprises might well be registered and the non-observed activities would become part of NOE type C2.

NOE type C4 also contains all enterprises that should be registered but for one reason or another want avoid government control completely, for example because they are producing illegal products or producing products illegally. Improvement of the register would not affect the registration of these enterprises. To cover such production, non-traditional estimation methods are needed.

NOE type C5 represents the production of own account enterprises. Such enterprises are typical of the informal sector. Most of the production here is not illegal, nor underground for taxation purposes.

If the number of own account enterprises (or households involved in own account work) is known from labour force or special surveys or the population census, an estimate of their activities can be made assuming that the per person characteristics are the same as for registered own account own account, or bear a fixed relationship to them. If there is no data available on registered own account enterprises, a minimum estimate can be made by assuming that the mixed income of households involved in own account work equals the minimum amount of money needed to make a living.

NOE type C6: production for own use by unregistered units

Production for own use by unregistered units, mainly households, is not very common in most Western European and North American countries. However, in many other countries these activities form a significant proportion of GDP. To measure their size, traditional business surveys and labour force surveys do not suffice. Additional observations are needed.

Extensions

The framework is not only of interest as a practical approach of the NOE, it is also of interest as a tool analysing the problems in implementing various extensions of the SNA. Although there is international agreement on the current production boundary of the national accounts, it is generally accepted that macro-economic indicators like GDP are not necessarily the only or the best indicators of welfare. Thus alternative indicators have been developed, building on the SNA. Examples are the so-called green national income and the total national income. The UN women conferences in Rio de Janeiro and Beijing strongly recommended the development of satellite accounts describing total production, including not only all paid activities, but also unpaid productive activities such as do-it-yourself, household work, and volunteer work, which are currently outside the production boundary. To cope with this last mentioned case, the unit and labour input framework could be extended by adding an additional row for unpaid labour, and introducing an additional NOE type C7 in the last column.

245

Non-Observed Economy: Documentation Template

A possible NOE recording structure inspired by the layout of the supply and use tables is illustrated in the following table. It is essentially a three dimensional matrix with industrial branches and size groups on the rows, the key data items on the columns, and the adjustments corresponding to each NOE category in layers of the table. The branch of industry breakdown is made to correspond with the branches distinguished in enterprise surveys, with a further breakdown by size class. If the smallest enterprises are not included in a survey sample, the smallest size class sampled should be shown separately. The same applies for branches of industry with a relatively large informal sector, for example trade, construction, furniture manufacture and services.

Data by industry, size, source and NOE category

Data by NOE Categories: Layer 0: basic data Layer 1: adjustments for NOE C1 Layer 2: adjustments for NOE C2 Layer 3: ... Layer Layer: national accts final value	Total production	Intermediate consumption	Primary cost			
			Wages and salaries	Social contributions	Taxes minus subsidies	Operating surplus
Enterprise surveys						
Agriculture						
2+ employees	–	–	–	–	–	–
1 employee	–	–	–	–	–	–
0 employees	–	–	–	–	–	–
Construction						
25+ employees	–	–	–	–	–	–
10-25 employees	–	–	–	–	–	–
1-9 employees	–	–	–	–	–	–
0 employees	–	–	–	–	–	–
...	–	–	–	–	–	–
Customs data:	–	–	–	–	–	–
Exports						
Imports	–	–	–	–	–	–
Tax data:	–	–	–	–	–	–
Wages and salaries						
VAT	–	–	–	–	–	–

The table contains layers corresponding to the NOE types. The first layer contains the basic data outputs of the surveys and administrative files after data editing and weighting. The next layer contains the adjustments for the first NOE type. The subsequent layers contain the adjustments for each of the other NOE types. The final (national accounts) figures are entered in the last layer. Each figure is accompanied, if possible, with a qualitative indication or quantitative measure of its quality and notes on alternative potential adjustments.

Annex 5

IMF DATA QUALITY ASSESSMENT – GENERIC FRAMEWORK

(Draft as of July 2001)

Quality dimensions	Elements	Indicators
0. Prerequisites of quality *(The elements and indicators included here bring together the "pointers to quality" that are applicable across the five identified dimensions of data quality.)*	**0.1. Legal and institutional environment** – *The environment is supportive of statistics.*	0.1.1. The responsibility for collecting, processing, and disseminating statistics is clearly specified. 0.1.2. Data sharing and coordination among data producing agencies are adequate. 0.1.3. Respondents' data are to be kept confidential and used for statistical purposes only. 0.1.4. Statistical reporting is ensured through legal mandate and/or measures to encourage response.
	0.2. Resources – *Resources are commensurate with needs of statistical programs.*	0.2.1. Staff, financial, and computing resources are commensurate with institutional programs. 0.2.2. Measures to ensure efficient use of resources are implemented.
	0.3. Quality awareness – *Quality is a cornerstone of statistical work.*	0.3.1. Processes are in place to focus on quality. 0.3.2. Processes are in place to monitor the quality of the collection, processing, and dissemination of statistics. 0.3.3. Processes are in place to deal with quality considerations, including tradeoffs within quality, and to guide planning for existing and emerging needs.
1. Integrity *The principle of objectivity in the collection, processing and dissemination of statistics is firmly adhered to.*	**1.1. Professionalism** – *Statistical policies and practices are guided by professional principles.*	1.1.1. Statistics are compiled on an impartial basis. 1.1.2. Choices of sources and statistical techniques are informed solely by statistical considerations. 1.1.3. The appropriate statistical entity is entitled to comment on erroneous interpretation and misuse of statistics.
	1.2. Transparency – *Statistical policies and practices are transparent.*	1.2.1. The terms and conditions under which statistics are collected, processed, and disseminated are available to the public. 1.2.2. Internal governmental access to statistics prior to their release is publicly identified. 1.2.3. Products of statistical agencies/units are clearly identified as such. 1.2.4. Advance notice is given of major changes in methodology, source data, and statistical techniques.
	1.3. Ethical standards – *Policies and practices are guided by ethical standards.*	1.3.1. Guidelines for staff behavior are in place and are well known to the staff.

Quality dimensions	Elements	Indicators
2. Methodological soundness *The methodological basis for the statistics follows internationally accepted standards, guidelines, or good practices.*	**2.1. Concepts and definitions** – *Concepts and definitions used are in accord with standard statistical frameworks.*	2.1.1. The overall structure in terms of concepts and definitions follows international standards, guidelines, or good practices: see dataset-specific framework.
	2.2. Scope – *The scope is in accord with internationally accepted standards, guidelines, or good practices.*	2.2.1. The scope is broadly consistent with international standards, guidelines, or good practices: see dataset-specific framework.
	2.3. Classification/sectorization – *Classification and sectorization systems are in accord with internationally accepted standards, guidelines, or good practices.*	2.3.1. Classification/ sectorization systems used are broadly consistent with internationally accepted standards, guidelines, or good practices: see dataset-specific framework.
	2.4. Basis for recording – *Flows and stocks are valued and recorded according to internationally accepted standards, guidelines, or good practices.*	2.4.1. Market prices are used to value flows and stocks. 2.4.2. Recording is done on an accrual basis. 2.4.3. Grossing/netting procedures are broadly consistent with international standards, guidelines, or good practices.
3. Accuracy and reliability *Source data and statistical techniques are sound and output data sufficiently portray reality.*	**3.1. Source data** – *Source data available provide an adequate basis to compile statistics.*	3.1.1. Source data are collected from comprehensive data collection programs that take into account country-specific conditions. 3.1.2. Source data reasonably approximate the definitions, scope, classifications, valuation, and time of recording required. 3.1.3. Source data are timely.
	3.2. Statistical techniques – *Statistical techniques employed conform with sound statistical procedures.*	3.2.1. Data compilation employs sound statistical techniques. 3.2.2. Other statistical procedures (*e.g.* data adjustments and transformations, and statistical analysis) employ sound statistical techniques.
	3.3. Assessment and validation –*Source data are regularly assessed and validated.*	3.3.1. Source data–including censuses, sample surveys and administrative records–are routinely assessed, *e.g.* for coverage, sample error, response error, and non-sampling error; the results of the assessments are monitored and made available to guide planning.
	3.4. Assessment and validation of intermediate data and statistical outputs.-*Intermediate results and statistical outputs are regularly assessed and validated.*	3.4.1. Main intermediate data are validated against other information where applicable. 3.4.2. Statistical discrepancies in intermediate data are assessed and investigated. 3.4.3. Statistical discrepancies and other potential indicators of problems in statistical outputs are investigated.
	3.5. Revision studies – *Revisions, as a gauge of reliability, are tracked and mined for the information they may provide.*	3.5.1. Studies and analyses of revisions are carried out routinely and used to inform statistical processes.

Quality dimensions	Elements	Indicators
4. Serviceability Statistics are relevant, timely, consistent, and follow a predictable revisions policy.	**4.1. Relevance** – *Statistics cover relevant information on the subject field.*	4.1.1. The relevance and practical utility of existing statistics in meeting users' needs are monitored.
	4.2. Timeliness and periodicity – *Timeliness and periodicity follow internationally accepted dissemination standards.*	4.2.1. Timeliness follows dissemination standards. 4.2.2. Periodicity follows dissemination standards
	4.3. Consistency – *Statistics are consistent over time, internally, and with major datasets.*	4.3.1. Statistics are consistent within the dataset (*e.g.* accounting identities observed). 4.3.2. Statistics are consistent or reconcilable over a reasonable period of time. 4.3.3. Statistics are consistent or reconcilable with those obtained through other data sources and/or statistical frameworks.
	4.4. Revision policy and practice – *Data revisions follow a regular and publicized procedure.*	4.4.1. Revisions follow a regular, well-established and transparent schedule. 4.4.2. Preliminary data are clearly identified. 4.4.3. Studies and analyses of revisions are made public.
5. Accessibility *Data and metadata are easily available and assistance to users is adequate.*	**5.1. Data accessibility** – *Statistics are presented in a clear and understandable manner, forms of dissemination are adequate, and statistics are made available on an impartial basis.*	5.1.1. Statistics are presented in a way that facilitates proper interpretation and meaningful comparisons (layout and clarity of text, tables, and charts). 5.1.2. Dissemination media and formats are adequate. 5.1.3. Statistics are released on a pre-announced schedule. 5.1.4. Statistics are made available to all users at the same time. 5.1.5. Non-published (but non-confidential) sub-aggregates are made available upon request.
	5.2. Metadata accessibility – *Up-to-date and pertinent metadata are made available.*	5.2.1. Documentation on concepts, scope, classifications, basis of recording, data sources, and statistical techniques is available, and differences from international standards are annotated. 5.2.2. Levels of detail are adapted to the needs of the intended audience.
	5.3. Assistance to users – *Prompt and knowledgeable support service is available.*	5.3.1. Contact person for each subject field is publicized. 5.3.2. Catalogues of publications, documents, and other services, including information on any charges, are widely available.